IN THE AVANT GARDE

The Prophetic Catholicism of Remi De Roo (and Politics Within the Catholic Church)

IN THE AVANT GARDE

The Prophetic Catholicism of Remi De Roo (and politics within the Catholic Church)

by

Patrick Jamieson

Ekstasis Editions

Samarhan Press

National Library of Canada Cataloguing in Publication Data

Jamieson, Patrick
In the Avant Garde

Includes bibliographical references and index.
ISBN 1-894800-02-8

1. De Roo, Remi J. 2. Catholic Church–British Columbia–Victoria–Bishops–Biography. 3. Catholic Church. Diocese of Victoria–Biography. 4. Victoria (B.C.) –Church history–20th century.
I. Title.
BX4705.D436J35 2002 282'.092 C2001-911658-6

Typesetting, cover design and photo layout: Louise Beinhauer, Word Works
Cover Photo: Foto FELICI, Roma

Published in 2002 by:
Ekstasis Editions Canada Ltd.
Box 8474, Main Postal Outlet
Victoria, BC V8W 3S1

Samarhan Press
P.O. Box 5715, Stn. B
Victoria, BC V8R 6S8

In the Avant Garde has been published with the assistance of the Canada Council and the Cultural Services Branch of British Columbia.

This book is dedicated to my parents and my children, Margaret and Jim, Sarah, Hannah and Martha and to Marnie Butler whose support created the conditions by which it could happen.

Special thanks are due to Jack Sproule, Louise Beinhauer, Michael O'Connell, Ken Bernard, Bruce Witzel, Fran Pastoreck, Ralph & Sue Rambow, Richard Olafson, Carole Sokoloff, Grant Maxwell, Bernard Daly, Janet Somerville, Doug Roche, Raymond Roussin and Remi De Roo, who all in their own way spurred me on. Thanks also go to Sarah Windsong Butler, Tom Claridge, Dave Szollosy, Dick Renshaw, Everett MacNeil, Tom Loring, Larry & Betty Rumsby, Deirdre Kelly, Gregory Hartnell, David Burke, the Dave Gallants, Lew MacDonald, Odosca Morgante, Don Caverley, Mike Kavanagh, Mary Kay Beeching, Andy Sinats, Sheila Fitzgerald McKenna, Lynn Carter-Hunter, Raymond Painchaud, Lew MacDonald, Phil Winkelmans, Grant Crosswell & Colleen Lissamer, Rev. Father Allen Jones, Alan Date, Ken Ramkeesoon, Rick Haughian, Bill Goodacre, Sarah & Alexis Puentes, Jamie Jenkins, Michael Peter and Laila Cubelic.

Above all, my five brothers and sisters Rita and Christine, Tony, Gene and Jimmy.

A Certain Risk

"There is a certain risk in becoming deeply involved in secular affairs, but there's also a risk in engaging in piety, which can make you hardhearted and unmoved by suffering," Gregory Baum said. "People complain about the Roman Catholic Church becoming political only when it criticizes society. When it blesses the existing order—'God Save the Queen'—no one notices that too is political. Religion always has a political role, either to stabilize the existing order or to raise critical questions. God's judgment is not only 'How many times do you masturbate?' but also 'How many unemployed are there?'"—Ron Graham's *God's Dominion, A Sceptic's Quest*, page 243.

What's Called Orthodoxy

"As long as we're open to discernment, to weigh the pros and cons in light of our traditions with experience and common sense, the Spirit will guide us," said Remi De Roo, the radical bishop of Victoria. "Our lay people are educating themselves, and some are better versed than some of the clergy. Rather than trying to control the emerging forces, we should let life move without worrying about the power struggles.

"After all what's called orthodoxy is only the perspective of certain powerful people in the Vatican. There's no monolithic interpretation of what orthodoxy means. We might as well settle down for a couple of rough decades ahead, without getting lost in fear or anxiety. The fear betrays a lack of faith in the laity. It presumes a super-class of ordained ministers and an ordinary class who can't be trusted. But where is the Spirit? Isn't it here today, working around and through us? We should be prudent, we have to listen to tradition, but we must trust in the Spirit, and go forward."—Ron Graham's *God's Dominion, A Sceptic's Quest*, page 165.

PREFACE

This book is approximately two years overdue. The delay is the result of a radical shift in the subject matter just about the time when the original text was about complete in the spring of 2000.

At that point the book had been two years in the making. In early 1998 a small group of writers acquainted with the Bishop's career decided to embark upon a biography of Remi De Roo. The bishop would be retiring in less than a year at that point, on his seventy-fifth birthday, February 24, 1999. Compulsory retirement at age seventy-five for bishops was introduced by Pope Paul VI following the reforms of the Second Vatican Council (1962-65).

Personally at the time I felt it was a touch premature as the bishop was obviously just readying himself for at least one more serious chapter, post-retirement, to the ongoing saga of Remi De Roo. For a number of reasons, however, I happily agreed to be part of the team.

For one thing I had just published a history of Catholics on Vancouver Island, including two long chapters on Bishop De Roo. So I was in the habit of reflecting on his significance. For another, I owed at least one of the other writers a serious favour which this might contain. All in all it seemed a likely project.

I did have a sense of déjà vu however. A similar sort of group had gathered itself in 1996 to write a history of the Catholic Diocese on Vancouver Island—with some of the same principals—but it had dissolved and I had ended up doing the project alone. Significantly the same thing happened with this book.

Fundamentally, in my own mind, I had agreed, in effect, to be a ghostwriter because I knew it was a project more important to the other writers at the time. I also knew that the book they would want was not the one I would do if allowed to follow my heart on the subject. Sure enough, when I showed the others my first five chapters—the ones that form chapters six to ten in this book—our partnership dissolved.

I must admit that I wondered at the time exactly why I was writing it quite so polemically, but as events unfolded I came to feel I could see just why. At any rate this book is that book.

Preface

I do not consider this book so much a biography of Remi De Roo per se, rather it is a study of the thirty year ongoing crisis of the Roman Catholic Church which began in 1968 with the birth control controversy of that day. This is a crisis that is far from resolved. In fact many of the measures which have been put in place for the purpose of 'resolving' it since 1978 have done little more than cover it over temporarily and thereby probably made it much worse.

This book uses the Canadian context and the life of a major Canadian player as a lens for deeper analysis of the current condition of the Catholic Church today. The social question is a good illustration.

After Vatican II, the Catholic Church launched itself into an effective program of global social transformation. Through the adoption of the theology of liberation and the subsequent liberation of theology, the world itself started to feel the real effect of harnessing this globally significant force of human energy, commitment and resources to bring about social change. For reasons that seem obvious now this could not be allowed to continue unabated. After 1978 forces were put in place to curtail this radically leftward bent. Remi De Roo was the principal Canadian prototype in the process. This book is the story of what he was about and how he was eventually dealt with in that overall context.

❧❧❧

By the end of February 2000, I could see that this book would be wrapped up by the fall of that year. For two years I had been working on it out of instinct and fundamentally letting the emerging parameters set its direction.

Admittedly it was 'very political', focusing on the left-right politics of the Canadian Catholic Church, which I sensed could only get me in trouble with (among other people) the publisher who I had in mind.

March 1, 2000, the horse and financial scandal broke, radically and permanently altering the story, and possibly the very way Bishop De Roo would be seen by history.

The financial scandal covered in Chapter Eighteen—*Smashing the Icon*—emerged quite suddenly. Because I had been precisely focusing on De Roo's life, meaning and career I was in a strategic position to track and study this fresh development. At the same time it obviously meant a delay for the release of the book. It had to be waited out in its implications. It also had to be integrated into the overall text.

In some ways the way I had been writing the book anticipated this sort of 'development'. Many who were experiencing the changes in the Catholic Church since 1978 half expected that one day Bishop De Roo would run into trouble. The emerging attitude toward money in the church, over and against pastoral priorities (such as social justice and internal church reform) augured this.

The supreme irony of De Roo getting caught out in this trap is revealed in an interesting fact. When he arrived in Victoria in 1962 as 'a boy bishop' at the age of 38, the net worth of the entire diocese was a quarter of a million dollars. Nearly forty years later when he left office it was worth approximately 110 million dollars. In all the public disclosure around the financial saga of the year 2000 no one mentions this perspective. The $1.1 million loss meant that, as one wag stated, if the diocese was worth a dollar, we would be talking about one cent worth of trouble.

All the work I had been doing on the book—as the reader will see—certainly presented me with a definite and unavoidable perspective through which to view the financial-horse scandal saga.

This tragic unfolding could be said to have vindicated the way I had been writing the story of Remi De Roo's prophetic Catholicism. Or, it could be said to have biased the way I perceived the financial scandal events. The reader can be the final judge of that. At any rate I was set up by the circumstance to write the book I have.

These are circumstances which go deeply into my own Catholic childhood. They also informed my very upbringing and eventual formation as a Roman Catholic Journalist. It is a book which I seemed by my family, childhood, adult formation, theological training and journalistic experience destined to write.

For some curious reason my family of origin was coincidentally intimately involved with the situations of three other

Roman Catholic priest figures in western Canada; all men who suffered the same ultimate fate as Bishop De Roo.

While these stories form an intricate part of his tale by my telling, at the time when I instinctively decided to integrate their stories into the story of De Roo—the stories of Archbishop Joseph Charbonneau, Eugene Cullinane, CSB and Father Bob Ogle—I had no idea De Roo would (or even could) suffer the same fate as these three.

Charbonneau was removed from his see as archbishop of Montréal for taking a prophetic social justice stand in the Asbestos strike of 1949. He 'retired' to Victoria, dying there ten years later.

For joining the CCF in 1946 Cullinane was banished from his Catholic teaching position in the Diocese of Saskatoon and spent the rest of his life on the margin of the institutional church.

Ogle died prematurely a few years ago as a result of being unilaterally and arbitrarily removed by The Vatican from his elected office as the Canadian Member of Parliament for Saskatoon East.

In each case, within the context of the church of their day, the situation reminds me of that dialogue from *Alice in Wonderland*:

"Now for the evidence," said the King, "then the sentence."

"No," said the Queen, "first the sentence, then the evidence!"

"Nonsense!," cried Alice, so loudly that everybody jumped, "the idea of having the sentence first."

In a way Remi De Roo's story prophetically wrote itself in the framework of an arcane yet common pattern.

After the watershed events of the horse and financial saga, as it was referred to unremittingly in the media, the Catholic population generally tended to find itself having to choose in their regard toward him and his legacy.

One group increasingly came to the conclusion that he was being politically crucified in at least the way the matter was handled publicly if not in the actual facts of the matter. They simply could not see the Remi De Roo they had experienced in the newspaper image that was so emotionally sickening to them.

The other group, probably by far the majority in the end, if only due to the relentless pummelling in the media, came to the sad conclusion that he had been, possibly inadvertently, the architect of his own undoing. This latter group included not only conservatives and traditionalists but also the liberals who, at the close, came to the defense of the institution rather than stand beside the individual, the leader who had meant so much to them over a number of decades. The liberals abandoned him in the end. Only the prophetic Catholicism following could not.

One of the priests of his diocese who deeply shared De Roo's proclivity for prophetic ministry (and the defense of the individual over and above the institution) was Father Jack Sproule of Saanich Peninsula. Sproule had many an intellectual wrestling match with the bishop over issues and priorities during their time working together. Plenty of strong opinion was shared in their dialogue.

Sproule has read through the text of this book and says he likes the way it raises so many necessary questions, especially in the area of the financial saga of the year 2000. He writes:

"Remi De Roo is my friend. As my bishop for nearly twenty years I have argued with him, 'wrestled with him', written him strong letters of disagreement. This was all part of our dialogue and at the same time I have learned much with and through him.

"Without hesitation I would say I have experienced 'God's grace' through this process. Perhaps nothing has caused more difficulties for the Catholic Church than what I call its addiction to perfectionism. I would say that the greatest truth I have learned from Remi is the truth of the Incarnation; that the locus of the divine is in the human.

"To be unwilling to accept another person's limitations is to deny my own humanity, and the reality of the Incarnation that the divine works in and through and with the human. To be human is to be imperfect. To be human is to always be part of unanswerable questions and yet to continually take up the courage and the curiosity to persist in asking them.

"This often leads to brokenness and that calls for healing and the possibility of wholeness. Trying to be perfect and expecting perfection of another is a most tragic human mistake. For me it is a denial of this most central religious truth, The Incarnation.

Preface

"What I like about this book of Pat Jamieson's is how it raises so many questions especially in that touchy area of the church today, the financial and the political. 'Live the questions', says the poet Rilke. The Catholic Church is far from perfect because the Catholic tradition is loaded with human beings. You are about to meet a human being, but one excitingly 'in the avant garde' and a social prophet. Enjoy!"

Rev. Jack Sproule, left, and Monsignor Leo Robert at a clergy session of the Diocesan Synod in 1988. In the background is Vicar General and Franciscan Father Sig Lajoie. (Jamie Jenkins Photo)

Table of Contents

First formal photograph of the 'Boy Bishop' in 1962.

Part One: The Elements of Fame

Chapter One: Five (or Six) Facts

1. BLOCKBUSTER

TORONTO—January 1, 1983. The *Toronto Star* features on its front page a blistering critique of the Canadian economy by none other than the Canadian Catholic Bishops. The next day the *Globe and Mail* gives the story just as much play and the rest of the media catch fire with the news.

A month-long debate—and years-long dissension—has been kicked off which result in the Bishop of Victoria, Remi De Roo becoming virtually a household name—certainly a countercultural icon.

He becomes a celebrity in the verbal battle during the mid-1980s. He is attacked by Prime Ministers, corporate and media tycoons and the head of the Business Council of Canada for his critical views of 'The Establishment'.

With the economy in the doldrums and the workers taking most of the body blows, De Roo takes a strong stand, based on recent papal pronouncements and the Canadian Bishops' own analysis, rooted in a Canadianized liberation theology cultivated over fifteen years.

Backed by community groups and labour unions, the argument catches on with the ordinary people, and De Roo is named the 'People's Bishop'. By most accounts he more than holds his own on the issue, despite 'not being an expert'.

He speaks from the point of view of the bottom level of society—ordinary workers, the poor and the various victims of the economic system—but with an uncommon passion and conviction. It's his 'fifteen minutes of fame' that goes on for fifteen months, the effect for fifteen years if not longer. He plays a key role in setting a counter-agenda for Canada in the face of the neo-conservative surge. He also will pay the price for crossing the powers that be, both within and without the Catholic Church.

2. ASSASSINATION

SAN SALVADOR—March 24, 1980. Roman Catholic Archbishop of San Salvador Oscar Romero is murdered while saying Mass in the hospital chapel where he serves as chaplain. It's a right-wing political assassination, aimed as curtailing liberation theology in Central America.

A champion of the rights of the poor in this war-torn region, Oscar Romero has been using the pulpit for gospel-based political messages. A convert from conservatism, the targeted archbishop is a victim of the sense of betrayal by the local oligarchy, but the assassins were trained at the School of the Americas in the United States.[1]

Three weeks prior to his death, although plainly exhausted, Romero consults late in the evening with Bishop De Roo who is in the region for the second time in recent years. On a fact-finding tour for the Canadian Bishops, De Roo publishes a booklet on the experience. He calls it his favourite book of the five published during his time as an active bishop.

Of Justice, Revolutions and Human Rights is a sociological analysis from the point of view of the emerging liberation theology model of Catholic social teaching. This 'prophetic Catholicism' has been adopted and adapted by the Canadian Catholic Church and Remi De Roo is one of its leading exponents in the Canadian hierarchy.

3. EARTHQUAKE

ROME—July 25, 1968. Pope Paul VI reveals his official pronouncement on artificial birth control and contraception, issuing a definite condemnation just when a different attitude was expected following the Second Vatican Council. Vatican II (1962-65) introduced revolutionary changes to the two-thousand-year-old institution, so hopes were high among church progressives for a liberalization of the church's teachings on birth control.

It is just the opposite, 'artificial' birth control is banned. The reaction is sharp. In North America opinion polls show that 85 percent of Catholics disagree with "*Humanae Vitae*," precipitating a profound crisis of confidence in the credibility of the central teaching authority of the church. It is a first of its kind in the history of the Catholic Church. How will the Canadian Bishops react?

In their pastoral response to the encyclical they emphasize the formation of conscience in the decision-making process of Catholics in their family planning. In complete conformity to the reforms of Vatican II, yet this is another surprise development that they did not automatically fall in line with the pope.

At the epi-centre of the week-long deliberations at Winnipeg in September of 1968 is Remi De Roo who co-chairs the theological commission which has responsibility for this issue for the national college of bishops.

De Roo's earlier involvement in this issue dates back officially to the Second Vatican Council where the most significant of his four written interventions at the four-year event directly speaks to the family planning concerns of Catholics when he addresses the topic of the sacramental nature of marital intimacy.

His work on this was revolutionary although largely unnoticed by the general public at the time. He had directly consulted articulate young progressive Catholic couples for feedback on this sensitive issue, an unprecedented approach in the Catholic Church.

4. SPECIAL FAVOUR

WINNIPEG—October 31, 1962. Rev. Remi De Roo of Saint Boniface is appointed fourteenth Bishop of Victoria. Pope John XXIII selected the youthful-looking thirty-eight-year-old, the youngest Canadian bishop of his day. On November 20, seven months before his death, the eighty-three-year-old pontiff makes clear his special favour by gifting De Roo with a papal ring. After an audience with the Canadian Bishops contingent in Rome, the pope calls him their 'Benjamin'.

The significance of this allusion to the biblical twelve tribes of Israel is not lost on the audience. Much is expected of this promising young trailblazer.[2]

De Roo takes these signs seriously, championing the rights of lay people and marginal causes during the four sessions of the Council, making four spoken and thirteen written interventions. These fashioned part of the lasting accomplishment of the Council, some were written into the final documents, forming part of a dynamic new direction for the enormous religious institution. De Roo would spend the fullness of his episcopacy at Victoria strongly implementing the reforms of Vatican II, which he typified as under the inspiration of the Holy Spirit of God.

5. RELIGION, WOMEN AND SOCIETY

VICTORIA—July, 1996—The University of Victoria officially opens its new centre for the Study of Religion and Society, originally a brainchild of Bishop De Roo. In the same year he appoints Kate Fagan, a twenty-six-year-old lay woman as chaplain to the students at the University.

It is his third straight appointment of a woman as chaplain since the death of Father Leo Robert in 1990. Robert, a magnetic university chaplain and De Roo's principal progressive collaborator among his diocesan clergy, died quickly and prematurely from an undiagnosed cancer in that year.

These two developments—the opening of the centre and the appointment of Ms Fagan as chaplain—signify the persevering innovative spirit of the bishop.

While many other Catholic bishops are ducking for cover under the new era out of Rome, De Roo is pushing ahead with the Vatican II program in various ways such as the dialogue with science, and the enhancement of the role of women within the church "up to the limits set by the pope," as he was partial to saying.

This has been his attitude on the women's issue at least since 1975 when the Vatican made a statement under Pope Paul VI that women's ordination was not possible while at the same time it officially admitted there are no scriptural grounds for the ban, simply Catholic tradition.

After 1978, for Pope John Paul II the entire topic became a complete non-starter, and he even tried to close down any serious discussion of the issue within the church. But the effect was only to move it underground for the season and fuel the debate by creating a deeper polarization around the issue.

In his last decade as Bishop of Victoria, these two events in combination with a thoroughgoing internal synod which consolidated the gains since Vatican II, were principal components of De Roo's program, countering a world-wide rightward swing within the Catholic Church universal.

6. DARK CLOUD DESCENDING

TORONTO—March, 2000. The *National Post* newspaper breaks the story that former Bishop Remi De Roo has incurred huge debts for the Diocese of Victoria by investing in race horses (actually Arabian show horses). The flagship newspaper of press baron Conrad Black is the first off the mark to give a strange, headline-grabbing spin to some financial losses of the diocese during the last decade of De Roo's administration.

An all but inevitable effort at discrediting the peerless proponent of Canadian prophetic Catholicism has begun. Other media follow suit. Distortion, exaggeration, vicious attitudes all emerge. De Roo keeps silence on the whole matter, choosing only to offer an apology for any pain and suffering he may have caused. Prior to retirement he went around to every priest in the diocese to ask for forgiveness for any difficulties he may have caused them during his four decades in office.

This was an act inspired by his study of Jewish customs. Immediately after he is out of office, entering into a retirement which he claims should offer him more time and possibilities to be speaking out, he is silenced for the first time by Rome. He was to speak at a married priests convention in Georgia but was asked by the papal nuncio not to do so and he deferred to his wishes. The nuncio had been instructed by the Congregation of Bishops in Rome.

Just when De Roo is fully prepared to change gears and enter what he calls his 'next career'[3] an outright attack is taken. This was just the start. For some reason his successor decides to release information about the financial difficulties in the external forum of the secular media rather than through internal channels and all hell breaks loose.

The diocese becomes a laughing stock in the broader community. The man put in charge of this process, the new diocesan administrator, was solicited from circles within the diocese that were hypercritical of Bishop De Roo in the area of his financial administration style.

These are the set that understand the church primarily as an institution to be run like a successful corporation. Speculation runs that if Bishop De Roo had been more favoured in these circles he would have been spared the subsequent humiliation, censure and personal embarrassment of such post-retirement disclosures.

The bishop's adversaries have a field day. He has been successfully discredited by all the bad press. The Canadian establishment, the church establishment and local critics have their way. Even the Canadian college of bishops turns against him.[4] He is offered no protection.

His program of church reform, progressive theology and social justice have been dealt a bad blow by this permanent darkening of the atmosphere around its principal symbolic figure. A figure of high regard has been reduced to one of contempt and derision in the public view due to the combination of the church's approach to the problem and the corporate media's interpretative spin.

De Roo's decision to remain entirely silent so as not to cause more difficulties and scandal for the new bishop[5] is reminiscent of another Catholic bishop forced into permanent exile to Victoria, Archbishop Joseph Charbonneau of Montréal in 1949. Charbonneau was removed by Rome for his socially progressive views and lived out his exile as a guest of the Sisters of Saint Ann at their institutions in Victoria.

INTRODUCTION TO A MAN OF DESTINY

For nearly four decades Remi Joseph De Roo of Swan Lake, Manitoba, by virtue of his natural abilities and appointed role as a Roman Catholic bishop, has been at the centre of significant historical events—ecclesiastical events, political events, spiritual events that have shaped the annals of his province, nation and the global Catholic Church.

Appointed the first chairperson of the British Columbia Human Rights Commission in the early 1970s, De Roo's reputation as a battler for human rights earned him the attention of the church worldwide, particularly in Latin America. Called the 'perfect human rights battler Catholic bishop' by one community newspaper in his adopted province[6], his leadership ability was not fully utilized or recognized by his church.

He was kept in a small if not tiny diocese when his talents were transparently required at a higher level to effectively implement the reforms of Vatican II—the reforms of Pope John XXIII's council—in larger and more lively centres across Canada.

On the other hand, by virtue of his being saddled only with lesser responsibilities of a smaller diocese, he had the time to head the social affairs commission of the Canadian Bishops Conference during its most energetic period.

This was during the years when the commission was adopting liberation theology to the Canadian context and taking tough prophetic stands on behalf of Native People, the underprivileged, indebted Third World nations and the ordinary workers of Canada.

As a result an extensive social justice network sprang up in the Canadian Catholic Church; and beyond. The church's social teaching took a giant stride forward in a direction long spoken of and promised but largely undelivered—direct social action.

De Roo regularly visited Central America during its most turbulent time. He became a key symbolic figure in the world-wide social justice network of the church. This extended network of social activists became so effective with its interventions based on an alternative intelligence gathering capacity, it was eventually squashed by moves from Rome in the late 1980s.[7]

But during the 1970s and early 1980s, lay people and religious orders in the Catholic Church formed an alternative perspective and radical grapevine of social activists.

Due to its far-flung nature the church had its own underground, consisting of on-the-ground information sources in all the trouble spots of the world. One measure of its effectiveness was the number of its martyrs in the Third World[8] including Archbishop Oscar Romero.

The significance of Romero's death was that he was a member of the hierarchy. The numbers of peasants and clergy and lay people who died for daring to take their faith seriously on the political plane are the fuller story behind the Romero headline.

Alert media voices learned to access church workers for behind-the-scenes intelligence during that period (and to this day). Jesuits, Dominicans, Canadian Scarboro and a multitude of other missioners were putting their talent, energy and commitment to work wherever the Church was attempting to bring its vision of non-violent social transformation to bear. Father Bob Ogle, MP was an example of a returned Canadian missioner who was converted to political action.

De Roo and Ogle had close friends—priests, nuns and archbishops—who were murdered in the cause. In the later part of his term Bishop De Roo was only able to observe as the struggle was systematically undermined from on high.[9] The Catholic social justice struggle was fundamentally dismantled as the Church was steered back toward the political right by forces within the institution that wanted a restoration of the pre-Vatican II church with its absolutist claim on certainty.[10] Ogle attributed his fatal collapse of health to this betrayal of his life's mission by the hierarchy of the church.

Notwithstanding, De Roo held a decade-long experimental synod in his own diocese. This was an elaborate process that reached out to the marginalized of society and tried to consolidate the gains of Vatican II as fully as possible.

Rightly identified as a prime irritant in their adjustment problems, De Roo was targeted by the ultra-traditionalist forces within the church. An anti-De Roo newspaper sprang up in his diocese in 1987; initiated by a couple who retired to the region expressly to counter his program.

In the midst of it all he stayed on course, seemingly undeterred and unrattled by attacks on his theology, personality and mission. Blessed with a famous equanimity and somewhat remote personality and nature, he rarely, if ever, took the assault personally.[11]

One example: When he was 'silenced' by Rome in 1999 for the first time—ironically after his retirement as an active bishop—he refused to comment, although he did provide a copy of the offending letter so it could be discussed publicly.

One of the most lasting charges by traditionalists was that he unduly influenced the Canadian Bishops' response to the birth control encyclical in 1968. *Humanae Vitae* became the first serious effort by reactionary conservative forces in the Vatican to derail Vatican II.

De Roo's original spade work prior to the Council led to his successful intervention on the issue of procreation at Vatican II. De Roo's work, it will be claimed, was a key element in expediting the crisis of confidence at the time of the 'Birth Control Encyclical'. He was said in certain quarters to have been undermining the respect for the hierarchy with democracy within the church. The Catholic Church is still an institution where being called a 'progressive intellectual' can be a pejorative epithet.[12]

His commitment to treat adult Catholics without a hint of the traditional paternalism—equals with only a distinctly different role—was very well received at the grass-roots level within the church. It also made him a bloc of enemies.

In a farewell interview with the local daily newspaper at the time of his retirement, he stated that many lay people came up to him at farewell events to say they appreciated this most about him. After nearly thirty-seven years in office, he said that nothing made him prouder.[13]

De Roo modeled a new way of being a bishop for Canada and in his own way the church universal. A unique Canadian contribution, this model reflects a permanent alteration to the way Roman Catholicism presently operates. Some nationalities were more prepared and suited to co-operate with the changes from Vatican II. Canada and the Canadian Catholic hierarchy were one such national church.

De Roo lived out the new paradigm introduced by the Council and in his own right was a force to be reckoned with due to his sharp focus and in-depth aptitude within the Canadian hierarchy. As a farmer's son his was a concrete theology, a 'way of doing theology' which he shared with the most outstanding Canadian Catholic theologians at the Second Vatican Council, Gregory Baum, a close friend, and J.M.R. Tillard, O.P.

As a bishop, De Roo was also radically centred in the gospel identification with the poor, a relentless trait that would more than passingly irritate the well-possessed.

As a Council Father at Vatican II, only the current pope served as long among those who attended all four sessions of the historic event between 1962 and 1965.[14] And that only because he was not required to submit to retirement at age seventy-five as De Roo was.

Some parallels with Archbishop Karol Wojtyla are illuminating and will be looked at later on. Many Canadians inside the church (and outside) feel that if there was ever an authentic Canadian candidate for papacy it was De Roo.

De Roo seemed destined to be at the event and he entirely identified with its commitment to church reform, the social struggle, to interfaith dialogue, and to ecumenical partnership. He persistently asserted that, in his view, Vatican II was a pure act of the movement of the Holy Spirit.

De Roo proved to be that rare combination of a man of action and a man of learning. The priorities of peace, championing the rights of poor and the voiceless were his in season and out—demonstrating a remarkable consistency. All of these traits have been attributed to Pope John Paul II as well but De Roo lived it out using a more mundane model.

At the same time, unlike his collegial superior the pope, De Roo adopted an entirely progressive theological stance, open to the idea (and practice) of the progressive development of doctrine[15] as well as challenges to and theological critiques of the church itself.

He took entirely seriously in an undeviating manner the challenge of Vatican II; challenges which others in positions of authority have worked to contain. Unlike the present pope, De Roo did not speak against the new emerging paradigm at the time of the Council.[16]

This is De Roo's story to be told in a fashion optimistically consonant with his style and priorities; that is, in a polemically sensitive manner. This book is an effort in the direction of biography but told with a controversial purpose. The Catholic Church, it will be argued, is in the midst of a persistent ongoing crisis of identity begun in earnest with the birth control controversy of 1968, with roots in The Second Vatican Council and beyond.

Less than three years after the official close of Vatican II, Pope Paul VI's *Humanae Vitae* demonstrated definitively things had changed for good within the Roman Catholic Church. The laity could no longer be relied upon to only 'pay, pray and obey', as the expression was.

Ten years later a new pope would be elected, one who would resist the direction of the change, who put his own distinctive stamp on the message of the Council event. This would be a pope who was dedicated by force of will to getting at least some of the genie back in the bottle.

However even as John Paul II nears his own final years it is still clear the crisis has not been entirely dissipated by 'containing' the progressive elements of Vatican II.[17]

There are plenty of powerful people inside the Curia and outside the church who never did want Vatican II to succeed.[18] It is no great surprise that Remi De Roo's progressive program has been sidelined for the time being; that there has been a systematic effort at discrediting him. The remarkable thing is that it had an opportunity to be tried at all given the history of the institution. Its very attempt indicates it can be resurrected when the conditions are correct again.

The verdict is still out. The story is far from over. For more than thirty-seven years Bishop Remi De Roo carried out his program in a way that brought encouragement to followers and animosity from opponents.

As the Catholic Church enters its third millennium, through the lens of De Roo's life, there is an opportunity to assess what has taken place and what is likely ahead; through the work of a remarkable Canadian pacesetter who broke down the walls between church and society in a pivotal if not permanent manner.

Obviously a definitive biography may well be in order in time. For now, with the bishop still intending to write further chapters of an active life, the purpose is to tell his story with something of the passion, courage and honesty that typified this Canadian figure of destiny.

Introduction to Pope Paul VI during Vatican II Session.

1975 audience with Paul VI with Canadian Bishops. (Foto FELICI, Roma)

Chapter Two:
1968 – The Watershed Year

1. A WARM SUMMER

It was a warm summer in Ottawa that year, so the country's Catholic Bishops held their usual summer gathering at a lakeside chalet outside the nation's capital. There was little to indicate what was just ahead.

As longtime staffer Bernard Daly recounts in his history of the bishops' conference, the well-planned agenda for the session "all became secondary in an instant" when the papal nuncio, (Archbishop Emanuele Clarizio) "opened his briefcase and handed out copies of Paul VI's finished work on an encyclical on human life."[19]

It was the summer of 1968 and the encyclical letter was the birth control statement, *Humanae Vitae, (On Human Life)*. An earthquake was about to happen in the Catholic Church, causing a permanent cleavage.

Issued on July 25, few if any papal statement caused the jolt this one would, not only on nearly one billion Catholics but on the consciousness of the modern world at large. This event would galvanize convictions and action around the options opened out by the sexual revolution of the Sixties.

The Canadian Bishops knew in that instant that their September meeting would be entirely given over to discussion of how to respond to this papal declaration. The meeting was scheduled for Winnipeg and its ultimate result would be almost as controversial as the pope's statement itself.

Bernard Daly himself would be scapegoated by groups who opposed the bishops' eventual stand, but who were not about to publicly take on a conference of bishops.[20] Instead it was said Daly had too much influence, thus occasioning his special section on 'tough issues' in his 1995 history book.

2. A PASTORAL RESPONSE

The Canadian Bishops' ultimate response to the troublesome encyclical was a nuanced one emphasizing the function of conscience in the adult Catholic. Catholics, it is taught, are ultimately responsible for the formation and updating of their own conscience. While due weight is to be given to official church teachings, the final decision has to be with the individual or couple as persons. Previously this emphasis was played down in Catholic teaching but work by Remi De Roo and the Canadian Bishops highlighted it at Vatican II.

The bishops spent an unprecedented full week on the deliberations in late September of 1968 and De Roo in his role as co-chair of the theological commission was admittedly a key player. He would have been deeply involved if only because of his general abilities and capacity with both official languages. For other prior reasons he played a crucial role in the largely unreported confidential proceedings of that week.

In the 1998 book *Even Greater Things* written in dialogue form of an exchange of letters with Mae and Bernard Daly, De Roo writes about the details of his interventions at Vatican II on sexual marriage partnership and procreation.[21]

3. THE PROBLEM OF MODERNITY

In line with the Canadian Bishops' statement of September 27, 1968, three years earlier at The Second Vatican Council in Rome, one of the four major documents approved was *The Church in The Modern World.* In it the Roman Catholic Church, virtually for the first time in its history, deliberately faced the modern world on its own terms.

For more than a hundred years modernity had dogged the church like a shadow aspect of its personality, one that it just did not know how to properly acknowledge. Vatican II was the moment when the Catholic Church made friends with modern society.

A principle axiom of the Council called by the astonishing Pope John XXIII was that the world had things to say to the church just as the church too had much, in its own view, to say to the world. This previously almost unthinkable idea of serious dialogue was precisely the purpose of the Council; an updating, in the Italian phrase an 'aggiornamento'; to begin in a whole new way the dialogue that would allow this ongoing exchange.

Part of the problem for the church was that there was no active dialogue, no one on the other side was listening to what the church had to say precisely because the church appeared to not be interested in what the world had to say. A great insularity resulted, hardened attitudes were the result. Finally had come a moment when the windows were opened wide, to 'let the wind of the spirit blow through'.

This was Pope John's adage and the result was to prove transformative. As a result much was expected from this birth control 'encyclical letter', so called because it is historically a form of communication circulated around the world through the local church.

A major sticking point historically in this non-dialogue had been Catholic sexual teaching as it affected procreation. As a consequence the eighty-some-year-old pope in his wisdom had reserved the issue of birth control to himself. He rightly sensed it would do nothing but divide the Council itself.

John XXIII died on June 3, 1963, after the first of four fall sessions which constituted the Council. His successor Paul VI was left to deal with the topic of contraception. Paul had admirably continued the work begun by John with the Council. Now in 1968 the touchy issue reserved to the pope would finally be confronted.

NOTEWORTHY SECTION

While the area of artificial contraception was preserved for papal perspective, there was a noteworthy section in *Gaudium et Spes*, Vatican II's *Pastoral Constitution on the Church in the Modern World* which was to prove very telling in the great controversy that was to arise from Paul VI's birth control statement.

Humanae Vitae was not defined infallibly. Its very weight as a teaching document became a prime source of controversy between left and right in the church. Its lack of collegiality was an issue as well.

As Gary MacEoin wrote in his popular-level book on the Council: "As far as Pope John was concerned, his ... concern was to revitalize the huge energy represented by the bishops, energy that had become progressively less since the declaration of papal infallibility in 1869 at the First Vatican Council.

"A solution effected by him would be no solution at all. It would simply confirm the claim of the Curia that the pope constituted the only centre of authority and decision in the church. The same consideration undoubtedly weighed upon Pope Paul, a man steeped in curial traditions.

"What is most extraordinary is that, with all these handicaps, the Council achieved so much."[22]

4. ON HUMAN LIFE

A standard element of Catholic teaching on sexual behaviour is that sexual intimacy is strictly reserved to marriage and that its proper aim is procreation which is to take primacy over any other aspect of marriage.

At least this was the pre-Vatican II teaching. This was certainly the general understanding: that partnership itself was entirely secondary to procreation. Without question this attitude reflected the major regard given to the near-absolute importance of the transmission of life in the Catholic view prior to Vatican II.

Obviously some—perhaps many—individuals and couples internally dissented from this narrowly-defined and exclusive view but this would be a private reservation; there is no record of public dissent prior to Vatican II. The church knew best and by 'the church' was meant the institution of the church—such was the regard of its general membership to its central teaching authority.

In this document on *The Church Today—Gaudium et Spes* by its Latin title—after a specific kind of preparatory groundwork a surprise segment was included—sections 49 and 50—ones that equated procreation with partnership in the area of conjugal love. Perhaps ambiguously as is the wont of Vatican documents, but a shift is definitely there.

The bishop principally responsible,[23] Remi De Roo of Victoria, Canada, was not about to publicly pronounce on its significance. To have it in the document was enough for the time. A few years later when the Canadian Bishops chose to respond pastorally to *Humane Vitae*, it would be brought forward in Winnipeg.

Naturally enough these paragraphs are directly alluded to in the Canadian Bishops' statement in response to *Humanae Vitae.*

❧❧❧

Paragraph 49 includes the sentence "Married love is an eminently human love because it is an affection between two persons rooted in the will and it embraces the good of the whole person; it can enrich the sentiments of the spirit and their physical expression with a unique dignity and ennoble them as the special elements and signs of the friendship proper to marriage."

It is significant that this preceded and thus conditioned paragraph 50 on the fruitfulness of marriage which states: "Marriage and married love are by nature ordered to the procreation and education of children."

The next paragraph of the section reads: "Married couples should regard it as their proper mission to transmit human life and to educate their children; they should realize that they are thereby co-operating with the love of God the Creator and are, in a certain sense, its interpreters... it also involves a consideration of their own good and the good of the children already born or yet to come, an ability to read the signs of the times and of their own situation on the material and spiritual level..."

These lines contain the new element, that 'in some sense' Catholic parents have to be the interpreters of family planning needs.

The teaching goes back and forth: "Married people should realize that their behaviour may not simply follow their own fancy, but must be ruled by conscience—and conscience ought to be conformed to the law of God in the light of the teaching authority of the church, which is the authentic interpreter of divine law."

This is followed however by: "But marriage is not merely for the procreation of children; its nature is an indissoluble compact between two people..."[24]

It is obvious that this is not an entirely unified approach to the question, the issue or the problem. In this way the problem of *Humanae Vitae* was forecast. Many hands, progressive and traditionalist, forward-looking and reactionary had a part in it. However, the ultimate thrust is in the direction of fresh development, new wind has blown through. Something permanent and new happened at Vatican II even in this area preserved for the pope. As

De Roo recently stated: "We achieved a certain breakthrough in church teaching about marriage at the Council."[25]

Like the Council itself, this new equation was revolutionary and would come back to haunt the debate within the decade. As one of the authors of this revolutionary change, the young Canadian bishop from the west coast Remi Joseph De Roo was thirty-eight years old at the time of his appointment and full of a startling potential.

5. AT VATICAN II

From the start De Roo was obviously a brilliant scholar. Reports from his seminary study days spoke of "his outstanding intellectual ability."[26] What was particularly significant about his 'conjugal love' intervention, however, was that it was not fundamentally a scholarly intercession. If it had been it probably would not have had the impact it did. Its power came from the fact it was direct feedback from people in real situations.

De Roo did have his doctorate in theology. In 1950 immediately following priestly ordination he was sent to Rome to complete a doctorate on the *Assumption into Heaven of the Blessed Virgin Mary*. This was a fact which would surprise both friends and foes alike within the church later, after he developed his reputation as a social radical and theological progressive.

Mariology often provided a blind behind which ultra-traditionalist right-wing Catholicism found its niche. Significantly in terms of this, the role of Mary was not directly dealt with in a separate document at Vatican II. It was generally recognized that her role had become exaggerated due to popular adulation.[27] Reference to Mary was integrated into the other texts, she was set up as the model in faith for the church not as someone far above it.

It was a long way from 1950 to 1965. Nothing shows this better than the new attitude toward Mary. But in those days, as he said himself, this was a very hot topic[28] in Catholic theological circles because the Pope of the day, Pius XII, had proclaimed officially the Dogma of the Assumption in 1950.

This was the first use of the doctrine of papal infallibility since its controversial adoption eighty years before. By contrast papal infallibility was not invoked for *Humanae Vitae* or at the Second Vatican Council.

In terms of modernity, The Assumption was a dogmatic declaration which the influential and decidedly non-Catholic psychologist Carl Jung welcomed. He saw it as a indication that Roman Catholicism, the great patriarchal religious system of the West, was now attempting to rectify its possibly inadvertent masculine-feminine dis-balance.[29]

Vatican II would be later understood as an advance in this direction and as such it would meet with great resistance; conscious and unconscious. In terms of birth control, it's no great stretch forward to move from the equality of partnership and procreation as enshrined in the documents of Vatican II in 1965 to the sort of mass resistance to *Humanae Vitae* in 1968.

6. FROM LIVED EXPERIENCE

This intervention by a bright Canadian Bishop was no accident. It reflected the changes that took place at the Council, both in terms of content and its central principles of collegiality and subsidiarity. It also sprang out of his own experience and emerging convictions about the direction needed for the Catholic Church in the last half of the 20th Century.

It was his debut onto the world stage. The next thirty-seven years would disclose a string of such progressive and prophetic intercessions, revealing an authentic revolutionary within the framework, at the very heart of the Catholic Church.

Scholars argue that the Catholic Church had been unconsciously preparing itself for the paradigm shift that took place at Vatican II. The same could be said of De Roo. Part of the purity of his emergence lay in the complete want of indications in his early life and formation that, like John XXIII, he would prove a prophet in the midst of such an institution; a new sort of church figure for the second half of the century.

∞∞∞

De Roo was the first graduate of his college to be appointed a bishop; from Saint Boniface College, the diocesan seminary in Winnipeg. At the seasoned age of thirty-eight he arrived in

Victoria December 20, 1962 after the First Session of the Council in Rome.

When he retired on February 24, 1999, his seventy-fifth birthday, he and the Pope, Karol Wojtyla as the former archbishop of Cracow, Poland were among the very few members of the Roman hierarchy worldwide who had attended all four sessions of the Council and were still active in their jobs.

In 1962 he looked at least a decade younger than thirty-eight, perhaps two decades. He was dubbed by a captivated media 'The Boy Bishop' but he was obviously no child intellectually or administratively. As stated, it was not from his scholarly work alone that De Roo formed his singular intervention.

The revolutionary aspect of his intervention on married love was that it was rooted in the lived experience of married couples: couples he pastored and listened to seriously. As a chaplain to the Christian Family Movement and Young Christian Workers in the 1950s he was a leader with these movements of young families and workers during the decades preceding the Council.

Out of their concrete experience these young married Catholics spoke candidly with trusted chaplains about their personal experience. These were the dynamics of family life as they found them, not so much as they 'ought to be' in the church's official view which was the usual disposition of ordinary Catholics in those times. Catholics were taught to always measure their lived experience against the church's lofty ideals.

This inevitably led to finding themselves lacking, falling far short of these often unreachable standards. This shortfall could be taken personally, that somehow it was all their own fault which would add a psychological burden to their own sense of deficiency. The attitude of the CFM couples was not the ordinary Catholic one of the time. Theirs was the attitude of the future, it was a pioneering movement in that way.

From this ongoing dialogue De Roo was prepared to act in an equally concrete way when the Second Vatican Council presented the opportunity. It was his pastoral opportunity to act on their expressed anguish; to honour the deliberations about the importance of loving partnership alongside procreative love. He had the means, the motivation and the opportunity to change history. He took it and was successful.

The significance of this intervention—which met with the approval of the three thousand bishops at Vatican II—was that by equating partnership with procreation in Catholic sexual teaching the Council had turned a tradition on end.[30]

Specifically to our present point, it logically and obviously opened the way to a succeeding step—a call for liberalization of the teaching on birth control. If a couple were to be given more direct responsibility for the ultimate meaning of their loving relationship then the pace of procreation and the means to regulate this would reasonably follow.

This was the face of modernity the church had traditionally foundered upon: the acceptance of its membership as full adults with a complete capacity for moral responsibility. The paternalism of the Catholic Church was challenged most directly on the birth control issue.

This faith maturity was the perhaps-not-surprising conclusion Catholics came to and acted upon in 1968. The floodgate had been opened by this tiny-seeming wedge. At minimum De Roo's successful intervention reflected the paradigm shift within the mass consciousness of the Catholic population, at least anticipating it by three years. The practical scholar had done his homework well. It was the quality of leadership that would characterize his term.

7. BIRTH CONTROL COMMISSION

This shift in consciousness was certainly the new understanding taken from the Council teachings by the birth control commission set up by John XXIII before his death in 1963.[31]

This was substantially the same commission that offered advice to Paul VI in preparation for his decree. It was a commission which included family life experts as well as ordinary couples plus the usual Vatican bureaucrats including an autocratic cardinal, Ottaviani, as chairman.

Their final deliberations were entirely disregarded by Pope Paul who was then shocked by the intense negative reaction that came from a world that had expected something much more positive on the issue. Knowledgeable, even conservative, commentators were astounded by the about face, which seemed to defy any consistency.[32]

In Germany for example, "a simultaneous poll among German Catholics at large found that 68 percent of them thought the pope was wrong on Contraception."[33] Greater numbers of polled Catholics in North America threatened to entirely disregard the teaching.

A permanent ongoing crisis of confidence in the authority of the central teaching office of the Catholic Church commenced from this moment. The ground has never been recouped. The internal reform of the church following the Council hit a wall.

That wall was the pope's seeming abandonment of the principle of collegiality just when it was most crucially required. In his final entry on this issue in *Even Greater Things*, De Roo states that the pope "may have lent support to those who now seem bent on undermining Vatican II's teaching on collegiality."[34]

Collegiality and its partner principle of subsidiarity are said to be one of Vatican II's chief accomplishments philosophically. Collegiality grants the colleges of national bishops an enhanced say in the local implementation of the church's universal teachings and principles. The Canadian Bishops's response to *Humanae Vitae* is an apt example.

Subsidiarity says that no higher level of authority should intervene when a subsidiary level can handle the issue on its own. In combination these two principles reversed over a hundred years of centralization of authority within the church.

The abandonment of collegiality at such a critical moment on such a crucial issue, less than three years after the Council, contributed to the credibility gap that ensued. The Canadian Bishops' challenging response to *Humanae Vitae* was its use of subsidiarity to try to compensate for the collegiality bust-up.

Having run up against a solid wall on internal church reform on the issue of birth control, the Canadian Bishops Conference changed its focus to a safer subject—social action. Safer for a while at least.

8. SHIRTSLEEVE BISHOP

When De Roo settled in at his diocese on Vancouver Island after the Council he utilized the scientific method of a survey of views to best determine how to implement the massive reforms of the Council. This was reported to have been the first time in its history that the Catholic Church had employed such measures, of actually systematically consulting the population affected by its rules.

He swiftly became known as the shirt-sleeve bishop for his direct and open consultation methods.[35] He became known as a leader who took seriously the views of his fellow Catholics and who had the ability to translate new emerging ideas into action.

As argued, it is not stretching the contention to claim that the work of Bishop De Roo (as a member of the College of Canadian Bishops) was at the instrumental heart of the credibility crisis in the world church. Certainly the style and content of the Canadian Bishops' response statement did nothing to contradict this idea.

At minimum the crisis illustrated De Roo's spirit, as a radically different sort of bishop with revolutionary ideas about the role and purpose (and even definition) of authority. All of which were in tune with the new theologies released by Vatican II. The new theologies out of Vatican II were actually vindicated older theologies which were condemned or suppressed during the immediately previous period. The revolution of Vatican II was said to be the theological revolution of all the suppressed great Catholic thinkers dating back a hundred years to John Henry Newman.

De Roo harkened back to this intellectual tradition. Ironically, in his personality and formation as a Catholic priest he cannot be faulted as a renegade, a rebel or even a revolutionary type. He was a fully formed and orthodox Catholic priest; perhaps too thoroughly formed for the good of the institution. Great institutions contain within themselves the seeds of their own reform and renewal. History conspired to put him in an unlikely role, but one in which he excelled and persisted.

While transparently orthodox and fully knowledgeable of the tradition and conservative practice of the church, circumstance placed him in this unique situation of manifesting a modern critical spirit just when the church decided to turn and face this reality. The Catholic Church to this day has not really begun to recover from this predicament of the crisis of 1968.

His years as a pastor and a chief administrator of the institution since 1968 exploited the necessary tension this involved. He pressed the changes to their limits while at the same time completely adhering to the roots of the tradition. Such was his prodigy;

to be able to walk that creative line on the margin of the institution while at the same time occupying one of its central offices.

The solution that was imposed ten years later with the election of an authoritarian style pope in 1978 was at best an intermediate measure. This pope, who was believed to have the charisma, talent, intelligence and wits to re-impose something of the old order—to provide 'A Restoration'—provided simply a temporary holding pattern of containment while he was still in charge.[36]

The new pope attracted a new sort of Catholic to join the church, fundamentally neo-conservative with neo-romantic notions of the nature and role of the church in the world. This medieval reversion flew in the face of activist spiritualities that arose out of Vatican II.[37]

But the fundamental problem was not ever resolved. It still lingers not far beneath the surface awaiting other leadership. The longer term judgment of history is still out in its final deliberation. This is because the twenty-one ecumenical councils, which historically have governed the Catholic Church over its two thousand years, happen on average every hundred years.

In this measure, only the next sixty-five years will tell the tale. In that time there will have been another four to five popes (customarily they average fifteen-year terms) and the result will come about through the twists and turns of an emerging leadership.

This scenario assumes that the very structure of governance itself, represented by the monarchic papacy, or the imperial papacy as some call it[38] will still be intact. Many argue that modernity here too will necessarily have its way and that great change will come as a result of the principles introduced at Vatican II to the system of the papacy's still very medieval monarchic style of rule.

Many believe that the eventual legacy of Vatican II will be a massive paradigm shift away from this permanent-seeming structure.[39] That indeed would be revolutionary, but it will not be without further great struggle.

The problem for the traditionalist is that they might be only enjoying a moment of fool's paradise, while the present regime is intact. If Vatican II is the new reality, as distinct from the contained Vatican II of the last twenty years, their misery has only begun.

For the progressives, on the other hand, since by and large they act as if the church is still the same as it was when they enjoyed it most, things can only get better or stay about the same; which is still tolerable compared with the pre-Vatican II era.

9. A 'REVOLUTIONARY'

At the time of Remi De Roo's retirement in 1999, thirty-seven years after 1962, a spate of articles appeared noting naturally enough his contribution. One piece in the daily newspaper of Victoria by Ian Dutton called him a persistent revolutionary.[40]

Another writer, in an article of the *Magazine of the Christian Taskforce on Central America,* Deirdre Kelly, told how De Roo had galvanized her into action in 1980. Kelly went on to become the director of the office for social justice of the Diocese of Victoria during De Roo's last decade at Victoria.

Her testimonial captures how De Roo as a man of history effected people at the grass roots, transforming their lives by his presence, words and experience.

BETWEEN DESPAIR AND SPIRITUALITY

"It's amazing to know the exact time one's life changes forever. I was in a room with some friends on Holy Saturday in 1980. We had met to pray and talk together as Easter drew near. Bishop De Roo had been invited to talk to us ... He came in needing no introduction. He sat with our small group of all ages, some of us living between a quiet despair and a budding spirituality.

"He began to talk, his eyes shining, animated. The stories he told us that afternoon have since become familiar to all of us. He had just returned from visiting Central America at a time when the region was burning in the heat of revolution and war. He had visited Panama, Guatemala, El Salvador and Nicaragua. The group sat riveted as he highlighted meeting Vincente Menchu in Guatemala, father of the now-Nobel prize winner Rigoberta Menchu.

"Bishop Remi recalled from his notes, 'The wrinkled, sunburned face of Vincente, a seventy-five-year old farmer, remains etched in my memory. After Vincente had calmly described the most horrendous tortures, the violations of women and children, the wanton destruction of homes and burning of farms by army personnel, he went on to say, *if we must die so our children can live, we are prepared to sacrifice our lives.*'

"Three days later, on January 31, 1980, Vincente and his companions were among the thirty-nine victims that resulted from the assault on the Spanish Embassy in Guatemala City by the Guatemalan police. Fire bombs were thrown into the embassy, claiming the lives of protestors who had sought refuge there.

"In El Salvador, Bishop De Roo met with Archbishop Oscar Romero after Mass in the room adjoining the chapel... the monseigneur was tired but they met for an hour, telling De Roo that his life was in danger, speaking of impending pressures Salvadoran church workers were feeling.

"It has been so many years since that Holy Saturday," Kelly recalls, "but I can still hear Bishop Remi say, 'Three weeks after I got back to Victoria, Bishop Romero was killed.'

"As a response to this horrendous event, and the widespread violence that characterized El Salvador at that time, De Roo formed the *Archbishop Romero Memorial Fund* and some of us from our small meeting got active, eventually organizing *'Tools For Peace,'* an ongoing aid project for Nicaragua's revolution, Nicaragua, the balm on the wound of war-torn Central America."

Formal episcopal photograph shortly after Second Vatican Council.

Greeting Bishop Samuel Ruiz of Chiapas at St. Andrew's Cathedral in 1998.

Media interview session during 'Ethical Reflections' debate, 1983. (Canapress)

Dr. Tony Clarke, Maude Barlow of The Council of Canadians and De Roo at the University of Victoria during Free Trade Debate of the early 1990s. (ICN)

Chapter Three: Politics and the Church

1. HAPPY NEW YEAR

I happened to be in Toronto over Christmas and New Years 1982-83. I was going out for dinner early on New Year's Eve when I spotted the front page of *The Star* newspaper. I could hardly believe my eyes.

Due to the work I had been doing during the 1970s and early '80s[41] I had been directly tracking the Bishops's social affairs statements and knew they were doing quality social justice work but I had hardly expected their statements would ever get this sort of front page play.

The banner headline read: **"CANADA'S UNEMPLOYMENT IMMORAL, BISHOPS CHARGE,"** the subhead read **"In a radical, blistering critique of Canada's economic strategies Roman Catholic prelates plead for worker's rights over profits."**

I knew where this was coming from as I had been editor of the *Prairie Messenger,* Saskatchewan's progressive Catholic weekly when Pope John Paul's social encyclical espousing humanist socialism had come out in 1982. I still remember the excited feeling from sitting up all night closely reading this lengthy and exacting document. I had a sense he was doing something new, and, as the English say, 'brilliant'.

Bishop De Roo had sent a tape of unsolicited commentary on that encyclical which we were only too glad to print. John Paul II argued for labour over capital on the philosophical basis of the higher priority of the transformative subjective process of labour over the end product of that labour, i.e. capital. "People before profits" was a slogan borrowed from this work.

As I looked over this front page story I could see why *The Star* featured the Bishops' statement. It corroborated what they were saying as a liberal paper about the human impact of the recent recession. *The Globe and Mail* would have picked it up not to be outdone on a dead news day. But then it took off across the country like a prairie wildfire in De Roo's home province of Manitoba.

It wasn't just the cover story, *The Star* was giving the statement a definite positive spin. Commentator David Crane inside the New Years' Eve edition opened his column with these words:

"The Canadian Catholic Conference of Bishops, in a year-end statement of concern for the country's 1.5 million unemployed and their families, has delivered a more important message on the economy than all our politicians, business leaders and economists."

The bishops had touched a deep nerve, that of fairness and social justice, something they had been saying and building up since the 1960s. Earlier in the middle 1950s the Canadian Bishops had issued annual 'Labour Day Statements', largely ignored but historically invaluable to understand the lead-up to this blockbuster event.

2. CANADIAN CATHOLIC SOCIAL TEACHING

After Vatican II there was a strong build-up of political analysis in church social teaching including its most famous offspring 'Liberation theology'. Implicitly this analysis had been there since the start in 1891.

According to Gregory Baum, in 1891 Catholic Social Teaching (CST) was a sort of noblesse oblige, with a high regard for the 'common good'. It was a kind of a Red Toryism in its 19th Century origin, but changes were impending in the 1950s.[42]

Modern methods and language had been employed replacing archaic medieval concepts and language but the general thrust never varied. Certainly the Catholic Church held strong beliefs that it had important insights about the correct social order. The Old Testament prophets were the basis of the tradition, together with gospel values about how the poor were to be treated by a righteous believer. More importantly CST recognized the power of social sin.

Eighteen ninety-one saw the first papal social encyclical. While the social encyclical of 1931—forty years later—targeted the problems of the Great Depression, the teachings, according to Baum, were at such a general and abstract level that they could be applied by left and right alike to justify their programs; and they were.[43] After Vatican II the prophetic tradition was revisited and because it was a critique of the established order, by and large, the church came down much more on the side of the left. Catholic social teaching had always been 'idealistic' inasmuch as it demanded faith, sacrifice and selflessness, outlining what ought to happen according to an abstract ideal of justice.

As a result the social statements by the Canadian bishops continued only to be general statements right up into the 1950s. For example, in 1956 the annual Labour Day statement was titled *"On Labour Unions—automation—housing advertising—consumption—credit,"* certainly an encompassing if general futuristic focus.

In 1962 it was titled *"Socialization"* picking up on that particular principle from Pope John XXIII's 1961 encyclical *'Mater et magistra' (Mother and teacher)* on the social role of the church. Papal encyclicals often set the tone and the current theme, just as John Paul II's had in 1982-83.

In 1966 it was *"Poverty in Canada,"* still pretty general. Only in the early Seventies did the focus and analysis tighten and become much sharper.

During the Seventies the convention of an Annual Labour Day Statement was abandoned in favour of occasional and much more frequent statements in direct response to emerging crises.

For example, in 1971 there were four major statements including: *"A Christian stance in the face of Violence,"* picking up on pacifism and civil disobedience and general social unrest of the era. Also in line with this was *"Christian formation for justice,"* while the major statement of the period was titled: *"Super States and Multi-national Corporations in a Developing World Community,"* the global context was front and centre.

Nineteen seventy-two saw another four statements: *"Social Justice in the Church," "Sharing National Income," "Implications of Political Choices," "Simplicity and Sharing."* All were hard hitting, left-leaning and focused on specific political change.

Between 1973 and 1979 there was a tremendous build-up with fifteen more on the issues of women, northern development, immigration, housing, social responsibility, transforming society, bank investments, unemployment, development, inequality, guaranteed annual income, all leaning well to the left.

By 1980 the analysis was very firmly focused with a clear direction. During the early Eighties it was politically targeted. Just prior to *Ethical Reflections*, the titles read: *"Unemployment: The Human Cost,"* (January 1980); *"On Oil and Gas legislation—A message to the Prime Minister,"*(March 1981); *"Towards a New International Economic Order—a Message to the Prime Minister"* (October 1981); *"The Neutron Bomb—Enough is Enough!"* (November, 1981).

In the same short period: *"A brief to the Standing Committee on External Affairs on External Affairs and National Defence: On Preparation for The Second Special Session of the United Nations on Disarmament"* (February, 1982); finally, *"To the Prime Minister: On Peace and Disarmament,"* (December 1982), and then *"Ethical Reflections on the Economic Crisis"* on January 1, 1983.

This concentration of statements indicated a new sort of thrust, one aimed at action not simply education. The Canadian Bishops had adopted the Liberation Theology model to the Canadian context, where education springs from action followed by reflection. It was the same 'See, Reflect, Act model' developed for the Young Christian Workers in the 1950s.

Remi De Roo chaired the social affairs commission all during this build-up period, adapting his previous experience to the new situation and bringing fresh insights wrought by the new practice. De Roo with commission staff person, Dr. Tony Clarke, engineered a new sort of approach to Catholic Social teaching, permanently transforming it in the process.

This new development of focusing directly on the politicians (rather than broad sweeping statements aimed at educating the general population of Catholics) proved effective.

Prime Minister Pierre Trudeau for one found it trying. From the Duplessis era in Québec he was already anti-clerical and this new clericalism from the left was just as irritating. When *Ethical Reflections* hit the headlines, Trudeau was the first to dismiss the bishops as meddlers in affairs they did not understand.

It did not end with *Ethical Reflections*. Before 1986 there were five more statements to follow up; one even harder hitting, to the MacDonald Royal Commission on Economic Union in late 1983. But it did not get the headlines.

By then the general public was used to seeing De Roo as an iconoclast on television and the impact of a savvy, articulate, left-wing Catholic bishop was not so sudden. Rather he had become part of the equation, and a cultural icon for the Canadian left.

3. PROPHETIC CATHOLICISM

So by December of 1982 the social affairs commission was ready to be heard and according to *The Toronto Star* and other key media, the country needed to hear it. From its response the public welcomed the discussion. Catholic bishops had shown their leftist populist leanings. Some columnists claimed they were trying to bring back adherents in a desperate maneuver.

It would all prove fuel for the fire, and the public discussion went on for most of the decade of the 1980s with Remi De Roo a key figure.

In his accompanying *Toronto Star* column on January 1, 1983 David Crane was far from cynical about the bishops' motives: "The bishops reminded us of two critical points. The first is that the economy is simply the means to the end. The way we run our economy and share its output reflects our basic values as a people. The bishops and many other people see economic activity as the achievement of social justice.

"The economy can be used to guarantee a level of well-being and dignity for everyone... The important point made by the bishops is that how we divide the economic pie reflects our values as a people.

"The Catholic bishops are reminding us that we need to step out of the intellectual strait jacket imposed by bankers, businessmen and academic economists. As the bishops correctly argue, we are in the midst of far-reaching economic changes that go well beyond the current problems of recession: a new economic vision is needed with new tools and new institutions...The bishops have challenged us with a strong call to action and change."

This sort of critique—severely anti-capitalist, long a standard element of papal social encyclicals and accentuated during the Great Depression in 1931—served to balance off the usually excessive anti-communism that had always been played up in Catholic circles.

The great shock for the ordinary church members was how far to the left the bishops had moved. But in actuality this had begun with Pope John XXIII and his introduction of the principle of socialization in the early Sixties.[44] After John XXIII socialism would be acceptable in Catholic thinking. After 1971 social justice work was claimed to be "a constitutive element of the gospels."[45]

John Paul II himself would advocate a form of humanist socialism in his 1981 social encyclical *On Human Work*.

With the progress of the Canadian Bishops, by the early 1980s, the focus had turned completely away from the symptomatic social problems and was centering on the political-economic root cause of the difficulty. All of this made the establishment very antsy about what they were hearing.

These were more than pious homilies, much more; and they were rooted in recent papal analysis that argues the problem lies in the nature of capitalism itself, within its framework of the national security state.

The Canadian Bishops' statements became more intense and penetrating. If the clock was ticking, the time bomb went off on New Year's Day, 1983.

If it was expected the bishops might not have that much more to say on the topic after their initial blow-out statement, the business community was sadly mistaken. The condemnatory dissection of neo-liberal capitalism was not well received but it was far from over. De Roo and Clarke made some permanent enemies during the furore, but also some staunch allies, and there was no looking back.

Big guns and paid hacks came to the rescue of the system, from media mogul Conrad Black on down. With all their considerable resources, they attacked the Bishops, the message and the messengers, particularly Remi De Roo. The reactionaries and the right wing had its firm allies within the church.

Cardinal Emmett Carter of Toronto, who had been upstaged in his hometown, so to speak, distanced himself from the social affairs commission statement as 'unrepresentative' but it had actually been cleared through the normal channels of the Bishops Conference. Carter had been caught looking the other way and he wasn't the only conventional leader to be caught offguard.[46]

The *Montreal Gazette* said in its January 4 editorial: "Emmett Cardinal Carter of Toronto unceremoniously rebuked the eight-bishop social affairs commission... But the bishops should be praised, not criticized, for not ducking controversy. Perhaps some people would prefer clerics to utter banalities from the pulpit..." On this one Carter and his Catholic initiate Conrad Black[47] formed an attacking team.[48]

Journalist Ron Graham described the phenomenon this way: "To judge by the press and the fury, however, the new message was not really heard until December, 1982, when the bishops' social-affairs commission under Remi De Roo produced its 'Ethical Reflections on The Economic Crisis.'

"The storm over its radical rhetoric and interventionist solutions demonstrated their novelty to much of the public, and much of the debate had less to do with unemployment or inflation than with the appropriateness of a Church statement on economics or the intrusion of the bishops into politics. The idea that economics could be separated from ethics proved to the bishops just how unethical liberal capitalism had become."[49]

4. SURVIVING CELEBRITY

Michael Higgins wrote in *Portraits of Canadian Catholicism*, "De Roo would survive the media blitz with commendable grace. If nothing else, he is a durable bishop."[50]

Bishop De Roo's executive assistant, Eileen Archer, said years later that the phones kept ringing for months with intensity and then for years with consistency.[51] De Roo and Clarke and Bishop Adolphe Proulx of Hull (for the French sector) proved versatile individuals, well able to handle the barrage of media interviews; using the attention to sustain their program, so long in the making.[52]

The Canadian Bishops had indeed been preparing their analysis throughout the late 1970s, honing it particularly since the 1975 statement, titled appropriately enough "From Words to Action." Higgins and Douglas Letson stated in 'Portraits': "all during that decade the social affairs commission had been issuing statements, well developed in their vision and analysis, which lead logically to the 1983 blockbuster."

De Roo's little biographical essay was the second chapter of their book, only immediately preceded by one on Cardinal Emmett Carter.[53]

5. PAPAL ENDORSEMENT

Significantly it was a papal social encyclical, *On Human Labour,* by John Paul II—perhaps the strongest, certainly the most progressive, statement of his papacy—issued in 1981 that gave the New Years' statement much of its primary punch. The pope had lain the philosophical basis for 'putting people over profits' as the social affairs commission insisted concerning the crisis of unemployment and recession.

The Canadian Bishops and John Paul were working in tandem even though they were coming from radically different social, political and economic histories.

It would not be the last time the pope would back up the social thinking of the bishop. His visit to Canada in 1984 was a definite validation of De Roo's leadership on the social question.

Tony Clarke's controversial book, *Behind The Mitre,*[54] provides exact details of the 1983 events that launched De Roo into media celebrity.[55]

More significantly for the church itself, Clarke spells out the reaction that set in, resulting in his own eventual and controversial removal from his position at the CCCB. (De Roo was also replaced in the late Eighties as chairperson of the social affairs commissions, though he claimed it was a routine procedure.)

Without doubt January 1, 1983 was the highest level of history by headline for the bishop, though the papal tour proved the peak promotion of the ethical pronouncement.

Tony Clarke gives this analysis: "For most of 1984 the work of the bishops' conference was largely taken up with preparations for the visit of Pope John Paul II.

"The twelve-day tour would be the longest papal visit in any country... Unlike papal visits in other parts of the world, the Canadian bishops did not want to turn this tour into a triumphal event. Instead the visit was designed to give expression to the diverse cultural and regional realities of the church from coast to coast...

"From the Commission's standpoint, much was at stake with this papal visit. As the time of the pope's arrival drew near, there was growing speculation in the media over whether he would openly endorse or refute the strong stands taken by the Commission and the Canadian bishops as a whole with respect to the economy."

"John Paul had become known as 'the workers' pope.' His encyclicals, especially *On Human Labour*, had provided the Canadian Bishops with inspiration for their moral critique of Canada's economy. But John Paul had not yet taken a clear position in support of liberation theology. Nor had he gone as far as the Canadian Bishops in criticizing capitalism and the role of transnational corporations. He was also wary of bishops committed to social activism and had warned against priests becoming involved in politics...

"The first clear signal of the Pope's endorsement of *Ethical Reflections* came during an ecumenical service with fishers at Flatrock on the coast of Newfoundland. With a flotilla of fishing boats in the background, John Paul declared that he stood firmly with the Canadian Bishops in deploring conditions of unemployment and their call for a 'restructuring of the economy, so that human need is put before financial gain.'

"In Toronto, while speaking about the moral order of the economy, he expanded on the bishops' list of ethical priorities. 'The needs of the poor,' he repeated, 'must take priority over the desires of the rich; the rights of workers over the maxification of profits; the preservation of the environment over uncontrolled industrial expansion; and production to meet social needs overproduction for military purposes.'...

"In Edmonton, John Paul focused attention on Canada's role in the global economy. Drawing upon Christ's account of The Last Judgment he warned, 'the poor South will judge the rich North; the poor people and poor nations .... will judge those people who take these goods away from them, amassing to themselves the imperialistic monopoly of economic and political supremacy at the expense of others.' ... He sounded like one of the ancient prophets delivering a passionate exhortation to his people."

6. THE SEVENTIES: DECISIVE DECADE

The 1970s build-up proved the key years in De Roo's preparatory stage for national leadership. In 1968 he was forty-four years old, by 1980 he would be fifty-six. Those twelve years of his peak power were his most creative period. It was during this time that his work transformed the nature of social justice work done in the Canadian Catholic Church and beyond.

Symbolically in the same year as the 'birth control fuss', as one headline called it, Saint Boniface Basilica in Bishop De Roo's home diocese burned to the ground. The post-Vatican II transformation of the church in De Roo's home diocese of Winnipeg and Saint Boniface was physical.

Headlines around the birth control situation read: *"Birth Control Fuss makes Bishop 'Uneasy.'"* *The Western Catholic Reporter*, out of Edmonton, gave the *"Story Behind the Bishops' Conscience Statement;"* and in October, 1969 the *Victoria Colonist* reported: *"Remi De Roo: Conduct on the Pill Grave Worry.'"*

At the end of the 1960s, Bishop De Roo was publicly expressing concern about an issue he feared could put a damper on the important progress wrought by the Council. If he had universal concerns, he did not pull back in his own diocese.

And internationally he upped the ante, travelling to Japan in January, 1970 to help establish a permanent World Conference on Religion and Peace. He was announcing that he felt there was a slowdown in both the ecumenical push and an underdevelopment in the variety of ministries undertaken by ordinary lay people in the church.

In the early Seventies the bishop was making speeches reported in *The Windsor Star, The Chicago Sun-Times* and *The National Catholic Reporter* of Kansas City that the Canadian Bishops were seeing their role as one of animating not coercing, of listening rather than telling, or encouraging clergy to be accountable to their parishioners, particularly women.[56]

Symbolically, at home in 1973 Saint Andrew's Cathedral spire was painted what were described only half-jokingly as psychedelic shades. The same year Saint Ann's Academy was allowed to close; it had been the pre-eminent girls school of the region since 1858 when the Sisters of Saint Ann first came to Vancouver Island.

De Roo's gentle program of nudging religious orders toward new roles and undertakings continued on schedule. He had been bishop on Vancouver Island a decade at this point.

It was then that De Roo was appointed by the new left-leaning provincial government as its human rights commissioner, the first for the province. For the next number of years the "Perfect Catholic Bishop Human Rights Battler" as he was designated in the weekly *Victorian* newspaper of September 29, 1976, put social fairness, if not social justice, front and centre in his community profile.

A curious case which offset some of the positive publicity was the protracted situation and eventual lawsuit with Mother Cecilia, an animal protection advocate and activist. Her attitudes were controversial, and the English Benedictine nun would not take any direction from the diocese or Rome on the matter.

Eventually she retreated from the Catholic communion after final defeats in both church and civil courts in early 1975. In the very end she did 'return to the Catholic Church' facilitated by a traditionalist clergyman just prior to her death.

'Mother Cecilia' was a cause celebre, made popular by the local press coverage. It was the first full scale instance of bad publicity for the bishop but proved more of a nuisance case than an actual issue. Later it would come back to haunt him when the separate trust fund set up from Mother Cecilia's Priory sale would be used for questionable investments.[57]

When he had first arrived in the throes of Vatican II, the press coverage was glowing and plentiful given his photogenic qualities and newsworthiness.

Ten years after the close of Vatican II, De Roo convoked a diocesan assembly called 'Interaction '75'. It would prove to be the first of a two-stage diocesan synod process. The second major five-year component would take place between 1986-91, but Interaction '75 served to consolidate the gains made during the previous ten years.

"Clergy, Lay people, being asked to take Part in Setting Catholic Policy and Goals," read the *Times* headline of February 15, 1975.

De Roo was among the very first bishops in the country to convoke a major synod, a practice which had fallen into disuse by the Catholic Church as a means of consulting the laity but was an ancient tradition of the historical church. Synodal church was a natural follow-up to Vatican II and De Roo was decades ahead of most Canadian dioceses which only got into the habit in the 1990s. Few of the other synods would have his thoroughness of consultation methodology.[58]

As outlined the rest of the decade saw the massively escalating involvement by the Canadian Bishops in the social justice issues of the day. Notably perhaps the Northern Pipeline moratorium of 1977; the death penalty debate of 1976; Canadian Immigration policy in 1974; and Latin American human rights which came to a crisis point with the murder of Archbishop Romero in 1980.

Romero's death was just at the time of De Roo's visits to that region as a human rights observer, his reputation preceding him from his provincial commission experience earlier in the decade. The irony of Romero's martyrdom was that the archbishop had been a cautious, conservative figure who only caught fire once exposed to the real plight of his people. He was educated by the people themselves and by the deaths of some of his key clergy who had made strong justice stands on the side of their parishioners. Vatican II had released a powerful and unpredicted energy in Third World Catholics.

When Oscar Romero was murdered in March, 1980, assassinated while saying Mass, the Catholic Church worldwide reached another post-conciliar turning point. Dozens of Jesuits, nuns, lay women and other missioners had been murdered for their justice stands, including the right to clean water, a semblance of housing, health care, et cetera. but this was an archbishop, a powerful symbolic figure. A crisis point had been reached. High level accommodations would have to be made.

Romero's murderer was trained by the American military at the School of the Americas in Fort Benning, Georgia. Many other martyrs had fallen at the same trained hands. These killings would only lessen dramatically when Pope John Paul II cut a deal with the Ronald Reagan administration of the American government.

In an agreed upon exchange the CIA bankrolled *Solidarity*, the Polish independent trade union under Lech Walesa, through

American Labour; which eventually led to the fall of the Iron Curtain in 1989. At the same time Pope John Paul II agreed to officially repress liberation theology in Latin America.[59]

7. JUSTICE AND POLITICS

De Roo was interviewed at length about "Faith and politics, church and justice, El Salvador and Nicaragua," particularly the situation in El Salvador, in 1981 by my youngest brother, Eugene Jamieson, then a Victoria journalist for a local magazine.

Monday magazine used some of the lengthy interview but we published it in its entirety in *The Prairie Messenger* in September of that year. The candid exchange focused upon the touchy role of the church in partisan (and non-partisan) politics:

Eugene Jamieson:

The Catholic New Times *quotes the papal nuncio in Ottawa, Monsignor Angelo Palmas, as saying the Catholic Church is always neutral in politics. Is that the policy of the Church as a whole?*

Remi De Roo:

"That has to be put into context. Obviously in particular political decisions affecting partisan politics the Church will remain officially neutral. Because the church's responsibility is not in the field of politics as such, and I am speaking now of partisan politics.

"The temporal, pragmatic decisions that have to be made by politicians as to how best use the power available to them to bring about solutions to specific temporal problems. But we must not confuse that with basic principles of truth, justice and the special love for our fellow human beings. When people are being tortured and the right to life is being ignored, to remain silent is to be guilty by complicity of horrendous crimes."

E.J.:

Where then do you draw the line between what is partisan politics and what is standing up for the basic principles of truth and justice?

R.D.R.:

"Partisan politics means, for instance, pertaining to specific political parties and advocating specific political policies that effect directly the temporal realm. It is not for the church to say, for instance, what party a Catholic should belong to or what policies a specific party should follow. That is not the role of the church. But it is certainly the role of the church, following the role of Jesus Christ, to proclaim the basic principles of justice, truth and love of neighbour, promotion of peace, without which you cannot have any democracy, let alone civilization."

E.J.:

There must be one particular party which is consistently more in line with Christian ethics than the others and thus more worthy of Catholic support than others.

R.D.R:

"As long as a political party does not posit or advocate actions which are directly contrary to the gospel, then Catholics have the freedom to adhere to that party and to try to work in that party to bring its methods of action and its solution for society's problems in line with the principles of the gospel.

"That is the basic responsibility for political life that everyone has on the basis of baptism and that is not only lay people, that is also the responsibility of clergy and bishops—everyone. We are all citizens of this world as well as members of the church and we have a basic political responsibility to try and improve society."[60]

This question and answer excerpt highlights the left-right tension in the church around the political question. Progressives like De Roo try to push the question to a deeper level to avoid the issue of the Catholic Church's traditional social conservatism which has been exploited by right-wing forces in society.

Conrad Black's conversion to Catholicism would be a good example of this appeal. One can imagine a not-so-hidden appeal for Black in becoming a Catholic through Cardinal Carter's auspices was to take on the role of De Roo's nemesis. De Roo's capability to deal with questions in depth disarms a great deal of this tendency and explains something of Black's venomous antipathy for the bishop's 'meddling in politics'.

When De Roo was viciously detracted after retirement, an academic explanation ran that he was suffering the consequences of hubris. Arrogant presumption was the source of his downfall, and perhaps Conrad Black and his *National Post* were the righteous agent of nemesis.

The more politically realistic understanding would focus on the danger for Catholic bishops to 'meddle in politics' even or especially when they have the sort of gospel-based prophetic understanding of the task that De Roo expressed above.

Gene Jamieson's first four questions in his interview focused on the problem of American intervention in the Central America region and how the church was able to circumvent the usual filtered information problem. De Roo's answers show him to be deeply engaged in and knowledgeable about the church's emerging alternative justice network.

E.J.:

The Canadian and American Catholic Bishops have been very critical of the current government in El Salvador and U.S. military aid to that country. Why is that?

R.D.R.:

"Basically because the present government is not bringing about a situation of justice for the mass of the people. The great majority of the peasants have seen no progress whatsoever in the last fifty years in trying to achieve basic social justice."

E.J.:

Why are the Canadian Catholic Bishops against U.S. military aid?

R.D.R.:

"Basically the Canadian bishops' stand reflects the stand made so clearly by Archbishop Oscar Romero in his letter to President (Jimmy) Carter in which he said what we have here is a necessary revolution. A solution can be brought about peacefully if foreign intervention stays out.

"He asked the United States to stay out. He said any military aid sent now merely shores up a discredited government and allows them to kill more people, delays the day when a true solution based on social justice will be possible and distorts what is basically a social problem into a military issue."

E.J.:

Do you think the problems in El Salvador could be solved peacefully if the American military aid was not there?

R.D.R.:

"In January of 1980 when I was in Salvador, the university called attention to the deepening coalition of popular forces that represented everything from left to slightly right of centre which was dialoguing with private business interests as well at the time.

"That umbrella organization—and I know it was supported by Archbishop Romero and a number of leaders I talked to among the peasants and churches—was the only popular force that would have the support of the people and could bring about a peaceful revolution. It is certain that if it had not been for massive military aid by the United States the junta would have crumbled."

E.J.:

The Church in Canada has primarily served as a source of information on the situation in El Salvador. How is it getting that information and how reliable is it? Is it more reliable than the information the Canadian government is getting from the U.S. Department of State?

R.D.R.:

"The church has a number of people working in Salvador. I have met a number of those people personally. They are missionaries, priests and sisters. There are a few lay people. And there is quite a number of European missionaries, many of them with degrees in social sciences. I have met and talked with a number of them.

"We also have direct personal contact. We had it with Archbishop Romero and we have it with his successor. I have personally visited with them at home. We have direct contact by mail, telephone, and telex with the legal department of the archdiocese, the director of which is now in exile having had his life threatened. But he still has channels into the country.

"The federal government sources rely on the interpretation of the American ambassador there. It is well known that the role of an ambassador is primarily political and tied in also with commercial interests. Consequently they will get their official information mainly from government channels. Because they are recognized as being closely associated with the government I can understand why representatives of the popular force should be somewhat reticent in talking with American representatives.

"These popular forces represent a coalition of some forty movements representing a great range of movements from peasants to farmers co-operatives etc. Canada has never had an embassy in El Salvador. Canadian officials are almost totally at the mercy of the American secretary of state. We don't deny the Canadian government's right to rely on the Americans but what we would like is for them to produce the evidence on which they base their conclusions so that it can be compared with the information we have."

8. THE CHIAPAS CONNECTION

Seventeen years later De Roo was keeping up the direct supportive link to the justice struggles in Latin America. The January, 1998 front page of *Island Catholic News*, the independent monthly serving Vancouver Island and the Diocese of Victoria, ran the headline "Diocese Forges Support Link with Chiapas."

Bishop Samuel Ruiz of Chiapas, the new Oscar Romero of that hemisphere, was in Victoria and was greeted and welcomed by De Roo at the Cathedral for a noon hour service. That morning the Mexican Bishop had been part of a protest march about Canadian Foreign policy in his region of Mexico.

The immediate event in Chiapas was that a few weeks earlier, on December 22, 1997 forty-five "innocent people were murdered by government-linked paramilitary troops," the story reported. These people were meeting in a village church at the time of the massacre and were lay educators who did religious instruction for the diocese.

Ruiz and his assistant bishop had been ambushed earlier in November and his sister was attacked in a separate but related incident. It was all understood by church authorities as a part of a process of intimidation. Ruiz chaired the peace commission mediation process between the Mexican government and the Zapatista Army for National Liberation which had been waging warfare against the state in that part of Mexico since January 1, 1994. When the North American Free Trade Agreement (NAFTA) came into effect, it eliminated traditional native land rights in the view of the popular uprising leaders.

Ruiz was believed to be too closely aligned with the issues being raised for negotiation by the Zapatistas. Chiapas is one of Mexico's poorest states with highest levels of poverty indicators. For example salaries were one third of the national average and the majority of homes lack basic electricity and water services.

De Roo had lead the charge as part of a popular coalition against the Free Trade agreement in Canada. Tony Clarke had written a book about it called *Silent Coup* and been the spokesperson for the Action Canada Network which was formed to resist free trade.

ණණණ

In the 1981 interview published in the *Prairie Messenger*, De Roo had answered questions which would come to bear on the Chiapas situation:

Is it the belief of yourself or the Canadian Catholic Bishops that social justice can be achieved in the social and political structure of modern capitalism? Or do you anticipate a need to shift to a new economic or political order based more upon the ideals of socialism?

"We, the Canadian Catholic bishops, have printed a paper on that very subject and in it we said that these decisions and options are for lay people.

"We have criticized communism, dialectical materialism just as we have criticized capitalism and indicated people should feel free to search for new ways. We are not canonizing any of the past systems."

"I think there is an increasing body of literature by very competent and serious people around the world that indicates society is moving toward another major form which is sometimes described as 'democratic socialism', which already has some interesting applications.

"... it is overly simplistic to divide the world into just two camps—democracy versus communism... Also we have to lay away the myth that what we call democracy is the only and pure form of human endeavour whereby we choose to close our eyes to the horrendous distortions of many so-called democratic regimes, where in the name of so-called democracy all kinds of injustices are perpetrated, even in Canada.

"I think we have to acquire the basic honesty that we be just as critical of our own system as we are of other people's systems."

In the meantime, then, it seems the violence is inevitable. As a Catholic bishop can you and Catholics in general, feel comfortable in supporting the violence in El Salvador?

"No I don't support violence. To me, any violent solution is only an extreme situation where all other means have been exhausted, and even then it rarely succeeds because it has been proven time and again that violence begets more violence.

"I ask them to honestly look at the different forms of violence and not reduce violence only to the actions of peasants who, in desperation, try to bring about justice in their country. What about the economic and social violence that has been perpetrated on the masses of Salvadoran people for the past fifty years beginning with the massacre of some 30,000 peasants in 1932.

"What about the violence imposed on Salvador by the distortion of its economy, like most of Central America, jokingly referred to as banana republics because their economy has been distorted into producing things like bananas and coffee for export to other countries while starving their own people..."

"All these forms of violence are conveniently forgotten ... Where is the real violence?"

To conclude this chapter on the bishop's connection with the revolutionary context of Latin America and to look ahead to the future tensions between his approach and that of the pope, let us look at his answer to Gene Jamieson's question about the pope's attitude to the Catholic priests who formed part of the revolutionary council that ruled Nicaragua in 1979 under the Sandanistas.

The press has generally interpreted the pope's message to Latin American bishops in 1979 as meaning the clergy can best achieve social justice by focusing on purely spiritual matters.

"I think that is a very narrow interpretation of the pope's remarks and I think it can be slightly less than honest to take a quote of the pope out of context. I think that if you take everything the pope has said, on balance, the pope comes out very strongly for involvement in social justice. He cautions priests to be wary of not getting involved in political activism for political activism's sake, and rightly so because they have a more important role to play in proclaiming the gospel.

"Also where the priests and bishops are concerned we must not forget priests have to be agents of unity in the Christian community. That means that a Christian community where the lay people may legitimately espouse a variety of political options they have to be able to look to the priest to speak the gospel in a way that is applicable to those options, not just to one. So if the priest publicly identifies with only one political option then he diminishes his role as a proclaimer of the gospel.

"The pope is quite right in insisting on the importance of that proclamation because the church knows there will never be a perfect political system. All political systems will have their weaknesses, which is not meant to knock politics but is rather putting it in its proper perspective.

"Also you have to realize the pope speaks of principles for the church universal. The practical application of those principles to specific situations is left to the bishops in a country. This is something people tend to forget when they start opposing what the pope is saying for the church universal. It is for these people to prove the pope has specifically repudiated any statement by the bishops.

"And I have yet to see a document in which the pope says, for instance, he rejects what the bishops of this or that country are saying or doing. I have not seen such a document and that is why I am asking men such as [then-Foreign Affairs Minister Mark MacGuigan] to provide the information on which they allege the Vatican has repudiated a bishop's stand."

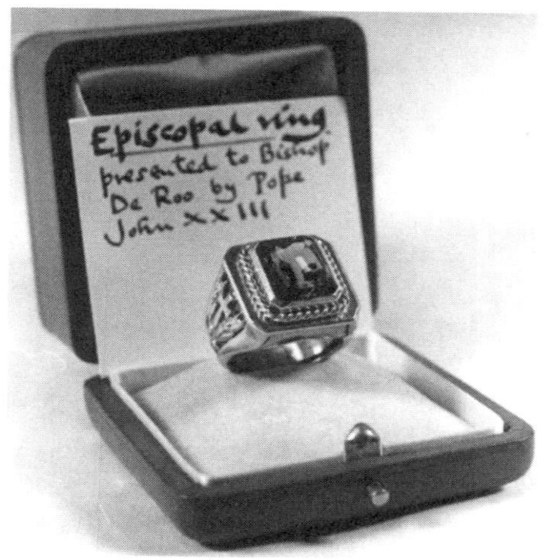

The amethyst ring presented by Pope John XXIII in 1962. (Jamie Jenkins)

Chapter Four: The Radical About-Face

1. VATICAN COUNCIL II

According to Richard P. McBrien in his *Encyclopedia of Catholicism*, the first post-Vatican II Catholic encyclopedia: "Vatican Council II was the twenty-first general, or ecumenical, council of the church (October 11, 1962 - December 8, 1965). The Council is regarded by many as the most significant religious event since the 16th Century Reformation and certainly the most important of the 20th Century."[61]

The Council was announced in late July, 1959 but not convoked for two and half years, ten months before the first of four sessions. The final session being held from September to December of 1965; the last three after Pope John XXIII's death in 1963.

While Vatican Council I (1869-70) had 737 delegates or 'Fathers' in attendance, the 20th Century council had 2,600 world-wide (2,908 were eligible).

Two hundred expert theologians attended the event, including Canadian Gregory Baum whose speciality at that time was ecumenism and relations with other faiths. Four hundred and eighty specialist theologians attended by the end of the Council. The expert theologians or 'periti' were in addition to the bishop's personal theologians.

While Vatican I was dominated by Europeans, Vatican II was the most 'ecumenical', meaning literally the 'whole wide world' in terms of nations and cultures. Eligible bishops numbered 1,089 from Europe, 489 South Americans, 404 North Americans, 374 Asians and Africans, and 84 Central Americans.

All sessions were conducted in Latin. By the final session there were 80 non-Catholic and 50 lay observers, including Eastern Orthodox representatives. This in itself was precedent setting.

It was the first council to be conducted by modern means of communication. The Council was unique in its stated purpose. It had not been called to 'combat heresy' or to deal with some serious threat to unity of the church.

2. A POSITIVE PURPOSE

"On the contrary," McBrien writes, "Pope John XXIII, in his opening address of October 11, 1962, said that the Council's goal was *to eradicate the seeds of discord and to promote peace and unity of all humankind, and not to repeat traditional doctrinal formulation or to condemn errors.*"

It was a new opening, a new day for the church; and the world. In this vein Pope John's special anointing of De Roo endows the bishop's extraordinary dedication to the reforms of the Council with an historical purpose.

Normally, on average, popes serve from ten to fifteen years. John served only five and thus appointed a limited number of new bishops. The relative few he did appoint carry an interesting spiritual distinction.

For example, Albino Luciani who became the ill-fated Pope John Paul I for thirty-three days in 1978, was one of John XXIII's first appointments as bishop in 1958. De Roo was among his last in 1962. On the other hand, John Paul II, Karol Wojtyla, was among the last appointed by the previous Pope, Pius XII, in July of 1958 just prior to his death.

REFUTING PROPHETS OF DOOM

During a concert in Victoria in 1994 the poet-singer-songwriter Leonard Cohen ironically described the 1960s as an event that happened a million years ago and lasted for fifteen minutes.[62]

Such is the vicissitude of the passing of time. But those fifteen minutes made all the difference. De Roo's relationship with John XXIII granted him a particular perspective on the changes in the church.

According to Richard McBrien and other historians, preparation for Vatican II was the most extensive in the history of the church. Ideas were solicited from every bishop and heads of clerical religious orders (though not women's orders). More than 9,000 proposals were submitted. Preparatory commissions met for two years between 1960-62, producing over seventy documents. These were reduced and combined to twenty for presentation to the pope and seven were circulated among the bishops of the world.

"The most dramatic and the most important of the four sessions was the first," writes McBrien, "with at least five significant moments: 1) the pope's opening address; 2) the refusal of the bishops to accept the curia's imposed order; 3) the debate on liturgy; 4) the debate on revelation; 5) the rejection of the curia's draft document on the church. Together these developments signalled a new mood and direction for the Catholic Church."

In his opening speech, John underscored the positive purpose and opportunities of the Council, namely to work toward the unity of humankind so that "the earthly city may be brought to the resemblance of that heavenly city where truth reigns and charity is the law." He explicitly rejected the advice of those close to him who "can see nothing but prevaricated ruin," who regard the modern era as worse than others and getting worse all the time and who are "always forecasting disaster."

He called them "prophets of doom." He also rejected their view that the Council should simply re-affirm traditional doctrine of the church, while condemning errors that undermine those teachings. "For them a council was not necessary," he said.

Instead these doctrinal formulations should be presented in new forms that reflect modern thought. And the most effective way to combat error is "through the medicine of mercy rather than that of severity." The church must show herself always as "the loving mother of all, benign, patient, full of mercy and goodness toward the brethren who are separated from her."

After that, bishops took control of their council from the curia. The division was between intransigent traditionalists and those who wanted legitimate and authentic progress; a major change in the balance of power became clear.[63]

The history of the machinations of these struggles has been portrayed in any number of close studies and histories including Xavier Rynne's famous book *Vatican Council II* which was originally published as a series in *The New Yorker* magazine during the

Council.[64] More recently a BBC TV/Vision Television four-part series titled *Absolute Truth*, is particularly good regarding how the first session was truly significant in the wresting of control from the Curia.

The self-image of the Catholic Church was about to undergo a radical transformation. The Council brought forth distinctive teachings that contrasted sharply with some common beliefs of the pre-Vatican II era.

The following are included in McBrien's list:

"a) The Church is first and foremost a Mystery or sacrament not primarily an organisation or institution;
b) The Church is the whole People of God not just the hierarchy, clergy and religious;
c) The Church's central mission includes action on behalf of justice and peace and is not limited to the preaching of The Word and the celebration of the sacraments;
d) The Church includes all Christians and is not limited only to the Catholic Church;
e) The Church is a communion, or college of local churches which are not simply administrative subdivisions of the church universal;
f) The lay apostolate is a direct participation in the mission of the church and not simply a sharing in the mission of the hierarchy;
g) There is a hierarchy of truths; not all official teachings of the church are equally binding or essential to the integrity of the Catholic faith;
h) God uses other Christian Churches and non-Christian religions in offering salvation to all humankind; the Catholic Church is not the only means of salvation..."

The revolutionary nature of the change is made explicitly clear from these shifts.

3. TWO POPES: JOHN & PAUL

As a bishop Remi De Roo was fashioned in a Catholic culture that was led by specific popes who lent an enormous influence to the tenor of their times, particularly within the church. John XXIII was the pope who appointed him and Paul VI was the head of the Catholic church during De Roo's first fifteen years as bishop. Both were intimately involved in the successful transition of Vatican II. Their story is critical to understanding De Roo's particular role, overall program and innovative style.

JOHN XXIII[65]

During the decade of the 1960s, the Catholic Church had two popes of extremely different temperaments but essentially of one mind on the central program of the church. John XXIII, the charismatic extravert who surprised everyone by calling the Second Vatican Council, and Paul VI, the anguishing introvert who surprised insiders by being so meticulous in his commitment to the reforms.

During his time in office Bishop Remi De Roo never tired of saying that The Council was without question under the inspiration of the Holy Spirit, and from a sociological point of view its very unlikeliness and total unexpectedness could confirm this conviction from faith.

Certainly John's life story rendered him a dark horse candidate to ever be elected pope and yet in a poll of church historians published in 1998 John was judged the most outstanding pope of all time.[66] The five categories of judging were: care for the people, zeal, defence of the church, collegial relations with bishops, personal holiness.

Born on November 25, 1881, the third of thirteen children in the Roncalli family in a mountain village in Northern Italy, Angelo graduated with a doctorate of theology at the age of twenty-three in 1904. He then served as secretary to the local bishop of Bergamo and was a lecturer in church history at the local seminary.

During the First World War he served as a hospital orderly and chaplain. In 1921 Pope Benedict appointed him national director of the Congregation for the Propagation of the Faith. In his spare time he composed diocesan history and a biography of Saint Charles Borromeo (1538-84), an aristocratic bishop who lived a simple and saintly life as an avid and youthful advocate of the reforms of The Council of Trent (1545-63).

Trent was the Council which sprang up to counter the challenge of the Protestant Reformation. John's study of Trent doubtless influenced his understanding of the value and purpose of a council.

Pope Pius XI launched Angelo into his diplomatic career. Roncalli served as papal representative in Bulgaria, Greece and Turkey between 1925 and 1944 where he established friendly relations with the Orthodox Church and government leaders, and worked hard to relieve distress and prevent deportation of Jews.

But the truth was that this lengthy posting in an obscure setting is seen as an early admonition of Roncalli, but whether for his views or his temperament is not clear.

In late 1944 he was appointed nuncio to France where he dealt tactfully but firmly, according to J.N.D. Kelly,[67] with the problem of the many bishops accused of collaborating with the Vichy Regime. He also looked favourably on experiments with worker priests. Worker priests were a pre-Vatican 'anti-clerical' development which sought to bring clergy closer to the lives of ordinary people.

From 1952 he was permanent observer for the Holy See at UNESCO, and in January, 1953 was named Cardinal patriarch of Venice, where he was known for his pastoral zeal, informality and firm resistance to communist maneuvers.

Only in 1958 did he complete his fifth and final volume on Charles Borromeo, and at the October conclave the same year he was elected pope and crowned on November 4, the feast day of his revered Charles Borromeo.

J.N.D. Kelly writes in the *Oxford Dictionary of the Popes*: "Almost seventy-seven, many regarded his appointment as a caretaker one, but it proved a decisive turning point." At his Coronation Mass John announced his desire to be above all things a good shepherd, and this was the hallmark of his pontificate.

He expanded and further internationalized the college of cardinals, but his outstanding achievement was The Second Vatican Council, the calling of which he attributed to a sudden inspiration of the Holy Spirit. Its purpose, he later explained, was to be a new Pentecost, a means of regeneration for the church, bringing its teaching, discipline and organization up to date, and opening a way towards the reunion of the 'separated brethren' of east and west.

He invited observers from eighteen non-Roman Churches, and at his opening address he urged the Fathers to expound truth positively without relying on anathemas. He intervened decisively and strategically on November 21, 1962, on the drafting of the key document on Revelation. He adjourned the first session in December, but did not live to see the resumption nine months later.

His own major encyclicals were more pastoral than dogmatic and included the famous *Mater et Magistra* (*Mother and Teacher*) (1961) which reinforced and brought up to date the social teaching of Leo XIII and Pius XI and called on richer nations to help the poorer ones. *Pacem in Terris* (*Peace on Earth*) (1963) addressed all humanity, setting out the recognition of human rights and duties as the foundation of world peace. In this document, John distinguished between Marxist ideology and the aspirations of communist regimes. This latter encyclical inaugurated a more open eastern policy.

During the Cuban missile crisis John publicly urged both the USA and the USSR to exercise caution, winning the respect of both President Kennedy, and Premier Khrushchev. More than any other pope, John wanted dialogue with the world, irrespective of creed. In terms of ecumenical gestures, he dispatched envoys to the Ecumenical Patriarch Athenagoras in Istanbul in 1961 and welcomed the Archbishop of Canterbury, Geoffrey Fisher in 1960, the first Anglican Archbishop to be so received. He also exchanged greetings with the Orthodox Patriarchy of Moscow and sent delegates for the first time ever to the World Council of Churches in New Delhi.

Warm-hearted and unaffectedly simple in spite of his erudition and command of many languages, attached to his humble origins and always retaining a peasant's shrewdness and jovial humour, John brought a wind of change to his office, relaxing its hieratic stiffness and, after decades of growing centralization, giving the worldwide college of bishops a new awareness of its importance.

Typically, at Christmas 1958, he revived the custom, which had lapsed in 1870, of visiting the Regina Coeli prison and one of the local hospitals. He also removed offensive language to the Jews from the First Friday liturgy and on one occasion introduced himself to Jewish visitors with the words; "I am Joseph, your brother."

When he died, after a prolonged and painful illness, *The London Times* commented that few pontificates had so captured the imagination of the world. Jewish philosopher and social critic Hannah Arendt wrote a long tribute commemorating his singular character, saying it was also a miracle that a true Christian actually was made pope.

This 'Joseph' who appointed Victoria's Bishop as his youngest brother 'Benjamin' was the key figure in changing so much symbolically and actually within the church.

It will be remembered that 1870 was the year that the pope of the day, Pius IX, declared himself a literal prisoner of the Vatican, and condemned roundly the world and all it had to offer. Everything modern was suspect.

PAUL VI

English Catholic writer Peter Hebblethwaite sub-titles his full biography on Paul VI, 'The First Modern Pope'. Paul was born Giovanni Battista Montini, and the dust jacket blurb to Hebblethwaite's book reads "Paul ranks among the most influential figures in the modern history of the Roman Catholic Church. When he was elected in 1963, he faced the awesome responsibility of guiding the Church through the conclusion of the historic Second Vatican Council. With the Council behind him, an overarching challenge remained: shepherding the Catholic communion during the turbulent aftermath of Vatican II—the after shocks of which are being felt throughout the Church to this day."

ↂↂↂ

Paul was the son of a prosperous lawyer who was also a political editor and a parliamentary deputy. His mother to whom he was devoted, was pious. She bore him on September 26, 1897. Shy and precarious of health, but with an appetite for books, he attended the diocesan seminary from home, and was ordained May 29, 1920, some four years prior to Bishop De Roo's birth.

He started off in the papal secretariat of state but due to health reasons had to leave that, though he eventually continued with the secretariat becoming deeply involved in the Catholic student movement until 1933. From 1931 he taught diplomatic history at the papal academy.

Every pope after Pius X, who died in 1914, up to and including Paul VI, was a career church diplomat, someone actively engaged with the modern world. This brought a new realism to the leadership of the Catholic Church. The present Pope, John Paul II, by contrast was not a career diplomat.

In 1931 Paul was made a domestic prelate to the Holy See and in 1937 was appointed assistant to Eugenio Pacelli, the future Pius XII. This relationship continued after Pius assumed the papacy, and in 1944 Montini was assigned charge of the internal church affairs. When promoted to Secretary of State in 1952, he declined a cardinal's hat when it was offered the next year, but was appointed Archbishop of Milan in 1954, which was an enormous diocese teeming with social problems.

This nomination has been interpreted as a sign of papal disfavour. J.N.D. Kelly writes: "Styling himself 'the workers' archbishop', but accompanied by his now-legendary ninety crates of books, he threw himself with immense energy into the task of restoring his war-battered diocese and winning over the disaffected industrial masses; for three weeks in November, 1957, he carried out an intensive mission aimed at reaching every parish in the city."

He also found time for experiments in Christian Unity, holding discussions, for instance, with a group of Anglicans in 1956. In 1958 the new pope, John, named him cardinal, the customary promotion withheld under Pius XII. As John's confidant he played a noteworthy role in the preparations for the Council, but he kept a distant attitude to the first session, travelling a great deal during that period.

At the conclave in 1963, the largest by far in history, with eighty cardinals, he was elected as John's successor on the fifth ballot, and selected a name which suggested an outward-looking approach.

Greatly under the spell of his predecessor, he promised to continue Vatican II, and at the second session significantly introduced important procedural reforms such as the admission of lay people including women as auditors, and the relaxation of confidentiality.

He proceeded with the third and fourth sessions promulgating key documents on the Constitution on the Church, the Decree on Ecumenism and the Decree on the Eastern Church in 1964.

He took special action to dramatically plead for peace at the United Nations, and establish permanent working arrangements with the Eastern Church, as well as set up a permanent synod of Bishops with deliberative as well as consultative powers.

To the *Dogmatic Constitution on the Church,* he had attached a note explaining the nature of collegiality of the bishops, that the bishops form a college which, acting in concert with and not independently of its head the pope, has supreme authority in the church.

After 1965 Paul began implementing the Council's decisions with great courage as well as an acutely felt sense of the difficulties. It was to his immense credit that he was able to steer the church through a period of revolutionary change without schism. He carried through the revision of the breviary, the lectionary, the order of Mass, sacred music and canon law and carried through the substitution of the vernacular in the liturgy without flinching.

He relentlessly pursued ecumenism as well as reorganized the curia and Vatican finances and confirmed the permanent offices for promotion of Christian unity, and relations with non-Christians and non-believers.

In May, 1967 he flew to Fatima to pray for world peace. He did this, he claimed, at the personal bidding of the Blessed Virgin Mary. Between 1965 and 1970 his encyclical letters dealt with the need for liturgical reform *(Mysterium Fidei),* the need for social justice in Third World-First World relations *(Populorum progressio,* 1967), the necessity of priestly celibacy *(Sacerdotalis coelibatus,* 1968), condemning birth control in 1968 *(Humanae Vitae),* and modestly relaxing the regulations for mixed marriages *(Matrimonia mixta).*

Humanae Vitae disappointed many in the church, not least because the vast majority of the pontifical commission appointed in 1963 to examine the subject had reported in favour of contraception in certain circumstances.

A few weeks after the anti-birth control encyclical the Lambeth Conference of the Anglican bishops rejected the encyclical, and while Paul remained confident of the rightness of his decision, he was profoundly shaken by the critical international reaction to it.

"After 1968," writes J.N.D. Kelly, "some detected a deepening shadow over the pontificate. Paul seemed to withdraw into himself, worried by such trends as international terrorism and by tensions within the church, such as the growing demands for marriage of the clergy, the defiant resistance of Bishop Marcel Lefebvre and others to liturgical reforms which highlighted the struggles between the traditionalists and progressives, the signs of the emergence of a new modernism. There were rumours of his possible resignation in 1974; but real though it was, his inner malaise, could be exaggerated."

The years after 1968, saw his widening international travel as the 'pilgrim pope', to Geneva to address the International Labour Organization and the World Council of Churches as well as to Africa and the Far East where he narrowly escaped assassination in Manila. It was Paul who proclaimed Teresa of Avila and Catherine of Siena as Doctors of the Church, the first women to be so entitled.

In 1970 he fixed the retirement age for priests and bishops at seventy-five years. Between 1971 and 1977 he convened collegial synods of bishops on priesthood, evangelization and catechesis, emphasizing the collegiality established by the Council. Also in 1977, he and the Archbishop of Canterbury, Donald Coggan, issued a Common Declaration which pledged united work towards unity which stopped short of the intercommunion which Coggan wanted.

Significantly in his latter period, he steadily enlarged and internationalized the sacred college of cardinals. When he was elected it had eighty members, by 1976 it was 138 with the Italian members a small minority and some Third World representatives.

Although not a man with a common touch, Paul had a flair for the dramatic gesture, yet he tended to leave an ambiguous impression, John XXIII had described him as "a little like Hamlet."

He was always torn between his forward-looking vision and his suspicion of any innovation which might undermine the integrity and authority of the church's teaching. He consistently emphasized the mystery and other-worldliness of the faith. He reduced the pomp and circumstance of the papacy, selling the tiara presented to him at his election, for the benefit of the poor.

In his last year he was profoundly disturbed by the kidnap and eventual murder around May 9, 1978, of his lifelong friend Aldo Moro, the Italian Christian Democrat statesman. Paul's last public appearance was to preside at Moro's funeral. Not long after he was stricken with arthritis and after suffering a heart attack while Mass was being said at his bed, he died on August 6, 1978.

4. HIGH EXPECTATIONS

When Vancouver Island Catholics were anticipating and speculating on the expected arrival of their new bishop, Remi De Roo, between the date of the announcement by Pope John XXIII, October 31, 1962, and the date of his actual installment as the 14th Bishop of Victoria, December 20, the level of expectation was unusually high.

Catholic city alderman Michael Griffin of Victoria was quoted in the *Daily Colonist* newspaper regarding his experience of the Bishop's ordination December 14 at the Cathedral in Saint Boniface. The predominantly French Manitoba archdiocese was home diocese for Father De Roo where he had served as priest for twelve years.

Griffin stated: "We of Victoria have been delighted by what we have seen and heard of the man ... We feel a new era in the history of the church in Victoria will start... when Bishop De Roo will be installed."

Alderman Griffin's words would prove more true than he could possibly know. While he doubtless visualized the St. Boniface priest as an exemplary candidate for the traditional role of bishop, much more would be called for in the short years ahead due to the Second Vatican Council and the exigencies of the times.

Remi De Roo, like Modeste Demers, the first bishop of the Diocese of 'Vancouver's Island' (as it was then called) was being dispatched from St. Boniface. And like the next three bishops who immediately followed Demers, De Roo was of Belgian descent.

De Roo, like all those bishops before him, was the youngest of his day at age thirty-eight, and he looked the part with an uncannily youthful appearance, so much so that he was dubbed 'The Boy Bishop' by a captivated media.[68]

It would have been impossible to predict that nearly thirty-five years later, at the time of the 150th celebrations of the diocese, he would still be bishop of Victoria, and still making headlines in the struggle to keep the overall program of Vatican II on track in an era of increasing ecclesiastical containment.[69]

Remi De Roo was appointed bishop by the unlikely, surprising, and charismatic Pope John XXIII in time to attend most of the first session of the Second Vatican Council. During the Council he took an extremely active role, making four successful interventions as one of nearly three thousand bishops worldwide who participated in the four-year process.

There is much good evidence that Pope John appointed De Roo because he recognized in him a prime candidate to carry out the program which could arise from his convoking of an ecumenical council. It is these general councils of the whole church that determine the dogmatic teachings which the pope, in collegial relations with all the people of the church, are called to implement.

This council would be no exception, instituting a program that would challenge the Catholic Church to adapt a fresh attitude towards itself and its mission in the world. According to informed commentators, The Church's very self-understanding would undergo a radical transformation.

This was to be no mere tinkering with superficial adjustments, rather, central categories of the church's identity underwent the adjustment of change that had been coming since the start of the modern age and the election of modern popes starting in 1914 with Benedict XV and continuing with Pius XI and XII.

THE BENJAMIN

When they first met in Rome, Pope John indicated that he knew that here in this vivid young bishop was the sort of leadership potential the new program would require.

In 1987, at the time of the celebration of Bishop De Roo's twenty-fifth anniversary as bishop of the diocese, William Power, Bishop Emeritus of Antigonish, himself a veteran of twenty-seven years as head of the small yet dynamic diocese of Antigonish, Nova Scotia, told of that first encounter.

Power recalled that at the Canadian Bishops' audience with the Pope in 1963, John XXIII referred to De Roo as 'The Benjamin of the Canadian Bishops', an allusion to the Old Testament story of

Jacob's youngest son and the youngest of Joseph's brothers who were founders of the twelve tribes of Israel.

To emphasize the point and underscore his favourable blessing, the next day, the eighty-one-year-old pope, in his last year of life, followed up by sending one of his rings to this 'Benjamin', a large amethyst ring which De Roo used as a teaching tool.

If the pontiff sensed in the youthful Canadian prelate the makings of a thoroughgoing and new type of bishop who would be a master disciple of Vatican II, he knew his man.

And Bishop De Roo, who already had achieved a sort of renown for his 'eloquence and scholarship', according to Catholic journalist Grant Maxwell, knew his subject well.[70] His entire service in office would be dedicated to the full implementation of the Reforms of the Council.

Dr. Tony Clarke

Chapter Five: The Paradox at Victoria

1. EARLY INDICATIONS

Ordained in 1950, De Roo served his apprenticeship as a cleric during the tail end of a triumphalist era, and yet he had a natural instinct for the new developments of his day. His work in that time included a doctorate in theology at the Angelicum University in Rome. He was twenty-eight years old when he received the degree in 1952.

The *Winnipeg Tribune* in November, 1962 reported on his appointment with this background information: "Born into a Christian family who immigrated to a homestead near Swan Lake, Manitoba, from Lembecke in Flanders during the late 1880s, the ambition to become a priest has been part of Monsignor De Roo's life ever since he can remember."[71]

"'There was no spectacular spiritual breakthrough and I always knew that in the ministry my line of vocation would be to teach the word of God and to devote myself to the pastoral care of souls.'"

The City of Winnipeg has three Catholic archdioceses: The Archdiocese of Winnipeg itself, the initially Francophone Archdiocese of St. Boniface and the Ukrainian Catholic Archeparchy. Leading progressive clerics, such as Cardinal George Flahiff, have been appointed to lead those dioceses. Certainly De Roo's mentor and patron, Archbishop Maurice Baudoux, was of that stripe.

According to Father Ken Bernard, a Winnipeg priest who relocated in 1979 to Victoria, Archbishop Baudoux was "a leading churchman of his time."[72] Baudoux was of Belgian Walloon stock.

Bernard said that being a European, Baudoux was able to provide him and other seminarians with the most up-to-date documents that were being prepared for the Second Vatican Council for study in the seminary.

De Roo, though a number of years ahead of Father Bernard in his priestly formation, benefitted in similar ways from his close association with the forward-looking archbishop.

During the 1950s De Roo was appointed director of Catholic Action for the archdiocese, director of the catechetical office, founder of the Catholic Information Centre's program for Non-Catholics. He called himself a 'Jack of all trades'.

At the time he was involved with so many new ministries that he said some of the older priest wondered if it did not indicate a sort of instability.[73] History would prove him out. These experiences were all in areas that Vatican II would underline as worthy of fresh attention. His experience in the lead-up period to the Council pre-figured his post-conciliar leadership.

Administratively his capacities were developed during that same early period when he served as general secretary to the Manitoba Conference of Bishops and vice-chancellor of the archdiocese. He was a diocesan consultor and pastor of Holy Cross, the large English-speaking parish in the Norwood area of Greater Winnipeg. He was being groomed.

Fluent in both French and English as well as his mother tongue Flemish, he taught as a part-time professor of theology at the major seminary. A summary of his career in the archdiocesan bulletin at the time of his selection as bishop mentions his "remarkable intellectual qualities." He was the first graduate of that seminary to be appointed bishop.

In the *Winnipeg Tribune* article by writer Manfred Jager at the time of his appointment, De Roo was described as: "A one-time Manitoba farmboy who drove a tractor and handled a combine as a youth, left for Rome to receive the robes he will soon wear as Roman Catholic bishop of Vancouver Island.

"The young prelate—'I'm a farmer and still drive trucks and like to tinker with them when I have time'—believes those 'separated' from his church are still Christian brethren. But that does not eliminate the need for mission as he sees it…

"There are 275,000 people on Vancouver Island, which is the diocese of Victoria, with less than 10 percent being Catholic.

"It opens a much vaster field of the apostolate, a much broader field. The majority of people in my diocese may not actually share my faith. But it will be both a privilege and a challenge on many occasions to work at mutual understanding those we call our separated brethren, as well as to present to them all the riches I have found in Catholic teaching and practice."

Another quote contained words that reflected his overall attitude:

"I believe God wants the salvation of all men. But Salvation cannot be defined in categories of human definition. The mysteries of salvation pass the narrow confines of the human intellect. But we have the personal responsibility of bringing to the attention of our fellow men the truths we have received by divine heritage."

His entire program is summed up in these words from the onset of his episcopacy. He was raised in a Catholic culture and as a result had the self-confidence to reach out extensively. Victoria, on the other hand, was a minority Catholic situation and had a history that revealed a defensive posture toward other religions and the community at large.[74] There would be tensions from the start.

Appointed to this minority and somewhat besieged Catholic situation on Vancouver Island, he would develop a distinct style of leadership that would not be without its resistances from within. The very nature of its success would fuel his critics. Many such commentators were paradoxically comforted by the awareness that he would not likely last long in such an outlying diocese. Victoria had a distinct reputation for short-term bishops, ones who used the Island as a training ground before moving on to larger Canadian centres.[75]

Ironically the more De Roo was publicized in his progressive theological and social positions, the more he was permanently digging himself in at Victoria as a consequence.

His new model of leadership made its enemies in high places and he was not successfully recommended to move on to Winnipeg, Vancouver, Halifax or even Saskatoon where some of his predecessors at Victoria had been elevated.

In Victoria itself, the *Victoria Times* and the *Daily Colonist*—two different newspapers at the time—in their coverage of the consecration event on December 20, 1962 indicated some of the anticipated expectations associated with the event.

The reporter wrote in a characteristic silver prose style of the time used for church affairs: "An expectant hush fell over those gathered to greet him at the residence on View Street."

Black and white photographs of the bishop's official reception, consecration and initial period of activity reflected images from an epoch of Roman Catholicism typified by elaborate ritual, a tone of pomp and protocol, and a high baroque manner of formal ceremony that accurately reflected the highly serious self-consciousness of the religion then. One Vatican II commentator called it: "Unseemly pomp of prelatial vestiture."[76]

To move so quickly from that approach to the informal 'shirt-sleeve bishop' style that soon followed the Council would have been jarring to the sensibilities of the essentially Anglo-Irish Catholics who had made up the mass of the diocese since at least the turn of the century. On the Prairies such informality might have been better appreciated.

But it was a new man in a new situation, with a mandated new program and he made the most of it.

As a full participant at the Council in Rome, De Roo was in a strategic position to foresee the magnitude of the change that was required. He also was endowed with the aptitude to be able to bring it about. His circumstance and ability would entirely define his role for the next forty years. He countenanced few distractions.

De Roo exercised a sort of lengthy antennae which picked up messages from all around the globe. Among his set of gifts was a singular receptiveness which allowed him to implement the reforms on this minor island diocese in a decisive manner that could serve, in effect, as an experimental model for the Catholic Church in the 21st Century.

2. THE SIXTIES

Between 1962 and 1969 the Western world changed irreversibly. Whether the Second Vatican Council had anything to do with the massive cultural shift which typified the Sixties is a question historians will need to address. What is certain is that the changes of Vatican II for the Catholic world and the revolution of social values associated with the coming of age of the 'Baby Boomer' generation did coincide; to the boon of both movements.

As Father Sig Lajoie wrote regarding that era: "It was a time of radical changes. The whole world entered into a very powerful evolutionary period of human history. The latter part of the '60s and early '70s saw a short-lived yet lasting impact on society."[77]

The Franciscan priest who served as Vicar General of the diocese recalled: "Bishop Remi encouraged us to pick up the hikers, seek to know the space they were in, what they felt toward the church. The point was 'the church' needed to go to the people to hear of their search and how best to respond."

"Bishop Remi's attitude was one of fearlessness. The changes perceived to be of long duration, encouragement was put forth not to fear to experiment; and keep him informed of the results... Just as we are providentially here as part of the Catholic Church of Vancouver Island, so was Bishop Remi a providential leader for our times and place."

❧❧❧

Young people were coming of age in the decade of the 1960s in such sufficient numbers that they, in the words of social critic and novelist Leslie Fiedler, were able to invent themselves in a way never before known, due to the developments of the modern world.

Fiedler states in his essay "The New Mutants,"[78] that the central categories of self-understanding in the culture—man, woman, work, duty, responsibility, race, creativity and leisure—what these mean, all were turned on their end for and by this new generation as a sociological group. Everything in some significant way was up for grabs.

The old cold war categories of east and west, capitalist and communist were challenged and expanded by the new vision. The Third World came into the lexicon, and the Third World nations changed the political equation worldwide. Canada aligned herself with the emerging nations as a smaller middle power. The country's identity shifted.

In an important way so did the 'country' of the Catholic Church. At Vatican II, the church reinvented itself in several central categories of self-understanding. Rather than imaging itself as a fortress over and against the world, the church was pictured as a 'pilgrim people' called to enter into and transform the world through engagement in social struggle. The people of the church were called upon to see themselves as the church not merely members of a world-wide institution.

There had been hints of this with the 'religious materialism' of the Antigonish Movement in eastern Nova Scotia during the Depression years.[79] There were other parallel and similar social movements fuelled by the papal social encyclicals, but now this was operating on a whole new level for the whole church.

The Second Vatican Council released among Catholic laity a startling magnitude of creative energy. The social justice movement was just one of many unanticipated new drives that were released with a liberating degree of energy.

In De Roo's diocese the rate of change and the level of excitement at his leadership were highly accelerated. As a result, Victoria became a paradigm example for North America. It was his first moment of serious celebrity, at this stage largely within the church. It was the first hint of the lasting structural change he envisioned.

June 1989 with United Church Presbytery officer William Howie, centre, and Anglican Bishop of B.C. Ronald Shepherd at Nootka for 200th anniversary celebration of Spanish missionaries arrival on Vancouver Island. De Roo had very close relations with these denominations throughout his years in office. (J.J.)

This is indicated some twenty-five years later by the movements that persisted through his first quarter century as bishop. The history of his diocese that was completed in 1997, after its first 150 years, gave a comprehensive list to indicate the degree of change.

From the pages of the Island Catholics News *were gleaned over three years's issues a list of nearly a hundred movements, organizations or persistent initiatives that were active between 1988-91. Few of these movements existed before the Second Vatican Council. Many did not exist elsewhere.*

A quick sampling indicates prison work, social justice projects, widespread local ecumenism, interfaith action, meditation practice and other new prayer styles utilizing Jesuit-developed techniques, links with Latin America, retreat houses offering the latest types of spiritual development techniques including the Enneagram, wholistic health care, basic communities, women as university chaplains, youth work, new schools and parishes structured strictly on Vatican II principles.

Parishes throughout the Island formalized their ecumenical arrangements. A number of parishes were started which shared accommodations with Anglicans and United Church of Canada congregations.

Christian meditation workshops were part of a worldwide movement. Hermit monk Father Charles Brandt pioneered conservation and ecological awareness by his lifestyle and writings. Brandt became a national figure through media coverage of his experiment which integrated meditation, conservation and environmentalism.

Refugee sponsorship, an ecumenical First Nations support program, the Charismatic Renewal Prayer Movement, The Christian Taskforce to Latin America. L'Arche, a movement of living with the handicapped, New Beginnings providing therapeutic retreats for separated and divorced Catholics. Christian intentional communities —permanent lay communities which banded together to engaged in the social justice struggles on the basis of gospel values.

Seniors and handicapped housing, along with the conventional soup kitchen. Support for the AIDS society. Pax Christi, the international Catholic peace organization. Creation spirituality. Rather than establish a separate Catholic family services organization, De Roo helped establish a provincial council for the family and a local secular family life agency.

Progressive religious education for children, lay pastoral ministry among the elderly including palliative care. These programs were part of the rise of the Catholic wholistic health care ministry where the institutional aspect of healthcare was played down, and the baptismal call to healing of all the People of God was accentuated.

Another significant phenomenon was the large numbers receiving spiritual direction including the integration of depth psychology into retreat work, adult faith education and spiritual direction.

In particular this was true of the Jesuits with their spiritual discernment exercises who integrated Sufi wisdom into their retreat work through the Enneagram, which became a controversial subject. Typically De Roo went on to become a trained Enneagram facilitator, a post-retirement project. The Prayer Companions Program of the Diocese was rooted in Jesuit Ignatian discernment practice.

Fundamentally De Roo was open to everything done in the spirit of Vatican II. There was a persistent radical openness to new ideas, tested by time, to the fruit which they bore; unexpected and unpredictable as the phenomenon would reveal.

3. THE CHANGES FROM VATICAN II

Every Catholic diocese was expected to begin to implement these changes. Some were slower than others due to the age and attitude of its leadership. Some had to wait until a new younger bishop succeeded one formed prior to the Council, who had built up unconscious resistance. The Council was not imposed on bishops, but rather, as one source put it, the bishops went to school for three years and it was their re-invention of the church.[80]

Some dioceses never did fully get on with the program due to the inability or nervous hesitation of its leadership.[81] Victoria, however, was well placed to attempt to fully implement the Council. The leading theologians of the day were brought in, attracted by De Roo's reputation and invited by groups who wanted to hear their ideas.

There was a group of young and motivated clergy. Religious congregations were small in numbers and flexible. The laity had historically been encouraged to participate.[82] Bishop De Roo at age thirty-eight in 1962 could look forward to twenty or thirty years of peak creative power in this process and during the 1960s he would have met very little if any internal resistance within the diocese to this push.

The younger clergy were given fresh areas of responsibility including the leadership training of laity in most of the traditional areas of spiritual development previously reserved for clergy. Older clergy were retrained as they saw fit. Religious orders redefined themselves and their commitments in light of the Council changes.

A massive de-institutionalization took place within the first decade. All the major historical institutions closed—Saint Louis College, a boys school; Saint Joseph's hospital was given to the public sector; Saint Ann's Academy, the girls school since 1858, was shut down.

These changes released large amounts of energy from the resources of the institution to allow the laity to go off in fresh directions. Religious education, particularly its adult learning side was a major commitment within the diocese.

De Roo was at the centre of the movement for change not only in Victoria but worldwide. He cut a strikingly youthful figure, perfectly appropriate to the new era, and was a speaker in demand far and wide.

As Benedictine Sister Bede Sullivan indicated in a 1982 summary of the first twenty years after Vatican II, it was "history by headlines" and a million miles of travel by the young bishop.[83]

❧❧❧

Sister Sullivan is a good example of the sort of people who were drawn to work with De Roo on his new program after the Council. She had been a student of communications guru Marshal McLuhan, himself a steadfast Catholic, in Toronto. She was a disciple in the spirituality of Thomas Merton, with whom she shared a birthday and a radical degree of openness to the world and everyone she met. She took on some responsibility for communications in the diocese.

Her work was not a formal or official appointment *per se*, but rather it was at her own initiative. It was typical of the way De Roo proceeded with these experimental projects. Once tested by time and starting to bear fruit, it would receive the informal blessing of the office of the bishop.

She ran the Thomas More Centre from her home. There she made tapes of important meetings and events and shared them with whoever wished to take advantage of the resource.

After she left Victoria to retire in the late 1980s she bequeathed the collection to a retreat centre library; preserving a valuable collection of De Roo's talks at Queenswood, the retreat centre of the Sisters of Saint Ann.

Sullivan's communication ministry of tapes and occasional publications filled a gap between the disappearance of *The Torch* in the late 1960s and the advent of *Island Catholic News* in 1987.

The Torch was the in-house diocesan newsletter from an earlier era, which was allowed to founder after De Roo arrived. It was always edited by clergy.

Island Catholic News by contrast was editorially independent, lay centred and completely supportive of De Roo's program, a fact which irritated some of the clergy and all the traditionalists.

4. THE COUNCIL IN THE DIOCESE

After the Council, changes coincided with those of the Sixties. An apt example is the story of the de-cloistering of the Poor Clare Sisters on Vancouver Island.

During the Council, Bishop De Roo addressed the community, then situated next to St. Patrick's Church in Oak Bay, the small preserved British enclave next to Victoria. In the discussion it was mentioned that the use of a heavy grille between the Sisters and broader community might not be entirely appropriate now.

That very night the superior, Sister Michael McMullon, removed the grille and a new era of more open relations began. As a result people across the Island started using the contemplative community as a spiritual resource in an unprecedented manner. This eventually resulted in their relocation of the monastery to the rural confines of Duncan, a small city an hour north of Victoria.

Twenty-five years after that dramatic intervention, in November, 1987 when the monastery was celebrating seventy-five years in the diocese, Abbess Clare Lewis said that enclosure and cloister had led to a misunderstanding of the group's purpose.

"Although enclosure is important it is seen as a means not an end as a support to prayer life. Now we live in a less hidden away type of life, but still prayer and contemplation are at the centre." The article quoted the nuns: "Emphasis is upon the value of depth dimension."[84] The rapport between the nuns and the bishop had added another depth dimension to their life after Vatican II.

For an activist bishop, De Roo had strong relations with contemplative communities, including a community of Catholic hermits who gathered from around the world to start a unique eremetical (hermit) experiment at De Roo's invitation.[85] The most famous monk of the 20th Century, author Thomas Merton, almost relocated to Vancouver Island as part of this episode.

HISTORY BY HEADLINES

Between 1962 and 1970 headlines cited by Sister Bede Sullivan tell the story in broad strokes, of an unprecedented opening by the Catholic Church to the world and other religious faiths.

In December of 1962 De Roo was cited saying 'humanity without God is not fully human and that tolerance is the key to the future.' "Bishop favours co-operation between faiths" was the *Victoria Times* headline. The media coverage in that period was entirely positive, an interesting contrast to how it soured in the mid-1980s after the economic critique; and became entirely inflammatory after his retirement, with the money uproar.

In the first half of 1963 the headlines were dedicated to Native relations.

The B.C. Catholic reported "You belong to us Indians, chiefs tell Bishop De Roo." Visits were made to the Saanich Peninsula reserves near Victoria. In June he made his first visit to the west coast of the Island where Native missions were strong and plentiful since the earliest days of the church on the Island. The first bishop of the diocese had come to the Island at the invitation of the local Natives[86].

In 1999 Cowichan Native elder Abner Thorne remembered De Roo this way: "To me, the bishop is very approachable, and quite open...if he sees you looking his way he will come over to you and talk as soon as he can. It's been like that from the start when our people received him as the new bishop back in 1963. I think it's important to put this in: We named him Chief White Swan because he came from Swan Lake, Manitoba. That was an outstanding event for our people at that time. Not long ago he came to visit up here... I don't know what the best word is, but I find him quite democratic."

PROGRESS IN THE SIXTIES

Nineteen sixty-four saw a very strong ecumenical push. The January 19 headlines in the *Daily Colonist* read: "Good time to be a bishop—Victoria's young prelate is both a symbol of the changing face of his church and a force in bridging fissures of Christianity."

A talk he gave five years later reiterated his attitude about the importance of the laity. He was speaking at Mount Angel College, a monastery in Oregon: "The role of the laity is not only to belong to the Church, or to be in the Church, but **to be** the church: that is not to just accomplish things, but to become complete Christian persons, to become members of Christ, united with him and together with him growing into the total reality that is Christ alive in his Church today." For De Roo the people were the church; the clerics, the hierarchy and the institutional format were secondary.

Sister Bede Sullivan, reporting on his 'basic insights' from Vatican II in her 1982 publication, lists them as: "a. Rediscovery of the Church as Mystery, b. The church as pilgrim journey, far from perfect, always in need of reform, c. The church is spirit endowed, that the Spirit of God is never absent, d. That the Christian life embraces the totality of human life, in all its relationships, e. That there is a hierarchy of truths. While all truth is important, not every document has the same primary relationship with the essentials of salvation. I make these basic points, De Roo said, to show the depth and significance of the reorientation of Vatican II."

LAST LATIN MASS

Nineteen sixty-five saw the announcement of the last Latin Mass in the March 6 headline of the *Daily Colonist* while on June 12, De Roo, speaking to the Kiwanis Club, made one of his first strong social statements. He told the service group that "Power Blocks Cannot Rule," revealing his Prairie roots where the small farmers and producers had banded together to resist the power of the eastern establishment during 'The Dirty Thirties' when he was growing up.

In the later half of the 1960s, with the Council over, he rolled up those shirtsleeve and decidedly put the words of the Council documents into action. The headline in the *B.C. Catholic*, for instance, read "Social Action needs action: Bishop De Roo." The early part of 1966 witnessed a continuing proliferation of ecumenical gestures.

In late January the cathedral in Victoria was overcrowded when 1,400 packed in to pray for the success of Christian unity. De

Roo was quoted in the *Victoria Times* as saying "let us all go forward in love." It was heady times.

The excitement for Catholics on the Island during this next half decade can hardly be overestimated. It seemed that there was a new development every few weeks. Headlines during this mid-Sixties period were monthly if not more often in the regular press.

A sample includes: "Bishop De Roo: Ecumenism not based on fear of isms" (*BC Catholic* 24-6-65); "Church element aghast at new look, says Bishop De Roo" (*Daily Colonist* 13-12-65); "For first time to honour Churchill prelates kneel together" (*Victoria Times* 30-1-65); "Drop old barriers, De Roo tells major superiors" (*Western Catholic Reporter* 11-7-67); "Senate of priests share bishops rule" (*Times* 26-11-66); "Bishop, People unlock ideas with talk, talk, talk" (WCR 25-8-66).

On the formal level De Roo was initiating regular ecumenical movement especially with the Anglicans which included the possibility of a joint theological college.

But also with the United Church of Canada, which celebrated its fortieth anniversary in June, 1965 by inviting the bishop to be a key part of the festivities at Metropolitan United Church in Victoria. The newspaper coverage was testimony to the hope seemingly all people were feeling from this new development.

Early in 1966 it was announced in the daily press that a community of seven hermits had established themselves at the invitation of the office of bishop. In late November, Charles Brandt was ordained as part of the group becoming the first hermit-monk ordination in three centuries within the Roman church.

❧❧❧

Certainly Victoria was breaking new ground. The diocese established one of the first senates of priests in the country. At the same time, the laity were given their voice in the overall direction and administration decisions of the diocese with a diocesan pastoral council which would give way in time to a permanent diocesan leadership council.

With De Roo the reforms were far from lip service or foot dragging reluctance. He restructured and de-institutionalised the diocese as quickly as possible. The headline read: "Victoria gives its bishop a Public Opinion Profile."[87]

Parishes were encouraged to establish pastoral councils and many other enabling structures would follow. The people were being given their lead and the responsibilities and collegial sharing of authority would follow. Marg Beaubien remembers those early years: "Vatican II was soon on the horizon after Remi arrived and he immediately called on us and other couples to assist him in developing his intervention on the intimacy of marriage. This was a time of great hope for many changes in the Church and we felt that Remi was the right man for the implementation of Vatican II at home. As part of the laity we felt valued and appreciated, not that there was agreement on particular issues."

"We found Remi to be tolerant and open to all our questions—and my husband Jim really appreciated this about him and would challenge him on many issues—celibacy, unions, homosexuality and feminism."[88]

❧❧❧

De Roo's penchant for such dialogue made him a sought-after speaker. During one typical short period in the mid-1960s the bishop was being asked to give presentations on his diocesan developments in Calgary, Mount Angel Oregon, Vancouver, Edmonton, Saint Paul Minnesota and Toronto.

In Toronto his address on May 18 was titled "Social Communication and the press." This subject matter would prove a consistent theme, the linking of social justice action and the communication that helps make it happen.

De Roo would become permanently linked with the leading lights in this field across Canada—Grant Maxwell, Father Bob Ogle, Mary Jo Leddy, Bernard Daly; all of Saskatchewan, who went on to provide national leadership in the field.

Another Prairie communications leader was Douglas Roche of Edmonton, who founded *The Western Catholic Reporter* in an attempt to develop a regional Catholic newspaper that would be finely tuned to the nuances of Vatican II in social communications. Roche was eventually elected a Tory Member of Parliament and consequently appointed Canada's Ambassador for Disarmament to the UN between 1984-89.

De Roo would write a number of books with these people, one with Roche as early as 1969, titled, perhaps unfortunately now that inclusive language is encouraged, *Man to Man,* which was introduced by writer Gary McEoin as a frank discussion between an informed layman and the bishop. In the early 1990s Grant Maxwell and Pearl Gervais would edit a book for the bishop, titled *Forward in the Spirit: Challenge of the People's Synod.*

The synod book was written in effect by over a hundred leading members of the synod process. Each of the two dozen major dossiers developed from the synod process were written by the major players in that ministry or area of interest.

The structure of all these books reflects what the bishops' executive assistant of more than thirty years, Eileen Archer, had to say about him on the occasion of his twenty-fifth anniversary as bishop:

"One characteristic that particularly stands out in my mind is Bishop De Roo's understanding of human nature and his acceptance of people as they are... He has always trusted people. He assigns a task and expects it will be done. No reminders, no interference. And he encourages people. I for one, have been challenged to do things I didn't know I could."

IN DIALOGUE

The significance of these books was precisely their dialogical if not dialectical method and format. De Roo dealt with people as mature adults, trusting in their capacity to grow if challenged and supported and encouraged in that challenge. He grew himself as a result.

Certainly his most controversial book was the one he co-wrote in 1992 with Doug Roche and former *Catholic New Times* editor, Mary Jo Leddy, titled *In the Eye of the Catholic Storm.* Leddy had provided laudable commentary for the CBC television coverage of the pope's visit in 1984.

The *B.C. Catholic*, the official newspaper of the neighbouring Archdiocese of Vancouver, refused on principle to run the advertisement sent to them by the book's publisher, Harper Collins. The book was a frank three-way dialogue about the issues of the church that were arising in the period of containment that began in earnest by the middle 1980s.

Ten or twenty years earlier there would have been no issue in all this, but the controversy was testament of the shifting historical tide. In fact the editor at *The B.C. Catholic* during that earlier period, Gerry Bartram, became the centre of a controversy on the Island when his feature piece in *The Globe and Mail* titled *A Sacred Gift from God* was reprinted in the *Island Catholic News*.

Bartram composed a sensitive reflection on just how he had come to consider his homosexuality a gift from God. Traditionalist Catholics took great exception to this and many other polemical theological positions taken by the newspaper as an extension of the program of Vatican II.

In each case De Roo tolerated, if not welcomed, the coverage of controversial ideas as the role of Catholic newspapers to engender discussion; which he considered part of the informal formation process of the church's magisterium or teaching office.

Mary Jo Leddy, a Sister of Sion and a member of a progressive Catholic family in Saskatchewan, in providing informed commentary during the television coverage of the papal tour, represented an intelligent feminist perspective common among women religious.

De Roo was her long-time friend and associate. The focus of *Eye of the Catholic Storm* was right on target in terms of the avant garde agenda developments following Vatican II. But by 1992 there were other serious storm clouds on the horizon, ones that would sidetrack their agenda for at least the best part of a decade.

With former Premier Dave Barrett at an educational event on the Chiapas situation in the late 1990s. Barrett appointed him inaugural Provincial Human Rights Commission Chairperson in the early 1970s. (ICN)

As part of a papal audience with Pius XII in the early 1950s.

Part Two: A Fixed Formation

BACKGROUND 1924-1949

Chapter Six: Advent

YOUTH AND FAMILY BACKGROUND

1. A DEATH IN THE FAMILY

In his family, he was among the first generation conceived in Canada. Both his parents had been born in Belgium: his mother a De Pape, his father De Roo. Nineteen families including De Papes and De Roos migrated to Canada from one village area in the old country.

One of his mother's brothers had married one of his father's sisters, not the only instance of such family closeness between branches of the extended family in the Swan Lake region. Swan Lake where he was born in south central rural Manitoba is still concentrated with members of this combined clan.

Remi Joseph De Roo was born on the family farm February 24, 1924; the second of eight children, five girls and three boys, two of whom became Catholic priests. The parents had both been born at Lembeke, Belgium, some six years apart. Raymond De Roo on the 5th day of November in 1885 and Josephine De Pape, March 5, 1891.

Their wedding photograph from November 30, 1921 shows the thirty-six-year-old Raymond standing beside his thirty-year-old bride seated holding a bouquet of flowers, ones that reflect in their fragility an undeniably sensitive face.

Raymond appears stalwart and determined. Contemplating this image one easily imagines how their faces reveal few illusions about the physical hardships ahead; and yet an open hopefulness is not entirely distant.

Their marriage would last less than seventeen years due to Josephine's early demise, but it was a happy union of a balance that issued in eight children between the dates of November 22, 1922 and June 14, 1934.

In one of those odd fortuitous coincidences their wedding date—November 30, 1921—happened to fall on the precise date of the 75th anniversary of the founding of the Roman Catholic Diocese of Victoria. Their first born son would one day lead this diocese for more than thirty-five years, including the year of its 150th anniversary, on November 30, 1996 which would have been his parents' 75th wedding anniversary.

Less than five years after the birth of her last child, Josephine would be dead, leaving Raymond with eight motherless children between the ages of four and sixteen.

Remi's only older sibling, Gerarda, would enter religious life as well, but only in 1949 after the youngest child had completed high school, serving as principal mother substitute in the upbringing of the family.

Raymond, the widower at fifty-four years, would survive another thirty-six years to age ninety, never marrying again, dying in 1975 at Saint Boniface after having spent his final few years with Remi in Victoria.

Asked by Grant Maxwell, in an interview for this book, which siblings he was closest to, the son Remi said: "The natural affinity would have been to my sister Gerarda and my next younger brother Michael but I can't say I would single out a favourite. I had no serious problems with any of them. There was little opportunity for rivalry. Everybody was busy because there was so much to do. We were a very disciplined family."[89]

The immediate family orbit, the extended clan of cousins in rural Swan Lake and nearby Bruxelles, the church circle and Saint Gerard's, the elementary grade school: these fashioned the entire crucible of formation for the young boy during his first fourteen years.

In his early teens his parents decided to send him to Saint Boniface for his high school education. He was there in his first year of studies when his mother died very rapidly from "pneumonia and pleurisy."

"She had come to visit me on my birthday... on the way home by train she caught pneumonia and died February 28, 1939." It had been his fifteenth birthday.

"It was a traumatic experience, no doubt about it," he stated looking back after more than fifty-five years, "but in those days, living in that environment, we stiffened our upper lip and kept going." The manner in which his mother's death was revealed to the boy is in itself symbolic of that season of 'stiff upper lips'.

"I was visited at college by a nurse, a cousin, who came to tell me I was needed at home. No details were given. When the train arrived at the village of Swan Lake, I walked to the De Roo grandparents house, which was just a couple of blocks away, near the church. Grandmother De Roo met me at the door, and said, 'Your mother is dead, now don't cry.' The next thing I knew we were in the church for the prayers before the funeral."

2. BELGIAN CANADIAN BUILDERS

On the hundredth anniversary in 1993 of the De Pape and De Roo families as "Belgian Canadian Builders," the family stories were collected by two of the clan, Marguerite Thomson and Sister Mary De Pape, under that title. The book is organized into essays on the major family units which focus on nine family branches including Raymond and Josephine's.

The role of religion in the Raymond and Josephine family segment is summed up by a sentence: "Despite losing Josephine, the family remained staunch in their Roman Catholic Faith, continuing to recite the rosary every night after supper."

Argument could be easily marshalled—both psychological and theological—that the death of his mother was a decisive experience for the young Remi in his acceptance of a priestly vocation. Eleven years later on June 8, 1950 he was ordained at Saint Boniface, age twenty-six and at that point embarked on two years doctoral studies at the Angelicum College in Rome. His thesis title: "Mary Assumed into Heaven."

As he later said about his doctoral subject, this was "a very hot topic at the time" as the doctrine of the Assumption of Mary had just been promulgated by Pope Pius XII. Still, it is not a very great stretch of the imagination to see the psychological appeal of the topic due to the connection of his earthly mother's own 'assumption into heaven'.

❧❧❧

Josephine De Pape, Remi's mother, was the youngest child of seven of Englebert (known as Ange) and Philomena De Pape, the original Canadian patriarch and matriarch of that side of the family. Raymond, his father, was the eldest child of Francis and Emma De Roo; the eldest of ten.

Because his father was the eldest child, the young Remi grew up knowing his paternal grandparents. Because his mother was the youngest, her parents were a full generation of twenty years older and were already gone by the time Remi became conscious.

It had fallen to Josephine's lot, as the youngest child, to care for her aging parents. At the time of her birth in 1891, Ange was already fifty-seven years old and her mother Philomena was forty-five. It was only after her father's death, at age seventy-eight, in 1914—seven years after—that Josephine married Raymond. For three years Grandmother De Pape lived with the couple; dying at age seventy-six in 1924, the year of Remi's birth.

In 1939 it was Grandmother Emma De Roo who told the young Remi of his mother's death. Some of her apparent bluntness may have been accountable in terms of her own very recent grief of widowhood. Francis De Roo, her husband of more than fifty years, had died the previous month on January 25, 1939.

Death was a constant visitor in the lives of Francis and Emma, as members of the pioneer generation. Toughness in the face of death was a requisite response if you were to survive. Four of their ten children died in infancy, all had been born in Lembeke where they spent their first eleven years as a married couple.

Remi's father Raymond was just one year older than his next brother, also named Remi. Uncle Remi died in his twentieth year from the hardship of developing the farm.

The text from the family history reads: "Through a combination of determination, hard work, endurance and timely assistance from Mother Nature; a viable farming operation was established... In the early years (after 1896), Francis and the two oldest sons, Raymond and Remi, cut and hauled wood during the winter to help defray expenses and through barter to expand the family farm stock...

"Dressed in blankets instead of coats, the boys endured considerable hardship on cold winter days while working in the woods. Family land holdings were expanded (but) Remi became ill and died in 1905 causing some family plans to be changed," the history finishes in its abbreviated manner.

Remi Joseph De Roo was the namesake of his father's next brother who died contributing to the original patrimony. It is not recorded what his paternal grandmother felt and thought about this third generation Remi. He was the intellectually gifted one focused on priesthood, sent out of the immediate region for his education, who required special arrangements to be brought home to be informed about Josephine's untimely death.

Emma only succeeded Francis for two years, dying in 1941 at age seventy-six. The history book recounts that Francis and Emma moved into the village of Swan Lake in 1918 to their property east of the present parish hall, "where they enjoyed a quiet yet full life in retirement."

"On their half acre, Francis developed a beautiful garden of fruit trees, strawberries, raspberries and vegetables... He also kept a few bee hives. One year he grew enough strawberries to supply the families of his children.

"We are told Emma enjoyed serving breakfast to her children's families on Sundays when they came to town to attend Mass."

Even in retirement they produce bountifully in the way they always had, as farmers of the land. The grandson Remi, with his scholarly abilities, is a departure from their norm. By 1942 both are laid to rest in Swan Lake.

3. BELGIUM

On the highest ground just south of the town of Lembeke were found flint artifacts between six and eight thousand years old, presumably left by nomadic travellers of that period. The earliest available record in this Belgium Catholic parish are from the 13th Century though the parish is believed to be centuries older than that.[90]

This small Flemish town situated between the larger centres of Ghent and Brugge in Belgium is critical to the history of the De Pape and De Roo families. It was from there they came to Canada in the early 1890s.

A village with a strong Roman Catholic tradition, prior to the 16th Century Lembeke was part of a wool weaving industry of renown; and after this a linen spinning industry prospered peaking toward the end of the 18th Century.

Coming under French occupation at this time, all medieval and feudal laws were absolved with the French Revolution, and when Belgium was constituted in 1830 it formed part of the new nation. The 1800 population figure of 2,400 people living in the parish was about the same one hundred years later, due in part to an experience of economic stagnation which resulted in the significant migration that included the De Roos and the De Papes. The De Papes were the first of nineteen families to migrate from Lembeke to South Central Manitoba.

Since 1975 the population figure approximates 3,700 due to several factories in the region of Lembeke. Saint Igidius' Catholic Church is the oldest and most prominent focal structure in the community. Built in the 13th Century, it was rebuilt after a fire in the late 1770s.

The importance of Roman Catholicism to the region is underscored by the church's geographical centrality and it is there that the De Pape and De Roo ancestors are buried adjacent to the church. As such, St. Igidius and Lembeke have continued as a focus of personal and family pilgrimage to this day for the Belgian Canadian builders.

There have been at least two waves of migration from Lembeke to Swan Lake and Bruxelles. Remi's grandparents on both sides were among the first generation to arrive. An uncle, August De Pape, eldest son of Ange and Philomena, travelled alone in the spring of 1893 to assess the possibilities presented by this new Belgian colony.

August worked in several places, found the soil fertile, and the climate and seasons agreeable. So, after seven months, in November he recommended his parents and siblings make the move. The result was "that faith in God and pioneer perseverance were the necessary qualities of a homesteader... these settlements at Bruxelles, Swan Lake and other nearby Manitoba locations soon flourished."

The element of religious faith in this situation was critical. As the history book reports: "The De Papes were very devout Roman Catholics who diligently adhered to the tenets of their religion. They were keenly interested in the church and attended Sunday Mass even under the worst of conditions. Sunday was considered a day of relaxation and meditation with only absolutely essential work allowed."

In Belgium the De Papes had operated a small grain hauling business as well as a small farm. On the religious side, there is a story told of Ange, the original Belgian-Canadian patriarch of the clan who died at age seventy-eight in 1914.

Shortly before his death, he received what he considered an extraordinary blessing from the Archbishop of Saint Boniface. The bishop, upon making his annual rounds of the parish, noticed Ange was absent from his usual place. So he paid a visit to the home of his dedicated, ailing parishioner to the latter's extreme joy; and the family's unbroken memory.

4. A LARGE FAMILY

"In those days it was desirable to have a large family to propagate the Catholic faith and to help with the farm work."—De Roo/De Pape family history.

Of all Remi's cousins none would feature more in his life than Martha De Pape Wytinck, third daughter of August, his mother Josephine's eldest brother.

Martha too was born on the family farm, November 12, 1912, some twelve years ahead of Remi. He explained her ongoing presence among the De Roos this way: "Martha spent a lot of time at our family home. She worked with mother quite a bit. Being twelve years older, she was becoming a young woman when I was a young child.

"Martha came at a relatively young age to help mother with some of her housework. Mother's brother August De Pape was her senior. It's natural that he would allow one of his daughters to help his younger sister. Especially at harvest time and for the birth of children. Mother died just after I turned fifteen. Martha would have been twenty-six or twenty-seven."

Even in her earlier childhood, Martha focused on providing care. Her school days were cut short so she could help her mother with the youngest of her twelve sisters and brothers, particularly Joseph born in 1925.

At age twenty-four she married Isidore Wytinck of nearby Cypress River but after ten years he died prematurely in 1946. After her four children were nearly grown Martha served as Remi's housekeeper both in Norwood, St. Boniface and Victoria from 1960.

Martha as such provided a close and ongoing connection with the distaff side of his life, and the De Pape side of his nature.

From his father Raymond he received the ability to be methodical, orderly, steadfast, from his De Pape mother came something of her intensity, humour and sensitivity. The De Pape side of Remi De Roo's nature is a subject worth particular reflection if we are to understand some of his later developments.

An interesting marriage union significant to our story was that of Charles De Pape and Marie De Roo, whose wedding was in 1909, anticipating Remi's parents union by a dozen years. The cousins from this marriage would bear an observable similarity to his own immediate family.

Charles and Marie's first child was a son, and another Remi. Remi De Pape went on to distinguish himself with a record of remarkable community service. Charles, the father, proved another creative individual. Similar qualities to these close relatives would later surface in Remi De Roo.

A brief consideration of some De Pape men may help reveal a side of De Roo that would emerge in his leadership style.

FOUR DE PAPES

Remi De Pape was born in a log cabin in 1910. He was the senior member of the first Canadian-born generation. From the earliest age he displayed inventive ways and ideas on how things could be done, exhibiting a creative resourcefulness to achieve these ends. An early and impish example took place at the age of six when his parents took him off to Bruxelles to boarding school.

Remi, it seems, was not entirely convinced of the immediate desirability of this new arrangement. While they were inside arranging with the Ursuline Nuns he successfully hid himself in the horse-drawn carriage and returned all the way home with his parents, necessitating another immediate long trip back to the boarding school.

The trick proved somewhat prophetic as he did leave school early to become a farmer at age eleven due to his father's illness. By age twenty he left that and started on a varied career as a horse breeder, then a carpenter; becoming a husband in the process, and again a farmer at age twenty-seven.

After ten years he became a grain buyer, a farm machinery salesman for Massey-Harris and eventually the owner of a feed mill.

Throughout this period he was recognized for his community service by being elected first mayor of Somerset, another village in the Swan Lake area. As inaugural community leader he established a progressive reputation for the new town, having water and sewage installed for the whole village.

Other civic accomplishments included a three-sheet curling rink, paving the streets and building a sports field, as well as constructing a senior citizens complex; all in an acknowledged spirit of overall co-operation. His was an inspired enthusiasm. His ability to speak and write in three languages was a distinct advantage.

"Remi's drive, energy and sense of duty allowed him to meet this challenges," his cousins wrote of him.

Remi's father, Charles De Pape, had married the eldest daughter of Francis and Emma De Roo, Marie, in 1909. A photo of Charles and Marie some seven years after their wedding reveals an intense unity blended from strong yet obviously complementary individualities.

From all appearances seven years had knit them together enduringly. A handsome couple, as the phrase would have it, Marie displays a vivid intelligence. The photo shows her more prominently as part of one side of Charles' face is in shadow.

He seems slightly interiorly preoccupied yet their shoulders interlock, melding a physical image of unity. They emerge very strongly together. Another photo of their grown tribe of children shows the same handsome vitality distributed among a large group that is obviously enjoying its time of being together.

CLEM AND SAMMY SAM

Another notable uncle-cousin combination on the De Pape side consisted of Charles' younger brother Clement and his son George. This family dwelled on Hornby Island, which is situated just off Vancouver Island not far from Victoria where cousin Bishop Remi would eventually be located.

Clem, Remi De Roo's uncle, was prodigiously physically strong, having worked in hauling in Belgium and in the United States. As the third son of Ange and Philomena, he was another of Josephine (De Pape) De Roo's older brothers.

If on the De Pape side of the family there was a strong streak of adventurousness and carefree creativity, then Clem and George (who had the nickname 'Sammy Sam') were apt examples.

All his life Clem sought the perfect utopia in western Canada and after a few false starts he felt he found it at Hornby Island. Hornby is a place which to this day has a reputation for utopian idyllism (and idealism) off Canada's westcoast, which itself is a part of the country—with its mild climate and natural beauty—well known for its dreamy distinctiveness.

❧❧❧

Clem was born in Belgium in 1874 and came to Canada at age 20 to help settle the family in rural Manitoba. He married Marie Hutlet in 1898 and for the next twenty-five years they searched with their growing family for that perfect place, finally settling on Hornby in 1925.

Dramatically (and perhaps typically) Clem died attempting to stop a team of runaway horses at age fifty-six. George De Pape was the ninth of Clem and Marie De Pape's ten children, born at Nanaimo on Vancouver Island in 1908. George and his wife Tatiana had fifteen of their own children.

George was a 'colourful character' as his nickname 'Sammy Sam' signifies. This branch of the De Papes spelled their last name in a variety of ways—de pape, Depape and the conventional De Pape—another indication of their creative restlessness.

Sammy Sam lived eighty years, much of it on Hornby where he built up an enduring reputation as an entertainer in a variety of ways. He published books of sayings and poems. He was a singing story teller. He ran a distinctive sort of primitive theme park called 'The Ghost Show' at his camp ground.

One of Sammy Sam's books was titled *The Colours of the Rainbow* and as a folk artist his originality seemed to run through the spectrum.

In most ways these two colourful characters might seem a long avenue from the type of individual the young Remi De Roo aspired to become. Catholic priests and bishops are not usually known for their psychedelic personalities. And yet these properties formed part of his family background and certain parallels could be seen to enigmatically emerge as he matured.

5. A BATTLEGROUND

According to Anke Van Zanten[91], Belgium has earned the nickname 'the cockpit of Europe' because of her long history of serving as a battle zone for European countries. A territory where the European balance of power was resolved, Belgium has been the site of more major European battles than any comparable area.

Despite repeatedly declaring itself a neutral country after its establishment in the 19th Century, Belgium was invaded and occupied by the Germans during both World Wars in the 20th Century. The country was invaded early in the First World War, on August 4, 1914.

Unprepared for invasion, Belgium quickly lost control over all her assets. Having devoted the pre-war years to becoming an industrial power, by 1914 Belgium was one of the world's most industrialized nations, with one of the densest rail and roadway networks. The Germans quickly destroyed the heavy industry and this was never totally rectified at the cessation of conflict.

Following the strife the Belgium people exhibited great determination in recovering from the ruin, becoming the most densely populated country in Europe after the war. The country is divided into two sections, the Flemish speaking people of Flanders in the northern part, and the French-speaking population in Wallonia in the south. Lembeke is in the north.

By immigrating to Manitoba, the De Pape and the De Roo families avoided the direct impact of the disruption caused by the Great War. The young Remi and his siblings enjoyed, as much as possible, a normal Canadian childhood for their time and social status. He did retain something of an old world formality and, according to one of his cousins, experienced an extended pioneer period of formation.[92]

As the second of eight children, he would enjoy certain advantages and satisfactions that were part of the security and dynamics of a large supportive clan; as well as some distinct responsibilities.

The family's first language was Flemish. He has described it "not unlike certain Low German languages. Over the last fifty years Belgium and Holland have unified their language into what is called Nederlands. The Flemish I heard as a child was more localized in East Flanders."

The family farm consisted of a three quarters section of land, mixed farming of grain growing and livestock raising, purebred shorthorn cattle and Belgium breed horses. The cattle produced both milk and beef. The milk was for their own use with some cream sold. In the early years the crops were wheat, oats and barley; later clover, alfalfa and flax.

The Great Depression certainly had a direct impact but, as he claimed: "Dad was a good provider. I remember him boasting he never owed anybody a nickel. Frugality was certainly a key word... No lavish presents at Christmas or any other time. I remember the day when a nickel meant something."

He experienced his mother as "a very sensitive person with a good sense of humour, somewhat frail and hypersensitive to the possibility of criticism." In contrast to this, referring to the brusque manner he was informed of his mother's death at age fifteen:

"That's the way things were done in those days. That was part of your training. The family did not show that much emotion. Dad was very stoic but a kind man. I never saw him violent or being cruel in any sense.

"I do have some memories of his reaming out any hired man who dared to be cruel to the farm animals. Horses in particular were seen as our partners, and they were treated with deference. The general attitude was one of respect and there was an element of stoicism."

Compared to his sensitive mother, De Roo typifies his father as "more serene, a solid character, a good provider, and kindly man who rarely raised his voice." His mother and father having come from opposite ends of the birth order of large rural families, this lead to some anomalies.

Again, Raymond was the first child of ten, born to the only grandparents Remi would know. Josephine was the youngest child of a man who was a quarter century older than Francis De Roo, Raymond's father.

With his mother dying during his mid-teen years and both his maternal grandparents gone shortly after he was born, his life might be assumed to be unbalanced in terms of his lack of exposure to the De Papes. However this was somewhat rectified by the sheer size of the many families of cousins, and the close contact he had with his De Pape cousin Martha Wytinck throughout their lives.

Both families were intensely religious. The young Remi's early religious formation was assumed. It was part of the spiritual landscape. "It was natural," as he liked to say about that period of his life.

Religion was in the very air he breathed. And as a result he just gradually—and naturally—knew he wanted to be a priest.

"Once my brother and I were big enough, we served Mass in the village church at Christmas Midnight Mass; and then again at dawn we helped celebrate it again together."

Asked if he had an early inclination to be a priest, he replied: "It came kind of spontaneously from my family in early childhood. I never really fixed on anything other than that."

He was not overburdened with choices as a child. "The only other option," he said, "was to stay on the farm and as the oldest son take over the farm."

This fell to his younger brother Michael, some twenty months his junior, who died well before his time (along with a son) from a farm accident in the 1970s. Remi as second child was born fifteen months after Gerarda. After Michael, the spacing of the children stretched out a bit more.

Clara, the fourth child and second daughter, was born nearly three years after Michael. Alma the fifth, was only seventeen months later in 1929, while Cyril was nearly two years afterward in late 1931. Cyril would also become a Catholic priest, ordained seven years following Remi in 1957. Failing health led to his resignation from the priesthood.

The last child Madeleine was born June 14, 1934, a full ten years after her eldest brother. Eight children in less than twelve years.

With cousin and housekeeper Martha Wytinck, right, and long-term executive assistant Eileen Archer in 1988. (Jamie Jenkins)

Chapter Seven: Nativity

RELIGIOUS VOCATION

1. BOOK OF GENESIS

Remi De Roo explained something of his religious vocation in the following way. "My parents listened to the advice of our parish priest, Father Deiderichs, a wonderful man from Alsace-Lorraine, who spoke four languages."

"Deiderich said to my parents: If your son wants to become a priest, since this is the Archdiocese of Saint Boniface, you had better send him to the French Jesuit College in Saint Boniface.

"So I ended up eight years as a boarder at Saint Boniface College where I took French immersion in what was then called a classical course based on Québec's college curriculum."

In another context De Roo spoke of Monsignor Deiderichs and his early years: "There has been a massive shift from what I knew as a farm boy, a member of a community in rural Manitoba. Our pastor was a benign dictator who knew four languages. He used everything he knew for the benefit of everyone. I never saw him rage at anyone but he was in control. He even advised the farmers when to sell their wheat, because he had a radio and could follow the grain futures market.

"He helped with wills, insurance policies, the whole bit. He knew which districts the banks and insurance companies had marginalized, where they wouldn't give loans or hail-insurance, because their maps showed too high risks of hail.

"I came out of the seminary ready to run my parish that way. I had all my books. The church had all the answers. I was comfortable. We just understood the way things were going to be. We had a basic security that if you did your work and said your prayers, all would go well."[93]

At age fourteen, the boy Remi made his first departure from the cultural enclave of his upbringing. The following February, just after his fifteenth birthday, his beloved mother, the sensitive Josephine, undertook her great leave taking, underlining the drama of his own passage.

As such the question arises: Had she died a year before, whether Remi would have left home in the same way? It is a moot point, the sequence coming in the order it did, his passage out was assured. Her passing probably intensified his commitment given that her final birthday visit would have seemed a blessing confirming the decision from the fall before. However it worked its way out, De Roo's priestly vocation seemed destined from the start.

A few years prior to his retirement as a bishop at Victoria, Remi De Roo confided to a friend that if he had not become a priest, he would gladly have become a farmer, taken over the family farm and raised a bunch of children.[94]

From a theological point of view, it could have amounted to the same thing. He would have been simply opting for the other predominant theology which has governed the thinking of Western Christianity since its inception; since the Book of Genesis actually.

Genesis being comprised of two distinct strains, one of which he followed by his religious vocation; the other, actually the older tradition, he was wishing upon in an understandable moment of lament tinged with wonder.

The farmer theology corresponds to the creation myth of Christianity, where the world as God made it has an integral perfection. Remi's early experience contained this sort of resonant wholeness.

In an interview he stated that "the family led a serene and regular life. By and large we got along well. We lived pretty well off the land. My father was serene, a solid character, a good provider, a kindly man who rarely raised his voice. Mother was a sensitive person with a good sense of humour."

Within a dependably supportive milieu they led the natural life, buoyed up by the environment, by Nature, they relied upon God's grace to do all the rest. As he said in the latter comment on

Father Deiderich, you do your work and say your prayers and 'all would go well'.

Of course, the natural life also has its stark realities.

"On the farm one was rapidly initiated into the realities of life and death. I remember having to get up in the middle of the night to help Dad attend to a cow that was calving and if I failed it might mean the difference between life and death."

Cirlot's *Dictionary of Symbols* says this about farming: "Among basic occupations, farming has a very special significance, not only because its activities takes place in the sacred world of seeds, buds, flowers and fruit, but also because it follows the cosmic order as illustrated in the calendar...

"The farmer is therefore the guardian of agricultural rites, seeing out the 'old year' and seeing in the 'new'. In spiritual terms this means that the farmer appears as the catalyst of the forces of regeneration and salvation...

"Farming was essential not only for the development of primitive economy but also for the emergence of a cosmic consciousness in Man. Mircea Eliade puts it most aptly: What Man saw in the grain, what he learnt in dealing with it, what he was taught by the example of the seeds changing their form when they are in the ground, that was the decisive lesson."

Remi De Roo never lost touch with these spiritual roots. His challenge of the economic system was precisely in the direction of the salvation of the 'primitive economy'. This was his primary religious calling or as Cirlot completes his entry: "One of the main roots of soteriological optimism was the belief of prehistoric, agricultural mysticism that the dead, like the seeds underground, can expect to return to life in a different form."[95]

De Roo's belief in unpopular causes was rooted in this resurrection theology that even what seems most dead and unlikely has the seeds of life and resurrection within it and his job was often to announce this improbable reality and work to support the conditions that could eventually bring it about.

When Remi left home on the path that ultimately led to priesthood, without really knowing it, he was abandoning that wholistic spirituality implicit in farm life. He was opting for that other theology pronounced in the Book of Genesis, that of the Fall from Grace and the subsequent need for Redemption.[96]

While one vision is of an unfettered wholeness, this second centres itself on the reality of brokenness and the need for rejuvenation. At the Jesuit college he would have been thoroughly instructed in this second theological bias, and subliminally it would have rubbed against his fundamental formation.

The priest figure in this second scheme is the great and necessary agent of redemptive grace. At least, this was assuredly the model employed by the Catholic Church in the period when he became a priest; and the model he said he had in mind for himself.

Changes since that time have attempted to rectify the balance, but this model peaked in its influence during his first decade as a young priest. While his parents may have somehow secretly subscribed to a form of creation spirituality, his grandparents De Roo self-consciously adhered to the formal framework of the fall-redemption paradigm. They were the religious gatekeepers.

"My paternal grandparents lived very close to our church, Saint Martin de Tours, in the town of Swan Lake. (I never knew my maternal grandparents.)

"The regular routine was to go to the De Roo grandparents' home before Mass to check in, as it were, and then go after Mass for a bite to eat. In those days we fasted and abstained from food and drink from midnight before receiving morning Eucharist.

"Grandmother De Roo was rather stern by temperament. Very definite in how she spoke. Grandfather was a quiet person who said less. However, both were kindly. I have nothing but good memories of them. They were very devout in a Jansenist way."

Jansenism in this context is an extreme form of the fall-redemption theology. It is the logical consequence of the weakness in the system. The need for redemption underlines the radical imperative of grace from God.[97]

Jansenism reflects the nagging worry that there may be circumstances under which even grace fails; that a human soul can't be too careful about not presuming that even God's grace might have its limits. Jansenism expresses the full doubt concerning the ultimately corrosive power of sin.

Given the vicissitude of the difficult life of the period, the insecurity of the pioneer life, its spiritual complementarity in Jansenism would have recommended itself heavily to the De Roo grandparents. Spiritually and physically there was no room for any mistakes in such a context, in such a time.

As a severely penitential form of spirituality, Jansenism is a spirituality rooted in a radical degree of fear, at war with the sort of peaceful security the other theology assumes; where grace unfailingly completes nature, and is almost a 'natural' aspect of creation itself.

2. CRUCIFIXES EVERYWHERE

"Religion always had priority," De Roo remembers. "Sunday was sacred. Although it was four miles to church in the village, we would go every week and more often in the months of October and May, months with special dedication to Mary. It meant going for vespers in the church unless there was some very heavy work on the farm."

What he meant obviously—from what he described—was that religious practice had priority over any other activity except farm work: "unless there was some heavy work on the farm."

Farm work itself would have been instinctively understood as a form of worship, perhaps the primary form of worship.

The truth was that the farming form of worship actually had 'priority' until Remi left home at age fourteen to study for the pastorate; and the farming form of worship was, naturally, rooted in a creation spirituality.

"We made the nine First Fridays; we would go before farm work, usually by horse and buggy. We said the rosary at home each night, mostly on our knees. We had holy pictures in the house and crucifixes everywhere. Always there were prayers before meals."

Their elementary school was situated on the farm. "Dad had set aside a couple of acres of our land along the road a quarter mile from our farm home, on pasture land."

Having the school so close at hand was partly a necessity as "roads were poor in winter and sometimes it was too cold to get the car started. Gumbo mud was another problem, so the car was something of a fine weather convenience."

All schools had to follow provincial curriculum "but effectively all pupils were Catholic in our school and we had a Catholic teacher who taught catechism. We walked to school through the pasture while some other pupils came about a mile and a quarter."

There were no children whose first language was English, mostly children of Flemish and French-speaking families. And no Protestants. "Very few as I recall. They were not a significant presence."

His most significant and excellent teacher was a cousin, Marguerite De Pape who had suffered polio and had one paralysed arm.

As a child he would have had no personal direct experience of having read the Bible, but rather, personal instruction was through "a little Flemish catechism we had at home, though we learned most at church where the sermons were long."

The child must have felt the benefit of long sermons because he liked going to church where "Michael and I were altar boys once we learned to carry the Missal without tripping on the altar steps." Sometime while avoiding such mishaps he settled on the feeling he wanted to be a priest.

"I don't remember a specific day, or a conversion in that sense. I think the parish priest, a wonderful man, had a lot to do with that decision."

It was only in elementary school he learned to speak English. Having the school on the farm contributed to the minimal amount of socializing he experienced beyond the immediate family.

Asked about particular school chums from those years:

"Our basic relationships were in the family. Occasionally we would visit neighbours. At school naturally I would be a little closer to the other boys my own age."

Asked about girls and any run-ins with school yard bullies, he replied: "I remember a cousin almost choking me to death, apart from that, no."

Girls: "Oh yes, it's only natural to be attracted to neighbouring girls, the 'puppy love' experience was part of life. However, dating was frowned upon unless one was older and seriously contemplating marriage. Casual dating was not encouraged."

It's interesting how often he tends to use the phrase "It's natural," or "It's only natural," regarding this phase of his life. It was a 'natural' life, self-sufficient spiritually as well as economically, idyllic in some important sense.

Until he left home the opportunities for exposure to non-family were very limited. "Besides there was little public recreation. We didn't go to dances. We spent almost all our time on the farm. When you're milking cows, cleaning barns, and seeding grain, you don't have the time. It was only later that some of the older guys started going to dances in town."

He did have plenty of time to reflect and meditate on the idea of priesthood it seems; and before he was one of the 'older guys going off to dances' he registered at Saint Boniface College, run by Jesuits.

All of the next twelve years of undergraduate studies, resulting in a Latin philosophy degree—and then theological studies at the seminary at Saint Norbert—were conducted in the French language. He left the language of his birth behind as he moved into his next stage.

3. ROAD TO ROME

Aside perhaps from military training, it is difficult to imagine a more focused program of preparation than a young man studying for the Roman Catholic priesthood, particularly in that period between 1938-1950.

When he entered St. Boniface College in 1938, the world-wide Catholic Church was about halfway through a most exceptional continuous leadership period, one that lasted most of four decades under two very similar and very talented popes, Pius XI (Achille Ratti) 1922-1939 and Pius XII (Eugenio Pacelli) 1939-1958.

The year the young Remi entered minor seminary was the time not only of his mother's death but of the pope's death, just eighteen days before hers. A turbulent period all around, in September, 1939 the world war started and this in effect closed the World Depression.

Pius XI, the pope during the Depression, issued a noteworthy social encyclical in 1931, marking the fortieth anniversary of the first great social statement by Pope Leo XIII in 1891. Leo's Statement was titled *Rerum Novarum* (*On the Condition of the Workingman*).

Papal statements are called encyclical letters if they are circulated among the leaders of the church for pronouncement among the laity. They are designated by their first few words in Latin. *Quadragesimo Anno*, the Depression Encyclical, ('After Forty Years') gave needed new impetus by releasing fresh energy from the Catholic population for particular Canadian social experiments of that time.

In the Maritime provinces, for example, the great push was in the form of credit unions and co-operatives among farmers and fishermen under the auspices of The Antigonish Movement, based out of a major Catholic university of the region.

On the Prairies this took the form of Catholic farmers getting behind the Wheat Pool, credit unions and co-operatives in the face of economic adversity from the central Canadian establishment. After *Quadragesimo Anno,* Catholics felt they could throw their weight behind these social movements without worrying about the socialist roots and connection of such movements.

Since the middle of the 19th Century the Catholic Church was the fiercest foe of anything smacking of socialism, communism or Marxism, which it uncritically lumped together. So fierce was this opposition that even democratically-run left-leaning political parties were tarred with the same anti-Communist brush. Any form of socialism was seen as a stepping stone to atheistic communism in the official Catholic view.[98]

In his 1931 social encyclical the pope tried to delineate a Catholic-Christian middle way between the excesses of monopoly capitalism and the dangers of totalitarian communism.

The political success of this 'middle way' idea was eventually very limited but at the time an alternative was being officially espoused, and it was tried particularly in the more underdeveloped regions of Canada such as the Prairies and the Maritimes.

Within that church context, the De Roos and the De Papes, both as a large extended family and as small farmers, would have been encouraged to recognize the value of small scale collective action regarding the means of production.

Pius XII who succeeded Pius XI continued this upshot within the new context of the Second World War and then, following that, the expansive era of the postwar period. Both these men had been career diplomats in church service and as such took a realistic view in terms of relating to the world.[99]

At the same time they were attempting to uphold within the church standards of Christian idealism which continued to set the church against the world's values in no uncertain terms.

❧❧❧

The pope at the time of Remi's birth was Pius XI (1922-1939). He would be the pontiff who served between the Great Wars, who would face a world radically changing, a world dealing with the dual spectres of world communism which had spawned in reaction the threat of global fascism and nazism. His manner of governing the church, and that of his immediate successor Pius XII (1939-58), would establish the Catholic Church's overall response to the modern world until The Second Vatican Council.

More immediately pertinent to our story was the style and tone of final spiritual authority which these two men cast over the universal Catholic Church during De Roo's period of upbringing. They were the prime exponents of the self-confident self-understanding of the Catholic Church as a perfect society over and against the world.

TWO POPES

Achille Ratti who took the name Pius XI was ordained in 1879. A scholar, he received three doctorates at the Gregorian University in Rome. A seminary professor, a library expert, he was also a keen mountaineer. As prefect of the Vatican Library until 1918, he was sent to Poland as Apostolic Delegate. This was a difficult time for the church in Poland, in August 1920 a Bolshevik revolution threatened Warsaw but Ratti refused to leave until the crisis was over.

Pope Benedict XV rescued him from a further untenable situation in Poland and subsequently elevated him to the See of Milan as archbishop in June of 1921. The next year at the conclave he was elected on the fourteenth ballot as a compromise candidate. His motto was interpreted as meaning that the church and Christianity should be active, not insulated from society.

His first encyclical inaugurated the era of Catholic Action which invited deeper participation of the laity, including the initiation of Catholic youth organizations. He was the pope who condemned contraception and in 1931 on the fortieth anniversary of Leo XIII's social encyclical, he reframed Leo's social teaching but extended it, going further in face of the global economic crisis and the escalating arms race. It was significant that the papacy engaged realistically with the modern world. This was a dramatic shift in relations.

With the help of the future Pius XII, Eugenio Pacelli, he regularized church relations with some twenty nations, culminating with the Lateran Treaty of 1929 which he negotiated with Mussolini and established Vatican City as an independent neutral state. For the first time since 1870, the Holy See recognized Italy as a Kingdom with Rome as the capital, while Italy indemnified it for the loss of the papal states and accepted Catholicism as the official religion.

The pope's attempts to check Soviet anti-Christian persecution had no effect, but it lead to a mistaken trust of Hitler when he negotiated a concordat with National Socialist Germany in July, 1933 which temporarily enhanced the prestige of the regime and curbed Catholic opposition to it, for which he was heavily criticized.

The break came in 1937 when he condemned Nazism as fundamentally anti-Christian. His attitude towards Italian fascism, shaken in 1931 when Mussolini dissolved Catholic youth movements, dramatically hardened in 1938 when the regime adopted Hitler's racial doctrines. Pius also supported Franco in Spain, due to that dictator's ultra-traditional Catholicism, adding to the impression that the church was soft on fascism.

Internally within the church, he required every religious order to engage in missionary work thereby doubling the number of missionaries in his reign. Like Pope Benedict XV just before him he pressed on with developing indigenous Catholicism, personally consecrating in the face of opposition six Chinese bishops in 1926, shortly followed by similar moves in Japan, India and China again between 1927 and 1933. Native clergy increased from three to seven thousand during his era.

The first scholar pope since 1758, he quietly eased the tensions arising from the anti-Modernist debate within the church rehabilitating some leading figures who had been demoted.

He modernized and enlarged the Vatican Library, founded the Pontifical Institute of Christian Archaeology and the Pontifical Academy of Science as well as instructing Italian Bishops to take proper care of their archives.

He delegated little, reducing the role of the Sacred College of Cardinals and was the first pope to use radio for pastoral purposes.

PIUS XII

Pius XII, who was pope from March, 1939 until October, 1958, epitomized in style the paradigm the church had become under his illustrious predecessor. This model of church was revealed in the language of its self-description as the 'Mystical Body of Christ'. The Catholic Church of that period adopted the self-image of the ideal or 'perfect society', very much a top-down spiritual prototype. The emphasis was upon its divine origins, playing down the 'merely' human side. Certainly its Supreme Pontiff successfully conveyed this understanding in all its regal implications.

Pius XII was a lawyer's son and the descendent of a long line of jurists. Born Eugenio Pacelli on March 2 (the same day he was crowned pope) 1876 and ordained to the priesthood in 1899, he entered the papal service two years later. He was instrumental in the codifying of the canon law between 1904 and 1916. For several years he taught international law at an academy for ecclesiastics.

During the First World War he also negotiated with governments about Benedict XV's (1914-22) abortive peace plan. In 1917 he was made nuncio in Munich and a titular archbishop. He worked on concordats with various nations during the 1920s and was named cardinal in 1929 after two decades of very busy years. In 1930 he was designated Secretary of State for The Vatican.

It was Pacelli who negotiated the Vatican concordat with the Nationalist Socialist Germany of 1933; all in good faith, but Hitler's repeated violations revealed his true intent. An accomplished linguist, Cardinal Pacelli paid official visits to Britain, Argentina, France, Hungary and an extensive private one to the United States.

With the Second World War threatening he was elected pope at a one-day conclave on the third ballot. He was the first secretary of state chosen since Clement IX in 1667 but he was the best known of the cardinals and possessed the gifts and experience that seemed called for.

The circumstance of war established the great test of the first six years of his pontificate. Pius saw himself as the 'pope of peace' and until September 1, 1939 strove to avert war by diplomatic moves. Through his efforts Rome was treated as an open city.

Although convinced that Communism was more dangerous than Nazism, he did not endorse Hitler's attack on Russia, and he deplored the Allies' demand in January 1943 at Casablanca for unconditional surrender. When Hitler occupied Rome in September of 1943, Pius made the Vatican City an asylum for countless refugees, including numerous Jews.

He has been criticized, however, for failing to speak out sufficiently firmly against Nazi atrocities, especially the persecution of the Jews. What remains clear is that the veiled or generalized language traditional to the curia was not a suitable instrument for dealing with cynically planned world domination and genocide.

Internally, he expounded in major encyclical teachings the nature of the church in terms of Christ's Mystical Body and he permitted the use of modern historical methods by exegetes of Scripture. This was important in terms of the church moving away from any fundamentalistic interpretation of Scripture.

He reformed the liturgy and called for intelligent participation by the laity in the Mass as well as standardizing relaxations of the eucharistic fast and the holding of evening Mass. Clearly, Pius unconsciously laid the groundwork for the great changes within the church that were to come.

Always Marian in his piety, he defined the Dogma of the bodily Assumption of the Blessed Virgin Mary into Heaven while at the same time leaving open the question of her mediation and co-redemptive role, always a touchy topic with Protestants. He was the first to appreciate the importance of the reported apparitions at Fatima, Portugal.

Politically he inveighed against communism, threatening members of the party with excommunication in 1950. In the moral field he condemned, with Germany in view, the concept of collective guilt, and in the medical field any kind of artificial insemination. Also he sought guidelines for the audio-visual media.

He canonized thirty-three persons including Pope Pius X, and created an unprecedentedly large number of cardinals, fifty-six in all, drawing them from many countries and reducing the Italian element to one third. The number of dioceses rose from around 1,700 to more than 2,000 in his era.

He somewhat relaxed his predecessor's negative attitude toward the ecumenical movement, recognizing it in 1949 following the formation of the World Council of Churches the year before.

Tall, slender, ascetic in appearance but friendly in manner, he made a profound impression on the millions who flocked to Rome for the Holy Year of 1950 and the Marian Year of 1954. He was the first pope to become widely known through television and radio. Authoritarian in style, he acted himself as secretary of state from 1944, and increasingly diminished the role of the cardinals. When he died at Castel Gandolfo his moral authority probably stood higher in non-Roman than Roman circles.

Pacelli was seriously gifted. Remi De Roo expressed a tremendous degree of respect for Pius XII, calling him a genius.[100] De Roo expressed admiration for how prophetic figures could exceed the limits of the given paradigm, cutting a swath of leadership into the future.

The political dimension of the church under this series of popes (starting with Benedict XV), who had served successfully as world diplomats and secretaries of state, was acutely alive. These were some of the parameters of the political theology of the Catholic Church at the time Remi De Roo applied himself for ordination.

"Yes, I went right from school on the farm to college. I never had high school. There was only one college class in English. Outside of that we were forbidden to speak English," he explained about this transition from one sort of radical seclusion to another.

"The college itself had been there since 1922. Most of the Jesuit faculty were from the east, that is Québec. Because of the war in the 1940s, I had to register as a seminarian. Four years at the archdiocesan seminary followed, primarily in French. I was ordained in 1950 and went straight to Rome."

These sentences are typical of the matter-of-fact manner De Roo tends to explain his early years in the interviews with Grant

Maxwell. He is very consistent in this. In another round, covering the same events he put it this way:

"My parents listened to the advice of our parish priest, who said you had better send him to the French Jesuit College at Saint Boniface. So I ended up for eight years as a boarder where I took French immersion in what was then called a classical course based on Québec's college curriculum. The last two years of philosophy prepared us for entrance to seminary. The first years began at St. Norbert but then shifted to the new seminary in St. Boniface under Archbishop Cabana.

"In the last year of studies I remember Archbishop Cabana meeting me on the street and telling me that the professors at the seminary had recommended me for further studies because they had to prepare more lecturers for the seminary. Would I be willing to go to Rome for a theology degree?

"I invited my father to come with me. We went to Belgium where he hadn't been for fifty years. We started by visiting the priest in the little village of Lembeke. Father recognized some of the places in the village where he had once lived. I took him with me to Rome where I attended the Canadian College."

At this stage his father Raymond De Roo would be nearly sixty-five. Somehow De Roo's filial devotion seems significant. Later Raymond would come to live with the bishop in Victoria for his final years.

At the age of twenty-six Remi was coming into his own, and yet was still a dutiful son who valued his family and rural Manitoba connections. Having Raymond on the trip to Rome granted a link with the fundamental family relationship. He had the regular intuition to keep someone close at hand as a vital link with the formative past.

The best example was the cousin Martha De Pape Wytinck, widowed young with four youngsters in 1946. Martha would serve some thirty-three years as his housekeeper both at Holy Cross Parish in St. Boniface and Victoria when he was appointed bishop.

Raymond and Martha, in turn, served as indispensable ties to his family roots no matter how far he would roam intellectually or geographically. It would be difficult to overstate the importance to his sense of identity of the company of immediate family members. He occupied a uniquely vaunted position in the De Pape and De Roo family myth given their heritage of religious dedication. In turn these vital rural roots fed his steadfast clarity of values.

4. RURAL ROOTS

Swan Lake lies within the canonical boundary of the diocese of Saint Boniface. Winnipeg is the lone large centre serving rural Manitoba, and the City of Saint Boniface is the French-speaking remnant of the original historical Red River Colony, now entirely surrounded by the urban megalopolis.

As such, most of Remi's classmates would have come from similar rural experiences. In that sense Saint Boniface was not a long way, culturally, from Swan Lake.

But Rome was another story. He later called Rome the world's market place where his ideas were expanded. It was there he outgrew his rural Manitoba roots intellectually, but he would never lose the moral anchor they afforded him.

At a much later stage, in his middle sixties, he would look back and comment extensively on the meaning of the small family farm to his ongoing values, to his interpretation of experience.

In an essay on the role of the church in the salvation of rural life, he would complain that "farming has drifted from its community and cultural moorings to become a business, producing commodities for a highly competitive and exploitative world economy."[101] For him, this was a deep betrayal of the true nature of rural life.

He identifies four principles—simplicity, proximity, balance and control—as meaningful to recovery of the original vision: the small is beautiful approach. These characteristics typified the family farm of his experience.

He also argues that "authentic change will only come from the involvement of rural people themselves, when they are no longer treated as clients of urban interest but rather as agents of their own future."

"Rural people have become conditioned by modern urban concepts and city-based popular values. They are constantly misinformed, overwhelmed by propaganda about the 'good life', and eventually numbed into subservience, rendered docile and powerless in the face of impending disasters."

"Many rural people have become alienated from nature... they no longer appreciate the land as gift, as source of life and meaning, as nurturing parent and friend."

A cousin of Remi's, Joseph De Pape, the youngest son of August and Augusta (and the baby brother Martha Wytinck left school to care for) had something similar to say in the family history volume in 1993.

Joseph, who was the last member of his family to work the family farm near Bruxelles, makes an piquant point that the stock market crash of 1929 delayed the completion of the pioneer era. He argues that the Depression extended pioneer-like conditions for another generation, the generation to which Remi belonged.

"The slowdown effect created by the Depression resulted in a widespread economic decline and type of poverty never witnessed before. We were still in the horse-and-buggy days. Electricity had not reached the rural areas, there was no running water. Most roads had not been gravelled, hardtop was unheard of." The bishop said the same, 'that a car was just a fine weather convenience'.

"Mechanization and farm labour saving devices were limited... There was virtually no money. Prices dropped to an all time low. Yet as the years progressed the younger generation appeared happy and unaffected because they did not know the difference between hard times and good times, never having experienced the latter. Because of the highly self-sufficient nature of the mixed farming operations around Bruxelles and Swan Lake, farmers in the area coped better than most Canadians during this period."

This was the key formative period of Remi's early teens. He was one of those younger generation 'who didn't know the difference' during the Depression. As a result he went away to seminary formed in the values of a pioneer prairie boy and shaped in his persistent attitudes by the extended-pioneer period.

It gave him bedrock values and a solidity of vision that persisted; eventually enabling him to make a significant national mark when his time came as a leader.

5. CENTRAL LIFE DECISIONS

During the next decade of the 1940s, Remi the boy became Father De Roo the man. In these ten years, within the culture of the seminary, he slowly arrived at his central life decisions.

He opted to forsake his direct relationship with the nurturing parental land; he rejected any possibility of a marriage partnership and children; he abandoned the idea of being able to earn a financial reward commensurate with his already indicated general abilities.

He chose to become a Catholic priest, forever committed to a higher spiritual authority within an institution which claimed to have a hold on truth with absolute certitude.

Looking back one can glimpse how the seeds of his future social concerns were planted in his youth. But at the time, there was no tangible indication he would ever become a bishop; or the national leader he did.

He was simply a young man from a modest background, modeled from his experience in a rural pastorate, encumbered with certain 'outstanding intellectual gifts', whose mother had died in his first year of seminary.

It was far from certain how he would make out. Following the conventional course of studies he graduated in a classical arts program and was prepared for ordination at the equally conventional age of twenty-six years.

BIBLIOTHECA PONT. UNIV. GREGORIANAE - ROMAE

ANNUS SCHOLARIS 1951/52

TESSERA N. 289

Dom. De Roo Remigius

Via Quattro Fontane 117

Praef. Bibl.

Student card when studying at the Gregorian University, Rome.

Ground breaking meeting with Anglican and Protestant clergy in Victoria following Vatican II in the early 1960s.

Chapter Eight: Grace Upon Grace

FOREGROUND 1950-1962

1. SWAN LAKE 1950

"A violent storm engulfed my home town on the night before my ordination to the priesthood. Lightning and thunder were followed by a drenching rain such as the residents of Swan Lake had seldom seen.

"Overnight the country roads became almost impassable. Happily, the storm blew over and brilliant sunshine lit up an almost cloudless blue sky. The green grass and lush fields of grain reflected the June promise of a bountiful summer.

"As people assembled from far and wide they shared their tales of struggling valiantly through seemingly endless muddy ruts. But nothing would prevent them from filling the village church for this important event in the life of our community.

"Ordinations were rather solemn affairs in those days. The presence of the Archbishop of St. Boniface called for a maximum of decorum. That is probably why I remember how surprised we were when a cousin of mine decided to play the clown.

"He appeared in the official reception line sporting a huge artificial nose. This gesture produced a round of laughs and the initial stern atmosphere became more relaxed. The prairie people quickly responded to the mood of rejoicing. My ordination day turned out to be a series of joyous encounters."

This recollection by Remi De Roo was made more than forty years after the event. He was officiating at the ordination of three young men for the Diocese of Victoria in 1992, and he used the opportunity to comment on the changed situation of the church since his first days as a priest. The focus was the still changing role of the priest, something he knew a great deal about.

"The essence of the hierarchal ministerial priesthood dates back to earliest Christianity. However the external form of the

Sacraments of Orders and the service it offers to society have known significant variations to meet the needs of a changing world.

"The essential elements remain, secondary aspects evolve. The Second Vatican Council clearly recognized the historical development and allowed for significant adaptation to ritual and practice.

"I recall the earlier incident of the clown at my ordination because 'imagination and creativity' help us to appreciate more fully the richness of our celebration. No matter what our age, the child in us is attracted to clowns. They invite us not to take ourselves too seriously, to enjoy the present moment. From a deeper perspective, they also remind us that all is gift. For there is nothing we have not received from God, grace upon grace."

❧❧❧

From the vantage point of 1992, he could look back and identify the importance of creativity and imagination but in 1950 at Swan Lake, Manitoba it was a radically different church in a radically different time.

The 1950s would prove the period of his making, and a conformist period it was. He could be described as a fully formed cleric of his time. He served just twelve years as a priest, and would accomplish three times that number as a bishop.

In those early days the Catholic Church worldwide was known as and prided itself in being the 'perfect institution', reflecting its deeper theological notion of the Church as the 'perfect society'. This concept was deep-seated within a medieval theology from an epoch when the Church had achieved a distinct integrity as a spiritual monolith.

Well into the 20th Century the Catholic Church was an elaborate institution set over and against the values of 'the world'. In this environment the talented and dedicated could quickly rise. In the twelve years between 1950 and 1962 when he served as a young priest, Remi De Roo was granted the privilege of the fullest formation afforded a priest by this global framework.

The fact that De Roo could see the value of the clown at the solemn event of his ordination represents his healthy respect for the shadow side of the institution. He demonstrated an almost uncanny objectivity in his perspective about the institution. It was an ability to see the blind side of the church and to work to integrate this into its development.

It is part of the reason why he would emerge at the end of his apprenticeship as a new sort of bishop figure; with the strength and advantages of one formed in the last days of the old prototype, and yet young enough to be ready for the major challenges of the transformation ahead. His years of study in Rome were an important part of the preparation.

2. DOCTORAL STUDIES IN ROME

At the behest of his archbishop, at age twenty-six, he relocated to Rome where he attended the Canadian College in order to be trained as a seminary instructor, possibly a future fulltime professor.

"Upon arrival at the College, a comprehensive oral exam earned me a bachelorate. I then plunged into studies for the equivalent of a licentiate in one year, and a Doctorate in 1952."

The licentiate is a pre-doctoral degree in theology which also includes a teaching license for Catholic seminaries. He entered upon an ambitious program of studies fraught with miscellaneous sorts of theological riskiness.

"In that year I had as moderator to direct me, a Father Geenen from Louvain (Belgium). His speciality was the 'development of doctrine' which in those days was a somewhat suspect subject field because the Vatican had not yet caught up with Cardinal Newman."

John Henry Newman was the leading 19th Century Anglican Oxford University man of letters who converted to Catholicism in 1845 at mid-life. In the process of thinking his way through to this decision, Newman contributed mightily to the eventual acceptance by the Roman Church of the principle of development within doctrinal formation. Newman is a paradoxical figure in the Catholic Church for this reason.

He is generally attributed with substantial changes in thinking that lead to and were enshrined in the Second Vatican Council, some seventy-five years after his death. For this and his writings on the freedom of Catholic conscience, he is understood as a progressive figure. For other reasons, notably his famous conversion and his deep regard for tradition and authority, he is also trumpeted by conservatives in the church as representing their cause.

He is an innovative traditionalist or a genuinely progressive conservative, somehow representing the paradoxical nature of the Catholic church in one exemplary personality. The same categories can be accurately applied to Remi De Roo both as a thinker and a leader.

It is no coincidence he was attracted by Newman's work so early in his career. Following his retirement in 1999, after he was 'silenced' by Rome from speaking at a married priests convention, he presented a talk to the Catholic Theological Society of America on "the Diocesan Synod as a means to develop Doctrine."[102]

De Roo's early intellectual formation under a scholar of Newman's work is significant to his story. Throughout his career, he is seen as, accused of, and generally misunderstood to be as a 'liberal.' But this is impossible.

Roman Catholicism has never tolerated 'liberalism' for a variety of reasons, a major one of which is that theological liberalism was a distinctly Reform Protestant development and as such was tainted for Catholics from the start. Roman Catholics invariably fall within the broad category of conservative, but of two very different sorts across a breadth of spectrum.

One pole is the traditionalist sort; the other the radical, as in rudimentary. The traditionalist has determined that a specific historical period—such as the High Middle Ages, say, or the early 19th Century—is normative for the church.

As a result this 'dated' criteria of judgment is held up as a permanent, unchangeable and unassailable accomplishment. A current example would be the Gregory the XVII movement which has sprung up in extreme opposition to Vatican II and what lead up to it.

Gregory XVI was the pope prior to Pius IX (1846-78); basically a medieval monk sort of figure. Ultra-traditionalists are harkening back to that era as the solution to why the church went wrong with Vatican II and as a strong antidote to the present era.

If we look at these two papal figures for a moment, it can go a long way forward in understanding the present predicament of modern Catholicism at the start of the 21st Century. These two popes formed an ultra-traditionalist sensibility which still plagues the church in its entirely unrealistic attitude toward contemporary society.

3. TWO MORE POPES

Gregory XVI (1831-46) and Pius IX (1846-78) were two dissimilar types of pope who reigned over distinctly different eras. And yet there was a definite sense of continuity between their two administrations.

Gregory, a Venetian, was born near the middle of the 18th Century. At age eighteen he entered a strict Benedictine monastery, the Camaldolese Order. He rose up in his order, becoming in turn a professor of science and philosophy, an abbot, and head of the Camaldolese Order in 1823. By 1826 he was a cardinal at age sixty-one.

As Cardinal, he was made Prefect of Propaganda and gave a new impulse to missionary enterprise during a period when Christian missionary activity (and Roman Catholic missions in particular) were undergoing a massive infusion of energy and human resources. Gregory had served closely the two preceding popes during the 1820s. Leo XII (1823-29) and Pius VIII (1829-31) were characterized by a 'less political' and 'more religious' orientation. Gregory continued along this line.

As pope himself he was an austere, learned monk who was hostile toward modern worldly trends and this would be said to typify his papal reign. But if Gregory was severe toward the world, Pius IX, who immediately followed him and became the longest serving pope of all time, was extreme.

Pius served an unprecedented thirty-two years between 1846 and 1878 and set the severe tone of Roman Catholicism for the next hundred years. His Syllabus of Errors (declared in 1864) and the definition of papal infallibility (at the time of the First Vatican Council in 1870) fundamentally set the church over and against the world in no uncertain terms for nearly a hundred years.

It would take the momentum of the Second Vatican Council (1962-65) to rectify the balance and serve as a corrective to Pius' program of antipathy toward anything of value which the world may have to say to the church.

In brief summary Pius' reign, in the words of J.N.D. Kelly's dictionary of the popes, sealed off the church from the world in a tight insularity which was a disaster politically and "left the church ill equipped to respond to the challenges but also left it profoundly changed and strengthened in its inner life." It was during this pope's era that the Diocese of Victoria became more or less fully established.

GREGORY XVI

Pope Gregory was the Bishop of Rome during the period of the uprising of the Papal States in Italy and this he put down by using Austrian troops. On May 31, 1831, nonetheless, the Great Powers intervened and the pope had to concede changes but he refused to grant elected assemblies or a council of state composed of laymen. The continued use of hired troops drained his treasury.

He was equally uncompromising in the realm of ideas denouncing the notions of freedom of conscience and of the principle of the separation of church and state; also condemning Catholic liberalism in 1834. His reign was a continuous struggle in the service of conservative ideals with a distinct horror of the revolutions occurring worldwide.

It was Gregory who insisted that the children of mixed religious marriages be brought up Catholic. This was in the face of steep Prussian resistance to the idea. The appointment of all bishops became centralized in Rome in his reign.

The 19th Century revival of missions dates from his era and in reorganizing them he brought them firmly under papal control. Through him some seventy diocese and vicariate apostolic were established including Vancouver Island: almost two hundred missionary bishops were appointed including Modeste Demers, the first Catholic bishop of Vancouver Island.

In 1839 Pope Gregory condemned slavery and the slave trade as unworthy of Christians and in 1845 encouraged a native clergy and hierarchy in mission territories. His concern extended also to Canada and the U.S.A.; he created four diocese in Canada between 1834-43 as well as reorganizing the See of Québec, Demers' home diocese. He established ten dioceses in the United States including Oregon of which Vancouver Island was suffragan for its first fifty-seven years until 1903. In fact it eventually took the intervention of the Prime Minister of the day, Wilfrid Laurier, to bring Victoria under Canadian control.[103]

About Pope Gregory XVI, J.N.D. Kelly summarizes: "Brought up as a monk, good-hearted but obstinate and narrow, with little comprehension of the contemporary world, he left his successor a grievous legacy both in the church and in the papal states."

PIUS IX

Pius IX, the longest serving pope, was cured of epilepsy as a youth. He served with a papal mission to Chile parts of three years (1823-25). He was originally thought to be a liberal due to his penchant for administrative reform and was elected as a moderate progressive against another reactionary candidate.

Although somewhat sympathetic to Italian nationalism and the movement for independence of the papal states he stopped short of establishing a constitutional state and in 1848 was forced to flee in disguise from Rome.

When he was able to return by the aid of French troops in 1850 he entirely discarded his liberal stance, becoming a 'prisoner of the Vatican' after 1870 when the outbreak of the Franco-Prussian war necessitated the withdrawal of his French Garrison. At that point the papal states were reduced in the face of the establishment of an Italian Kingdom.

J.N.D. Kelly summarizes: "Politically, Pius' pontificate, the longest in history, might seemed to have been a disaster but viewed ecclesiastically it was full of positive achievements."

This was the period when the church under his leadership felt the need to turn in upon itself to a degree never before known and as such set up a parallel 'perfect society' as model for itself, from which it only began to emerge after a hundred years with the reforms of Vatican II.

Pius established over two hundred new dioceses and vicariates notably in North America. A feature of the reign was an increasing centralization of authority, facilitated by modern means of transport but encouraged by the bishops' loss of political power within the church and their consequent need to work closely with the pope. He carried out an unprecedented number of canonizations and beatification and on June 16, 1875 consecrated the Catholic World to the Sacred Heart of Jesus.

According to Kelly:

"Three events stand out as particularly significant. The first was his definition of the Immaculate Conception of the Blessed Virgin Mary, that is, her freedom from Original Sin, on December 8, 1854. Made without mention of episcopal approbation, this gave a powerful stimulus to Marian Devotion. Secondly... he published the 'Syllabus of Errors', which denounced 'the 64 principal errors of our times' including the view that the pope 'can or should reconcile himself to, or agree with progress, liberalism and modern civilization.' This dealt a fatal blow to liberal Catholicism... thirdly, he summoned the First Vatican (20th General) Council (1869-70)."

"The Council declared the definition of the popes in faith and morals to be infallible in their own right, not as a result of the consent of the church, thereby completing the doctoral development of centuries and removing all conciliarist interpretations of the role of the papacy. This owed much to Pius' personal intervention..."

Pius was the first pope to identify himself wholeheartedly with ultramontanism, that is, the tendency to centralize authority in church government and doctrine in the Holy See. Its triumph led to an outbreak of anticlericalism in Europe generally, to the point that after his death a Roman anticlerical mob tried to fling his casket into the Tiber river.

This unbalanced political state for the church is the deep background which was only fully rectified by the Second Vatican Council (1962-65).

J.N.D. Kelly writes of Pius:

"When he died he had effectively created the modern papacy, stripped (as he never ceased to deplore) of its temporal dominion, but armed with vastly enhanced spiritual authority in compensation. His own mind being closed to modern political trends, he left the church ill-equipped to respond to their challenges, but he also left it profoundly changed and strengthened in its inner life. Whether at the level of the clergy or of the great body of the faithful, his reign witnessed a vigourous spiritual regeneration."

4. A RUDIMENTARY PERSPECTIVE

While it seems clear what the conservative traditionalist Catholic is about, the radical, on the other hand, such as Newman himself, looks back to the roots of the religion for a persistent perspective of evaluation. The gospels and the Early Church, plus possibly the Patristic Period (300-600 AD), are the primary measure.

Into this camp falls Remi De Roo and most of the significant theologians who shaped Vatican II. The Second Vatican Council was said to be a vindication of Newman's work and as such was an attempt to rescue the church from the 19th Century and the ongoing paralysing and destructive reaction to the Protestant Reformation.

As De Roo states, in the middle of the 20th Century, more than a hundred years after Newman's publication of his *Essay on the Development of Doctrine,* the Catholic Church was only finally getting around to accepting the idea of a developmental perspective.

After his retirement in 1999 De Roo addressed the Catholic Theological Society of America on the development of doctrine as it emerges from the lived experience of the people.

Pope Pius XII, whom De Roo typified as a genius, made the first major move in the 1940s when he encouraged scripture scholars to be open to modern critical thinking in their work.

Again this was a significant departure because it signalled a new openness to ecumenism. Historical-critical thinking in scripture studies was originally a Reform Protestant development. But it was the Second Vatican Council under Popes John XXIII and Paul VI that fully introduced the developmental principle into the everyday life of the church.

Without the developmental principle, theological thinking was very static and tended to occupy a mindset that turned against progress of any sort; finding it threatening to already established 'orthodox' concepts of spiritual and social reality.

Newman thought his way into the Catholic Church by use of comparative analogies. He reasoned there must be some authentic continuity between the early Christian Church and its authentic successor. So he tried to successfully identify it from amongst the dozen or so post-Reformation claimants among the leading Christian churches.

Ultimately his reluctant conclusion was that, although much changed through legitimate transformation as well as decadent accretions, in the Western World the Roman Catholic Church was the true successor to the title of the original church.

It proved a very difficult decision for him personally, as well as professionally because he was far from entirely welcome in the anti-intellectual atmosphere of the English Catholic Church of the time. It also ran entirely against the Anglo-Catholic sensibility he had carefully cultivated for thirty years but it was a spiritual conclusion he believed he could not evade.

Only after the progressive Pope Leo XIII succeeded the arch-reactionary Pius IX in 1878 was Newman acknowledged with the red hat of the cardinal. This sent an important message to the Catholic world, and the western world generally, that progressive thinking was now being willingly suffered at the highest level.

Change comes very slowly within the Catholic Church and not without protracted controversy. De Roo would become a symbolic figure of this sort of struggle within the church, but at the time of his doctoral work in 1950 the risk-taking was more intellectual and personal; not yet political.

The irony that he was on the verge of becoming a Marian expert, a domain which is normally the intellectual and theological preserve of traditionalist if not reactionary thinkers, cannot pass without comment.

"I took a doctorate in Mariology because in the 1950s the Assumption (of the Blessed Virgin Mary) was a big issue (due to its then recent promulgation as an official doctrine by the pope). Plus the fact that I had practically no schooling in Mariology while at our seminary.

"I made a judgment which in retrospect was a disastrous mistake, academically speaking, because you normally do your doctorate in your strongest suit, not the one you know least about. But with Geenen's encouragement and very close surveillance I managed to plough my way through in a year."

He states at another point that after his final oral exam he was so tense he had to walk all day to settle himself down. The work itself was not ground-breaking in any sense, but typical of the static theology of the day.

"The thesis was on the relationship between Queenship and The Assumption. Was Mary assumed into Heaven because she was

Queen of the Universe or is she Queen of the Universe because she is assumed? Historically that meant reviewing the history of Mariology and Marian devotion, in both the eastern and the western church all the way back to the origins.

"The thesis itself is inconclusive but that's what doctoral thesis are all about. You research a certain very fine point in a certain field and you research it definitively so no one else has to do it over again. You leave it saying it's inconclusive, not conclusive from the evidence."

While the topic was 'hot', his methodology could not be controversial in those days. It was strictly apologetics, the part of theology that tries to show the reasonableness of Christian faith.

"The Dogma of the Assumption was proclaimed by Pius XII in 1950. So I was writing on a hot topic. Remember this was pre-Vatican II. We had been brought up in a fairly conservative theology that raised no questions. Theology then was largely biased toward apologetic.

"We would start from canon law, or the practice of the church and rationalize that according to Thomas Aquinas, to prove we indeed had the right doctrine and were in the right church and all that. We then used Scripture itself moreless as proof texts. The idea of calling into question the Catholic teaching on an issue was simply unheard of."

It was the time of the tried-and-true method in Catholic theology, and in the daily practice of the church. His expertise on the role of Mary in the salvation of the world he would use again late in his episcopacy to attempt to allay ultra-traditionalist and anti-Vatican II devotional practices that were welling up.[104]

But at the time it was a lot of hard study that had no intention of breaking new ground, just plenty of research proving some inconclusive point. It did provide him with a Doctorate in Sacred Theology, a solid accomplishment, and, of course, it trained his mind for future responsibilities.

One world-famous dynamic thinker who would have an interesting reaction to the promulgation of The Assumption in 1950 by Pope Pius XII was Carl Jung, the psychologist and psychoanalyst. He stated jubilantly at the time that there was a deeper psychological significance to this proclamation.[105]

Jung believed that the Marian dogma served to rectify an unstable imbalance in Catholic dogma, particularly represented by the doctrine of the Trinity, which in his view as a psychologist was much too heavily weighted against the feminine in the direction of the overly-rational masculine principle.

For Jung, who studied Medieval alchemy and early church history for his own scholarly purposes, the Trinity, as the central Christian teaching, is an unstable concept because the number three is incomplete in the natural order of things. Three is an incomplete number which always naturally tends toward completion in four.

The greater stability and more natural completeness of four is revealed in its symbolic propensities. Four is symbolic of totality, as represented by the earth's four elements, the four seasons and the points of the compass etc. In its equation with the square, the cube, and the cross, it is the number associated with tangible achievement.

In other words, through the promulgation of this 'infallible' dogma of The Assumption of the Blessed Virgin Mary into Heaven, the Christian Trinity achieved a more feminine balance through greater completion, in the quaternity. The Assumption for Jung represented a move in this more stable and balanced direction in Catholic teaching and he welcomed it as such.

Though not a Catholic, Jung had deep respect for the Catholic Church as a means of achieving the symbolic life, which in his view is necessary for the wholeness and complete self-realization of the individual and society as a whole. Jung called this process 'individuation', and also suggested the importance to the continued development of Catholicism the integration of its shadow side in this way. De Roo's candour and objectivity about the dual nature of the church went a long way to furthering this end.

Of course there is nothing of this in any of De Roo's doctoral work. But if Jung was expecting a great leap forward by the church as a result of this rectifying development, Vatican II would have proved him correct in his analysis and De Roo demonstrably lived out the new paradigm, which eventually got him into a certain amount of trouble within the church.

After his two years of study, the twenty-eight year old Remi was called back to St. Boniface by the appointment of a new archbishop. He missed out on some-hoped-for travel and pursuit of other interests while in Europe as a result of returning early to Manitoba.

"I was recalled to Saint Boniface at the end of my second year. We got a new archbishop when Baudoux replaced Cabana. The parish of Holy Cross was desperately in need of an assistant who could speak English. The pastor prevailed to get someone, so I was an assistant for one year while I polished my doctoral thesis so it could be published." This juxtaposition of pastoral duties with ongoing scholarly work became De Roo's life pattern.

5. JACK OF ALL TRADES

After completing his doctoral program the young priest was called home to help out at Holy Cross, the largest English-speaking parish in the French diocese and the parish he would stay directly connected with until he left the region.

The majority of seminary colleagues were fluently bilingual but their first language and cultural preference would have been Francophone. Able clergy who were fully fluent in English would have been harder to come by.

It was agreed he would prepare his doctoral thesis for publication during the first year back and serve as an assistant to Monsignor Charles Empson, running the eleven-hundred-family parish.

He was soon given other lesser assignments, "other sideline hobbies," he called them, but he maintained his weekend presence at Holy Cross throughout the decade of the 1950s. In 1960 he was appointed pastor there for his final two years prior to Victoria.

During the activity year of 1952-53 he was full time doing parish work but during 1953 he was appointed Director of Catholic Action where he "particularly liked working with young lay people in Catholic Action, including the members of the Young Christian Workers movement."

One young leader from that time was Pearl Gervais who later took on key leadership responsibilities for him when he was bishop in Victoria. In 1953 he was twenty-nine years old with an open approach and a youthful dynamism which inspired lay people in their early twenties.

Gervais describes her initial experience this way: "He introduced himself as the new Catholic Action chaplain and asked us what we expected of him, how he could enhance our calling as lay people working in the world. Right away his trust in lay people was there. We didn't feel we had to be old to be accepted. It was a very powerful message."

Somewhere De Roo had gained the ability to ask engaging questions as a leadership figure. He was soon seconded to other diocesan responsibilities. The new archbishop, Maurice Baudoux, appointed him as secretary to his own office and then in 1954 as vice chancellor, a position he filled for three years in addition to his Catholic Action chaplaincy role.

Pearl Gervais had come to Winnipeg as an enthusiastic youngster from Bellegarde, Saskatchewan near the Manitoba border, to become a teacher at the Manitoba Normal School.

Part of the purpose of the Young Christian Workers and Young Christian Students was to continue the Catholic formation when young people departed the safeguard of hearth and home and entered the workplace and 'the world', as it was designated in Catholic parlance.

Gervais continues: "In the spring of '53, a YCS worker asked me if I would take on some responsibilities at the archdiocesan level while I was at Normal School. Remi became chaplain for all Catholic Action groups at that time."

YCS and YCW were two wings of a movement of Catholic Action that sprang up at the initiative of Pope Pius XI in the early 1920s. The pope wanted to take steps to counter the general passivity of the Catholic laity in the face of the predominant structure of the church. He also wanted to capitalize on the powerful potential of the masses in the development of the church.

Under the teaching of Catholic Action, the people were mandated to participate more fully in specific functions of the hierarchy. They were invited to share in the work of the hierarchy. This was a limited anticipation of the full mandating that would come with the Second Vatican Council (1962-65), but the young Father De Roo caught the drift of the movement, applying a more radical degree of openness than most of these young people had been raised to expect from priests.

Pearl Gervais: "A lot of spiritual work was done in a co-operative collaborative way in CA groups. There was time for fun and prayer especially when we organized study days and retreats."

"We were trained to use this Catholic Action method developed by Cardinal Cardjin—'See, Judge, Act' which means: See what you can observe; Judge to decide what needs to be done from what you observe; then act together for clear ends."

It was a methodology that would lead to political action for a great many of its practitioners in time, but Pearl Gervais' memories of De Roo from that time were more specifically pastoral.

"One of my clearest memories of Remi was during the summer we all went to Windsor and Montréal to meet with CA groups in those places. It happened at a lake. He would go out alone on the lake in the evening to say his daily breviary prayers which priests were required to do.

"When he came back, he said this one time: 'It's a very good place to pray.' That's the dominant image I had of him very early; as a man of prayer. He loves the music of the psalms, loves to listen to music, loves the contemplative place."

With cosmologist Brian Swimme and event organizer Pearl Gervais at St. Andrew's High School, Victoria in 1997. (Joan Brown)

The young Father De Roo (Napoleon Photo Studio, Winnipeg)

Chapter Nine: Ordinary Time

1. AN EXPERIMENTER

At this point Father De Roo began an innovative experiment which would indicate his style. One of the needs Pastor Charles Empson required at Holy Cross was a response to the increased demand for objective information about (and instruction in) the Catholic faith. Remi De Roo was put in charge of this. He organized it in a manner which accentuated an imaginative outreach to the general population.

He opened a store-front office near the St. Boniface General Hospital. While there was not enough traffic to warrant its long term continuation, the significance was its direction: he designed the program to engage non-Catholic interest. This early effort in wider dialogue included "Mennonites, Bible-carrying Protestants and other stripes," he said.[106]

His other area of special concentration was the empowerment of the laity, which came with the hat he wore as Director of Catholic Action. Another essential aspect of CA was the Christian Family Movement.

CFM lasted approximately twenty-five years between 1949 and 1974 and was described in a recent history with these words: "The effect was exhilarating. Young professional couples, whose lives had been dominated by an ethos that extolled material culture, found through CFM a tool with which to transcend and transform not just the structures of family life but their culture."[107]

"CFM was a major force in raising the consciousness of its women members about their role in society," wrote Robert McClory in his review of Jeffrey Burns's *Disturbing the Peace.*

As to its demise, McClory gives this explanation: "The malaise that affected Catholics, particularly liberal Catholics in the early 1970s, was widespread. CFM did not decline in a vacuum. The church in the United States was in decline everywhere. The decline was severely exacerbated by Pope Paul VI's encyclical *Humanae Vitae*, banning all forms of contraception.

"The encyclical shattered the hopes of many that the Catholic Church could change, writes Burns who stoutly denies that the Crawley's (founders of CFM) well known personal dissent from the encyclical was itself a cause of CFM decline."

In his role as chaplain to members of the Canadian branch of CFM, De Roo would have been well exposed to the same critique of the church's sexual teaching. He was rubbing shoulders with lay leaders in the Canadian Catholic Church. These included many who would go on to occupy high political office including Claude Ryan, Québec provincial Liberal leader and Marion Dewar, future mayor of Ottawa and a federal New Democrat Member of Parliament, who both got their grounding in Catholic Action. CFM proved a preparatory school for many liberal and radical Catholic politician/social leaders in Canada.[108]

Also typical of his associates in those times but on the Christian apolitical if not anarchic side were Tony Walsh, founder of Benedict Labré House in Montréal, who was a direct influence on the Vanier family and future prime minister John Turner; Catherine Doherty, founder of Madonna House in Combermere, Ontario, an international lay movement with a social aspect; and Romeo Maione of Ottawa, who went on to found the federal government's Canadian International Development Agency (CIDA).

Maione had been a youth leader with Young Christian Workers in Montréal with Father (later Bishop) William Power. He was also the first president of The Canadian Catholic Organization for Development and Peace in 1968. CCODP was the Canadian church's response to Pope Paul VI's social encyclical on Third World development in 1967, known as *Populorum Progressio*.

In these circles it was an intense period for energetic young devotees who saw an opening for new ideas and fresh approaches within the church. Like any movement they made a special effort to keep in touch with each other, forming a vital network in terms of the changes ahead with Vatican II.

De Roo remembers: "In Montréal at the Young Christian Workers conference we met Monsignor (later Cardinal) Cardjin, head of the Catholic Action worldwide.

"At the Vatican Council, I saw him again and he shared with me his frustration in trying to get certain basic insights of the lay apostolate into the documents of The Vatican Council. So some of the groundwork was being laid before Vatican II."

Even as a student De Roo had picked up on this new emerging openness. He took note of Pope Pius XII's new realism regarding the importance of the ordinary lay person in the church. He was quick to take encouragement from the signs when they were given in the early 1940s. He could sense a significant shift in the wind:

"Pius XII made a statement in February 1946, speaking to the college of Cardinals. He said the laity are in the forefront of the church. The pope stressed repeatedly that the laity not only belong to the church but they are the church.

"He repeated this. I expect it went over the heads of most cardinals. Pius XII was a man of genius. Another example was his 1943 encyclical permitting critical studies of Scripture."

This acceptance of a historico-critical approach to Scripture bore much fruit at Vatican II because after 1943 Catholic theologians and scholars were more free to think in a critical new manner in their work and this lead to many of the reforms. Up until this time much of the new theological thinking by Catholic theologians was suspect due to the strange atmosphere created by the Modernism crisis of 1907.

To gain a general sense of 'the modernist crisis', it might be sufficient to cite a March 1990 article *The Crisis of Modernism* by Roger Haight in the monthly Canadian Jesuit magazine *Compass*.

Haight makes the following generally accepted assertions about Modernism and the odd spell it cast on the universal church: "In condemning Modernism in 1907, the Vatican created the heresy it was denouncing... Catholics who were fearful that new ways of thinking would undermine faith itself looked beyond the Alps for a papal pillar of security... It is difficult to find anything in the thought of the leading modernists that is seriously objectionable or that is not held, perhaps in modified form, today... The papal document was politically brilliant, deadly effective, intellectually dishonest, and totally comprehensible in the historical situation... ('modernist' leader) Alfred Loisy proposed a radically historical view of the Catholic Church. The problem was that the church did not conceive itself as a product of historical development."[109]

As a result of this modernist crisis, most of the condemned theologians of the first half of the 20th Century were only able to work in integral freedom after the time of Vatican II. The documents of the Council reflect their pent-up brilliance and overdue acknowledgement. The first sign of the new openness were from 'the genius' Pius XII in the 1940s.

An important new openness to some significant level of change had been in the mind of the pope early in the 1940s and for the young student De Roo, it represented a direction to which he could relate.

Catholic Action, the initiative of the previous pope, was fully endorsed by Pius XII. The very idea of another general ecumenical council for the whole church had also been in the minds of both these popes. Like John XXIII after them, they recognized the need to move the church more realistically into the modern world.

The First Vatican Council (1869-70) had been the gainful attempt by the pope of the day, Pius IX (1846-1878), to keep the church in the medieval mould with his office as the infallible arbiter of severe standards. In a revolutionary social period he lead a rigid reactionary assault against what 'the world', as such, had to say to the church.

While this led to internal renewal (in terms of spiritual strengthening) as such periods invariably do for religious institutions, politically it was a disaster. By the middle of the 20th Century the Roman Catholic Church was in danger of becoming functionally anachronistic.

The popes knew this themselves but the moment to decisively act only came with John XXIII. The church would have to rely upon a fresh sort of visionary leadership at the clerical level to help make it a reality. De Roo was formed in this transitional time. John XXIII's special recognition of De Roo underlined the likelihood of his playing a special role.

Nothing much would shift until the 1960s with the advent of the Second Vatican Council but during the twenty years leading up to that time, groundwork was being laid. Critical ideas were being put forward, and Remi De Roo's involvement in Catholic Action put him at the cutting edge.

The significance of Catholic Action was its outward orientation. The focus was on the spiritual role ordinary working Catholics played in their day-to-day life in the world. CA was not an internal church program. It was radically different. It was about the quality of their active engagement with the world in the process of bringing about social and personal transformation.

The direction of the social transformation was spelled out in Catholic Social Teaching beginning from 1891. Catholic Social Teaching would preoccupy Remi De Roo's episcopacy. He would become known as its strongest and most penetrating advocate among the Canadian bishops of his day.

2. CATHOLIC SOCIAL TEACHING

Historically, Catholic Social Teaching could come about only after the departure of Pius IX in 1878. Pius had resolutely condemned all social progress in his Syllabus of Errors of 1864. The church was not the product of a historical process in his view, but rather always stood over and above the mundane, judging it by higher standards; with the papacy serving as the final arbiter of values.

His definition of Papal Infallibility in 1869-70 was a direct step toward the deification of the authority of the pope within the church. The Syllabus consisted of sixty-four specific anathemas condemning socialism, liberalism, progress and every other noteworthy social development of the previous hundred years. It was medievalism extended until the last quarter of the 19th Century.

The Syllabus is perhaps best typified by its final anathema that the pope "cannot and should not be reconciled and come to terms with progress, liberalism and civilization." There are still many Catholics today who are instinctively suspicious of any social progress. This would be the residue of Pio Nono's work.

In this view the church is primarily a transcendent reality, well above all civil developments. This declaration together with the definitive statement of papal infallibility from the First Vatican Council in 1869 provided a complete encapsulation of the otherworldly attitude persistent in Catholicism since the feudalism of the High Middle Ages.

By necessity, the Catholic Church's rejection of progress, revolutionary change and social development in general could obviously go no further in this extreme direction. Since the Vatican had been deprived of all temporal power with the loss of the Papal

States in 1869, and the pope was literally a prisoner in the Vatican, some sort of shift in bearing was all but inevitable.

Since Pius IX proved the longest serving pope of all time—thirty-two years from 1846 to 1878—it was not a swift passage, but the succeeding pope, Leo XIII also served for a lengthy term—twenty-five years—and he wished to directly engage the modern world in an entirely different manner.

He did so in 1891 with the first of what became known as the social encyclicals. Basically Leo simply recognized the legitimacy of electoral democracy and the workers' rights to organize, achieve just wages and humane working conditions. He did this on the basis of the church's historic recognition of the common good.

Leo put the moral weight of the papacy behind the social struggle. Thanks to the toil of the two previous popes, this weight was considerable, both within the church and its impact on the world. The effect within the church would be a continuous development until the late 1980s.

For many, Leo's response to the problems of the Industrial Revolution all seemed a bit late, but for the church it was a huge step forward. It would be another forty years before another pope would add substantially to this social teaching, prompted by the worldwide Depression.

In 1931 Pius XI extended Leo's analysis and proscriptions in the face of the collapse of international capitalism and the incipient arms race. His major social encyclical approved a middle way between monopoly capitalism and atheistic communism, as they were portrayed, endorsing a sort of co-operative middle path as the most ethical economy.

Certainly the rise of co-operativism in Canada was given a huge boost by this new emphasis in church teaching. This was especially true in the Canadian hinterlands where statistics revealed an insurgent increase in the numbers of co-ops, credit unions and their membership lists in the decades following the papal encyclical. Remi De Roo's home region in rural Manitoba, for example, felt this impact directly and beneficially in the form of marketing boards, wheat pools, et cetera.

Later Catholic social teaching would get much more positive about socialism itself with the advent of Vatican II and the teachings of later popes. Certainly with John XXIII, Paul VI and John Paul II, democratic socialism would become fully acceptable but when De Roo was a young priest in the 1950s this was the transitional phase when church social teaching was largely critical and condemnatory of the two emerging world systems.

During the 1950s the English-speaking Canadian Catholic Church conducted leadership education in this field, something the French Canadian Church had been doing for thirty years at that point, after a fifty-year example of the Catholic Church in France. To this day the Catholic Church in Québec has continued to be more *avant garde* in the social field. De Roo always followed their developments with special care.[110]

ꕥ

On November 16-18, 1958 the sixth annual social life conference on the role of training leaders was held in Winnipeg. Remi De Roo is listed as a participant.[111]

Under the sponsorship of the conference of bishops in Ottawa, these events featured leaders, personalities, celebrities and well-known speakers in a successful effort to draw social leadership candidates from across the country.

In 1958 the spirit was high after the selection of the new charismatic Pope John XXIII, elected less than three weeks before on October 29. Claude Jodoin, president of the Canadian Labour Congress was the keynote speaker. Montréal Canadien's hockey broadcaster Danny Gallivan and federal cabinet minister Davey Fulton were among the better-known stars.

The organizers were trying to make the subject better known within the church; a popular phrase of the time was that 'Catholic Social Teaching was the church's best kept secret'.

Thirty members of the hierarchy attended including leaders of the socially progressive movements in the church. These included Bishop John R. MacDonald of Antigonish and the previously mentioned Father William Power of Montréal who headed the Young Christian Workers nationally. MacDonald's diocese was home of the world-famous Antigonish Movement and Power would eventually succeed him.

At this particular conference, the Prairies were represented by speakers John Francis Leddy and Grant Maxwell, prominent lay leaders in Saskatoon and Abbott Jerome Weber of the Benedictine monastery in Muenster, Saskatchewan, home of the socially progressive weekly newspaper *The Prairie Messenger.*

In Weber's talk he alludes to comparative statistics, how the number of chartered credit unions in Canada nearly doubled during the decade between 1945 and 1954 from 2,219 to 3,920 with individual membership nearly tripling from 590,794 to 1,560,715 officially. He also listed parallel increases in co-operative figures.

The conference drew two hundred clergy and seventy-five nuns (who had not yet started to focus on social issues) plus three hundred lay people nationwide. There were particularly large delegations from the Prairies including De Roo, who, interestingly, was not on the program, indicating that events like this were still largely formative for him. This particular conference would have been a turning point, given the program and disposition of the new pope and the role he would give De Roo in four years time.

The style of the event was pure pre-Vatican II. There was an exchange of cables between Winnipeg and the Holy See in Rome with the pristine pope. In the formal language of such communications of the time, Cardinal McGuigan of Toronto wires:
"Sixth national English-speaking Catholic social life conference convened at Winnipeg sends sentiments of profound loyalty to your holiness and humbly begs apostolic blessing."

The Vatican Secretary of State wired back: "Sovereign Pontiff warmly appreciating devoted message prayerfully invokes illuminating guidance on Holy Spirit deliberations..."

3. WORKING WITH THREE GIANTS

Such events indeed were close to the new pope's heart, as his own social encyclicals would make very apparent in the next few years.[112]

During this exact period the changes that would typify the Catholic Church for the next two decades were honestly being born. It was in the air and De Roo was stirred by this new vigour.

He was working out a non-traditional style for himself as a cleric; one that featured higher leadership capacity. He did not aspire to fill the traditional role as a pastor in a solitary parish. Rather, his superiors were training him to use his gifts to provide leadership for the new movements that were emerging in the post-war expansion period.

These movements that sparked the imaginations of progressive young Catholic clergy, nuns and lay people were seven in number: the liturgical movement[113], the biblical movement, the social action movement, the Catholic Action or lay apostolate movement, the ecumenical movement, the missionary movement, and the movement for theological renewal.

In the early 1950s some of these were officially sanctioned and some were canonically suspect; all were signs of new life.[114]

Remi De Roo was knowledgeable about, committed to, or directly involved with each of these. They were all aimed in the direction of church reform, progressive theology or greater openness to the world beyond the strict confines of the Catholic Church. At the time he would have been going against the grain. He was risk taking although he had the support of some specific superiors.

All of these movements would be integrated into and given official sanction by the documents of Vatican II but in this period he was part of a riskier, ground-breaking and developmental push without which the final vindication at the Council could not have occurred; and was not in any sense assured.

This period of leadership required the courage and vision of youth and an injection of daring. By comparison, the work of implementing the reforms of the Council afterward only followed logically and probably more easily than the earlier innovative efforts. In other words he had already been doing what seemed so new and fresh after the Council. As he said reflecting back on the Council: "Everything about Vatican II that seems new has deep if hidden, roots in our history and tradition. And all of it can be celebrated as the work of the Spirit."

"Vatican II didn't just pop out of the blue. We mentioned a number of charismatic leaders, starting with John XXIII. However, we must also acknowledge how many other streams of influence ran into the Council. Some people complain that it was too sharp a break with the past. Actually everything about it has deep if hidden roots in our history and tradition."[115]

His work and leadership abilities were not going unnoticed. It was an exhilarating time and he was given support and opportunity from his three bosses in Manitoba, three archbishops all centred in Winnipeg. He refers to this period as his time of "working with three giants."

From 1954 to 1956 he had been serving as secretary to Archbishop Maurice Baudoux and as vice-chancellor of the archdiocese. And the next years gave him additional "exciting responsibilities," which he explains:

"In 1957 the Royal Commission on Education was a significant event in Manitoba. We had been assured by the premier of the day that if the majority of the commission favoured the restoration of the rights of Catholic schools, that would be done. So the Roman Catholic bishops got together and at that meeting I was named secretary of the Catholic Conference of Manitoba."

He ironically claimed this happened because he happened to be the only priest brought along by a bishop for that meeting. A further irony was that later he would be said to not favour Catholic education while in Victoria, but by then the whole context of the church had shifted.

"That opened up one of the most exciting chápters of my life. Here I was working closely with three giants: Archbishop Hermaniuk, the Ukrainian Eparch (who died in the middle 1990s); Archbishop Philip Pocock, who later went on to Toronto; and Archbishop Baudoux. Three archbishops who lived within a stones throw of each other, but who never threw stones. Wonderful men, all three. Working with them broadened my mind."

His relationship with his own archbishop was particularly significant to his development. "Baudoux was the most Christian bishop I'd ever known. To a great extent he was self-educated. Born in Belgium he came to Prud'homme, Saskatchewan with missions at Vonda and St. Denis. At the time he worked with Bishop Pocock of Saskatoon. First Baudoux became bishop of St. Paul, Alberta; then he was named Archbishop of St. Boniface.

"Self-educated with a vast intelligence, particularly interested in history, literature, canon law. Working with him as a secretary those years was the equivalent of a university experience. He had a lot of trust in me and we remained very close friends down through the years."

He was directly being prepared for his own thirty-some years as a bishop during this seasoning with Baudoux but he bristles at the suggestion of favouritism as a 'protégé'.

"I guess you could use that expression. But I wouldn't want it to imply special favours. If anything he was a very demanding man. He worked like a locomotive and smoked non-stop until his doctor forced him to quit.

"I remember working in his office with books spread all over the floor. He wrote all his stuff in heavy handwriting. He used pencils on heavy paper. We sometimes worked until two o'clock in the morning. He wrote in French. I'd have to translate it into English and type it, then make copies on the old Gestetner, the oldest version; and then get all that into the mail.

"I worked under pressure but learned a lot. Archbishop Baudoux had a wonderful sense of humour. Some lived in fear of him because he was a formidable man—six feet four inches and quite outspoken. That scared off some people."

It was during these years that De Roo gained the reputation as someone who slept in his office overnight, working almost around the clock. If he was Baudoux's protégé, as the term was bandied about, it never did quite come to successful completion, that he actually take over as archbishop of his home diocese of Saint Boniface.

4. TEARDROP AMETHYST

Secretly the thirty-four-year-old priest yearned to serve as a foreign missioner. When John XXIII as the new pope in 1958, called for 'papal volunteers' to go where priests were needed most in the Third World, De Roo asked to be considered.

"I was Baudoux's secretary then. He called a meeting of all clergy to talk about volunteering for priestly work in Latin America. I left on the corner of his desk an envelope. In it I volunteered to go as a missionary. He didn't accept it. Four other young priests went.

"When I became a bishop these missionary priests sent a beautiful teardrop amethyst stone which I had placed on my mitre to remind me that I'm meant also to be a missionary." The ring given to him by Pope John in 1962 was also an amethyst.

For the Greeks the name amethyst meant 'not drunken' as they thought the amethyst mysteriously prevented intoxification[116]. *This provides an interesting unconscious comment on Remi De Roo's supremely sober personality.*

His personae in its natural reserve and aloofness presented its own sort of formidability as a bishop figure in particular to those not initiated to his personality traits. This was all in spite of his own efforts at informality in the role.

❧❧❧

As he stated, the missionary call was worked out as he went along.

"In the mysterious design of providence I was to go to Latin America on three occasions for various reasons. I wrote a short book on my Latin American experiences in 1980."[117]

Nineteen eighty was the year of the assassination of Archbishop Oscar Romero by Salvadoran para-military forces. In the 1950s Catholic archbishops in Third World countries were not being executed by right-wing governments for their social justice stands. The change that brought all this about started precisely in 1958 with the October 28 election of Angelo Roncalli as Pope John XXIII following the death of Pius XII on October 9.

John proved a surprise choice. He was definitely seen as an interim transitional figure but he would surprise the world by effectively turning the Catholic Church on its ear. By the time of his death (after five short years), the very self-understanding of what it means to be a Roman Catholic had undergone nothing short of a radical transmutation. And it was all in the direction De Roo had been heading.

The Second Vatican Council, the event by which all this was accomplished, caught everyone by complete surprise. This was one of the signs, Bishop De Roo would claim, which proved that the event was inspired by the Holy Spirit.

Afterwards, patterns were identified which indicated its necessity and probability, but at the time it was entirely unexpected. And when it was called nothing much was foreseen for it. A rubber stamping at best of some Curial controlled modifications; just a housekeeping agenda.

The Vatican would ratify the old ways, some minor insignificant tinkering would be accomplished, and that would be that. The surprise element is best understood by examining the personality of Pope John who would prove the most popular pope in modern history.

His attitude and program was a far and distant cry from that of Pius IX from a hundred years before. As Richard McBrien wrote in *Catholicism,* the first post-Vatican II general encyclopedia: "The distance between Pope Pius IX's *Syllabus of Errors* (1864) and Vatican II's *Declaration of Religious Freedom* (1965) is more than chronological. They inhabit two different theological universes."

John XXIII had a remarkable charism. He was completely ego-less: a certain sort of holy man. As Jewish intellectual Hannah Arendt wrote in an essay on him in her book *Men In Dark Times,* he was literally a humble Christian. How he ever got to be pope is considered by many evidence that God still bothers with the world.[118]

One of John's many small surprises was his selection of the thirty-eight-year-old Remi De Roo as bishop of one of the oldest and stuffiest English Catholic dioceses in western Canada. As De Roo himself stated at the time: "You could have knocked me over with a feather."[119]

Popes pick new bishops to reflect their values, priorities and attitudes; so that their programs will be fully implemented at least during their lifetime. But John XXIII served such a short time —the shortest reign of any previous pope in the 20th Century—that he did not have that much time and he did not appoint that many bishops.

He could not appoint anywhere near as many as Pius XII, who served almost twenty years, or even his successor Paul VI who was in office fifteen. One of his first appointments was Albino Luciani in December 1958, the future Pope John Paul I (John Paul II, by contrast, was among the last appointed by Pius XII earlier in 1958) and late in his papacy the eighty-three-year-old pontiff picked the thirty-eight-year-old De Roo another far from casual choice.

To display his special approval he called him their Benjamin during an audience with the Canadian Bishops and the following day sent him a large ceremonial ring to indicate special papal favour.

The symbolism of the ring is such that "like every closed circle, the ring is a symbol of continuity and wholeness. This is why it has been used both as a symbol of marriage and of the eternally repeated time-cycle."[120]

John XXIII was nearing the time of his death. He would be gone within the first year of De Roo's episcopacy. This special anointing near the end time reflected the repetition of a time cycle where the intent of the noble program of the old man was laid on the willing shoulders of the young and able enthusiast.

De Roo's first encounter of the Council sessions "was a little overwhelming," he admitted. This was because "there was a sense of the presence of the Holy Spirit. You could just feel it in the worship."

5. AT THE COUNCIL

As a young man he was dropped into the company of "over two thousand bishops from all over the world, of every race and colour" at what was arguably the most important deliberative and direction-setting event in the history of the two-thousand-year-old institution.

Having been fast-tracked through all the preparatory steps toward episcopacy, this experience of submersion in an historic assembly had the permanent impact of a ritual initiation. It was an eventuality he could not possibly have been fully prepared for in advance.

Suddenly all his instinctive innovations during twelve years as a priest were being justified, all the unconscious intuitions that had been driving him toward some sort of destiny were being ratified at the highest level within the church. It is a small wonder he felt he experienced the movement of the Holy Spirit.

The nascent vision behind his actions as a creative cleric within a huge megalithic institution on the verge of a watershed moment in its history was being fully realized.

An institution the age and grandeur of the Catholic Church normally moves at a glacier-like pace. But if it has been snagged for an unconscionably long time (such as a hundred years) when it does move again it is like a sudden leap forward compared to its usual rate of motion. Shock and reaction to such 'sudden' change by the

Catholic population became a permanent part of the legacy of the young bishop.

De Roo knew that in this sweep of the change of history the central focus of his life's work was being worked out. In some important sense, the next thirty-five years would be the everyday unfolding of the detail of the grand plan revealed at the Council. At least that was the way it would be for the first twenty years. His was far from a passive role at the Council. Not only did he make a disproportionate number of effective interventions but he was selected to serve as a point man for the Canadian Bishops' team, due to his articulate nature and direct youthful style.

He made four oral and thirteen written submissions, which effected permanent change in the church's policy toward conjugal love, hermit life, the role of the priest and the responsibilities of the laity. The rest of his episcopacy would entail the unpacking the implications of these interventions. It is one thing to get ideas on paper, quite another to oversee their successful implementation over decades.

~~~

Just prior to the Council and his appointment as bishop, he had succeeded Charles Empson as pastor of Holy Cross, serving between 1960-62. At Holy Cross he directed a team of younger priests. As well he taught ethics to nurses at Saint Boniface Hospital, instructed at the seminary and conducted lectures to lay adults.

Prior to Vatican II Catholic daily life was overlaid with elaborate procedures and well developed rituals both in liturgical worship and pastoral application.

It was often all a young priest could manage to do to keep up with hearing confessions, his own daily breviary recitation, saying Mass, counselling people, running parish committees, supervising liturgies, working with young people, keeping up as much as necessary with diocesan and Vatican policy pronouncements, conducting devotional groups et cetera, et cetera.

This was in addition to attending to his own spiritual growth and monitoring new developments within the life of the parish. Leadership development could be a slow process in such an elaborate ongoing format.
~~~

All of this was being accomplished within a fiercely formal framework of centralized teaching and disciplinary authority. The distinction between the clergy and the members of the hierarchy was very great indeed.

When Remi De Roo said his first bishop, Maurice Baudoux, was a very kind and charitable man with a stalwart sense of humour, he was saying a good deal. These could be sanity-saving traits in such a serious milieu, where 'the salvation of souls' was the business at hand.

The Catholic Church took itself with grave seriousness prior to Vatican II. It was only then it started to change from being "The Church" in its own mind, shifting to a more balanced perspective.[121]

For Remi De Roo to move so quickly through its ranks at such a time in history, with no real evidence he was particularly ambitious, said a great deal about his general abilities, and something about Baudoux's capacity to cultivate and utilize these.

In hindsight, all the signs were there that he would be appointed bishop in time. Yet when the news came, as the headline in the *Winnipeg Tribune* read, he was genuinely surprised.

This is credible because there is something supremely existential in De Roo's sensibility and outlook despite his critical capacity for envisioning the future. And yet in his presence you do not get any feeling of a dreamer, but rather of a practical efficiency that conflicts with the view of many critics.

Somehow—mysteriously in his own view—he had been given license to have a direct and active hand in the changes ahead. Providence surprisingly granted him a chance by which to conduct an interesting and important creative spiritual experiment.

Chapter Ten: Eastertide

"If I were asked to give a lecture on Bishop Remi De Roo, I would present him as a bishop who embodies the spirit of Vatican Council II."—Gregory Baum[122]

1. A NEW KIND OF CHURCH

The Second Vatican Council (1962-65) was arguably the most important event in the history of the Christian Church in that it completed the work of the first thousand years when the whole church—East and West—was united and governed by general ecumenical councils of which Vatican II was the 21st.

More importantly it rectified the distortion of the second thousand years represented by two major splits, between the Eastern and Western church at the start of the 13th Century, and then the Protestant Reformation in the 16th Century. Vatican II prepared the overall framework of Christianity for the third millennium; for the possibility of a full recovery.

Until the split with the Eastern Church, Christianity was generally and uniformly governed by synods; general universal assemblies that settled disputes, clarified teachings, established doctrine into permanent dogma and set overall direction for the following period, on average a hundred years or so.

However, after the East-West split in 1202, xenophobic tendencies arose in reaction within Roman Catholicism that were politically exacerbated by the rise of nationalism in Europe. Another major irritant was that aspect of the Enlightenment antagonistic to the Medieval concept of religious faith. This resulted in the 16th Century schism, the Protestant Reformation.

After these events of the 1520s, for more than four hundred years the Catholic Church tended in an authoritarian direction with an exaggerated importance given to the papacy over and against Protestantism. This has been said to have culminated in the

19th Century with Pius IX's *Syllabus of Errors* and the Definition of Papal Infallibility at Vatican I (1869-70), as discussed.

This tendency to over-exaggerate the role of the pope was known as ultramontanism, literally 'over the mountains' in that Europe looked over the alps to Rome for true guidance and direction; resulting in an overcentralization of authority.

After 1870, things could really go no further in that direction; that is, away from the conciliar governing practice of the first thousand years of Christianity. Vatican II was the requisite re-addressing to rectify the balance.

Circumstance, talent and effort dictated that Remi De Roo happened to be at Vatican II and play a notable role in the outcome of the Council. The upshot was that his life as a bishop in the most westerly Canadian diocese would be played out striving to fully implement the reforms of Vatican II.

He would have about twenty years clear and free to do this before a reaction of general theological and political containment of Vatican II would be imposed by the regime of the new pope, after 1978. Due to his formative resolution, he would be able to continue relatively unhampered for his full term, but he would become almost an exception, and would pay a severe personal price for his perseverance.

Most of the church in Canada and beyond would be seen to dramatically slow down on the complete implementation of Vatican II. His work would prove to serve as a target model for the restorationists who emerged after 1978. It also encouraged the reformers who saw it as a prophetic model—one that would eventually be vindicated.

Directly out of Vatican II would come, of course, one of his strongest pushes internationally, in the fields of human rights, social justice and opposition to the arms race in its distortion of the world economy.

The reforms at Vatican II emerged in sixteen distinct documents but it is generally agreed that four contained the major thrusts and are the most important. These four tend to subsume all the others and focus upon the major areas of: Liturgy; Revelation; the Constitution of the Church itself; and the Church's ongoing role in the contemporary modern world.

De Roo's own evaluation of their importance coincides with the general consensus. The news of this radical change and his gift for clarity of communication generally explain why he was such good copy for the regular media and progressive Catholic newspapers alike as they reported on the changes immediately after Vatican II.

2. THREE MONSIGNORS

"Inevitably there was speculation on who would succeed Bishop Hill... I don't think I was ever a serious candidate compared to some of the possible appointees in Vancouver, Calgary, Edmonton... When Remi was named, Archbishop Pocock and Archbishop Baudoux were thought to have been instrumental in the appointment. At least that was the talk..."

During the 1950s Victoria Diocese had a number of local candidates ordained to the priesthood. The speaker, Michael O'Connell, was one of these. During the sixteen years of the previous bishop's tenure he had proven a very able and helpful cleric to the ailing bishop James Michael Hill who had been diagnosed with a heart ailment ten years prior to his death in 1962. As a result O'Connell was appointed to the domestic prelature (made a monsignor) in 1963, one of the Bishop De Roo's first formal actions.

"I was with Bishop Hill almost daily for twelve years. We all lived at the cathedral then. One thing about Bishop Hill, he had a certain dignity and formality. There was a lot of warmth in conversation with people he knew. He enjoyed visiting with the priests. He was very kind.

"[On the other hand] you wanted to be well prepared if you had a special request about a difficult marriage [case]. You were very aware that he was the bishop and you were a young priest."

ෙ෴ෙ

Another young priest who was a local ordained by Bishop Hill also in 1950 was Philip Hanley who was also elevated to the rank of domestic prelate through talented service, though twenty years after Monsignor O'Connell.

"The designation that has been most apt through the years in describing Bishop Hill is that he was a 'perfect gentleman'. He came out of the Depression (in the Maritimes) and that had an impact on him as rector of a college in hard times.

"A lot of things happened in his term. He was very supportive of social life conferences... He was very pastoral... He was not demonstrative. He initiated behind the scenes. He delegated," stated Monsignor Hanley.[123]

ಞಞಞ

James Michael Hill was not a western Canadian. He was a Maritimer, born in 1899, who successfully ran a small Catholic liberal arts college in an impoverished part of rural New Brunswick for twenty years during the toughest financial times.

One reason he was supportive of social life conferences was that Catholic Action in the form of co-operatives and credit unions were critical to the economy of the region around Chatham, where Saint Thomas College was then situated at the mouth of the Miramichi River in New Brunswick.

As Michael O'Connell states: "In financial matters he was very conservative. He was very conscious of the Diocese's heavy debt... He was very good at saving funds so that the essential could be done but otherwise very anxious to save money...

"He was very gracious in welcoming people. He had an annual New Year's Reception which brought many leading citizens to his home. I give Bishop Hill credit that many leaders in Victoria appreciated him very much."

Philip Hanley: "The annual priests' meeting with the Bishop on the feast of Saint Andrew [November 30] was quite hilarious [in hindsight]. We would meet in the basement of the Cathedral. Bishop Hill would take out all the circulars he had sent out during the year and read them to us, just in case we hadn't read them. Looking back I think he didn't want discussion.

"It was quite a change moving from Bishop Hill's way of doing things to the way of the new bishop. Hill was cautious, the other daring. They were as different as day and night."

Michael O'Connell: "He didn't drive. Then Remi arrived. He drove his own car, so you could see right away that he was less formal. He wasn't chauffeured. He was energetic. He had pastoral and diocesan experience. Vatican II inspired many of his policies."

After Hill died, the weekly scheduling of the priests' Sunday Mass duties at the cathedral was found written out in his own hand. This gives an indication of the hands-on administrative style and the scale of the operation that would allow this of its chief administrator. It was only after 1962 that Vancouver Island moved beyond its missionary status, led by a young bishop who assumed his priests could and would read for themselves.

A third monsignor who was present in those transition days was William Bulloch, though ordained for the diocese in Toronto by Cardinal MacGuigan during the era of the previous bishop John Cody in 1944. He remembers it this way: "When Remi came into the diocese he looked very young, like a kid. But he was very much a bishop and expert in all things. He knew everything. There's a lot to the man. I certainly wouldn't want to get rid of him... He has a certain humility too."

Reading between the lines there is a good deal to be picked up in the comments of these veteran priests that are typical and characteristic of Catholic clergy. Generally among clerics only compliments of the left-handed variety are given, especially about their immediate boss.

De Roo was not what any of them could have expected. An enigmatic figure they could not help but admire his giftedness, but his reluctance to fit into conventional categories was far from comforting. They could not quite be sure they liked what they received in the way of a leader. He took some getting used to.

With his 'I certainly wouldn't want to get rid of him' comment, William Bulloch is referring to the reputation De Roo quickly gained nationally as a leader who was radically implementing Vatican II. Many traditionalists among the laity (and the clergy) liberally exercised their right to disapprove of him.[124]

"Once I went to a parish in Ottawa. One person said, 'So you're out there with that pagan bishop.' I told him I never allowed anyone to say a word against Bishop De Roo. He's our bishop and you have to keep your loyalty."

On the other hand, many unlikely types were fascinated by De Roo. Certainly William Bulloch might have appeared at first look an unlikely fan; a convert to Catholicism, like an Englishman in style with his proper manners, yet he became a very progressive liturgist, and theologically open to the changes. De Roo wrote of him: he "has proven his ability to adapt readily to changing situations."[125]

De Roo enabled these particular priests to develop and contribute their talents but he was far from the patriarch they might have felt more comfortable with initially.

ぐぐぐ

Monsignor O'Connell: "We became aware that the Vatican Council was the most significant event of the century. I was one of the key people in ecumenism. I was asked to start going to meetings of the council of churches.

"Bishop Remi was the first bishop here who was a native of western Canada. He brought with him a certain informality. He was very much at home with people in all kinds of situations. Very relaxed and confident. He always encouraged lay participation in justice issues and in parish decisions."

Philip Hanley: "It was a very exciting time. This diocesan emphasis on Vatican II was great stuff because it fitted in with what was happening in the universal church. I think we came through the period after Vatican II 'articulating aspirations and ventilating frustrations'. Now we are into the hard realities."

ぐぐぐ

These interviews, conducted in the middle 1990s, still freshly recalled the excitement of the historic new start despite the encroachments of 'the harder realities' as Philip Hanley calls them.

More than simply a leader who wished to administer a diocese; one who encouraged and enabled priests and lay leaders in pursuing their individual personal goals and projects, De Roo had a major vision of the diocesan and universal church, which had sprung out of his experience of the Second Vatican Council.

He saw the possibility of it returning fully to its synodal roots as functioned in the period of the Early Church (100-600 AD) and he had the ability and aptitude to attempt to actually bring it about. He set about developing Victoria as a permanent model along these lines.[126]

3. AN ECUMENICAL CHURCH

Ecumenism was the major thrust of the 1960s in the Canadian churches. This was no major bombshell. Vatican II, in a surprise departure, had included fourteen official visitors from the other major Christian denominations.

The general direction of the documents was an unprecedented openness toward the non-Catholic Christian world. Pope John announced prior to its opening that he wished the Council to be without 'anathemas', the negative condemnations of earlier councils, particularly the 19th Century Council, Vatican I.

This very positive attitude toward the 'separated brethren', as Pius XI had phrased it, had to be the first item on the agenda. Four and a half centuries of discord had taken its toll in terms of the credibility of Christianity. If the Christian message was to be even effectively communicated, unity was of the essence. The groundwork had to be lain during this golden opportunity. The rancour and the acrimony of the past had to be dissipated.

Bishop De Roo became a leader in this area, not only in Victoria but throughout the continent, speaking regularly by invitation throughout the west and beyond. In Victoria he immediately initiated historic gestures and events. He presented gifts to the leaders of the other major denominations, particularly the Anglicans who were the predominant group due to the English enclave nature of Vancouver Island.

Throughout the Sixties, this unprecedented opportunity for openness and sharing was exploited, even celebrated in a series of events that marked the new rapport. De Roo himself spoke at the Victoria Council of Churches, an unprecedented move.

Because of his openness he quickly becoming a permanent favourite with the United Church of Canada and the Anglicans. Speaking to the Council of Churches was a first for a Roman Catholic bishop. All of this was covered as real news by the mainstream media.

On January 19, 1964, for example, the *Daily Colonist* reported in its headline *"Good time to be a bishop—Victoria's young prelate is both a symbol of the changing face of his church and a force in bridging fissures of Christianity."* Fifteen hundred people had attended an interdenominational prayer meeting on the theme of Christian Unity. A month later the opposition daily, *The Times*, announced that *"Bishop De Roo makes history at Council where he said that interchurch unity means striving for truth."*

It was not only in the comfort of his own backyard he was making strong statements regarding reconciliation but at the highest historic level.

Within his own denomination, at the Council, of course, and at the Anglican world gathering at Lambeth in 1968, as the Canadian Catholic Church's representative he was presented to the Queen. He must have been feeling his oats as a young bishop, displaying a penetrating confidence: He was a man for the times and a type of the future.

As a consequence he was called upon to speak throughout the continent, certainly consistently across Canada. He accepted the speaker's fees from these invitations and placed them in a contingency fund so that when he had to travel "it wouldn't be a burden on the diocese," which was always perceived to be far from affluent.

4. NOT AN UNTROUBLED PAST

The Diocese he had come to run had its own unique past, not an untroubled one. The bishop he succeeded served for a respectable sixteen years but the previous fifty years had been intensely unstable. During one five-year period Victoria was elevated to metropolitan status for the province and shortly after was threatened with suppression with its removal.

Between 1900 and 1923 two bishops had been removed by Rome—a far from common occurrence in Canada. Twice during this same time span the diocese was threatened with suppression, presumably to be attached to Vancouver.

It had been elevated and demoted from the metropolitan status of archdiocese during that five year period between 1903-1908. Sir Wilfrid Laurier had to step in to have it made a Canadian diocese as Vancouver's Island, as it was then called, was still attached as a suffragan diocese to Portland until 1903. During a later fifteen year period (1923-1937) there had been five bishops averaging less than three years each. Another earlier one had lasted only seven months in 1899.

Besides the political problems, Victoria by and large was a proving ground for bishops who would be quickly moved on to larger dioceses. Bishops had gone to Portland, Edmonton, Saskatoon, Winnipeg, London and Halifax after apprenticing at Victoria for three to five years during the modern era.

The same was expected for Remi De Roo, given his general ability, and the recognition he was receiving both at the grassroots and the highest level within the church.

However things rarely go that smoothly or predictably even within the Catholic Church, which at any rate was quickly shedding the monolithic image which had facilitated his meteoric rise. Pluralism was entering the Catholic Church Universal.

By serving nearly forty years as head of his diocese, De Roo inadvertently lent it an unprecedented stability. His thirty-seven years far exceeded even the longest terms of the original pioneer bishops (between 1846-1896) when ordinaries more regularly died in office at the site of their initial appointment.

Victoria has its own distinct saga. It is the oldest Canadian diocese west of Toronto. According to diocesan historian Vincent McNally it was erected so early due to the vicissitude of chance. As one of two suffragan dioceses of Portland (along with Walla Walla, later transferred to Seattle), it was an American diocese for its first fifty-seven years.[127]

In the United States only Baltimore was established as an archdiocese earlier than Portland. McNally argues that this was all the result of a smooth selling job to Rome by the initial archbishop of Portland, Norbert Blanchet who accompanied Modeste Demers to the Willamette Valley in Oregon in 1838 from Saint Boniface.[128]

Portland was erected as the second oldest metropolitan see after Baltimore due to exaggerated claims about the number of Catholics, according to Father McNally. 'Vancouver's Island' had as its first bishop the thirty-eight-year-old Modeste Demers of Québec. Demers was so intimidated by the prospects of his life's work that he only arrived in the diocese for the first time after a seven-year delay.

Demers served his twenty-five years and died in office as did most of the other pioneer period bishops. Archbishop Charles Seghers, for example, was murdered by a follower in Alaska, which was part of the huge uncharted domain of the diocese at the time.

The then Diocese of Vancouver's Island included the Queen Charlotte Islands, all of the British Columbia mainland (then called New Caledonia), Alaska and the various bordering islands of Puget Sound, the Gulf of Georgia and islands of Johnstone Strait.

Charles Seghers, the second and fourth bishop of Victoria (he was appointed to Portland as second Archbishop but returned a few years later in time to meet a tragic end) was not the only early bishop to die in foreign parts. John Lemmens the fifth bishop, who had the present cathedral constructed at great cost, died from contracting malaria in Guatemala in 1897 while fundraising to pay for the building.

Money and politics almost seemed a curse regularly visited upon Victoria's Catholic leaders. One bishop, Alexander (Sandy) MacDonald of Cape Breton (1908-1923), uncannily met almost the exact same end as De Roo over money matters and Vatican church politics.[129]

De Roo was not expected to stay long in the little diocese. Ironically it was the very behaviour that alienated so many local right-wing Catholics and traditionalist clergy which resulted in his spending the balance of his career in such an out-of-the-way place. Perhaps if they had not complained so much to Rome, they might have been rid of him sooner.

De Roo utilized the opportunity for advancing the causes with which he became identified. He quickly sensed the limited parameters of the situation and used the fact Victoria was such a minor diocese in such a non-Christian (not to say non-Catholic region) to apply himself to a national and international program.

In 1970 when ecumenism was seen to begin to wane, he started to move things in fresh directions. For example he was a founding member of the World Conference on Religion and Peace in Kyoto. A little later in the same decade he was appointed the first Chairperson of the British Columbia Human Rights Commission. Ecumenism and internal church reform gave way to social action.

He became the longest serving and easily most effective chairperson of the Social Affairs Commission of the Canadian Bishops Conference in Ottawa. He redefined what Catholic social action meant in the Canadian context.

During much of the middle 1980s, when he was the national celebrity defender of the Bishops' ethical reflections on the crisis of the economy, he challenged in a incisive manner the conventional wisdom of the market economy. He was immensely effective in an unprecedented manner at broadening and lengthening the debate.

By becoming a permanent burr under the saddle of Corporate Canada and the federal government, he attracted the baffled ire of back-door-Catholic Conrad Black, Canada's self-styled media mogul and answer to Lord Beaverbrook.

Black entered the church by skirting the normal entry process[130](the Rite of Christian Initiation for Adults also called the Catechumenate) and it cost him in the debate as it became quickly evident that he did not have a clue about the church's social teachings. Nevertheless Black did not let his culpable ignorance stop him from displaying inordinate reserves of particular antipathy for such 'a meddling priest'.[131]

ꕥꕥꕥ

Given all this, De Roo seemed an improbable figure to bring such long-term stability to such an unlikely diocese. The local anguish over this previous insecurity was identified by Monsignor Michael O'Connell. As a child O'Connell watched several bishops come and go with an alarm which was general to the tiny Catholic population of the island.[132]

Somehow O'Connell himself might have seemed a more sensible and likely replacement for his mentor Bishop Hill, or even the affable Philip Hanley, but the winds of Vatican II blew the church in a different direction.[133] De Roo certainly emerged an inscrutable champion to these men.

Financial shortfalls had been a constant lesson for the leaders of Victoria Diocese. As mentioned Bishop John Lemmens (1888-97) died as a direct result of his effort to pay off the original cathedral construction debt in the 1890s.

Lemmens is noteworthy for his strong penchant for social justice teachings, becoming identified in his day with the labour struggle and the right of workers to a living wage. Much of this was the direct result of his adherence to the teachings of the first social encyclical (*Rerum Novarum*) of Pope Leo XIII in 1891.

Another strong leadership figure from that era was Bishop Alexander (Sandy) MacDonald, the Cape Breton priest who served from 1908-1923. Bishop MacDonald, also an intellectually gifted individual, waged a ten-year legal and fiscal battle with the City of Victoria over its 'single tax system', which was particularly punitive to downtown churches between 1910 and 1920.

While the church building was tax free, the property it sat on was not. The policy was driven by a peculiar sort of anti-religious mentality that took root on the westcoast where many individuals had come to escape the reaches of established religion.

This strange struggle (which was ultimately won by the church at the level of the Privy Council in London, England) broke the diocese financially and resulted in Bishop Sandy's removal by Rome.[134] The financial problems actually were probably more of a pretext. He was in fact removed for 'modernism' because he dared to challenge the predominant thinking at The Vatican.

As a theologian MacDonald argued effectively—too effectively perhaps—with the Vatican's interpretation of authority within the church, which had became enshrined in a code of canon law in 1918. He refused to go to Rome for his five year *ad limina* report on the basis that the diocese could not afford to send him and that he had already been exempted from attending due to the difficulties of travel during the First World War.

Bishop Sandy, as he was known, was a respected theologian, certainly the most accomplished English-speaking theologian among the bishops of his day. It was this very smartness which got him into hot water and had him removed.[135]

In an interesting irony, the financial cost of the court victory benefitted all the other Christian churches in the region while nearly eliminating the Catholic Diocese. This was one of the times when suppression of the diocese was most threatened.

Bishop Sandy's (and Bishop Lemmens') financial history cast a permanent pall over the mentality of clergy of the diocese. Certainly as a legacy it influenced Monsignor O'Connell's style. Both De Roo's predecessor James Michael Hill and his successor

Raymond Roussin were extremely cautious about finances, acting as though they were under orders to make this a priority item.[136]

It must be said De Roo took a more balanced approach. While hardly spendthrift, he had his definite priorities which were going to be funded. His central concept of the church and of his role in it had a pastoral emphasis rather than administrative. He was appointed in an era which did not require the sacrifice of ideals to practicalities and this probably suited his temperament.

5. THE FISCAL CONSERVATIVE

These lessons of fiscal record would hardly be lost on De Roo, a student of history and always a fiscal conservative within his own administrative practices. Unlike some 'princes of the church' he consciously lived at a very modest level. "At the same level of income exactly as every priest in the diocese," he proudly declared.

In his interviews with Grant Maxwell, he took some pride in the fact that he drew the same salary and allowances as 'the youngest priest' in the diocese.

"When I arrived here I learned that Bishop Hill had been running the whole diocese on one Pentecost Collection yearly. There was no organized system of diocesan taxation. I had to negotiate with the clergy to set up such a system. We started, if I remember, with a modest levy of seven percent, eventually moving it up to where it is now (in 1997) at fifteen percent."

As a group Catholics generally have never been known as generous givers. Part of it being the obligatory nature of attendance at Sunday liturgy, where members are forced into a provisional situation. Another factor is the accurate assessment (or inaccurate, as in the case of Victoria) of the overall immense wealth of the institution. De Roo typifies Catholics as "modest givers" and admits that his controversial prophetic Catholicism over the years may have hurt the diocese financially.

"I think Andrew Greely (an American priest sociologist) has established quite clearly that Catholics are not particularly outstanding when it comes to generosity toward the church. Many other Christian groups almost double the offerings that Catholics give.

"You draw your own conclusions. If a bishop comes in with policies that are a bit upsetting because they are moving forward, then the well-heeled population that tends to be more conservative is not going to get excited about supporting them financially."

At the time of this interview the financial administrator of the diocese was Muriel Clemenger, a former pharmacy manager who had previously also been a foreign missionary to India. After converting to Catholicism she eventually sought the position at the diocese and as with many other key diocesan positions, De Roo filled it with a talented laywoman.

As he might have said about himself, he never seemed to have any problem with women. In fact people have noted that he regularly surrounded himself with women as key advisors, something that irritated certain sorts of clergy.

But on the financial side, one of the disappointments for Muriel Clemenger over the more than ten years she spent as administrator was "not being able to get the level of generosity I had hoped for [from the parishioners in the diocese.] Perhaps my perception was incorrect; it's still a puzzle to me."

Her associate Al Heron, who worked with the Catholic Church in Regina prior to coming to Vancouver Island, did not claim to be so puzzled. He felt that it was due to the hierarchial nature of the church where the majority of laity still feel their only real power is that of the cheque book.[137]

⁂

To return to the early 1960s when De Roo first arrived and saw the need to shift the bases of regular giving: "Let's say it wasn't very easy to get people with parochial mindsets to begin to appreciate their diocesan responsibilities. However, they did gradually respond."[138]

"I also started a contingency fund of my own into which I put all the monies I could get from my lectures, and out of which I would pay for my own travelling in such a way that I would not be a burden to the diocese.

"My own revenue from the diocese has been exactly the same as the clergy get. The youngest priest to the most senior and the bishop all get the same stipend."

Asked about his relations with his clergy over the years, based on the collegial model which came out of Vatican II: "By and large I'm not complaining. I'd be the last person to complain about the clergy. I think we have a good group. We're all human beings, as in every diocese."

He established one of the first Priests Senate in Canada, sharing his authority as far as possible under canon law. (The code of canon law resulting from Vatican II was only authorized in the early 1980s).

One large category of clergy on Vancouver Island were those who relocated from elsewhere. Aside from an unprecedented number of seven local clergy ordained by Bishop Hill in the 1950s, priests transferred from other dioceses, drawn in large part by his popular perception as a progressive leader. There are claims that traditionalist young men left the diocese to be ordained elsewhere but given their conservative nature, outright statements to this effect are hard to come by.[139]

Ken Bernard, a priest of the archdiocese of Winnipeg, described his experience of transferring to the diocese in 1979: "After hearing my reasons for coming west, Bishop Remi cautioned me about taking advantage of the diocese. Several priests had asked him the same thing as I was asking, and he had said yes to them, and many did not stay."

"In a sense they had only used the diocese as a stepping stone out of the priesthood; something that was hard on the bishop and stressful for the people of the diocese. After I had been on the Island for some years I realized that Bishop Remi had been more than generous to priests requesting to come and work here.

"He has trusted what they were saying. He has accepted their weaknesses, He has always said yes. While that has meant that a large number of clergy have just 'passed through', it has also meant that many of us have come here to stay and work. A bishop's generosity towards priests is always something to remark [about]. It is a characteristic to praise."[140]

He became a sign to clergy of a court of last resort when they were nearly ready to leave the priesthood due to frustration with narrower definitions of the role elsewhere. One of the areas where he may have had cause to complain about clergy was this idea of his diocese as a stepping stone on the way out. In the late Sixties and early Seventies huge numbers were leaving worldwide.

One priest he did ordain who was from Vancouver, Charles Joerin, remembers his first encounter in 1976 this way:

"I do like to recall the time I phoned the bishop after I had made the decision to ask him if I might study for the priesthood under the auspices of Victoria Diocese. I was very startled to hear, not a secretary's voice, but his own: "Bishop De Roo here; can I help you?"

"After I picked myself up off the floor I said 'Yes' and went on to request an interview with him. I went over from Vancouver that same week and was welcomed most graciously by Monsignor Bulloch who took me out to see the bishop at his old home on Arbutus Road.

"It was a good meeting, but most surprising. Among other things, we discussed married clergy. Or I should say the bishop asked me what I thought of the idea and I remembered mumbling something incoherent as I hadn't thought about the idea at all, and said so. I was invited to stay and meet many of the clergy who were having a gathering that day but declined saying I had to get back to Vancouver. That was, of course, just an excuse but I'd had enough of clergy for one day!"[141]

De Roo stated in the interviews with Grant Maxwell there were no major scandals in his diocese in the Eighties when the sexual abuse charges and dismissals were reaching epidemic proportions in other not-so-distant dioceses[142].

"You can look at the historical record. I don't think there have been major scandals among our clergy." At the time of this writing there are rumours of upcoming court cases on the issue, but these would have been centred in the very institutions he was quick to close or allow to close during his first decade in diocese. These intuitions having proved accurate.

❧❧❧

Concerning that early period, author and editor Gary McEoin summarized De Roo in his introduction to *Man to Man,* the 1969 dialogue volume with Catholic journalist Douglas Roche:

"In the six years since he became Bishop of Victoria... De Roo has won a reputation in the United States as well as Canada as one of the most dynamic and forward looking members of the

Catholic hierarchy in North America. I first met him in Rome during the Vatican Council.

"Gentle in manner to the point of shyness, he was never the less conspicuous by his availability to help in every project, big or small, that promised to promote the purposes of the Council. He was an assiduous listener. He stated his position clearly, frankly, briefly. He was skilled as a catalyzing formulator of the common content of apparently divergent viewpoints.

"Of his various interventions in the General Assembly, the most commented upon stressed the active function of the laity in the Church and urged his fellow bishops to give more weight to the beliefs and practices of the people when attempting to formulate moral rules."

McEoin says he would classify De Roo as a moderate progressive, "certainly no far-out radical." He describes the changing context of that time—and the difficulty bishops were having with it—in these terms:

"In many parts of the world, and specifically in North America, the bishops seem to have found great difficulty in adjusting to the techniques of social communication. Steeped in a tradition of a two-class society, in which those in authority commanded and the others simply obeyed... a form of monologue frozen in a language and a style guaranteed to turn off even those in agreement with the ideas expressed."[143]

This was the style of leadership of De Roo's immediate predecessor that certain local clergy preferred. The top down approach was fuelled by a certain mentality, not to say theological reasoning. At the risk of caricature, the attitude could be described to say that since the Church had the real truth anyway, it was better to force people into doing the right thing; manipulate them into the right form of behaviour rather than risk the loss of salvation.

This completely paternalistic approach overlooked the central moral issue of freedom of choice, without which no moral value is possible. The need of progressive education in the face of this entrenched obduracy was certainly De Roo's persistent dilemma.

Having been appointed just at the time of the Council, he attempted to sidestep some of this. To some extent he was able to avoid the difficulty by utilizing other communications vehicles, moving directly into the use of sociological surveys, open consultation with the population, direct dialogue utilizing the commented upon listening skills.

ᯅᯅᯅ

Aside from the instigation of a Priests Senate to 'share the bishop's role' as the headline read, lay leadership councils were set up to run parishes with the pastors, and the diocese itself with the bishop. It had all been put on paper at Vatican II but here it was being put into practice immediately.

Much of this had to do with time and place. The West Coast of Canada has always had a healthy skepticism about 'organized religion', as the expression goes. Diocesan historian Rev. Vincent McNally claimed that British Columbia is the most pointedly un-churched—or to use his expression 'pagan'—part of North America, a continent not un-renown for its secular materialism.[144]

De Roo's attitude toward this was open and accepting, far from defensive, as distinct from the extremely protective posture practiced by nearby Vancouver diocese. He leaned into it instead. Recognizing the nature of the landscape and the futility of the conventional challenges. Instead, following the lead of John XXIII he sent out non-judgmental signals of encouragement to people of good will, and attempted to work with them as fully as possible.

Pope John XXIII had done the same thing in his major encyclical letters. These statements *Pacem in Terram (Peace on Earth)* and *Mater et Magistra (Mother and Teacher)* had been the harbingers of the fresh attitude and a new realism within the church.

The Sixties were a period of rebirth and renaissance in the western world. Society generally was looking for original leadership figures, ones who broke the old mould, who understood this new social reality and were willing to work with it in a creative fashion.

De Roo caught the public imagination both within the church and without. The demand to hear him speak was ongoing and during this period he would fly to address gatherings across North America, Europe and the Third World about the new vision.

6. PUBLIC OPINION POLL

He was the first Canadian bishop to employ modern sociological methodology. His reference to sociologist Andrew Greely's work reflects a deep respect for modern social scientific procedures, which he himself would utilize.

In 1966 he had conducted a public opinion poll within the diocese to get accurate feedback from the people themselves. This may have been the first ever done within the Catholic Church universal.

The major mass circulation Catholic newspapers throughout North America reported extensively on this novel idea. He was pictured as 'the shirt-sleeve bishop', casting his permanent public image as a socially attuned, grass-roots-oriented leader who listened because he really wanted to hear.

This may be De Roo's most radical instinct: taking seriously the experience of ordinary people, actually working to expose himself to the truth contained therein. He was persistent with this passion throughout his career.

This phenomenological approach runs against the grain in the Catholic Church. Historically the church has enshrined the reasoning process which starts with set ideas, first principles which condition the results toward an established end.

First principles, or set points of view, as De Roo said in describing his postgraduate style of theological studies, tend to be defensive and apologetic in purpose: explaining and defending the given order; expecting the listener to accept the standard explanation, granting it the due weight of authority.

The Catholic Church as a two-thousand-year-old institution has a great deal to defend and explain in any attempt at dialogue. There are always good reasons at the time why decisions are taken but these do not always stand up in the light of historical critical scrutiny. Without a certain intellectual and political humility, the situation quickly degenerates into off-putting defensive posturing, a characteristic the public has grown to classify with the church.[145]

De Roo was able to avoid this pitfall by basing his decisions not solely on traditional principles but balanced with realistic perceptions from the people affected. He would take unpopular stands as time went on but normally in the direction of the prophetic tradition of the church, not in the direction of defending no longer credible practices. De Roo, like his patron John XXIII, was not guarded in his fundamental attitude.

John's famous adage that the church must heed the signs of the times and bring it up to date, favoured De Roo's image as "a bishop who comes to listen in sports shirt and slacks." This image was nearly revolutionary in its impact upon the imagination of ordinary Catholics. The sort of negative reaction mentioned by Monsignor William Bulloch, from his reported visit to the Ottawa parish, was almost to be expected.

On the other hand, to be revolutionary in the social atmosphere of 1960s was almost expected; in style and gesture at least. But to persist with this into the 1990s invited derision and contempt. After the 1980s theologian Richard P. McBrien wrote that the Catholic Church under Pope John Paul II settled into an era of containment of the 'progressive practices and ideas of Vatican II'.[146]

De Roo was much too deeply steeped in these principles to be able to afford to cut his cloth to the precepts of the day.

Ecumenical Councils such as Vatican II cannot be erased but they can be contained for a period by a pope, especially one who had grave misgivings about the central direction of the Council in the first place. This was definitely the case with John Paul II who as Polish Archbishop Karol Wojtyla stated at the time he did not see how the paradigm shift could work in his homeland.[147]

In Poland the church was a bulwark against the Communist regime and the new concepts seemed entirely inappropriate apparently for that reality. Much of John Paul II's administrative style is best understood within these unnegotiable parameters.

A significant indication of De Roo's persistence of attitude occurred when *Catholics of Vision Canada* issued its public statement in 1996 inviting ordinary Catholics to sign a petition pushing for the logical consequences of Vatican II—married clergy, women's ordination, greater tolerance of sexual orientation, greater openness in sexual teaching, lay consultation in the selection of bishops, and greater emphasis on social teachings.[148]

The reaction to this call for greater freedom all around, within the hierarchy and even the so-called liberal Catholic press, was severely condemnatory. It was as though they were instinctively over-reacting in lock-step anticipation of the iron hand of Rome.[149]

On Vancouver Island, the independent *Island Catholic News*, developed in the late 1980s to support the bishop's overall program, stood strongly behind the *Catholics of Vision* statement, publishing the entire document, the only Catholic newspaper in Canada to do so.

Given the overall atmosphere in the church since the special synod of 1985,[150] this might have been a telling moment when even Bishop De Roo could have been expected to duck for cover.

However it was not to be that way. When one of the local leaders of the *Catholics of Vision* campaign sent the bishop a copy of a radio program interview on the issue, De Roo received it positively, thanking the individual for sharing the information and commending him on how adeptly he made his case.[151]

De Roo was a consistent believer in the fundamental principles of Vatican II whether they happened to be in or out of season; or at any level of favour within the church. Because his experience of Vatican II had been personally and spiritually transformative, he was convinced that these teachings could work the same effect on the whole church given the chance.

It is part of what he meant when he regularly claimed the Council had been the work of the Holy Spirit. As late as November, 1997 he undertook to thematically explain the thirty-five years following the Council in terms of the major shifts and trends in a manner that demonstrated he had not lost sight of the vision or relegated an ounce of fervour.[152]

As a result of *Humanae Vitae*, the 1970s would have an entirely different emphasis because of the difficulties prompted by this document. Its challenge to the direction of central authority served to place severe limits on the ecumenical movement. As discussed, the Catholic Church underwent its traumatic post-Vatican II crisis of confidence around this issue of birth control. Why this was so 'traumatic' for the church is an important point.

7. AD INTRA AD EXTRA

Spiritually the Catholic Church's most vulnerable spot is in its attitude toward central teaching authority. Its highly structured centralized authority mechanism is its great foundation, but this leads to its equivalently weighted vulnerability. If it is effectively challenged, the results can be catastrophic.

The shadow side of being so rigidly lined up in terms of governance is that when a weighty teaching is successfully resisted, confidence in the whole structure is shaken. Such was the situation with the issue of contraception and the structural crisis which ensued. Never before had a Catholic Church Teaching of this stature been publicly refuted by the overwhelming majority of the Catholic population.

Pope Paul VI, so courageous in completing and implementing John's council, foundered on birth control. De Roo was not comfortable with this claim or the conventional image of Paul as like Hamlet, indecisive. De Roo expressed great respect for Paul.[153]

At the time of the Council, Pope John reserved that area of church sexual teaching to himself. He struck a widely representative commission to study the issue but died before he could rule upon their findings. Paul continued with the commission which included many experts but also regular lay people.

De Roo did somewhat the same thing during the Council when he held in-depth consultations with married couples in preparation for his important intervention on conjugal love.

The difference with Pope Paul was that he entirely disregarded the recommendations of the vast majority of the commission. The commission recommended the direction spelled out in Bishop De Roo's intervention. De Roo's intervention that there are two equal aspects of married love, the procreative and the partnership, seemed to correspond to the thinking of most Catholic couples, but the pope's teaching could not reflect the new reality.

❧❧❧

In Catholic doctrine marriage is a sacrament. This means the church teaches that it involves a special manifestation of

Christ's active presence in the world. The sacramental aspect centres in this three-way relationship, the two marriage partners with Christ. Vatican II's document on the Church in the Modern World finally formally accepted that too much focus on procreation can destroy the fundamental unitive relationship; that is, threaten the sacramental nature of marriage.

The complete expectation was that Pope Paul's teaching would be consonant with this development. For some reason he reverted to a particularly narrow interpretation of the church's natural law foundation which declared that every conjugal act must be entirely open to the possibility of procreation. This totally ruled out most forms of birth control and up to eighty-five percent of Catholics in North America refused to go along with it, according to public opinion polls done at the time.[154]

The crisis of confidence was the deeper issue. The Canadian bishops conference was placed in a delicate position because they had been one of the leaders in the practice of the principle of collegiality, one of two major principles enshrined by Vatican II. Collegiality states that national colleges of bishops have a key teaching role in the implementation of universal church policy. This principle had been blatantly disregarded in the process of issuing the birth control encyclical. The document was not circulated ahead of time for input by any national colleges of bishops.

In view of this, rather than agree or disagree with *Humanae Vitae* per se, the Canadian Bishops issued a pastoral statement on how the birth control teaching could be realistically applied within the Canadian context. As De Roo stated, the pope later agreed that this was the appropriate action.

A major aspect of the 'pastoral statement' focused on the question of the proper weight to be given papal documents in the formation and exercise of a mature Christian conscience.

Bishop De Roo was a central figure in the playing out of this touchy issue, as he explains:

"I was co-chair of the commission (which drafted the Canadian Bishops response) ... I was in that sense a central person in the event. The pope acknowledged that while he had to speak at the level of the church universal, it was the proper domain of the bishops to speak from the pastoral perspective of their own people.

"The Canadian statement was accepted as balanced. Basically it takes in fundamental principles of moral theology: to the primacy of the individual conscience before God; with the need for that conscience to be well informed.

"The basic principle that we espoused was that when people of good will find themselves facing a conflict of responsibilities where it is not possible for them to meet every demand, then they may legitimately before God decide prudently what they can do in terms of balancing the many goods related to marriage."

"Procreation is central but it is not the only good. There is the unitive sacramental dimension of marriage, which was discussed at great length at Vatican II. People have to balance these goods and try to do their best to achieve that which is prudently possible in their context.

"So we said that when people, having weighed all these factors prayerfully in considering their responsibilities, and having decided to act in a certain way, we would respect this as a decision of conscience. It was not for anyone else to jump on them and condemn them and refuse them absolution or whatever."[155]

~~~

The Canadian bishops with De Roo in a central leadership position had bitten the bullet of collegiality and taken a significant position in the direction of confidence in the spiritual and moral adulthood of the laity.

It also indicated the direction they would go on the social question during the next decade and beyond; a direction that would only start to shift after the death of Paul VI in 1978, the year of three popes.

Within the Canadian conference the push was fundamentally unanimous, he said:

"I am not aware of any (Canadian) bishop acting contrary to the conference decision as a whole. To my knowledge the only man whose name came forward was Archbishop James Carney of Vancouver. He did indicate quite clearly that he couldn't accept some of the things the other Canadian Bishops were saying. I'm not sure he had completely pondered the significance of what the Canadian Bishops were saying."
~~~

8. VANCOUVER VERSUS VICTORIA

Many have noted the intriguing irony that the most progressive diocese in Canada and the most traditionalist (if not reactionary) were situated geographically next to each other on the west coast. This has been an ongoing subject of comment and speculation, and continued well after Archbishop Carney's death in 1991 when he was succeeded by Adam Exner, OMI.

For example, in 1997 the *Vancouver Sun* newspaper carried an extensive comparison and contrast of the two dioceses; one that favoured Victoria and De Roo if only because Exner refused to grant an interview for the piece.[156]

Doug Todd's comparison of Vancouver and Victoria summarizes the most significant high points of De Roo's career as a national leader bishop figure. He provides a useful jumping off point in succinctly recounting his views and revealing the subtlety of his mind. The great usefulness of the piece is its expression of De Roo's general public image and reputation.

The editorial introduction to the piece, titled *A tale of two dioceses,* explains: "The Roman Catholic diocese of Victoria is considered the most radical in Canada, a direct extension of its bishop, Remi De Roo. By contrast Vancouver archdiocese historically leaned conservative on key church issues, as it has continued to do since the arrival of Archbishop Adam Exner six years ago. *Sun* Religion reporter Douglas Todd compares the two men and finds they may have more in common than do the districts under their authority."

"Vancouver Archbishop Adam Exner is 'a very intelligent well-read, personal friend,' says Victoria's Remi De Roo, but the longest serving bishop in English-speaking Canada cannot resist adding with a puckish smile on his lean, lined face, that Exner 'is inclined a little bit to be black and white.'

"Like all bishops, De Roo and Exner, both prairie born farm boys, choose their words carefully. But De Roo, who has made an international name for himself as an advocate of social justice, is not meek. Speaking of Exner, a dedicated crusader against abortion, De Roo says: 'You need not always agree with someone to respect someone.'

"The Roman Catholic diocese of Victoria is known as the most radical and avant garde in Canada—an adventurous offspring of the emerging freedoms of the Second Vatican Council; for putting much energy into advancing the role of women, denouncing oppression and encouraging what some Catholics think is too much diversity of ideas.

"On the other side of the Georgia Strait, meanwhile, Vancouver ...is seen as a dutiful servant of doctrinally strict Pope John Paul II, known for its lack of dissension and for rigorously enforcing Catholic bans on such things as abortion and homosexual activity...

"The gap between the two remains wide... It may explain why some Catholics in Vancouver have been unwilling to tolerate De Roo. In 1992, the *B.C. Catholic* newspaper refused to run ads for De Roo's book, *In the Eye of the Catholic Storm.*

"'De Roo gives the constant impression of undermining the church,' said Father Vincent Hawkswell, long time editor of the official Catholic newspaper in Vancouver (there is no independent Catholic newspaper in Vancouver). Although Hawkswell said he had not consulted with Exner on the ad ban, Hawkswell insisted: 'I have no qualms saying the book is not worth reading.'

"Although observers believe Exner is more likely, in private, to toe the Vatican line on doctrine, De Roo also says he 'refuses to play the dissident' for over-eager journalists or malcontents. Any bishop knows that expressing bald disagreement with central Catholic teaching would require his resignation. As well, De Roo believes everything he does and says fits, in some way, with Catholic tradition, which, unlike many, he considers 'flexible.'"

"De Roo's career can be characterized by his life-long devotion to social and economic justice. De Roo made arguably his biggest impact in Canada when he chaired the social affairs commission of the Canadian Conference of Catholic Bishops, which issued a 1983 report that infuriated then-Prime Minister Pierre Trudeau.

"It declared chronic unemployment 'a moral crisis' and said it, not inflation, was the economic catastrophe of the day. When

Canada's unemployment rate was just two points higher than today's nine percent, De Roo criticizes political and business leaders for spreading 'propaganda that high numbers of unemployment were unavoidable.'

"'That's what we said then, and it's all come true,' De Roo says, 'Only it's gotten worse.' De Roo, who follows the Bible's prophetic tradition of criticizing those in power, will tell anyone who listens that society is heading for destruction because of unemployment, free trade ideology, corporate greed and a widening chasm between rich and poor...

"De Roo makes a point of expanding his 'pro-life' philosophy to include opposition to not only abortion, but capital punishment and war, (and) has subtly criticized militant anti-abortionists as insensitive to women struggling with unwanted pregnancies."

"The striking contrast between the leadership styles of De Roo and his Vancouver counterparts may be just as revealing as their divergent approaches to specific topics of contention.

"The reaction of De Roo and Exner to *Catholics of Vision* offers insights to the two diocese's characters. The headline grabbing reform group is rattling the church this year by sending around a petition calling for married priests, female priests, elected bishops and greater freedom of thought.

"'I advise you to and exhort you not to co-operate with *Catholics of Vision*,' Exner told Catholics in a statement. 'As Catholics we cannot support it. I see their petition as an expression of dissent and protest.' He went on to decry any attempt to 'democratize' the Catholic Church.

"While Exner was one of many Canadian bishops trying to ostracize *Catholics of Vision*, De Roo has let it roll. He has allowed the *Catholics of Vision* statement to be discussed in full. The Vancouver *Island Catholic News,* which De Roo never censors, became the only Catholic newspaper in the country to run the full text of the *Catholics of Vision* statement, says staff member Pat Jamieson.

"'Over the years Remi has spoken in favour of all the points made by *Catholics of Vision,'* Jamieson says. Like many Island Catholics, Jamieson raves about how De Roo has instituted a long-term discussion forum called a synod.

"The synod is a startling notion to many in the Catholic Church because it invites the entire community to offer ideas on how the church should be run. At the recent five year anniversary of the first synod, De Roo proudly says he received more than a thousand suggestions for improvements from parishioners."

NOT A MONARCHY

"While De Roo agrees with Exner that the church is not a political democracy, neither should it be a monarchy. He refers to the church as a 'sacramental people'. That means, he says, the church is called to follow the form of community of the early Christians—who met in a circle, considered each other equals, and engaged in self-criticism. 'Every member of the church is equal in dignity and class,' De Roo says. 'The only class is the class of Jesus.'

"De Roo says he respects those who disagree with him. If a priest breaches Catholic discipline, De Roo says he will be told about it and expected to rectify it himself.

"'I like to deal with people as adults, and respect their freedom within the limits of the tradition, which I think is flexible,' De Roo says. 'The church is a mysterious body moving through history; it will be here in two thousand years. But that doesn't mean we don't criticize. The pope has powerful influence, but the church is not a monolith. Popes can declare doctrines all they want. But the critical test of a doctrine is that the people receive it.'"

"Diverging styles are also reflected in the prominence De Roo gives women in the church. While the Vancouver diocese struggled until recently ... over whether to allow altar girls... Exner has posted women to some key committees, but women do not serve mass at Vancouver's Holy Rosary cathedral...

"De Roo, on the other hand, has busily advanced the role of women since he began in 1962. He allows females (and male lay members) to perform almost every duty and sacrament usually reserved to priests.

"University of Victoria Catholic chaplain Kate Fagan, twenty-seven, says she performs weddings and baptisms, preaches, presides at mass and counsels people (which comes close to hearing confession). The only thing Fagan leaves up to priests is consecration of the bread and wine.

"Fagan, who was raised in Vancouver Diocese, says some Vancouver Catholics are frightened by the power De Roo allows women. 'Remi teaches you have to decide whether you are going to act from love or from fear. Victoria is refreshing because there's no fear here. To some Catholics in Vancouver, he's a terrible rebel bishop. But there are other Catholics who just drool when they hear what he does.'

"De Roo, for example, was the driving force behind the creation of the ecumenical, no-theological-holds barred Centre for Studies in Religion and Society at the University of Victoria. Director Harold Coward, a prominent Canadian religious scholar, said De Roo 'is a visionary and a catalyst to make things happen. And he doesn't get in the way of his vision by trying to control it.'"

THE ENNEAGRAM

"The Enneagram, in which De Roo has become a certified trainer, is based on a personality-type system said to be rooted in mystical Judaism, Christianity and Islam. It was largely introduced to North American Christian circles by Jesuits. Through the Enneagram De Roo has discovered he's a 'perfectionist'. He often feels guilty when he takes it easy—'and deep down there's a little anger'.

"He's trying to loosen up. 'I'm allowing myself to be humanly imperfect, rather than perfectly inhuman,' he says. Asked about Christian resistance to the Enneagram, De Roo acts as if he can no longer waste time fretting over such things. 'Most people,' he says, 'don't really want to know who they are.'

"Many Catholics consider Vatican II the most significant religious event since the 16th Century Reformation. It was a dramatic effort to try to make the church's hierarchal structure more flexible and open to differing views.

"'I was appointed in the euphoria of that ecumenical movement,' De Roo says. He insists he is not disappointed that Vatican II has not yet been fully realized under John Paul II. 'I'm just realistic. There was bound to be a counter-reaction. It's sometimes said it takes a hundred years for a council to be lived.'"

❧❧❧

"When De Roo is asked his views on such things as sex outside marriage and artificial contraception, he tends to say, 'Catholic teaching is very clear on them.'

"Asked if he personally accepts such Catholic restrictions on sex, De Roo responds that many people are caught in the culture of individualism and instant gratification, which leads them to become addicted to easy sex, as well as drugs, alcohol, food, sports, TV or movies.

"But De Roo opens the window for some value other than the rule of law to decide such sensitive matters when he adds: 'My pastoral concern is for the spiritual well-being of the total human person.'

"'There are three key things in the gospel tradition: We have to pursue truth as we know it; we have to love one another; we have to practice compassion. Those are the gospel fundamentals. They don't change.'"

❧❧❧

Todd closes his comparison of the two dioceses: "If Exner had allowed himself to be interviewed for this article, it's easy to believe he would not have disagreed with his colleague across the water that love, in the end, is ultimate."

❧❧❧

"The bishop is a man of faith, convinced that the message and the work of Christ are relevant to every aspect of human existence, including the life of society...the bishop is guided by a new understanding of mission found in the documents of Vatican II: to proclaim God's coming reign; to announce God's judgment on sin and injustice, God's gratuitous gift of forgiveness, conversion and new consciousness and God's promised rescue from poverty, misery and oppression."—Gregory Baum[157]

"Catholics have fallen out of the healthy old habit of reminding each other how sinful Popes can be...Authoritative as a Pope may be by his office, he is not impeccable as a man—he can sin, as can all humans."—Garry Wills from the Introduction to *Papal Sin, Structures of Deceit*

Part Three: The Cost of The Containment

CRUCIFIXION—The symbolic meaning of the crucifixion—which does not oppose or alter the historic fact, but provides further explanations of it—seems to be related to the suffering which is at the root of all contradiction and ambivalence, especially if one bears in mind the practice in medieval iconography of showing Jesus on the cross surrounded by symmetrical pairs of objects or beings.

These paired items are sometimes, but not always, based upon the actual witness of the scene. Thus the cross may be shown between the sun and the moon, between the Virgin and St. John, the good and the bad thief, the lance and the cup or chalice (or sometimes a stick and a sponge soaked in vinegar), and of course between heaven and hell.

At St. Andrew's Cathedral in the late 1980s. (Chuck Groot Studio)

Chapter Eleven: Night Battles

1. PIONEERING POLITICAL PRIEST PASSES PAINFULLY

SASKATOON, May 1998—Rev. Robert J. Ogle, priest of the Diocese of Saskatoon, missionary to Brazil, and former Member of Parliament for Saskatoon East, died April 1st here as a result of medical complications arising from a brain cancer suffered nearly fifteen years ago, when he was forced to leave electoral politics by the Vatican in 1984.

"Father Bob" as he was known to his constituents would have been seventy on December 24. He resided during the last months of his life in a Catholic seniors' residence in Saskatoon where I was able to visit him on March 20. In his room was a computer on which he surfed the Internet keeping in touch with old friends and associates and world events.

On the walls were blown-up photos of him shaking hands with celebrities he met as a priest and social democratic politician, including Pope John Paul II in 1982 and Fidel Castro the same year. He was rather affected by the fact that these two men had shaken hands for the first time just prior to our visit.

A life-long traveller and pioneering sort of personality, Father Ogle regularly stated that he had pretty well met everyone in the world he had ever wanted to meet due to his missionary work in the 1960s, his political career in the 1980s and his own intrepid nature.

He wrote a number of books on his life experiences, including an autobiography in 1987, *North/South Calling*, its title alluding to his life-long preoccupation with social justice restructuring between developed and underdeveloped nations, as well as his own priestly calling.

LOYAL TO HIS CALLING

During a period of history when many Catholic clergy sought laicization once drawn into the political realm, Father Ogle was always loyal to his religious vocation as a priest. It was as if his priesthood was so central to his personal identity that despite the unendurable stress he encountered staying true to its hold on him, he could never let go.

He openly stated that it was the stress from the arbitrary and unilateral decision by the Vatican in removing him from his elected political office that broke his health. Ultimately Ogle was torn between the discipline of his first calling and the subsequent developments that priesthood led him into, following the changes in the Roman Catholic Church after the Second Vatican Council.

Vatican II lead him to believe that as a priest he was entitled to the freedom to serve as an elected representative in a western democratic country.

As a result he suffered as directly as anyone the consequences of the radical about-face in the church's policy that took place shortly after he was elected when the neo-conservative containment of Vatican II began in earnest, and was ratified by the extraordinary synod of 1985.[158]

STRONG PREMONITION

Significantly, he had a strong premonition of personal trouble for himself at the time of the election of Pope John Paul II in 1978.

"I remember well the day the pope was elected. I was in Saskatoon. I walked in the rectory door at Saint Paul's (Cathedral) and two ecstatic priests told me that a new pope had been elected and he was Polish. At that moment I had a deep premonition that the election of this pope was going to mean trouble for me.

"Premonitions are not normally part of my life. I don't go on premonitions; I go on facts. But here all of a sudden, I had a deep premonition that I was going to have difficulty with this Polish pope and that never went away," he wrote in *North/South Calling*.

It certainly didn't; and that was six months before his first electoral victory in May of 1979. Ogle's books reveal a strong and distinct sense of his strength, limits and destiny.

He was born in the small borough of Rosetown, Saskatchewan in 1928, one of five children in an Irish-Catholic and therefore Liberal family. He reported in the autobiography that his association with the New Democratic Party alienated him permanently from certain members of his extended family in Rosetown.

He did his seminary studies in London, Ontario and was ordained in 1953 in his hometown. He was a missionary to Brazil between 1964-70 and it was there he underwent his complete conversion to social democratic principles. The year before he left Brazil, in 1969, he co-ordinated a large scale flood relief and house building program in that country. He never seemed to be able to forget the impact of that experience of Latin America.

His election in 1979, and re-election in 1980, was notable in that he defeated the sitting member, the federal cabinet member Otto Lang, also a Catholic. Ogle wished to serve as external affairs critic but was appointed health critic though he kept a profile in international relations.

SEAMLESS GARMENT POLICY

From the start he made it clear he was taking a dissenting position with party policy on the abortion issue, and extended that to all human rights which he considered all of one piece, a position statement he worked out with his close friend and former colleague Grant Maxwell.

His autobiography contains all the documentation on the capricious nature of his removal from politics. It literally tore him apart, creating a tension which severely damaged his health and resulted in his premature death.

He published another book in 1990, titled *Man of Letters*, which comprised of his correspondence with people around the world. His third volume was an earlier one in 1977, *When the Snake Bites The Sun*, comprising tales from his experience in Latin America.

He founded *Broadcasting for International Understanding*, utilizing his media contacts and international focus. He also hosted a series on *Vision Television* called *Ogle and Company*; always an Irish flair for the play on words.

He was assisted by his younger sister Mary Lou, a nurse, from the time of his political years when she served as his executive assistant in the Saskatoon office when he was Member of Parliament. It was during this period when I got to know him personally when doing freelance work between jobs after being removed myself from the *Prairie Messenger* where I had served as its first lay editor for a year in the early 1980s. He let me use his office when he was in Ottawa and it was a very helpful kindness during a difficult passage.

He was a frequent visitor to Vancouver Island as he had family there and was a regular preacher at Saint Andrew's Cathedral. In 1992 he gave a talk there entitled "What are you going to do when you get better?" It addressed his own health struggles but widened the topic out into the general question of the social responsibility that arises from spiritual development.

In the later years honours and recognition were bestowed but so did the health problems worsen. The nurse Mary Lou Ogle was able to monitor his condition and assist him right to the end when his blood complications led to the last hospital admittance.

❧❧❧

During my March 20 visit, ten days before the end, his physical condition was obviously much more fragile than I had ever seen in him, but his intellectual curiosity and general spirit were of the same intense focus I had always noted in my encounters over the years.

We spoke for an hour in his room. We located the references to himself in a book I had published. He joked about his brother, a Reform Party supporter, who had brought him a large poster of Alexa McDonough, the federal NDP leader, that adorned one wall of his space. We spoke about his visits to Vancouver Island and he chuckled as he remembered the "What are you going to do when you get better?" theme.

I wheeled him down to the chapel where he had a special place to sit in the doorway during the daily Eleven O'clock Mass. Then I had to leave to walk downtown to see my children who reside in Saskatoon.

It was an unseasonably warm and melting kind of morning so I walked for an hour thinking about all the changes I had seen him go through over twenty years, and the favourable effect he had on my life and many other people.

I was glad that I had said that to him before we had parted, although he replied in response that he did not know about the truth of it. I also wondered when I would see him again.

2. QUARTET ON THE LEFT

Father Bob Ogle is just one in a series of Catholic clergy in western Canada who moved too closely to the fires of left-wing politics. For a certain kind of variety of religious faith it is an irresistible attraction at a specific stage of faith development.[159]

Perhaps the most famous case is Archbishop Joseph Charbonneau of Montréal who was forced to retire to Victoria. Basilian Father Eugene Cullinane, who died in 1997 at the age of ninety after fifty years at Madonna House in Combermere, Ontario, is another well-known case.

Cullinane, an exemplary figure of Catholic piety and traditional holiness, was removed from the Diocese of Saskatoon in 1948 for daring to join the socialist Co-operative Commonwealth Federation in Saskatchewan.

Father Gene, as my family called him, had done his doctorate on the CCF and had come to the uncomfortable conclusion that they were the party which most closely espoused gospel values.[160] *When I was growing up in the Yukon, he was our parish priest.*

Bishop De Roo fits into this tradition although escaping—on the surface at least—from the perils of exile, banishment and virtual elimination of Cullinane, Charbonneau and Ogle. Charbonneau's presence in Victoria for his last decade (1949-59) prefigured De Roo social justice works after The Second Vatican Council. Ogle and Cullinane shared the western Canadian experience which made the CCF an all but inevitable part of the tradition of prairie populist politics.

If you study the details of their journeys, it is easy to conclude that the combination of their intelligent inquiry and faith integrity led them into situations where they would be blindsided (not to say crucified) by the persistent residual prejudice within the church about partisan politics.

They became symbolic figures who facilitated the advancement of their cause, the cause of spiritual maturity in the face of the overwhelming problem of structural sin. Each moving it through their sacrifice one more step in the direction of acceptance and legitimization within the institution.

The 'containment period' of the church called for the sacrifice of the vision of the church De Roo had assiduously worked up his entire career. Fundamentally hopeful, in one of his final interviews before retirement in 1999, De Roo is seen this way:

"While the Catholic Church, like many other churches, is suffering from declining attendance, De Roo isn't worried. He points out that the young people he speaks to these days demonstrate a deep concern about their spirituality.

"It might not look like the church of yesterday but a church of the Holy Spirit. On the question of women priests within the Catholic Church, De Roo says he has no problems with such a development if that is what is meant to be. I wouldn't object if the Holy Spirit moved us in that direction."[161]

It seems that it was precisely this sort of declaration that ensured he would not be able to continue with his overall program of proclaiming an uncontained Vatican II.[162]

3. THE FIRST POPE JOHN PAUL

If Pope John Paul I had lived, serving ten to fifteen years, there may have been more of a need for the second John Paul who succeeded him within thirty-three days in 1978.

There is every indication that Albino Luciani, a.k.a. John Paul I, would have continued to extend the program of Vatican II in line with his two immediate Italian predecessors. There was no indication that he would have moved directly to contain it as did his Polish successor, Karol Wojtyla AKA John Paul II, the "universal pastor of the church," his chosen title upon election.

Even a cursory glance at Luciani's biography indicates that he would have continued the left-ward direction of his two immediate predecessors, as signified by his choice of a combination of their names. He was going to continue their era with a fresh pronunciation betokened by his invention of the historically new papal appellation 'John Paul'.

'GOD'S CANDIDATE'

One of the shortest papacies in history lasted thirty-three days in 1978, between August 26 and September 28. Albino Luciani was born October 17, sixty-six years before, in 1912, to poor working-class parents. His father frequently travelled to Switzerland as a migrant worker and his family were known as outspoken socialists. Albino was ordained July 7, 1935 doing doctoral studies at the Gregorian University in Rome.[163]

For ten years he taught and served as vice-rector at the diocesan seminary in Belluno, after serving as pastor in his native parish. In 1949 he was put in charge of catechetics for the Belluno Eucharistic Congress, recording his experiences in a book, *Crumbs from the Catechism.* He was known to have a good working relationship with local communists and was appointed bishop in 1958 by John XXIII.

His pastoral ministry was exercised in a markedly grassroots manner. He played a background role at Vatican II, but became known in the Italian Conference of Bishops as an active member of the Doctrinal Commission.

On December 15, 1969, largely in response to local demand, he was named Patriarch of Venice, John XXIII's former position. During nine years there he hosted five ecumenical conferences including the meeting of the Anglican-Roman Catholic International Commission which produced an agreed statement on authority in 1976.

He moved unobtrusively to the right politically, declaring during an Italian election of June 1975 that communism was incompatible with Christianity. During this period he published *Illustrissimi*, a series of whimsical but pointed letters to authors or characters in history or fiction such as Pinocchio and Figaro. The book revealed a fondness for Charles Dickens and his character Mr. Pickwick. Journalism was said to be Luciani's second career choice.

From 1972-75 he served as vice-president of the Italian Conference of Bishops and was elevated to Cardinal on March 5, 1973. A defender of *Humanae Vitae* and conservative in theology, he was also a defender of the rights of conscience, but he had no use for ecclesiastical display, encouraging parish priests to sell precious vessels and other church valuables for the benefit of the poor.

In 1971, he proposed that the wealthy churches of the west should give one percent of their income to the impoverished churches of the Third World.

He was elected on the third ballot on the first day of the conclave in August, 1978 although almost unknown outside Italy. His candidature moved into the foreground once it became known that the majority of cardinals wanted a completely new style of pope, without connections with the curial establishments.

After the election the prevailing mood of the electors was one of unrestrained joy, and it was said that the one they had chosen was 'God's candidate'.

From a prepared text he stated that he was taking his name as a decided commitment to the progress of the Council, but also preserving "intact the great discipline of the church." A more spontaneous act was to hold a press conference during which he held the thousand journalists present spellbound.

Always impatient of pomp and outward trappings, and transparently humble-minded, he dispensed with the traditional papal coronation. Three weeks later, about 11 PM on Thursday, September 28, he died of an apparent heart attack while lying in bed reading some papers containing personal notes.

J.N.D. Kelly reports on the death and subsequent speculation: "His light was still on when he was found dead about 5:30 AM next day. Rumours of foul play, fanned by the lack of an autopsy, were later (1984) blown up into the claim that he was poisoned because he planned to clean up the Vatican Bank, demote important curial figures, and revise *Humanae Vitae,* but the evidence produced was a tissue of improbabilities.[164]

"The first pope of demonstrably working-class origins, a man of practical common sense who captivated people with his friendly smile, it is impossible to guess what kind of policies he would have pursued had he lived."[165]

With Pope John Paul II during *ad limina* visit in the early 1990s, some fifteen years into the pontificate. (Foto FELICI, Roma)

Indtroductory visit of the fifty-four year old De Roo and the fifty-eight year old newly-elected pope in 1978. (Foto FELICI, Roma)

Chapter Twelve: A World Of Paradox

COLLAPSE OF THE SOCIAL JUSTICE FRONT

"Controversy, at least in this age, does not lie between the hosts of heaven, Michael and his angels on the one hand and the powers of evil on the other; but it is a sort of ***night battle*** *where each fights for himself, and friend and foe stand together."* —John Henry Cardinal Newman, Sermons.[166]

1. SIMPLE UNEXAMINED ASSURANCES

DENVER, COLORADO (August 14, 1993)—On this the eve of a major Marian feast, the Assumption, Pope John Paul II issues forth a clarion call to the North American youth, if not the world, encouraging them to engage wholeheartedly in the struggle for peace and social justice. Tens of thousands of Catholic youth including many from Canada have flocked to what the mainstream media report as a major religious 'love-in'.

There is an ongoing struggle between the Pope and the media to control the reported agenda of the papal visit. His final talk from the three-day gathering is a hard-hitting reprimand on the subject of abortion.

The media have been trying to divert the pope's focus on youth toward the many issues it has identified as tearing the church apart—many of them sexually-related ones such as priestly celibacy, ordination of women, cases of sexual abuse by clergy, homosexual rights within the church and also abortion.

In the face of this, Pope John Paul II issues a call to youth about the evangelical nature of social justice work in the world today. It should be enough to warm the hearts of the Catholic Church's social justice community—those in the Canadian Catholic Post-Vatican II Church who have taken this call to heart for more than twenty-five years since the close of the great Council in 1965.

But, is it? There seem to be too many questions in the air today for such simple unexamined assurances. Is this call from the highest office in the church actually a furtherance of their twenty-five years of radical commitment to a social transformation? Or is it something else?

Is the Pope in tune with the phenomenon of the 'People of God' that sprang unpredictably at Vatican II—as if from the Holy Spirit—becoming known as social justice ministry in its diversity of forms?

Or, does this pope have in mind something more to do with a restoration of Catholic values, with a retrenchment of a new 'integralism' with its 'perfect society' concept of church: a model favoured by the 'traditionalist' and 'revivalist' Catholics who most favour the key aspects of the pope's overall program.

FALLOW TIMES

In Canada, in the early 1990s the social justice ministry of the Roman Catholic Church has fallen on fallow times. A 1993 series of articles in the *Catholic New Times,*[167] the country's national social justice newspaper, reported that at least five diocese have closed (or not restaffed) their social justice offices since 1990.

The Toronto Archdiocese relieved its director of fourteen years, saying that other related departments could pick up the slack; without any increase in their budgets.

Victoria fired its director of seven years; saying that it is awaiting the emergence of a new model of doing social justice ministry. This is in the wake of its recently completed five-year synod deliberation process where 'collaborative ministry' emerged as a key operative term for any new paradigm.

Saint John, New Brunswick, simply has not replaced its departing staff member after more than a year and a half.

Those are the reported facts, but a deeper malaise has also surfaced. Like the ecumenical movement, to which it is deeply connected, there is a sense of stall and discouragement in the social justice movement today.

For the first twenty to twenty-five years following the Second Vatican Council (1962-65), the social justice work of the Catholic Church flourished. It was the direct consequence of a release manifested in the emergence of the 'People of God' concept being integrated into mainstream Catholicism. It was a new Catholic 'way of life' for thousands.

At a 1971 world synod of bishops in Rome, the church stated that social justice work was a 'constitutive' element of the gospel, not a mere add-on. In other words it is an necessary aspect of religious salvation in the Catholic system.

The Vatican Council had deliberately enshrined this theological concept of the church as 'The People of God'. A biblically based concept, it took hold with a spectacular fervour in the direction of lay ministries, social justice action and the Catholic charismatic renewal.

By formally defining itself in this open and inviting manner, the church called forth a remarkable amplitude of energy, enthusiasm and adult faith development among the laity and clergy who were most in tune with this astonishing effect of the spirit. However, with the election of John Paul II in 1978, the famous year of three popes, a fly surfaced in the ointment.

2. A DISSENTER

At the Second Vatican Council, the record shows that the future Pope John Paul II actually spoke against the enshrining of this key concept in *The Constitution On The Church*, long held as the most significant accomplishment of the Council. The electoral cardinals seemed to forget that he had made it abundantly clear this was not the type of church he wanted for his native Poland (or the world).

In her 1989 book, *People of God, The Struggle for World Catholicism*, the late Penny Lernoux found this fact both extremely significant and worrisome in terms of the future of the church under John Paul II. Earlier in the decade, Peter Hebblethwaite, Vatican correspondent for the *National Catholic Reporter*, identified the problem in his 1986 book, *Synod Extraordinary, the inside story of the Rome Synod, November/December 1985*. This was the event when Vatican II began to be seriously contained.

John Paul II himself admitted in an interview that the cardinals did not know what sort of man they had elected as pope. As it started to become apparent what he meant, one long-term Canadian Catholic churchman commented slyly in the early 1980s:

"You cannot make a silk purse out of a sow's ear, and that's a biblical quote".[168] Karol Wojtyla was not going to continue business as usual.

THE POPE'S PROGRAM

At the very heart of the difficulty lies the program of Pope John Paul II. Penny Lernoux argues that he is an old-style 'integralist', that is one who subscribes still to the authoritarian model of church, almost the military model which was perfected in Poland under totalitarian communism.

The operative word here is 'perfect' as in the idea of the church as a 'perfect society', a characteristic of the integralist model in its classical mode. It was a view of the church deliberately eclipsed at The Second Vatican Council.

In the Pope's view, the western social democratic response to the contradictions of late capitalism, as embodied in the social justice movement, is seen as inadequate if not irrelevant. John Paul II's pyramid model of church does not mix well with the implications of the social justice movement—ecumenical, more democratic, open to women's ordination and grassroots consensus model of decision-making.

In the world today it is no overstatement to claim that the Catholic Church in Eastern European countries is the most backward in terms of the full implementation of the reforms of Vatican II, Poland notwithstanding.[169]

This condition of deepfreeze due to communism renders John Paul II highly suspicious of any Marxist influence in movements for social change within the Catholic Church. He and Cardinal Joseph Ratzinger have made very plain their distaste for the Theology of Liberation movement and its leading intellectual leaders, theologians who have come under hard scrutiny of Ratzinger's Congregation For The Doctrine of the Faith.[170]

3. THE CANADIAN CONTEXT

According to Gregory Baum, liberation theology underlies the model of social justice officially adopted by the Canadian Bishops, and by inference the Canadian Catholic Church.[171]

On the other hand, Baum has delineated the Pope's own remarkable social justice credentials as established by the landmark Papal Encyclical *Laborem exercens*, published in September, 1981.[172]

When John Paul II visited Canada in 1984 he definitely furthered the social justice agenda of the Canadian Bishops—liberation theology and all—with very powerful speeches, especially at Newfoundland, Ontario and Edmonton in Alberta.

At the same time, Pope John Paul II has given heart and limitless encouragement to the enemies of prophetic Catholicism. These so-called Revivalist Catholics are in full accord with any revisionist interpretation of Vatican II implicit in the papal program. They are also fully in favour of the Ratzinger initiatives at curbing 'excesses' by progressive theologians particularly in the areas of liberation theology and sexuality.

Catholic man of letters Garry Wills had John Paul II figured out from the start it seems: "I went over to Rome in 1978 when he first became pope. I wrote a long piece for *New York Magazine*, and I said he's going to be another Pius IX (the all time longest serving pope between 1846-78, and the most extremely reactionary)... Pius IX was uneducated and not very bright. John Paul II is very educated and very bright. But they both feel the world is against them and they have to be the last bastions of truth."[173]

CATHOLICS AGAINST THE CHURCH

According to Michael Cuneo's book *Catholics Against the Church*, a 1989 study of the *Anti-abortion Protest in Toronto, 1969-1985*, the revivalists identify the current pope as just the figure to lead a 'Restoration' to pre-Vatican II Catholic values which they believe have been betrayed and inexcusably abandoned.

The rise of this revivalist Catholic culture, called 'Catholics Against The Church' because of its alienation from the official church, especially the Canadian bishops, is in direct opposition to the Vatican II social justice thrust. This radical contrast was a clear prefiguring of the ideological conflict at the heart of the social justice crisis.

Using the abortion issue as a shibboleth for 'true Catholicism', this extreme right-wing movement within the cast of the old Catholic religious mentality grabbed hold of the moment under the current pope. While non-reflective of the middle-of-the-road Catholics, the revivalists are radically committed to undermining the progressive direction of the Vatican II Church.

The extremist pro-life movement, as described by Cuneo, concretely manifests the dilemma. He writes:

"In contrast to Revivalists, who conceive themselves as defenders of an ancient yet beleaguered orthodoxy, Progressives regard themselves as a Catholic avant-garde charged with the responsibility of advancing the process of modernization within the church that was ostensibly set in motion by the Second Vatican Council.

"Thus, they prefer a church that would have a democratized authority structure; that would give women access to the ordained ministry; that would accommodate a greater range of doctrinal, liturgical and ethical pluralism; and, above all, that would be broadly ecumenical."[174]

Gregory Baum's comment in *Compassion and Solidarity*, the 1987 CBC Massey Lectures, places the revivalist misgivings in the fuller context of the intent behind the degree of openness in *The Constitution On The Church*, by an acknowledged Vatican II *periti* (expert):

"It is no wonder that some conservative Catholics were unhappy with the new teaching of Vatican II. They feared that the Church had become excessively preoccupied with worldly issues and their relationship to outsiders. The true task of the church they said, is to proclaim God's Glory. They felt the church's concern had become too horizontal, that it should be more vertical.

"The answer to these misgivings is that the Vatican Council did make important statements about God. Implicit in the call for universal solidarity is the affirmation that God is graciously present in the whole of humanity. All people, wherever they may be, the Council proclaims, are touched by the Spirit and enabled, in a manner known only to God, to participate in the redemption made visible in Jesus Christ."

OGLE: AN EXAMPLE

Father Bob Ogle, the Canadian Catholic priest ordered out of partisan electoral politics by the Vatican, is a revealing example as a casualty of this cold war heating up. Besides the loss to the Canadian parliamentary process of this able figure, Ogle claims that the subsequent complete breakdown of his personal health was a direct result of the arbitrary order.

Ogle had been six years as a missionary in Brazil for the Diocese of Saskatoon and he came back full of social justice fervour. Through a process he outlines in his 1985 autobiography *North/South Calling*, he was selected to run for the New Democratic Party for the riding of Saskatoon East in 1979. Always a fierce competitor, he defeated a sitting cabinet minister and fellow Catholic, Liberal Otto Lang.

Ogle's stance on the abortion issue, as a member of a left-wing federal party, placed him in a unique and distinctive position to contribute the perspective of the Catholic-Christian value system to the shaping of the national debate. He explained it in *North/South Calling* this way:

"The abortion question didn't go away once the vote on the Constitution had been taken. It was a constant problem for me. Interestingly enough, I was never harassed by the pro-choice people. They knew my position and they never tried to interfere with it—probably because they knew it wouldn't change. I had discussed the question many times with pro-choice members of Parliament and other people.

"The difference always boiled down to a difference of language and understanding. One side focused on the rights of the unborn child to the exclusion of other factors—the future of the child, the well-being of the mother, family support. The other side focused exclusively on the mother—her circumstances, her well being, her future. They saw the foetus as an intrusion into her life. There seemed to be no common ground for discussion.

"The people who kept after me were the *Campaign Life* people, the militant wing of the pro-life movement. They were holding out for a total ban on abortions. Having observed the aggressive, implacable attitude of these people in numerous meetings when all three parties were present, I concluded they were a hindrance to the pro-life movement.

"They didn't understand that it takes a long time to change a law, and that it's better to get a little change than no change at all. These people, along with the people who didn't like the New Democratic Party, showed up wherever I went. They would argue that my being NDP was a sign that I was not sincere as a priest, because the New Democratic Party had passed a convention resolution calling for the removal of abortion from the Criminal Code.

"I always replied that I had made my pro-life position absolutely clear prior to being nominated, that I was against the party position and I continued to act according to my personal conviction in the House of Commons."[175]

Ogle might also have added that the CCF-NDP had a proud tradition of allowing dissent on matters of conscience dating back to its founder J.S. Wordsworth who opposed Canada's participation in the Second World War on this very basis.

Due to Pope John Paul's Polish political sensibility, Ogle was ordered out of federal politics, and his own bishop refused to go to the wall for him as he could have done in terms of the collegiality principle of Vatican II. Due to this process, Ogle's comprehensive moral perspective on abortion within the broader social justice context of being 'truly pro-life', was eliminated from the federal Parliamentary process.

It is difficult to perceive how this helped further the integration of Catholic values into the Canadian cultural milieu, an activity that is vital to the relationship between faith and culture according to what the Pope himself stated while in Canada in 1984.

Ogle actually had a well-thought-out position on pro-life and abortion. It reflects some of the deepest and longest moral traditions of the church on this issue. He spelled it out in his book:

"I took a very strong pro-life position. In my Commons speech, I quoted from my nomination speech of September 17, 1977, 'I will defend human life from its conception until its natural end.' I went on to say: 'This means I am opposed to: first, abortion; second, euthanasia; third, capital punishment.'

"And although I do not have it included in the document from which I read at this time, I am also against death from starvation, from war or from any other act in which the human right to live is violently taken away from some other person.

"The human rights which I support are: first, the right to be born; second, the right to adequate food, housing, medical care and education; third, the right to live in at least frugal comfort within one's cultural traditions; fourth, freedom of conscience, worship, expression, political participation and peaceful dissent; fifth, equal treatment in public job markets and courts regardless of sex, age, ethnic origin, marital status, religious or political beliefs, social and economic status; sixth, the right to social assistance when age or other circumstance made self-support inadequate; and seventh, the right to die with dignity.

"I believe that all human rights are all of a piece; ignore one right and you jeopardize all the others. That is why a single-issue approach to rights will not work. If we are really pro-life, we have to protect human life from conception through to death. This requires an active life-long concern for a just social system."[176]

4. REVIVALIST CATHOLICISM

The principal thesis of Anne Roche-Muggeridge's 1986 book *The Desolate City* (subtitled *The Catholic Church in Ruins*) is that the true Vatican II has been lost amidst the media-hype-and-jive version that came to be widely accepted as the real thing. An unabashed advocate of the counter-revolution, she spells out the tenets and sources of encouragement for the counter-revolutionaries without apology.

When Roche-Muggeridge spoke at Victoria in May, 1987, her topic was provocative enough: *Revolution and Response: The Lay Apostolate in a Revolutionary Society*, if somewhat vague sounding. I covered the event for *Island Catholic News*, and found it very difficult to locate what church she was defending against the revolutionary onslaught—it seemed to have totally disappeared.

I remember thinking that it is going to be very difficult to pass this on to her children when they have had no direct experience of it; nor are they likely to. All her responses seemed extremely emotionally driven, filled with archaic language and poetic imagery. Romantic idealism *par excellence*.

I came to the conclusion that she was—for whatever reason —inordinately attached to her experience of being Roman Catholic in the 1950s. She seemed to have a clear attachment to the romance and spiritual security of the era of Pope Pius XII, the quintessential integralist.

In her fifth chapter of *The Desolate City, (*her earlier book (1975) is titled *The Gates of Hell, The Struggle for the Catholic Church)* on 'What the dispute over *Humanae Vitae* was really about,' she writes: "The two principles of authority cannot long co-exist within a church."

THE POPE VERSUS 'THE PEOPLE'

The assumption contained in this statement reveals her permanent attitude toward the church—authoritarian, a-historical, *a priori*. In other words: What's the big fuss all about? There is really only one way to look at this, after all. Let's just get back to the basics, which have all been settled.

Paragraphs from my newspaper report of June 1987, read: "The speaker said it is the freethinkers who visualize the church in only human terms, who speak in terms of 'paradigm shifts' when they mean the revolution which threatens to wound even the true Bride of Christ.

"Roche Muggeridge explained she is in favour of 'the letter of Vatican II', that it is the 'so-called spirit of Vatican II' which has led to the abuse."

"She said the reforms will only come from the laity, whose job it is to 'save the essentials, pray for reform, and offer up the rest'."

PARADIGM SHIFT

While the term paradigm itself simply means 'pattern', in this context it has come to mean the dominant pattern of thought; so that *People of God* became the new paradigm through the work of the Second Vatican Council.

What is meant by 'paradigm shift' is something much more significant. We are talking here on the scale of the Reformation or the Enlightenment periods of history, a significant shift that happens historically only every four hundred years.

At a conference on the future of the church held in Victoria in 1992 on the occasion of the centenary of St. Andrew's Cathedral, Anglican Dean Herbert O'Driscoll, a poet and Christian visionary, presented a schematic overview of the past two thousand years. He concluded that once again humanity is in the throes of a major paradigm shift; another gigantic change of pattern is under way as evidenced by the breakdown of the global systems—political, economic, ecological, spiritual—and the emerging new thought.

O'Driscoll claimed this paradigm will combine the essence of science and religion in a whole new mix, and that the church's response will be very important to the shape and acceptance of the whole new configuration.

5. CATHOLIC POLITICAL MYTHOLOGY

The difficulty for the Roman Catholic Church in all this is that historically it has not responded well to change, especially massive complex change on this scale. The contempt for change, or talk of the nature of change, exhibited in Anne Roche Muggeridge's writings is not her own invention.

Her attitude is an accurate reflection of a deep strain within the tradition of the church toward the effect of shifts in the political order; especially in shifts to the left. The social justice movement of the Canadian Catholic Church moved much too far to the left for the comfort of its opponents.

Michael Cuneo writes: "As Gregory Baum has observed, the social teaching of the Canadian Bishops has undergone a noticeable 'shift to the left' during the past decade and a half. The emerging social theory of the bishops, Baum writes, has been under-girded by two ethical principles, namely 'the preferential option for the poor', and the 'value and dignity of labour'."[177]

The traditional response to this sort of flirting by social activists within the church has been the declaration that there is a Catholic middle way between the left and the right. In the integralist model of church, there is definitely such a middle way. This is not a new idea even within the 20th Century. However J. M. Cameron in his 1960 book *Night Battle* and Gregory Baum in his sociological treatise of the church and left-wing politics from 1980: *Catholics and Canadian Socialism—Political Thought in the Thirties and Forties*, have shown the idea to be thoroughly discredited.

In fact it was largely the collapse of so-called Christian Democratic parties in Italy and Latin America in the 1960s that gave rise to a fresh attitude in Catholic social teaching under Popes John XXIII and Paul VI toward socialism. Ironically John Paul II's stellar labour encyclical, *On Human Work* in 1982, advocated a humanistic, i.e. non-Marxist form of socialism.

At the same time, his new integralism presents a massive contradiction to this political option, just as the Pope's inner reservations about the central concept of *The Constitution On The Church* contradicts the fact that he was elected to lead the full implementation of this paradigm.

These central contradictions will not be resolved or rooted out during his reign. The question becomes: How much will be lost? How much will be permanently lost? What will be the extent of the roll-back? What are the prospects of recovery in the next papal era?

THE THIRD WAY

Another question arises: What's so unworkable about this third or middle way?

There is a residual historical temptation within Catholicism to somehow stand above and beyond the political fray: to advocate and cling to a mythical third way between the greed of capitalism and the tawdriness of socialism. Why cannot there be a Catholic integration of the best of both sides, a perfect society rooted in Catholic values and principles?

In theory it sounds interesting; in practice it has always abdicated to the right. The so-called Catholic middle way has always capitulated to the pressures of the powers that be; the very forces that gave rise to the prophetic resistance and condemnation that took the form of the social justice movement in the first place.

Such efforts have been tried and invariably found wanting.[178] At best they result in a questionable neutrality that feeds into the perpetuation of the injustice implicit in the status quo. At worst, they are a self-protective alignment with the ruling elites, manifesting itself with abstract condemnations and invocations to justice while at the same time taking no clear stand with the poor or the persecuted. Prophetic Catholicism solved this moral problem through a level of active engagement that clarified the neutrality question.

J.M. Cameron relates a pertinent anecdote in his essay *Catholics and Political Mythology*: "During the [Second World] war a Swiss priest was asked what he would do if there should be either a Soviet conquest of Switzerland or a Nazi conquest. He replied: 'If the Communists were to come, I would stay with my people, for I know I should be faced with an anti-Christian power. If the Nazis were to come, I would try to escape abroad; for fear I should deceive myself'."[179]

6. BRIDE OF CHRIST

A Jewish convert, who had been making a retreat with us at Maryfarm, said some weeks after, "It is hard to live in the upside-down world of the Gospels." Truly it is a world of paradoxes, giving up one's life in order to save it, dying to live. It is voluntary poverty, stripping oneself even of what the world calls dignity, honour, human respect."—Dorothy Day, September 1945.

As for wounding the Bride of Christ, Dorothy Day has a meditation on that from January 1967. The founder of the Catholic Worker movement at the height of the World Depression in the Thirties, she was the prefigure for the post-Vatican II prophetic Catholicism in North America and beyond. Her life of radical commitment to the justice and peace dimensions of the Gospel underlines her meditation:

"There is plenty to do, for each one of us, working on our own hearts, changing our own attitudes, in our own neighbourhoods. If the just man falls seven times daily, we each one of us fall more than that in thought, word and deed. Prayer and fasting,

taking up our daily cross and following Him, doing penance, these are the harsh words of the Gospel.

"As to the Church, where else shall we go, except to the Bride of Christ, one flesh with Christ? Though she is a harlot at times, she is our Mother. We should read the Book of Hosea, which is a picture of God's steadfast love not only for the Jews, His chosen people, but for His Church, of which we are every one of us members or potential members. Since there is no time with God, we are all one, all one body, Chinese, Russians, Vietnamese, and He has commanded us to love one another.

"'A new commandment I give, that you love others as I have loved you' not to the defending of your life, but to the laying down of your life.

"A hard saying.

"'Love is indeed a harsh and dreadful thing' to ask of us, of each one of us, but it is the only answer."[180]

7. THE SECOND POPE JOHN PAUL

The first Slav pope, and non-Italian one since 1523, was born eight years after John Paul I, on May 18, 1920 at Wodowice, an industrial town fifty kilometres southwest of Krakow, Poland.

From a modest family, his father was a retired army lieutenant living on a pension. They were especially close since Karol's mother died when he was a small boy. He proved an outstanding student and sportsman, keen on football, swimming, canoeing and later skiing. He also loved poetry and had a flair for acting.

At the age of eighteen, in 1938, father and son moved to Krakow where Karol entered the Jagiellonian University studying language and literature, excelling in acting and writing poetry. When the Germans occupied Poland in September 1939, the university was forcibly closed down, and Karol studied through an underground network. He studied incognito, wrote poetry and had an attachment to a girl.

In the winter of 1940 he was given a labourer's job in a limestone quarry and in 1941 was transferred to the water purification department of a factory. These experiences were to inspire some of the more memorable of his later poems.

In 1942, following his father's death and after recovering from two near-fatal accidents, he felt the call to priesthood. During the war he studied theology clandestinely until the Russian liberation of Poland in January 1945, when the Jagiellonian University was reopened.

Ordained November 1, 1946, in March of that year his collection of poems, *Song of the Hidden God*, was published. He studied at the Angelicum University in Rome, obtaining his doctorate in June 1948, for a dissertation on the concept of faith in Saint John of the Cross, that is, mystical faith.

He served three years as a parish priest between 1948-51, returning to the Jagiellonian to study the philosophy of Max Scheler, the Christian existentialism of Gabriel Marcel and also the personalism of Martin Buber.

During this period, to 1958, he also lectured in social ethics at Krakow seminary and ethics at Lublin University, becoming acknowledged as one of Poland's foremost ethical thinkers. On July 4, 1958 he was nominated auxiliary Bishop of Krakow by Pius XII.

❧❧❧

The pairing and parallels with Bishop De Roo are worth noting: four years his senior, Wojtyla was also made a bishop after only twelve years of priesthood. Both lost their mothers at an early age; both taught ethics with a special interest in social justice; both have a capacity for languages and a singular personal charism for leadership that caught the notice of those associated with them.

While De Roo was passed over for promotion and elevation due to his progressive positions despite his formal European manner, Wojtyla was elevated precisely because of his appeal as an eastern European traditionalist who put on a modern face.

❧❧❧

In his position as Bishop of Krakow, Wojtyla revealed himself as a politically astute and formidable adversary of the repressive communist government. On June 26, 1967, Paul VI named him cardinal after elevating him in late December 1963 as Archbishop of Krakow.

In 1960 he had published *Love and Responsibility*, a pastoral treatise on sexuality which influenced Paul VI in his work on *Humanae Vitae*. At Vatican II he became a prominent figure internationally. As a member of the Preparatory Commission, he attended all four sessions and made his most influential contribution to the debate of religious freedom, contending that the church must grant to others the liberty of thought, action and speech she claimed for herself.

After the Council he was active in implementing it in Rome as well as Poland, attending four of five general episcopal synods. In 1971 he was elected a member of the permanent steering committee.

In these decades he repeatedly visited North America, getting even better known. In Poland he co-operated with the Primate Cardinal Stephan Wyszynski in a broadly successful struggle to secure some tolerable legal status for the church from the regime.

In 1976, at the invitation of Paul VI, he gave the traditional course of Lenten Addresses to the pope and the papal household, which were subsequently published as *Sign of Contradiction*.

In the October, 1978 conclave he received an overwhelming number of votes (103 of 108) on the eighth ballot when no Italian cardinal was seen to be achieving consensus. So at a relatively youthful age of fifty-eight, he was made pope. As such he pledged himself unreservedly "to promoting with prudent but encouraging action the exact fulfillment of Vatican II."

His first encyclical, *Redemptor Hominis*, in March 1979 was an eloquent statement of Christian Humanism. His second, *Dives in misericordia*, December 1980, called on humanity to show mercy in an increasingly threatened world. On May 13, 1981, while being driven in a jeep in Saint Peter's Square, he was shot and seriously wounded by a young Turk, Mehmet Ali Agca. He recovered after major surgery, convalescing until October.

In his third encyclical, *Laborem exercens* of September 1981, (a commemoration of Leo XIII's *Rerum novarum* ninety years before) which he revised while recovering, he called for a new economic order, neither capitalist nor Marxist, but based on the rights of workers and the dignity of labour, insisting on the primacy of people over things.

Prophetically, his fourth encyclical, *Slavorum apostoli* in July 1985, appealed to the people of Communist eastern Europe to resolve divisions on the basis of a common culture and religion.

But John Paul's favourite, immensely successful, method of impressing his message on the world has been to make spectacular, skillfully organized journeys by air around the world. By August 1985 he had made twenty-seven such journeys including Turkey in 1979 where he attended liturgies with the Ecumenical Patriarch; Britain in 1982, the first visit ever paid it by a pope; and Canada in September 1984, when he appreciably furthered the social agenda of the Canadian Bishops.

As time went on the reception was not always as unconditionally enthusiastic as the more traditionalist elements of his long-term program made itself known.

The visits followed a common pattern, with the pope kissing the ground on arrival, saying Mass in front of enormous crowds, preaching sermons carefully attuned to the local situation, and giving full reign to his skills as an actor and to his outgoing personality.

Among the later biographies written of his life, was one co-authored by journalist Carl Bernstein of Watergate revelations fame. While he admired the pope, Bernstein revealed how closely John Paul worked with the Central Intelligence Agency of the United States of America in bringing about the collapse of the Iron Curtain in 1989. This in itself will probably determine that he will be seen by history as a 'political' pope rather than the 'spiritual' one he might have rather preferred as a permanent image.

In line with this, in his 1995 *General Encyclopedia of Catholicism*, the general editor, theologian Richard McBrien, summarizes the contribution of John Paul II in these words: "Although committed to the Second Vatican Council, much of his pontificate thus far has been dedicated to the containment of progressive ideas and practices following that council.

"For that reason he has been called a restorationist pope, a strong and deeply spiritual leader guiding the church toward a new century and a new millennium."

While the pope was taking the universal church in one direction, Remi De Roo was pushing forward in another.

❧❧❧

CRUCIFIXION — On occasion, there is the added symbol of the Holy Spirit balancing Adam's skull. These pairs of opposites then, only serve to emphasize the essentially binary system underlying the cross itself. The horizontal limb corresponds to the passive principle, that is, to the world of phenomena. The vertical limb denotes the active principle, that is, the transcendent world or spiritual evolution.

The sun and the moon are the cosmic representatives of this dualism, echoed also in the symmetrical placing of the Beloved Disciples and the Holy Mother (of opposite sexes) who stand also for the outcome and the antecedent of the life and work of Jesus, and hence for the future and the past.

The two thieves represent binary symmetry on the moral plane, that is, the two potential attitudes between which Man must choose: penitence leading to salvation and prevarication leading to damnation.—J.E. Cirlot, *Dictionary of Symbols*

Praying the rosary with members of the Catholic Women's League in Nanaimo at a Marian celebration in 1989. (ICN)

Chapter Thirteen: Gathered to the Centre

1. A SYNODAL CHURCH

In the middle of the key month of the year, the healing month of June 1997, something very modern, yet very ancient, took place in the Catholic Church on Vancouver Island. The bishop established his diocese as a synodal church.

The ancient tradition of the synodal church had been re-established some thirty-five years earlier at the Second Vatican Council (1962-65), the event which made possible this sort of restoration of the Roman Catholic Church to its most ancient roots.

Being a synodal church meant that the diocese was to be governed through collegial consultation at every significant level. Gone are to be the days when the bishop operated as some medieval ruler might, by simple decree with no necessary local accountability.

The evolution of the Catholic church to this point has been a slow and arduous process; and also been the purpose of the historically longest episcopacy of Victoria's fourteenth Bishop.

2. BEGINNING AT BETHLEHEM

It is Tuesday, June 17, 1997. At 9:30 AM thirty members of the Diocese of Victoria begin a day-long assembly at Bethlehem Retreat Centre near Nanaimo. They have been invited to this pastoral setting by Bishop Remi De Roo, who will be thirty-five years as bishop of the diocese later in this same calendar year.

The group representing every geographical region of the Island diocese is here for the purpose of preparing a final statement for formal promulgation from the eleven-year synod process which was officially convoked in 1986. It includes diocesan theologian Patricia Brady, University of Victoria Catholic chaplain, twenty-seven year old Kate Fagan, and reporters from *Island Catholic News*, which was founded in 1986.

Bethlehem Centre itself was begun that same year. The Island diocese had long felt the need for a mid-island retreat and meeting facility. Many in the more northerly regions—the Comox Valley, Campbell River, and the far North as well as the west coast—found it too far to always have to be travelling to Victoria to take part in overnight diocesan events.

Certainly the Island population warranted a second centre. By the middle 1990s the fastest growing populations centres would all be north of Nanaimo, two hours north of Victoria. In the four decades of De Roo's episcopacy Vancouver Island's diocese has prospered financially as well as theologically under his management. From a 'shoestring operation' when he arrived, the financial assets of the Catholic Church now exceed a hundred million dollars.[181]

His critics would state that this was through no fault of his own, it was simply due to the natural economic development of the Island, but the facts speak for themselves. Officially Victoria moved from mission status when he arrived to a prosperous if small unit of the universal Catholic Church. While his style of management irritated traditionalists and conservatives, the idea of possible mismanagement would only surface after he had let go of the reins of power when others antagonistic to his ideas were in a position to build a case against what they had not liked all along.[182]

Bethlehem Retreat Centre anticipated these shifting demographics by a decade and today it is being utilized for another future-oriented purpose.

In terms of population statistics, while the 1991 national census indicated that more than 90,000 people called themselves Catholic who were living on Vancouver Island, at this gathering the bishop discloses that only 30,000 of them are actually registered in parishes. And only a third of that number attend liturgy on any given Sunday.

The longstanding tradition of Catholics relocating to Vancouver Island to put distance between themselves and the institutional church continues from the earliest part of the 20th Century.[183]

More significantly, among De Roo's introductory comments to the assembly was his statement that he considered the Diocese of Victoria "now to be operating as a synodal church," the roots of the word mean "walking together," he explained, also "gathered to the centre of a circle."

The Catholic Church is conventionally imaged as entirely hierarchal but De Roo is calling upon the deeper tradition which Vatican II rediscovered for the universal church. His diocesan theologian, Dr. Patricia Brady published her doctoral thesis in 1986 on this subject under the title: *Has Anything really Changed?—A Study of the Diocese of Victoria since Vatican II.*

3. HAS ANYTHING REALLY CHANGED?

Between 1986 and 1991 the entire diocese underwent an intensive, structured, three-stage Synod process utilizing community development principles. This resulted in the animation of all the Catholic population (and beyond) to participate in this literally thought-provoking undertaking.

By this was meant not only Roman Catholics, but all those of good will, other Christian denominations, and some who had intentionally disassociated themselves from the formal church. It was similar to Pope John XXIII's ground-breaking gesture in his social encyclicals.

These categories included the marginalized in a number of senses: those impoverished within society, those who seek a new age spirituality and those alienated by the 'spirituality' of containment which is increasingly seen to be defining the Roman Catholic Church worldwide.

The initial two-year animation process produced some four hundred resolutions, suggestions, proposals and recommendations from the lived experienced of the participants. Local Sisters of Saint Ann provided trained professional facilitation. The third year was used to formalize the results of the very informal discussions held throughout the Island.

The final two years between 1989-91 involved bi-monthly gatherings at Bethlehem for approximately one hundred delegates who represented every parish, region, major organization, as well as many minor ones. It proved an interesting balance of efficiency and inclusion. Most conclusively the extensive exercise demonstrated the collective level of faith maturity steeped in the principles of Vatican II of the Catholic population under twenty-five years of De Roo's leadership.

Synod Vision

We,
the Synod of the Diocese of Victoria
reaffirm our belief
that we are created in love
and called to enter the Reign of God
through the mysteries of the Incarnation,
Death and Resurrection of Jesus Christ.

Through our common baptism in the Church,
the Holy Spirit empowers us
to witness to Gospel values
and to the wisdom of God
revealed in all creation.

We, delegates or participants,
commit ourselves to live the vision
we have prayerfully discerned,
and in solidarity with the oppressed
to foster unity
with all people of good will.
We invite our sisters and brothers
to join us in this quest.

Significant Shifts for the Synod

People:	from task to person.
The Poor:	from doing for to welcoming and sharing wisdom.
Ministry:	from tasks for others to shared service.
Education:	from information to formation.
Spirituality:	from Church only to all of life.
Power:	from one or a few to all sharing power and responsibility.
Decisions:	from decisions by one or a few to consensus.
Structures:	from maintenance management to transformation.

For a diocese its size, Victoria had a disproportionately large number of mature faith leaders due to De Roo's gifts. Adult education was probably his area of greatest strength. As laicized priest François Brassard wrote of De Roo: "The greatest personal and episcopal gift of Remi De Roo is his ability to teach. More than just communicate information clearly, he stimulates deep spiritual reflection... In terms of process, he has often preached collegiality and dialogue.

"When one remembers The People's Synod, the image of Remi quietly listening comes to mind. Rare was his intervention and it was usually to clarify an issue or to stimulate further discussion. Unfortunately, Remi is a bishop of the Roman Catholic Church with its present papal insistence on the administration and enforcement of Canon Law..."[184]

This synod deliberation resulted in the formal recognition of the eight major shifts of direction of Vatican II but at the level of the local church where the people actually lived.[185]

4. THE PROCESS

As a result the changes of Vatican II had thoroughly been worked through the whole mix of the diocese. A process of collective systematic reflection, employing adult education principles, and spiritual discernment practices (perfected by the Jesuits) arrived at a consensus determination for the diocese as it approached the threshold of the next millennium.

The diocese was well equipped to accomplish its end, having been one of the leading areas nationally in pioneering methods of adult faith development following Vatican II. Its level of faith maturity and spiritual development was found to be comparatively high due to the years of De Roo's leadership style.[186]

The very small size of the diocese gave it the flexibility to make a disproportionately large contribution to many of the emerging lay ministries including social justice, liturgical revitalization, parish restructuring as well as adult faith development including theological formation despite limited budget.

Within the diocese, the bishop's most significant, long-term contribution to the 150-year history of the diocese could well be judged this comprehensive shift to a synodal church.

The central shift within the Catholic Church as a result of Vatican II was precisely in this direction of enhanced faith maturity for the laity. The synod being the effort at comprehensive completion of De Roo's work in this direction.

THE PEOPLE OF GOD CONCEPT

Diocesan theologian Patricia Brady, in her published doctoral thesis on the development of the diocese after Vatican II, contends that the roots of the synod went back to an earlier effort in 1975, when an attempt was made to consolidate growth within the church since the Council.[187]

In 1975, after thirteen years as bishop, De Roo called *Interaction '75*, an event which amounted to a preview or mini-synod of the whole "People of God" on Vancouver Island.

"People of God" was the Biblical image the church adopted for itself at Vatican II. The image of a "People of God" appears more than three hundred times in the Old Testament alone, and is developed and utilized by many New Testament passages.

An entire chapter was dedicated to the concept of "The People of God", in *The Dogmatic Constitution on the Church.*

Placement of this chapter generated one of the most dramatic conflicts at the Council, with the eventual placing of it before rather than after the chapter on the hierarchy.

According to *The Encyclopedia of Catholicism*, such a strategic placement was to emphasize that the church is a community with a hierarchal structure rather than a hierarchial body with spiritual subjects.[188]

This strategic placement underlined that everyone in the community—laity, clergy and religious—participates in the threefold mission of Christ as prophet, priest and king. This principle of collegial co-responsibility is something that traditionalist Catholics since 1965, contrary to the Council itself, have found threatening to the church's traditional governance pattern.

In terms of the official teachings of Vatican II, the diocesan synodal process is for the purpose of offering the bishop advice. The Code of Canon Law which arose out of the Council does not require but allows it. Like Victoria, some diocese have used it in such a way as to involve a wide number of groups and individuals in the process of renewal in the local church. Some have simply gone through the motions with a rubber stamping single weekend to ratify a set agenda.

Under Bishop De Roo's leadership, "People of God" was fully celebrated as the emerging paradigm of self-understanding enshrined in the teachings of The Second Vatican Council. Its complete actualization lay in this lay-centred synodal church.

In his introductory preface to Brady's book, De Roo wrote: *"The Second Vatican Council was a prophetic period in the life of the Church. Its impact continues to be felt around the globe... The Diocese of Victoria has been profoundly affected by the Council. Many changes resulted in many areas of church life...*

"Vatican II was inspired to renew the ancient tradition of Catholicity, as unity in diversity, made manifest in the variety of local diocesan churches. Renewal can be recognized as a movement towards greater communion.

"It passes through four phases: a) structural reform, b) emerging lay ministries and small communities of faith, c) renewed growth of ecclesial mysticism, d) strengthening of the prophetic dimension expressed in social outreach by the promotion of justice directed to a civilization of love."

De Roo's "People's Synod" was the closing effort at consolidation of his 'movement toward greater communion'.[189] While this went on, at the same time resistance was allowed to happen within the Catholic Church on Vancouver Island, sometimes even within the formal structure.

5. TWO VISIONS IN CONFLICT

Twenty and thirty years after Vatican II two genuinely contrasting sorts of parishes opened a decade apart in the diocese: Holy Cross in 1983 in upscale Gordon Head, Victoria; and in 1992, Christ the King Catholic Community of the Comox Valley, four hours north of the capital, demonstrated the diverging ecclesiologies.

The divergence between them illustrates both the traditionalist shift in the worldwide church during that interval, and the radical developments underlying the diocesan synod.

Holy Cross could be said to have caught the final fullness of the last wave from Vatican II, while Christ the King reflected a new emerging neo-conservatism. This was in spite of their actual physical facades. The very architecture of their buildings belied the problem as much as the internal adaptation it revealed.

Church buildings constructed in the diocese during the 1970s and '80s tended to be severely unostentatious in appearance; so as to be purely functional in a contemporary way. Christ the King proved a departure in reaction to this self-conscious constraint.

For example, Trinity Nanaimo, Sidney's Saint Elizabeth's —starting from the time of Duncan's Saint Edward's in the early 1960s—and Holy Cross, were more all-purpose buildings than conventional-looking churches. Ascension Parksville, Saint Joseph's Victoria and Saint Mary's Ladysmith had been constructed along similar lines.

There was no set diocesan policy, rather the buildings style reflected the new model of church.

Toward the north end of the diocese from Victoria, Christ the King was an amalgamation during the 1980s of the three historic mission parishes at Cumberland, Comox and Courtenay. It featured a freshly-designed modernistic structure facing and architecturally reflecting the magnificent glacier of the Comox Valley.

Placed high on a hill, in a cul de sac named after a veteran priest of the region, the church building intentionally makes a statement reflecting a particular ecclesiology.

While Father Ken Bernard did the original spadework of the amalgamation, it was completed by a talented young cleric John Laszczyk; and that final ecclesiology was very much Father Laszczyk's.

A native of Duncan, of a traditionalist family, Laszczyk was an individual ordained in the early '80s but with a difference. Not a 'late vocation', at a time when young men generally were not entering the Catholic priesthood, he sought ordination as a younger man, flying in the face of the prevailing winds.

It could be argued that if De Roo were not quite so avant garde, traditionalist families would not have felt so pushed to react. Some such families sent their sons to study for nearby Vancouver diocese. Vincent Hawkswell, long time editor of the *B.C. Catholic*, would be an apt example of an antagonistic, home-grown, expatriot cleric.[190]

Laszczyk stayed however and became a priest under De Roo. In doing this task of building Christ the King, he formed a committee to work closely with a young female architect to put fresh ideas into the design and imagery of the edifice. A gifted individual with strong ideas about the nature and purpose of the church, Laszczyk had a strong influence on some of the younger seminarians and most of his considerable energy was neo-conservative in intent. At a time when the diocese had been moving in other directions, Christ the King revelled in a new face of defiant triumphalism.

Proud on a hill, as a beacon of Catholic truth in a secular setting, the church building symbolically reflected the natural glow of the facing glacier, but granting it a supernatural hue. The architectural design integrated colour schemes and a layered effect that accumulated into this mountain top theology.

A NON-PARISH PARISH

Holy Cross, on the other hand, was deliberately and comprehensively structured from the grassroots up, in its upper middle class and university community confines. Father Joseph Jackson, a retired African missionary, was the founding pastor. He was ably assisted by a Sister of Charity out of Edmonton, Patricia McMahon, and a younger priest, Leo Robert, the first university chaplain appointed by the diocese.

Robert, a native of Winnipeg, died prematurely at the age of fifty-three from a fast-acting, undiagnosed cancer just six weeks after being raised to domestic prelature status, as a monsignor, in May of 1990.

A dynamic personality, Robert lead a symbolic life, acting out the new paradigm of the church in both lifestyle and ministry. When he died there were three funeral events. His funeral proper was at the cathedral, while a moving memorial service was held at the parish.

The surprise aspect was that he had arranged to be buried in the Anglican Christ Church Cathedral crypt as a permanent ecumenical gesture. A third liturgy and testimonial service was held there.

Robert in many ways lived out the fullest manifestation of De Roo's model of church, so it seemed more than simply appropriate that his grave marker is a permanent symbol of the earliest daring ecumenism of De Roo in the 1960s.

In the development of Holy Cross, these three extraordinary individuals headed an ongoing discernment process at every stage of the parish's evolution. This included an ongoing determination whether the 'parish' structure concept was the appropriate mechanism to express the faith of founding members of the community. Some decided it was not and an 'underground church' called the Thomas More Society persisted. It was friendly to the bishop and he to it, calling it his visible underground church because he respected their freedom and judgment.

This was very much a lay-centred theology with all decision-making broadly based and integral to the vision of church which had evolved in the diocese over twenty years.

One of the key discernments was that the parish organization would not be arbitrarily divided along gender lines. This decision ruled out the presence of the traditional men's and women's parish organizations.

Holy Cross had neither a Knights of Columbus Council nor a Catholic Women's League chapter. This in itself indicates just how far from traditional Roman Catholicism Victoria had come. For most lay Catholics the Knights and the CWL were central to the identity of being 'Catholic', to the definition of being lay Catholics. In Victoria it was recognized that the Knights of Columbus in particular was still rooted in a traditionalist vision.

The men's organization never distinguished itself as having come to terms with the reforms of Vatican II. The women, on the other hand, were among the most co-operative with the reforms of the Council.

THE BEAUTIFUL POLARITIES

Jesuit poet-priest and anti-war activist Daniel Berrigan used to describe the divisions within the church as 'beautiful polarities'; beautiful in that they help with clarifications and provide valid reality checks. In Victoria Diocese De Roo did not strive to cover

over the differences but allowed and even encouraged them to flourish.

Traditionalist priests were allowed within wide limits to continue to practice the faith according to their outdated theologies. Neo-conservative ones such as Laszczyk were welcomed if they wished to be ordained for the diocese.

The freedom that De Roo posed was not a convenient affair or mere lip service. Even as an institutional leader, as the administrator of a large organization, he had little problem integrating his own spirituality which required the actuality of freedom as the basis for authentic spirituality.

(Novalis Publication)

A Study: The Diocese of Victoria since Vatican II

by Patricia C. Brady, Ph.D.

with a Foreword by Bishop Remi De Roo

(Wood Lake Books)

Chapter Fourteen: Spiritual Predecessors Cullinane and Charbonneau

1. PRAIRIE POPULISM

W.L.Morton's *Manitoba: A History* has this to say about the establishment of Swan Lake:

"The Plains had become one solid wheat field by 1881... East of the Red River, settlement stopped along the wooded ridges, for Manitoba was 'the Prairie Province where the pioneer had only to sink his share in the sod and run his furrow as he pleased.' For future settlers of the north and east, a heavier task was in store... In the upper Red River Valley... the difficulties of farming and living in the open, long-grass plain were overcome...

"On the Southern Uplands, while the good vacant lands of the older districts were being taken up by purchase or homestead, the general movement of settlement was across the Pembina Valley and northward toward the Tiger Hills. Beaconsfield, Somerset, Belmont, and Swan Lake date from these years, as do the French settlements of Notre Dame de Lourdes, Bruxelles and St. Alphonse, the last like some Italian town with church and houses huddled on its hill...

"While the farms spread over the province, the methods and aims of farming were changing. The subsistence and mixed agriculture of the first years of settlement began to give way to wheat as the railways furnished a means to export."[191]

Remi De Roo's grandparents originally settled in Bruxelles and Swan Lake in the 1890s, and in the 1920s his father was still doing mixed farming; subsistence farming rather than the wheat exports. As mentioned by one of his cousins in a family history volume, pioneer conditions persisted for Remi's generation due to the effect of the Great Depression of the 1930s.

The failure of capitalism in that region bred a deep feeling for left-leaning prairie populism. Taking the matter into your hands meant small scale collective action. Locally this meant co-operative stores, credit union banking; regionally it translated into not-so-small-scale action with the wheat pools and marketing boards.

Even the most ambitious farmers were well aware of how much they needed their neighbours. Others like the Catholic De Roos and De Papes had a special feel for community, and communal ways of operating as it was built into Catholic social teaching. An emphasis on the common good paralleled the Protestant commonwealth idea.[192]

On the Protestant side, it is no accident that the Cooperative Commonwealth Federation (CCF) was founded by Baptist and Methodist clergymen—in a heartfelt gospel value response to dehumanising conditions. The radical gospel roots of prairie populism was the focus of a political theology conference held in Saskatoon in 1977, organised by United Church of Canada professor of Church and Society Ben Smillie, who taught at Saint Andrew's College in that city.[193]

Nineteen seventy-seven was in the peak period of ecumenical social action on the part of the five mainstream Christian Churches in Canada following Vatican II. Catholic leadership was provided chiefly by the social affairs commission of the Canadian Bishops Conference chaired by Bishop De Roo and based in Ottawa. Social theologian Gregory Baum represented the Catholic radical tradition at this particular event in Saskatoon.

It would be difficult to overstate the importance of prairie populism in the formation of Remi De Roo's social analysis. It is undeniably the bedrock experience upon which his social thinking rests. If he had been made a prairie bishop, there would have been more implicit understanding of his strong left-leaning populist stands.

In Victoria however, with the Catholic church in such a minority position, 'left-wing' was viewed with suspicion in the Anglo-Irish Catholic culture because the westcoast was so politically polarized and the left in British Columbia was traditionally dominated by communists and radical socialists, not Fabian socialists.

De Roo's Manitoba childhood was grounded in a combination of factors including the absolute necessity of interdependence among prairie producers in concert with communal Catholicism at the village level. These factors were within the context of large extended families critically dependent on constant co-operation and common concern. All this was further compounded by the unifying nature of his European migrant family experience reinforced by their practice of the tradition of Catholic social teaching.

This crucible effect was quite complete and enduring. As a result, Remi De Roo had an almost old-worldly air of formal courtesy. It could be off-putting in the world of western Canadian informality, which he adapted to only in his own studied way. De Roo's childhood formation was more European than North American in its values, sensibility and Catholicism. Its air of detachment would have been a key factor in the almost uncanny objectivity of his analysis.

Catholicism, by and large, has not distinguished itself in its objectivity about society and its mores. It looks at them through non-rose-coloured glasses. Its leaders, with some notable exceptions, operate within a worldview that they may well have learned at their mother's knee. While bishops look like anyone else in a position of authority, appearances can be deceiving.

Blindspots appear in predictable patterns. Certain bias regularly reasserts itself in recognizable ways, such as clinging to archaic concepts that fly in the face of commonsense and reason, or an antediluvian obstinacy about a specific social issue.

For the modern listener it can be an embarrassing anachronism. De Roo was a refreshing change from the usual in this area. He spoke out of an exasperatingly contemporary sensibility. One traditional example would be the persistent attitude which Catholicism took toward depth psychology, viewing it with a fear that it would prove corrosive to religious faith. De Roo knew the difference between theology and psychology and in his later years as bishop took courses in Jungian and other human development practices including the ancient teachings of the Enneagram. In fact he became an Enneagram teacher and scholar.

An inability to fully understand the impact of technology on medical procedures such as abortion is another case in point. One of the reasons De Roo was suspect within the church was that he did not suffer from these endemic ailments of intellect and spirit. He did not spend a lot of time looking over his shoulder.

He was a leader in the fullest sense. He was prepared to explain and defend his newly arrived at positions on topics, challenging the conventional wisdom of the day within the church and without. Invariably he attacked it by broadening the perspective.

An example of this refreshing directness would be his Easter 1985 pro-life pastoral statement, *Our God is The God of Life*, which opens: "There is a mood running through contemporary society which is hostile to life. It is anti-life, almost as if the modern world was haunted by a death-wish. The dramatic increase in suicide rates among youth is one illustration of this contemporary despondency. Cut backs on various aspects of social security network which protects the poor, the frail and the handicapped, the marginalized victims of our competitive market society, are further examples."

"Pressures for a return to capital punishment, the nuclear arms race, the star wars campaign, are again illustrations of the insanity that advocates violence as a solution to violence, be it military, political, cultural or economic. These attacks on life in its many forms, economic, social, cultural, political, even religious represents forces of evil, modern death-dealing Idols, rising against the God of Life."

He was post-modernist in both senses of the term. Within the church he was a pioneer if not a prophet in honestly expressing his understanding of the nature and inevitability of change—social, personal, institutional, global.

The bedrock of this was his farmboy's experience and understanding of the meaning of nature. The influence of his childhood experience remained vivid to his imagination and manner of expression. As recently as 1995, in his talk to Corpus, the national married priests' conference in Victoria, he still liberally illustrated his ideas with distinct anecdotes from his rural Catholic ethnic experience growing up in Swan Lake.[194]

2. PERSONAL SYNTHESIS

Apart from its global significance, Vatican II proved his personal synthesis, rooted in this prairie gospel tradition. Central to his consciousness was the doctrine of 'The Church in the Modern World' with its emphasis on the revolutionary principles of collegiality and subsidiarity—'revolutionary' to the Catholic church—focused on bringing the church up to date with modern developments.

This fuelled his leadership experience internationally with an energy that often springs from gospel value social consciousness as spurred on by liberation theology. He was there at the beginning of a major paradigm shift within the church, and he was instrumental in its successful communication at large. The shift was in all the directions he had been preparing himself for, so he was a natural leader. The thrust was definite.

An unforeseeable development was the legitimation of socialism. So long the *bête noire* of Roman Catholicism, serious consideration of socialism became almost de rigueur in left-wing Catholic circles after Vatican II. After the Rome synod in 1971—which declared that the pursuit of social justice is a 'constitutive element' of the gospel—socialism aided and abetted by liberation theology would achieve a new status in Catholic social teaching. This development would eventually result in a reaction and containment that was more severe than perhaps anyone could anticipate; but for twenty years it resulted in a wonderfully unpredictable flowering of the church's social teaching.

APOCALYPTIC TRADITION

The advancement of the legitimation of socialism would set off a reactionary containment in the 1980s, but in 1977 at the political theology conference in Saskatoon, Professor Ben Smillie put forward the commonly held assumption and shared analysis which declared Canadian political theology a necessity in the jointly held social teaching of the mainline churches.[195]

In his introduction to the conference Ben Smillie explained that the thinkers at this conference "follow the western theological apocalyptic tradition, which sees events in history building up to an overwhelming burden of domination and oppression, and envisions a perfect community that follows as the passing of the old order."[196]

Excluded necessarily, he said, "are many Canadian writers who stand in a rational liberal tradition." The key to understanding this apocalyptic tradition according to Smillie is the "nagging question" of American domination of the Canadian economic political culture.

"This problem of satellite status, a kind of kept state of economic privilege, due to capitulation to foreign ownership" is a problem of foreign policy as well as domestic, Smillie explains. It involved Canadian complicity in manufacturing war materials for the Vietnam War, then just ended, supporting the American-backed overthrow of democratically elected socialist President Salvador Allende by General Augusto Pinochet in Chile, etc..."

The tradition that Smillie and De Roo follow then is in "increasingly strident opposition to the American domination in Canada."

Psychoanalytic images of its effect on the country, in line with Smillie's metaphor, include "arrested maturation, prolonged dependency" and finally "a mid-life crisis."

This "taken-for-granted mistress" status, theologically, is a moral disorder for these gospel thinkers. "Canada lives ... in the same condition as Israel did in biblical times when it considered itself free."[197]

❧❧❧

In the mainstream Catholic tradition, the equivalent post-Vatican II development is liberation theology which Gregory Baum, in his five part 1984 CBC Radio series, claims was fully adopted by the Catholic Bishops to the Canadian context. Baum explains that the bishops combined it with the 1981 papal encyclical *On Human Labour* to issue their New Year's Day 1983 blockbuster moral critique of the economic crisis then underway in western capitalist polity.

In these traditions—Protestant and Catholic—"Nations are called to account for their deeds in the name of a righteous God in the tradition of the biblical prophets such as Mica and Amos," Smillie says. Canada lives in the bondage of a "Babylon Captivity" in the "worship of fecundity and production, the Old Testament versions of idolising the Gross National Product."[198]

3. THE PROBLEM OF SOCIALISM

While Canadian Reform Protestantism has married up easily with various forms of democratic socialism, Roman Catholicism, until Vatican II, condemned even democratic forms of socialism as stepping stones to atheistic communism. It was to be regarded with wariness at best.[199]

Even today the stigma remains, hampering the more progressive voices. Criticism of left-leaning social democratic parties such as the NDP, as Father Bob Ogle found out, often takes the form of anti-abortion sentiment which is a cover for good old fashioned Catholic suspicion of socialism.

Gregory Baum studied this problem in his 1980 book *Catholics and Canadian Socialism*. He dedicated the book and most of the writing itself in the fifth chapter on "Catholic Support for the CCF in Saskatchewan" to a Basilian priest, Father Eugene Cullinane.

Cullinane, a very saintly man,[200] a teacher and scholar, did his doctoral work on the CCF. In the process he came to realise how much the party platform had been based on gospel values. This recognition and his own integrity cost him dearly.

As he tried to live out his new awareness—teaching courses at Saint Thomas More College in Saskatoon, speaking out publicly, following his conscience and eventually joining the party—he suffered grievously for his expressed views.

Largely due to the influence of powerful Catholic Liberal laymen, Cullinane was removed from his teaching position, removed from his diocese, ostracized within his religious order and effectively eliminated from any position of ongoing influence within the mainstream church. He was pushed to the extreme margin, although temperamentally he was of an even disposition and quite charismatic as an individual. In the end he came to live out an even more radical attitude in a Catholic anarchist community called Madonna House situated in the Ottawa Valley.

Originally an American from Michigan, Cullinane came to Canada to study at Windsor's Assumption College, receiving his BA and MA at the time of the start of the Great Depression, in 1931.

"The Depression touched his life profoundly. His own family was greatly affected by the economic disaster, since his father had already died, it was his task as the oldest son to assume a position of responsibility. At that time he learned there was something radically wrong with the current economic system," writes Baum.[201]

In 1932 he entered the novitiate of the Basilian Fathers in Toronto and studied theology there until 1936. "There he associated with various groups of people moved by the present misery and committed to radical social change. He was greatly impressed by the presence of Protestant ministers among the activists, and regretted the absence of Catholic priests.

"Yet some Catholics were moved by the social question and responded vigorously to the unjust system. Cullinane was particularly impressed by the teaching and the social witness of the great French thinker Jacques Maritain, who came to Toronto in those years. It seemed to him that Maritain's call for a new humanism (was directed) toward the struggle for social justice and the rebuilding of society...

"He thought Maritain was opposed to the free flow of economic competition, criticised the present capitalist order and advocated a more rational planning of production and distribution in accordance with the needs of the community.

"Later on in the Thirties, he saw Maritain exhibiting the extraordinary courage of supporting the Republican side in the Spanish Civil War, while the body of Catholic opinion was wholly identified with Franco's cause."

Baum's book, given the period under study—the 1930s and '40s—is necessarily a study of the few but significant clusters of dissent within the Catholic tradition. De Roo, despite his high office, fits into the dissenting tradition.

Just as the dissenting theological and social voices within the church of the '40s became the mainstream voice at Vatican II two decades later, De Roo's 1980s critique, vision and broader-based dissent is expected by his followers to bear fruit beyond the present period of containment. De Roo's strategy from his last fifteen years could be seen as a clever tactical maneuver to outflank the containment period, however, if it was, it was also to meet fierce opposition.

❧❧❧

Eugene Cullinane's identification with the ideals of social democracy was opposed by a group of mainstream Liberal Catholics in Saskatchewan. These pillars of the church pressured a seemingly somewhat reluctant Bishop Philip Pocock into issuing a clear statement in 1948, forbidding priests from getting involved with politics.

"We regret that it has become necessary to legislate that political activity of a partisan nature is strictly forbidden to all priests residing in the Diocese of Saskatoon."

Thirty years later, after Vatican II, these words would be repeated in the case of Father Bob Ogle who went so far as to get himself elected as a socialist Member of Parliament. However in Ogle's case the orders came directly from Rome with the local bishop merely wringing his hands on the sidelines.[202]

"Cullinane, a man of obedience," wrote Baum, "intended to follow the new ruling, but when a letter he had written prior to the decree was published in a CCF newspaper, the Bishop of Saskatoon ordered him to leave the diocese." This perplexing episode in the history of the Canadian church paralleled what happened to Archbishop Charbonneau in the same historical period, as though ordination vows of a voluntary nature could extinguish fundamental human rights.

Cullinane eventually joined the Catholic anarchist social movement associated with the Baroness Catherine De Hueck.[203] Started in Toronto as a response to the Great Depression, De Hueck's group eventually settled in northern rural Ontario and ran along the lines of The Catholic Worker Movement in New York where De Hueck had made the acquaintance with Dorothy Day, co-founder of *The Catholic Worker*.

While Day was a socialist who found herself in the unlikely situation of conversion to Catholicism, 'The B', as De Hueck came to be called, was a deposed Russian aristocrat from the Russian Revolution (although a recent biography has lead to some revisions of this piece of mythology).[204]

Madonna House, a Christian intentional community, undeniably persisted on providence and prayer. Over many decades this was the daily experience of its followers, demonstrating to them at least the radical truth of the gospel imperatives.[205]

Gregory Baum describes Madonna House as suiting Cullinane's journey: "Their Christian philosophy based on fraternal love, included a radical critique of contemporary economic systems. These movements did not favour socialism, as it was based on large organisations and thus could not be trusted... It was a Catholic anarchism that despised major economic and political institutions and sought the reconstruction of humanity through small groups, whose operation embodied a new logic of love and simplicity."

Cullinane lived at Combermere for nearly fifty years. Earlier he did "his doctoral work by interviewing the radical wing of the CCF in British Columbia, including Harold Winch who was portrayed in the mainstream media as 'Terrible'."

Cullinane wrote from his experience: "Even here in this hot bed of Marxist socialism, the CCF does not conform to that brand of socialism of 'Socialism' condemned by Leo XIII and Pius IX. The mentality of most Catholics I have met across Canada, including the clergy, is infected with a terribly distorted view of the CCF reality."

Cullinane was having to face a hard reality in his own life, as did De Roo in his own time. The facts of their hard study did not match up with the reality of a distorting infection of prejudice. Catholicism, like any other competing ideology within the western Capitalist framework, had to make certain accommodations that covered over contradictions in the prevailing culture and in effect legitimised systemic anti-gospel values.[206]

Towards this end Catholicism automatically pre-judged socialism. This would come to a head once again in the early 1970s with the onset of the Latin American based Christians for Socialism movement within the church and the global phenomenon called Liberation Theology which was altogether sympathetic to socialism.

Cullinane, the precursor, wrote in his doctoral dissertation: "The result is that Catholics generally are afflicted with a deep-rooted although unconscious prejudice against the CCF. It is virtually identical with the kind of prejudice against Catholics found in the typical Ontario Protestant of twenty years ago. Catholics by and large condemn the CCF for something it is not. They are enslaved by the tyranny of a single word—'Socialism'."

In Cullinane's day, the prevalence of the prejudice resulted in the Catholic Social Teaching remaining "a great untold secret."[207] It would remain that way until the arrival of another generation which, due to the change in attitudes of the 1960s, could be inoculated against the virus. But in the meantime, according to Cullinane, "Catholics tend to fall into a mould of political and economic thought quite out of line with that of the papal encyclicals on the question."

The prejudice blinded Catholics not only against "Protestant tainted CCF but against an accurate or true reading of their own social teaching." It was a persistent prejudice. Other-worldly Catholicism regularly reasserted itself. The conservative force exists side by side with the progressive. As Gregory Baum expressed the paradox: "While religion is usually a conservative force protecting the present order, there have always been times when religion was prophetic and utopian, when it released people from the present and instilled a yearning in them for a more just, an alternative, society."[208]

Remi De Roo's reputation was built on his leading role as the builder of this New Jerusalem. He is viewed by the public perhaps as a utopian idealist, who dedicated twenty key years of his life's work to inspiring and leading a social justice movement within the Catholic church. As such he became a symbol and a target. His last decade in office revealed undeniable signs of what was in store.

In the early 1990s the social justice substructure within the Canadian Catholic Church was virtually shut down and shut out of the central work of the church. This was a definite blow given the previous strong emphasis and full flowering of this form of action following the Council. However, after the mid-1980s, mainstream Catholic social justice activity became increasingly a casualty of the containment policy of Vatican II taken by the Vatican.[209]

4. ROOT OF RECENT RESISTANCE

After Vatican II, when the social teaching landscape was so obviously altered, when a transformation toward a greater openness seemed all but entirely inevitable, the same sort of prejudice (or the roots of it) took an intriguing tack in the winds of change.

According to Michael Cuneo's 1989 study of the question, contraception and abortion became the new shibboleths of true Catholicism for the popular Catholic social right. His book is titled *Catholics Against The Church*, referring to the right-wing resistance to the bishops' leftward slant. One standard bearer was Alphonse De Valk, who Cuneo calls "the foremost critic of the bishops' approach to the Canadian political process."

De Valk, a Redemptorist priest, forms an exacting counterbalance to De Roo in the area of the social question after Vatican II. Similar to De Valk, Cuneo is critical of the relative diminishment given in his estimation to the issue of abortion by the Canadian bishops. De Valk eventually founded a traditionalist monthly newsletter, *Catholic Insight*.

One of the fierce points of resistance in the social teaching field was to 'the seamless garment approach' to pro-life issues. The seamless garment idea was advocated by the Archbishop of Chicago, Cardinal Joseph Bernardin. It was an attempt to broaden the pro-life sensibility beyond the anti-abortion fixation. Pro-life in the seamless garment approach included all life issues from conception to the grave, including peace, poverty, capital punishment, human rights, euthanasia as well as abortion. De Roo's previously cited 1985 Easter Pastoral would be a key example.

Once the overall context had shifted, as it had with the reforms of the Second Vatican Council, then a 'seamless garment' approach to all social issues contextualized specific issues; and abortion suffered in its pre-eminence within the new perspective. This resulted in the inevitable reaction by those who could not (or would not) follow the significance of the contextual shift.

In fact nothing seemed to make traditionalist anti-abortion pro-lifers more furious than this seamless garment business. It seems to make them smell Satan. For example, Tom Aussenegg is quoted in an April 5, 1988 full page feature in the Victoria *Times Colonist* to this effect. The article was examining the troubled relations between the Diocese and a maverick right-wing Catholic newspaper called *The Trumpet*.

"One of *The Trumpet's* editorial board members is Thomas Aussenegg, who criticized St. Andrew's (cathedral) in Victoria last year for having "Satanic" influences.

"Aussenegg says in the latest issue of *The Trumpet* that a pastoral letter on abortion from De Roo is "at best lukewarm, diluted by unnecessary references to other unrelated issues" such as the death penalty and economic justice.

"Aussenegg criticizes the position that people fighting abortion should be equally vigourous in fighting capital punishment, nuclear weapons and other life-related issues.

"This propaganda should be recognized as a devious way to defuse the energy of the abortion campaign by imposing imaginary duty on its volunteers," writes Aussenegg."

❧❧❧

The seamless garment argument seems particularly touchy to traditionalists because it exposes their blind side and the fundamental weakness of the logic of their argument against any idea of extenuating social factors in the abortion issue. It is all much simpler if abortion is entirely isolated from any other social factors or related pro-life issues.

In his book Michael Cuneo does a good job showing how and why the Catholic right consider sexual issues such as abortion and contraception the Achilles heel of this 'false' sort of approach to church and politics. Abortion, for these people, is the ultimate measure of any sort of social morality.[210]

For the left-wing culture within the church, this sort of thinking constitutes just one more example of an obsession with 'pelvic morality' issues that embarrasses them. In the view of the Catholic left culture, this is an approach to issues that has characterised the narrowly self-serving and myopic view of the traditionalist Catholic right and its resistance to social change. Cuneo summarises the dilemma:

"There is no room then, in the ecumenical consensus for the abortion issue. The bishops no more enjoy being cast as cultural cretins than anyone else, which in the present historical period is the likely consequence of aligning oneself with the anti-abortion movement."[211]

This contrasts with the favour gained: "They have captivated the media with their economic critique, have won the approval and sometimes praise of their denominational counterparts, and have come to enjoy a hitherto unprecedented reputation for compassion. It would be difficult to sacrifice all of this for the sake of taking a harder and more visible stand against abortion."

Reflecting on each item listed, whether he acknowledges it or not, it is Bishop De Roo that Cuneo is speaking about. De Roo spearheaded the economic critique that captivated the media, he has been praised indeed from the early 1960s by his denominational counterparts, and he has been publicly typified as the compassionate people's bishop.

But Cuneo gets it wrong about De Roo's attitude toward the abortion issue. If he did not take "a harder and more visible stand," it was not out of fear for losing any standing but because it would not be consistent with his inner self and approach to the question of social issues generally. More to the point, such a stand would be seen as confusing the symptoms for the cause which in his analysis lies in the deeper political economy of capitalism.[212]

This is typical of the sort of misunderstanding of De Roo and his positions taken by critics. He was the consistent target of shadow projections by academics and ordinary Catholics alike.[213]

These were people who were ideologically opposed to his program and no amount of discussion was going to change their palpable ignorance or predisposition to the matter. They had prejudged the situation and with the change of atmosphere in the Catholic Church after 1986 they felt complete freedom to attack his record with impunity. Dialogue was not possible if only because to them 'dialogue' itself was seen as symptomatic of the blight which De Roo's version of Vatican II had brought into the purity of the Catholic Church.

Significantly Cuneo's book covers the period between 1969 and 1986. Coincidentally after 1986 everything could be seen to radically change. Pope John Paul II had been in office a full seven years and the dictates and repercussions of this were becoming apparent. His hard line of containment of the more progressive aspects of Vatican II were being fully felt.

This pope's program could be seen to have fully kicked in. A neo-orthodoxy and neo-conservatism, which in effect was counter to Vatican II, was being served under the generic title of 'The Restoration'.[214]

After 1986 Bishop De Roo could be seen at age sixty-four to start to retreat into at least a new strategy. The focus was diocesan or local, even if the program was along the same lines. He put his talent to work at shaping a diocesan synod that would bear his stamp and that of an entirely thoroughgoing accommodation to the more progressive prescriptions of Vatican II.

He was taking a deeper tack and the intent, upon examination, was the permanent establishment of a model of church that was entirely based on the Ancient Church of the first four centuries in concert with the reforms of Vatican II. His new program, one that might not be appreciated for some time to come, was the internal reform of the Catholic Church in accordance with its great moment of enlightenment at which he happened to be key player.[215]

Trumpet publisher Mark Toth in 1987 distributing his paper outside St. Andrew's Cathedral. (Jamie Jenkins)

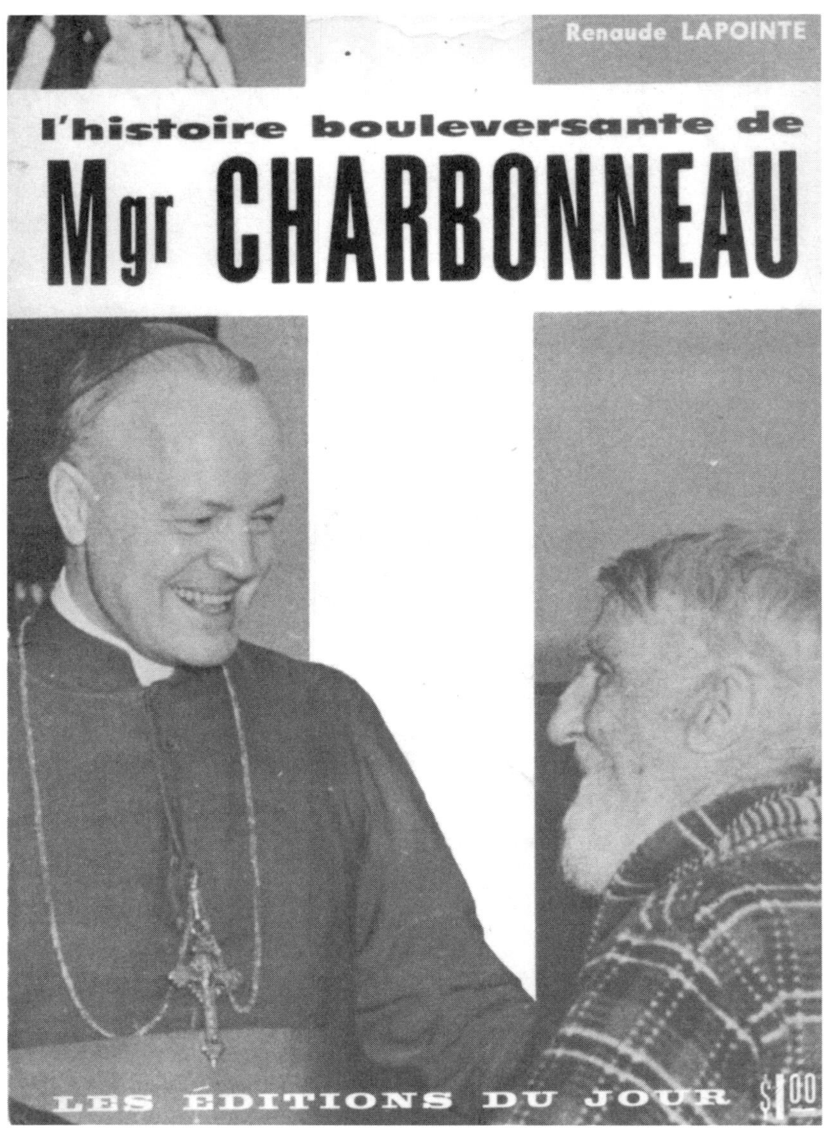
Renaude LAPOINTE
l'histoire bouleversante de
Mgr CHARBONNEAU
LES ÉDITIONS DU JOUR
$1.00

Chapter Fifteen: The Archbishop Charbonneau Saga

1. JOSEPH OF MONTRÉAL

The Cullinane situation revealed a recognizable pattern. There was a familiar ring to the fact of this struggle. Particularly within the Canadian Catholic Church in Quebec; and it would be especially familiar to Bishop De Roo.

"Joseph Charbonneau came into our lives in Victoria when he was required to retire from his position as Archbishop of Montréal," states Sister Catherine Moroney.

Moroney, a hospital administrator and health care professor, as a Sister of Saint Ann helped to care for him during his last years between 1949-59 when Charbonneau served as chaplain at Saint Joseph Hospital and Saint Ann's Academy girls school in Victoria.

"As I learned his history and observed his conduct, he became for me a living example of Catholic/Christian social teaching in action, and still more, in self-sacrifice," explains Moroney in an interview for this book.[216]

"My father who had been a college professor in Australia had a deep interest in this (Catholic Social) teaching. *Rerum Novarum* (1891) and *Quadragesima Anno* (1931) and their main principles were quite familiar to me when I was a teenager."

"Although many within the church made determined effort to teach and put them into practice, my father deplored the fact this teaching and practice was not more developed and deeply rooted. Their exponents too often met with suspicion and fear by those with substantial financial assets, and with an interest in maintaining the status quo."

By the time of this interview Sister Moroney was well into her ninth decade and living at a retirement home in Victoria owned by her religious order.

She said she was feeling some acute need to get her version of the Charbonneau story told publicly. One of the reasons Charbonneau would have chosen the Sisters of Saint Ann was their deep discretion about his right to privacy in his final years. Their distance from Montréal would have been a key factor as well. The Sisters of Saint Ann were founded and based in Lachine, Québec but had come to the far west in 1858 to Victoria to establish hospitals and schools.

Sister Moroney said the local newspapers in Victoria had established an intelligence system within the hospital to get them immediate information at the first sign of Charbonneau's demise. Such was his fame for confronting Premier Maurice Duplessis in the 1940s. Exile and ignominy in Victoria were his reward.

Moroney and the Provincial General of the 1950s, Mary Luca Kirwan, SSA (1953-59) had granted an extensive interview in the early 1980s to a Québec biographer but the material had not been published. 'Luca', as she was called within my family, was a family intimate from the time my mother had studied at Saint Ann's Academy in the late thirties and early forties.

My youngest brother Eugene, a freelance journalist at the time, keenly wanted to get Sister Luca's version of the Charbonneau saga but she took it to her grave. Catherine Moroney respected Mother Luca's wishes but being her junior outlived her mentor.

Sister Moroney's keen sense of personal and social justice obviously put pressure on her from within to tell what she knew. Moroney had served on the board of the independent Catholic monthly *Island Catholic News* on Vancouver Island and so utilised the established channels to get her story released and published.

The older generation of leadership of the Sisters of Saint Ann, including Sisters Moroney and Kirwan were governing the Order at the time of Vatican II. The change caught them like everyone else in the church unawares and the adjustment was considerable, given their vintage and formation.

The two previous bishops to Remi De Roo—John Christopher Cody (1937-46) and James Michael Hill (1946-62)—were far different sorts of men, though both were progressive in their own ways. These were the style of bishop the Sisters of Saint Ann on Vancouver Island were used to at the time of Vatican II.

The de-institutionalising 'boy bishop' would have posed a special challenge to their traditional sensibility. Some Orders on the Island such as the Poor Clare Sisters were small enough to more easily make a radical about-face in response to his leadership. The Sisters of Saint Ann had been in Victoria for more than a hundred years, establishing the first schools and hospitals on the Island from the pioneer period. They were a major institution in themselves, and ran many of them, including Saint Joseph's Hospital where Charbonneau lived and served as chaplain during his final decade.

Certainly Mother Mary Luca (Kirwan) was a strong minded blend of the old and the new and was known to express certain discontent with the disruptive effect of De Roo's early years of administration on the work and priorities of her Order.[217]

While she fully welcomed Vatican II,[218] Mother Mary Luca was always particularly solicitous of Archbishop Charbonneau's request that there be no public scandal about the way he was treated by the church.

However when Luca died in the middle 1990s, Sister Moroney had the leisure to rethink her commitment to such secrecy, especially in light of the admirable job she judged Bishop De Roo to have done in her beloved social justice field; and also in light of the obvious containment of the reforms of Vatican II which were befalling the church since the early 1980s.

When a Catholic bishop moves within his office to put some serious weight behind the church's prophetic stand for social justice, as Remi De Roo had between 1965 and 1985, he was bound to feel the truth of Sister Catherine's insight that not all Catholics are progressive idealists; he would discover rudely just how very few were.

A certain number have a large vested interest in the liberal capitalist system, and Bishop De Roo would be made to pay for his strong stands. This was not only nationally at the hands of the antediluvian Conrad Black and the anti-clerical Pierre Trudeau but in his own diocese where fund-raising drives consistently came up short despite special efforts. Wealthy business families held back their contribution as a not-so-passive-aggressive way of punishing De Roo and stating their disapproval of the new church.

Muriel Clemenger, the financial administrator who served with Bishop De Roo during his last fifteen years in office required a long time to understand this elementary vengeful attitude.

Clemenger, who converted to Catholicism from the Evangelical Christian tradition where tithing and extreme financial generosity were relatively common, stated that she felt for a long time that the problem must be one of simple communication.

However when a viable communication vehicle was established for the diocese in the middle 1980s and nothing really improved, she was forced to conclude something deeper and less understandable was at work.[219]

2. TRUMPETERS AND THE SWAN

"A Roman Catholic newspaper in Victoria has almost certainly broken canon law by speaking for the Church and challenging the authority of Bishop Remi De Roo, the bishop's legal counsel said Monday.

"Kevin Doyle said in an interview The Trumpet *does not have authorization from the Diocese and that its editorial views are its own.*

"Doyle said the paper routinely suggests that De Roo has strayed from the Church's true teachings.

"He said The Trumpet's *February edition compares De Roo to a shepherd inviting a wolf into a flock.*

"The most recent issue of the monthly paper accuses the bishop of being soft on abortion..."—**Stephen Hume, Times Colonist,** Tuesday April 5, 1988.

Island Catholic News, an independent pro-De Roo newspaper, itself had to struggle for its funding due to this attitude once it was perceived to be in favour of the bishop's overall program. In the environment created by the *Island Catholic News* initiative, an extreme right-wing traditionalist element in the diocese started up their own reactionary newspaper, *The Trumpet*, in 1987. However *The Trumpet* did not make convincing inroads due to its simple neglect of developmental strategy when becoming established.

That paper foundered largely due to its own insensitivity to community development principles. In a diocese where the lay leadership had embraced the value of consultation, self-monitored fair practice, doctrinal accountability as hallmarks of the post-Vatican II church—of how a viable project operates within the church—*The Trumpet* failed to take many fine points of such procedure into consideration. Theirs was the path of righteous indignation.

As a result many of the clergy became alienated by the perceived negativity of *The Trumpet's* attitude.[220] Lay progressives were alarmed at the implications for what they had built up over the decades since Vatican II. The advent of *The Trumpet* proved to be more a sign of things to come rather than the almost amusing anomaly it was seen to be at the time.

The Trumpet could be said to have been hoisted with its own petard. By setting up as an independent project which was not accountable to the local bishop, it attempted to utilise the very principles to which it was so acrimoniously opposed. As a result ordinary lay people became confounded by the message and ultimately dismayed by the self-contradiction.

In its odd twirl of irony *The Trumpet* brazenly used the reforms of Vatican II to argue for their elimination. In a church run on the principles which it advocated, *The Trumpet* would not have been allowed to say what they were saying, or do what they were doing; especially attacking the person of the bishop, whom they transparently held in contempt. *The Trumpet* phenomenon provided a supreme example of the sort of shadow projection De Roo would increasingly carry for the rest of his mandate.

Obviously buoyed up by confidence from hearing how the bishop was viewed in their own circles, as Kevin Doyle stated, in fact *The Trumpet* did go well beyond attacking him personally. Great details of this contention by the diocese's legal counsel were carried in the pages of the Victoria daily newspaper.[221]

According to Doyle, the editor and publisher came perilously close to attacking the very office of the bishop, an action which by definition would remove them from the 'communion' of the faith.

As a result they were ultimately threatened with action that might have lead to excommunication. Public knowledge of this information could be gleaned from The *Times Colonist* which did an extensive feature on the antagonism which had built up. The feature article included an interview with counsel Kevin Doyle (but not Bishop De Roo) who used the opportunity to issue a not-so-veiled warning.

This warning shot across the bow seemed to have the desired effect as the newspaper owners soon retreated out of the diocese. But perhaps the most telling encounter in this antagonistic atmosphere was between *The Trumpet* and the Catholic Women's League in the late 1980s.

After the Second Vatican Council no large mainstream lay organisation within the Canadian Catholic Church embraced the new model of church more comprehensively than the Catholic Women's League nationally.

After a few issues of *The Trumpet*, the Diocesan League President of the day responded, as reported in the *Island Catholic News*, to what she called "Negative distorted reporting" of the activities of the league in the renegade newspaper.[222]

Perhaps nothing could be so convincing an indicator of the success of De Roo's grassroots adult education program than this countervailing leverage on his behalf by the most mainstream women's organisation in his diocese against what became the most sustained and directly organised attack against his general program during his tenure as bishop.

The Trumpet represented the start of a portentous phenomenon in the Catholic Church during the containment period of Vatican II under Pope John Paul II. Its content was less significant than the very fact it would dare to exist, given its belief in the almost divine authority of bishops. While the genie of Vatican II could not be put back into the bottle, the right-wing resistance to its reforms took on this curious hue; they were empowered by the developments they detested.

Their rhetoric read that they were against the recent and widespread abuses of the reforms, but there was very little more abusive than their own distortions of the license granted. The irony was thick with hypocrisy and self-contradiction. The conservatives were indeed very liberal in their utilisation of the tools they insisted should not have existed in the first place.

3. THE POOR MAN

Catherine Moroney continues about the situation of Archbishop Charbonneau in the 1950s. The ordinary of the time was De Roo's immediate predecessor, the mild-mannered gentlemanly former college president James Michael Hill of Newcastle, New Brunswick. Hill served from 1946 until 1962 when he died from a heart condition, something he suffered from for a decade prior to his parting.

Hill would have been an appropriate and gracious host to the exiled archbishop; at the same time swallowing without any public questioning concerns he might have about Rome's treatment of the social justice martyr. Hill himself had been a leader as a priest in the co-operative and credit union movement in his home region of the Maritimes during the Dirty Thirties, to the point of being called a local hero.[223]

In her taped interview with this author, Sister Moroney explained just how the local media were alerted about Charbonneau's death before it was known throughout the hospital staff itself. The newspaper had staff vigilant to notify them of the first indications. As a result, moments after his death the administrator of the hospital received a telephone inquiry.

Moroney happened to have been the one in 1959, who passed the archbishop the evening newspaper bearing the headline announcing Québec Premier Maurice Duplessis' death. Charbonneau's reaction, which so impressed Sister Moroney, was to simply state: "Oh, the poor man;" about the individual who had engineered his removal.

❧❧❧

"Archbishop Charbonneau was obliged to leave his diocese and retire in the West because of his championship of workers' rights. As a true follower of Christ, he lifted insupportable burdens from the backs of the poor, and suffered crushing humiliation and pain."

At this point in a written statement, Catherine Moroney makes a post-Vatican II theological distinction between the institution of the church and the People of God as the contemporary Body of Christ. "He would always want us to remember that what happened to him should not be blamed on the church 'per se'. He knew that he was the church, just as every one of us is the church, each in one's own way.

"Those within the church organisation who bowed to political pressure and abetted his removal from Montréal betrayed the Church as much as they betrayed him, but he would never speak out publicly in retaliation for fear of increasing divisions that would mislead many people and alienate them from the faith."

This is an excellent summary of the classic rationalisation that characterised the thinking of the period on the problem. It also consists of a reading back into history insight derived during a later period of development. It was only at Vatican II that the church adopted the paradigm of self-definition of the church as The People of God. Prior to that the dominant image was The Mystical Body of Christ with its explicit top down model of authority.

In this sense it is open to criticism and yet it does express her deep sympathy for the man in his horrible situation, one that killed him prematurely according to the view of Moroney's Provincial General at the time.

Mother Mary Luca Kirwan insisted that "Archbishop Charbonneau died of a broken heart." Certainly photographs of the man in his final years reveal a thoroughly crushed individual, from the transparently self-confident prelate of a decade before.[224] Luca Kirwan served as superior from 1953-59 and would have been entirely privy to the most confidential information of his situation. It was her order that hosted him as their permanent guest for ten years and she spoke out of her direct experience.

She inherited the situation when she took office. The details of what she knew she took to the grave nearly forty years later. Although her 'second family', as she called them, consisted of a number of journalists—church and secular—she refused to speak of the situation except in the most general terms. She was possibly sworn to secrecy at the time, and came from a period when such oaths were permanent, their moral appropriateness never being questioned.

Sister Moroney and 'Mother Luca', as she always referred to by her close friend, did give a series of controlled interviews for the purpose of a biography. This work faltered apparently, Moroney reported, when Charbonneau's family refused access to his medical records which Moroney stated on tape "could have obscured the matter by an undue emphasis on Charbonneau's health issues." Moroney, who often spoke in set pieces of phrasing for sensitive aspects of the case, repeated that phrasing a number of times in the interviews and other discussions with this author.

Obviously Charbonneau's opponents knew they could utilise this attitude he had about avoiding scandal in the church, scandal which would weaken people's faith. It was an attitude used against him and in Mary Luca's phrase, breaking his heart, and his health.

The ethics of this sort of manipulation of moral sensibilities were an issue in the case of Father Bob Ogle when he was forcibly removed from electoral politics in the 1980s; and elements of it could be detected in De Roo's own case when he kept complete silence at the time of his own orchestrated discrediting after retirement.

Certainly in Charbonneau's case, the Sisters of Saint Ann loved, supported, respected, admired and deeply pitied the archbishop. Catherine Moroney explains their position as sympathetic and entirely empathetic hosts:

"When his resignation was demanded by the church authorities, however, he would not pretend he was retiring for health reasons or any other excuse. He simply came west, where the Sisters of Saint Ann had been asked to receive him. Their Superior General having been asked to arrange this, and he kept his self-imposed silence to the end."

Catherine Moroney described the situation in that deferential manner used by those who exist comfortably within an institution and therefore are guided by a need to balance the modicum of respect expected with any real reservations they maintain within; and so therefore need to speak in a necessarily modulated manner. Sister Catherine emitted an air of measured refinement that applied to her intellectual expression.

"Joseph Charbonneau was a tall, handsome man of great dignity without any pomposity. He had a warm smile, a twinkling eye and a hearty laugh. He also had a strong personality and a veritable passion for justice. His chief opponent when he was Archbishop of Montréal was the premier of Québec, Maurice Duplessis, a dominant personality of a totally different nature from that of Charbonneau.

"Whereas Charbonneau strove to lead the people through fostering a better understanding of their faith and the practice of justice and charity, Duplessis bound people to him by the fear that if they did not remain a practically closed society, resisting the federal government, they would be deprived of their language and culture and their religion would follow suit.

"Charbonneau's crisis arose from his championship of the miners working at the Manville-owned asbestos mines. These workers had no union or effective means of negotiating. In desperation they finally went on strike. Duplessis sent carloads of police to force the miners back to work. Charbonneau ordered that all churches in his diocese to take up collections every Sunday for the support of the miners' families. The battle was truly joined."

4. A MEMORABLE SUNDAY

"On a memorable Sunday the Archbishop spoke forcefully from the cathedral sanctuary during the Sunday Mass condemning the abuse of the miners by the government. A nun who was present told me he spoke with great force, at times pounding the floor with his crozier to emphasise his words. When the congregation was leaving after Mass, she heard a great buzz of excited comments and recalled one man declaring loudly and sadly: 'He's finished. Duplessis will get him for this. He will have to go.'"

The paternalism of the period is evident from Sister Moroney's words. De Roo would act out a different model from Charbonneau, but would be served the same fate, the passionate advocate who was blindsided. Charbonneau represented somehow a faltering symbol of a disappearing paradigm, one that Pierre Elliott Trudeau objected to as a clerical version of what he objected to in Duplessis; and he habitually applied the same anti-clericalism to De Roo.[225]

"Joseph Charbonneau's stand against Duplessis was not in vain. In the end the miners were allowed a union and certain other improvements. The dangers of asbestos were becoming well known in North America and millions of dollars would be spent to eradicate the problem... largely too late for those already severely ill... all over the continent workers ... claimed compensation. A few years ago the affluent Manville Company declared itself bankrupt, thus avoiding much compensation.

"But in the 1950s another result occurred. Through means never clearly revealed, the church authorities empowered to appoint bishops were pressured in asking for Charbonneau's resignation. For reasons still unknown he did not seem to have been granted an opportunity to make an effective appeal.

"It was a crushing blow to him as he was still vigorous and full of plans to lead the way to sorely needed improvements in Québec. Rather than make a public protest, he accepted his cross, came west, and dressed in a plain black suit, served as a teacher at St. Ann's Academy and assistant chaplain at St. Joseph's Hospital as long as his health allowed."

❧❧❧

The lesson of the Charbonneau saga was a well heralded lesson in the Canadian Catholic Church. A play '*Charbonneau and the Chief*' was published by a Dominican priest John Thomas McDonough.[226] It is one of those stories that does not go away.

On one level, the story itself served as the object lesson it was meant to, reflecting Rome's nervousness about clerics straying too far to the left in the political arena. On the other hand, paradoxically, it serves as a clarion call within the left culture of Catholicism where idealism is always tinged with a realism that crucifixion for speaking out is never entirely avoidable.

Often these sorts of removals were screens for theological conflicts over the nature of authority within the church. An earlier equally intelligent bishop of Victoria, Alexander 'Sandy' MacDonald was removed for challenging the prevailing notion of authority in the first decades of the 20th Century. Someone as politically susceptible as De Roo, a keen student of history, and formed in the period of 1939-62, was well aware how to tread softly in the touchy magisterial areas. After all he was a bishop, and there was the perception of transformation that characterised Vatican II. He was the one on the Canadian scene to see how far the Catholic moral critique of late capitalism could be taken, even in the face of the historical right-wing default position of Rome.

While the Catholic Church traditionally issued high sounding statements about justice and peace, and was the source of many a martyr to these causes, it would never want to be seen as playing into any ideological camp. Its justice advocates insisted that they stood on the firm ground of Catholic social principles, that it was the dupe of neither left nor right. Traditionally, however, as we have seen, this has translated into a permanent wariness of the left and a definite degree of self-deception that defaulted to the right.

English Newman scholar J.M. Cameron, American church journalist Penny Lernoux and Canadian social theologian Gregory Baum have all written extensively in recent years about this structural political problem of Catholicism: How this very attitude of seeming neutrality itself plays into the hands of the powers that be.

As mentioned, Baum's theological analysis of papal teaching on socialism exposes the default mechanisms in traditional Catholic social teaching, but J.M. Cameron's essay *Catholics and Political Mythology* may be more pertinent, examining the problem in the context of the Spanish Civil War. Penny Lernoux's study (*The People of God–the Struggle for World Catholicism*) bares the problem in practice since Vatican II, especially in Latin America.

For Baum the great pioneers in Canadian social teaching and action always took the papal teaching one step further than its original intent. For example Doctors Moses Coady and Jimmy Tompkins, priests of the Diocese of Antigonish in eastern Nova Scotia during the 1930s, pushed the Catholic teaching of their day well beyond its recognisable limits:

"The Antigonish Movement was created by two imaginative and powerful personalities Tompkins and Coady who were greatly disturbed by the growing Depression and powerlessness of the region. They devised a new philosophy of adult education, based in part on English and Scandinavian models, that envisaged a movement from the university to the people. Coady believed that people were intelligent enough, even when they had little formal education, to analyze the reasons for their poverty and organise for co-operative action. Coady presented his own ideas in the context of Catholic social teaching, yet went considerably beyond it."[227]

The same was true of Remi De Roo in the 1970s and 1980s. He too learned his co-operative socialism early; during the Great Depression as a child growing up in rural south-western Manitoba where the small farmer depended on interventionist economic structures such as co-operatives, credit unions and the wheat pool grain elevator system.

His life's work—his prime achievement in a way—would be to take post-Vatican II social teaching in the Canadian Catholic Church "considerably beyond" any previous parameters worldwide. His contribution amounts to a permanent achievement; a landmark starting point for the next stage of development once the present fog clears.

Contrasting features: Above, Archbishop Joseph Charbonneau in 1946, as self-confident chief pastor of Montréal; below, 1958, the year before his death, at a meal in St. Joseph's Hospital, Victoria, where he served as chaplain.
(Les Éditions du Jour)

Oblate Father Terry McNamara with members of the Cathedral Native ministry team in Victoria. (Jamie Jenkins)

With Oblate Bishop Hubert O'Connor at St. Andrew's Cathedral in the early 1990s. Rector Terry McNamara on the left. At right is Oblate Bishop of Whitehorse Thomas Lobsinger, who died in a small plane crash in April 2000. (ICN)

Chapter Sixteen: Traditionally Touchy Topics

1. THE NATIVE QUESTION

Douglas Todd has a section on the Native question near the end of his feature on the two westcoast bishops in the *Vancouver Sun*:

"Yet, despite discordance, De Roo and Exner have struggled together, on similar wavelengths, through some complex moral and social issues.

"The native decor throughout De Roo's office and home hints at his long history of action on native Indian causes. He has stood with native chiefs on Parliament Hill. De Roo, along with Exner, signed a statement two years ago supporting the creation of land treaties with natives.

"And despite—or perhaps because of—his radical reputation, De Roo has publicly expressed more reservations than Exner about how natives are trying to achieve their political goals. To De Roo, justice for natives definitely needs to be seen in shades of gray.

"Exner—who became highly sensitized to abuse issues because he led a national Catholic panel to combat priestly sex transgressions—publicly apologized, with all the sincerity he could muster, for the abuse of teenage female residential-school students by former Prince George bishop Hubert O'Connor.

"But De Roo, who has been offering O'Connor pastoral support in Duncan, has taken a tougher line. He says he's disturbed many natives have capitalized on sexual abuse at church-run residential schools to blame all their problems on Christianity and the federal government. De Roo criticizes native leaders who play up cases of sex abuse in the defunct residential schools "to the hilt."

"Some native leaders, De Roo charges, are promoting a 'victim' identity for natives to further their land claims.

"Similarly, despite his progressive tag, De Roo ... with Exner organizing an all-out push to stop the legislation ... signed a joint statement by B.C.'s Catholic bishops, which said that calling same-sex partners 'spouses' undermines 'the sacredness and indispensable social role of marriage and the family'.

"But both De Roo and Exner insist they continue to believe in full rights for homosexuals. And De Roo softened the blow of the joint statement further by issuing his own conciliatory letter to the homosexual community, suggesting its goals could be furthered by conversation with Catholics and by being sensitive to the church's traditional heterosexual understanding of 'spouse'."[228]

On these two issues, so 'touchy' for the church, De Roo combines his prophetic stance with the elder-educator role granted by the Natives (and his reputation for 'liberalism' in the gay community) threading a needle to stitch together a fabric of reconciliation without compromising the integrity of his office as a Catholic bishop. It is a fairly typical example of his creative capacity and reputation for finesse.

Overall it is true, as Todd claims, that De Roo has been a favourite with the First Nations people since 1962, and it is this reputation that allows him to play the creative critic part.

THE SPIRIT OF A DIOCESE

In preparation for the 150th anniversary celebrations of the Diocese of Victoria during 1996-97, Villagers Communication of Toronto was contracted to produce a half-hour video production, titled *The Spirit of a Diocese.* It was part of their *Catholic Journal* series for *Vision Television* and was broadcast repeatedly on national television. The video was in two parts: *Dreams* and *Memories.* It provided an overview which included a focus on historical relations with the First Nations people.

In the program, De Roo is recorded candidly stating:

"The relationship today between the Native People and the Church is going through a painful and difficult phase. The image that was given the Native people years ago needs complete revision. We came here with a superior attitude that had an overlay of European racism in it. At the same time, there were many Native people who accepted the faith, found it quite compatible with their own beliefs.

"We have a real challenge today, with our Native People, to see how those religious values they embraced could be experienced, more meaningfully to Native People."

Vancouver Island, under Remi De Roo, has been held up as an interesting model of integration of Catholic and First Nations spiritualities. When he first came to Vancouver Island he made headlines with his relations with the indigenous peoples of the Island. The *BC Catholic* of February 14, 1963 featured the headline: "*Ceremony in Big House ... 'You belong to us Indians,' Chiefs tell Bishop De Roo.*" The *Victoria Times* headline of the same date read: *"Bishop rides war canoe... Big Welcome given 'High priest Swan'.*"

White Swan was the name given to De Roo by the Cowichan in their longhouse ceremony. It corresponded to the name of his birth place in Manitoba and the site of his last twelve years in Victoria. The pastoral centre where he had an apartment overlooked Swan Lake, a wildlife sanctuary in Greater Victoria.

As Todd noted, De Roo especially cherished the keepsakes that the natives presented him during this inaugural stage. He kept them prominently displayed in the Diocesan Pastoral Centre. The glass case also exhibited the ring specially given to him at The Second Vatican Council by Pope John XXIII following an audience during the first session in the fall of 1962. The swan symbolism has followed De Roo since birth. As an archetype it reflects something central of his destiny.

2. SWAN SYMBOLISM

According to authoritative sources, the swan is a symbol of great complexity. For example, the dedication of the swan to Apollo, as the god of music, arose out of the mythic belief that it would sing sweetly when on the point of death. Almost all meanings have to do with its whiteness. In poetry and literature the swan is often the image of a naked woman, of chaste nudity and immaculate whiteness.

A deeper significance lies in its blend of masculine and feminine, a mysterium conjunctionis of alchemy. The movement and the long phallic neck is masculine while the rounded silken body is feminine. In sum the swan always points to the complete satisfaction of desire. The swan song being a particular allusion to desire that brings about its own death[229].

Upon appointment to Victoria, De Roo's mythological quest, identity and destiny became permanently linked with the original purpose of his diocese. According to its historians the church on Vancouver Island was directly if not exclusively tied to mission to the Natives.[230]

In the Villagers video, Cowichan Native elder Diane Modeste is quoted as saying that in the latest census ninety-two percent of the people of her Nation identified themselves as Roman Catholic. She said that through special efforts by the church the situation was constantly improving. One such outreach was the Native Studies component of the curriculum at Queen of Angels School in Duncan. There the majority of the student population at the largest elementary school in the diocese was made up of Cowichan children.

The best known Cowichan leader in terms of the integration of Cowichan language and spirituality within the Roman Catholic faith sensibility during De Roo's term was Abel Joe of Duncan. As early as the late 1940s Abel Joe wrote hymns in the Cowichan dialect; in the 1960s he composed and performed publicly a Cowichan musical drama titled TZINQUAW. Chief Tzinquah was a legendary early Cowichan leader.

In the 1980s the gifted Joe led the Cowichan Tzinquah dancers and drummers at all major diocesan liturgical celebrations at Saint Andrew's Cathedral and other key locations throughout the Island.

A feature on Abel Joe in the *Island Catholic News* just prior to his death in 1989 stated: "Abel Joe is seen as an example of the compatible qualities of contemporary Roman Catholic Christianity and Cowichan religious practice from the traditional period before contact with non-Natives."[231]

At his funeral more than a thousand mourners and nine Oblate priests from throughout western Canada attended. The clergy including Terrance McNamara, vicar for First Nations people in the diocese. The write-up on the funeral contained these words: "In the brilliant warm sunshine of the day, young and old, Native and non-native stood in silent solidarity in honouring the man who touched their lives with his cultural and spiritual gifts."[232]

However after his death this whole approach—manifested by Abel Joe's life work—eventually became controversial within the local parish community due to the same inherent conflicting visions of the church we have been discussing. Traditionalist parents complained that the school was teaching pagan myths, even to the point of the removal of one principal, a former Sister of Saint Ann, who strongly advocated the full integration process.

At the same time the progress continued on other fronts. One example is that earlier in the decade, in 1993, church property and land at Chemainus was transferred to the Cowichan Nation in the region as part of the same lengthy process of rehabilitation of relations.

The polarization of the situation was a principle feature of De Roo's final decades at Victoria. He continued with his program, and the resistance and forces of containment mounted as though heading for a giant collision which finally exploded onto the scene one full year after his retirement, early in 2000.

❧❧❧

In its fall 1995 edition *Mission Canada* magazine featured De Roo's reflections on his experience of Saint Ann's Native parish in Duncan. He said it was always "like coming home to a very special part of my family—my spiritual family," that part of his family which named him "Great High Priest, White Swan."[233]

Traditionally he would visit the Cowichan at the time of their Corpus Christi annual celebration "which is a very ancient tradition associated with honouring the Blessed Sacrament on a day of general rejoicing which included canoe racing."

"There is a longstanding tradition here of blending native spirituality with Christian liturgy. We no longer make the black and white distinction between the native mass and the white people's mass. It's quite common to have a blending of both with singing in native tongue as well as English."

De Roo was not always so radically open to such innovations. It started "shortly after my arrival, the leaders of the fifteen different tribes gathered and held a very special celebration at which time I was given an Indian name, Siam Lepletes Soken, which translates as the Great High Priest, White Swan. To this day, the native elders will greet me by the name of Soken.

"I came out of a fairly conservative traditional white society in Manitoba that had very little understanding of the native people. When I came here and met the different tribes, I came to appreciate in a new way their richness and their compassion, their sensitivity toward one another.

"As a result I have been able to acquire a much deeper sensitivity to the diversity of ways in which God can be worshipped.

"I recognize the living presence of God visible in Jesus Christ in my native brothers and sisters. They are to me Jesus in their own culture, in their own language, with their own insights. If Jesus were present in our midst, we would see him preferentially spending more time with those people that would be considered minority cultures.

"The native church has already influenced the mainstream church in Canada considerably, partly because they have given us a deeper sensitivity into the personal, compassionate and communal relationships which should be part and parcel of our religion. They are less hung up on formalities and on the strict regulations that sometimes mark our white type of religion."[234]

❧❧❧

Later in the same year in Hull, Québec Bishop De Roo apologized once again for the Catholic Church's ill treatment of Natives at a conference with national native leader Ovide Mercredi. *The Prairie Messenger* of December 18, 1995 had the lead page headline "De Roo apologizes to native leader."

"An emotional address by national native leader Ovide Mercredi, raised a Roman Catholic, brought an immediate apology from a Canadian bishop at a Sacred Assembly aimed at 'healing and reconciliation' between natives and non-natives.

"In apologizing to the native leader, De Roo said: 'Those people who told you the drums were evil, that sweet grass was evil, were not speaking the true Catholic message. They were forgetting their history.'

"De Roo said 'I stand here as a brother to Salvadoran Archbishop Oscar Romero who gave his life on the altar because he dared to speak for his native people. I want to stand here as a brother to the bishop of Chiapas, Samuel Ruiz, whose life today is on the line.'

"De Roo also said he was aware that some missionaries forgetting their own scriptures and their own history, have dared to make remarks such as Mercredi mentioned."

"They have mingled the racism of the eurocentric culture with the integrity of the gospel, and I can only deplore it."

"Turning to Mercredi, De Roo said: 'I apologize for the terrible things that were said. They are not Catholic teaching. I would like you to accept my apologies.' Delegates applauded as the two men shook hands."

3. A SYMBOLIC FIGURE

A key contemporary story within this context was that of Terrance McNamara, OMI. McNamara, born in Northern Ontario, served as a religious brother within the Oblates of Mary Immaculate, teaching First Nations children in various locations in the province.

After twenty years as a brother he sought ordination with the encouragement of Bishop De Roo. He was ordained to the Catholic priesthood July 15, 1979 in a Cowichan Longhouse ceremony in Duncan.

Seven years later McNamara took on a six-year term as rector of the cathedral at Victoria. While there he hired two First Nations women as pastoral agents for the Native community in the city. Other imaginative unfolding featured the commissioning of sanctuary art of Native design.

Charles Elliott, a Native artist and graduate of the local boys' school, Saint Louis College, constructed two large specially-designed cedar bentboxes as the base of the central altar. The eight side panels displayed Native images corresponding to the central Christian Mysteries. These are rotated in liturgical season and form a permanent aspect of the cathedral sacred aesthetic.

For an Oblate to serve as rector of the cathedral was an unprecedented and symbolic development. To do this he had to receive special approval from his religious order. Historically in this part of British Columbia, Oblates of Mary Immaculate (OMI) tend to prefer to serve in dioceses where the bishop is one of their own, such as Vancouver, Prince George and, at one point, Kamloops have been. Adam Exner of Vancouver is an OMI.

Traditionally Catholic religious orders of men have experienced a political conflict around authority when serving under bishops who are not a member of their order. Where does their first loyalty lie? With the local ordinary or with their general superior in Rome who has direct links with the pope.

In Victoria, originally the Oblates came in 1858 but stayed only eight years due to a conflict of this nature with Modeste Demers, Victoria's first bishop.[235]

They eventually returned to serve on the Island in more outlying areas in the 1930s, but in the church, history is not quickly or willingly forgotten; often for valid reasons. Normally to break a tradition there has to be an extraordinarily good argument.

Part of the argument on behalf of McNamara's serving as cathedral rector was as a symbolic gesture toward reconciliation during this protracted period of difficult relations between the church and the Native community.

However, this was not the only exceptional permission McNamara's 1979 ordination required. The previous year, 1978, the church had been shaken by the eyebrow-raising 'Year of Three Popes'. When the dust had settled, the Catholic Church had its Polish Pope.

A strong theme of John Paul II, particularly in his first decade of papacy, was that Native acculturation of the Catholic faith should continue unabated. Here he was following the emphasis given by all previous popes for at least a century and a half. Certainly it was a noted theme of the pope's 1984 visit to Canada.[236]

Terry McNamara, in the long tradition of the Oblate Order, became deeply immersed in the Native culture of the people he had come to serve. He was fully accepted and as a consequence he was initiated as a spiritual dancer in the Coast Salish tradition—one of three distinct Native Nations, each with its own language and custom, who have resided historically within the boundaries of Victoria diocese.

Having become a Native 'spiritually', ongoing accommodations had to be made to the protocol of the situation. As Pat Brady PhD, wrote in her study of the diocese: "Brother Terrance's initiation into the Long House required him to be present weekly during the dancing season (a period that extends fully between Christmas and Easter each year).

"This made attendance at seminary very difficult. Having taken this into consideration, Bishop De Roo permitted Brother Terrance to pursue his studies for the priesthood under his direction, with the assistance of qualified resource people."[237]

Patricia Brady as diocesan theologian was one such resource person. A condition of McNamara's taking on the cathedral's rectorship in 1986 was that Brady be part of his pastoral staff.

This major concession is typical of the attempt by De Roo at rectification of the faulty attitudes and practices within the diocese as underlined by diocesan historian Vincent McNally in his historical overview of diocesan relations with the First Nations people.[238]

Clouding this development, in 1999 Terrance McNamara was named in a residential schools court case against his order on the abuse issue, although these alleged incidents were eventually dismissed. A full blown reaction set in against extensive prosecution of the church as relatively 'easy' targets—as mentioned by De Roo in the Doug Todd *Vancouver Sun* article.

McNamara's fellow Oblate priest, Bishop Hubert 'Hub' O'Connor, was convicted. O'Connor has the dubious distinction of being the highest ranking Canadian Catholic clergyman brought up on charges of this nature; the only bishop to date. As this incident gained public notoriety, the media discussion revealed some of the hidden dynamics of the issue.

Doug Todd, for example, wrote a critical piece in the *Vancouver Sun*[239] at the height of the controversy explaining why he felt O'Connor more or less got what he deserved; that he brought it on himself due to his "arrogance." I took exception to this perspective as being too narrowly defined and wrote a lengthy rebuttal of some of his points. Some of this follows.

4. DOUG TODD VERSUS BISHOP O'CONNOR

There is no doubt, as Doug Todd wrote in his piece on Bishop Hubert O'Connor's conviction, sentencing and legal appeal tactics, that the Roman Catholic Church in Canada (and worldwide) suffers from a tragic prideful hubris, which is what I take Todd to mean when he uses the term "arrogance."

There are moments in the reading and rereading of the piece, however, when I wish Todd would hesitate and more carefully choose his terms. The piece jumps out in some journalistic cliches in what was otherwise surely meant to be reflective in tone. What it isn't is pastoral; rather it appears a moralistic diatribe.

It was handed to me as a former Catholic editor with the words that Todd had been very hard on O'Connor. From my experience, it is accurate and intelligent but entirely unforgiving, as matches the general mood in the country.

By way of perspective I also happen to have served on the board of a residential treatment centre on Vancouver Island for religious and clergy which we were forced to close for lack of utilization, particularly by clergy. Not one priest from Western Canada ever took advantage of the program, and this was during the height of the revelations of sexual abuse scandals in the late 1980s and early 1990s. This level of denial is indication of such hubris.

In actuality this particular therapeutic centre could not have handled those sorts of problem—though there are places that do—but at the time the irony of the situation did not go unnoted.

I suspect that O'Connor received the legal counsel to avoid apologizing at this stage. For lawyers the pastoral value of the apology would be pretty pale in its entreaty if it imputed guilt. This is just one example of a conflict of Christian values with secular ones brought on by legal proceedings.

From what I was able to glean from newspaper accounts, thirty years had done little to sharpen the detail of memory of the recounting of the actual events. So much has changed in that time.

The late Sixties were politically charged in the opposite direction from the 1990s which proved a period of conformism. Defying and abandoning the vestiges of authority were the order of the day in 1968. Today's blend of misdirected political correctness would have been laughed off stage then.

In the Catholic Church it was a period of intense change. It was the era after Vatican II when even sexual mores were being questioned. The ill-fated birth control encyclical would founder from defiance by ordinary Catholics in 1968. Many younger urban Jesuits of my acquaintance were seeking 'girlfriends', often as a first step to leaving the priesthood in droves over the celibacy question.

It is not difficult to imagine a young and virile thirty-eight-year-old Father Hub O'Connor looking for that sort of love in his own context; perhaps not exercising the nuanced ethical scrupulosity of the urban Jesuits.

It is not hard to imagine that he was even attractive to some of his charges. After all, the lines of authority were being blurred in the political climate of the time. It was a period of intense sexual experimentation, and democratization along lines of authority within relationships.

Even hard-bitten clergy were not immune, from what I recall. There was even a thing bandied about in the media called 'free love', or 'free lust' as the church might say. Heady times.

STRANGE AMALGAM

What would have been hard to imagine then was this strange amalgam consisting of a blend of simplistic gender feminism, Native liberation headiness, an ongoing credibility crisis within Catholicism itself, and a serious sort of late-capitalist self-righteous media triumphalism.

Admittedly it would have been impossible to anticipate how all these odd developments could come to coalesce to create a climate where the criminal conviction of a bishop (as a symbolic figure) would be their curious common conquest.

My own sense is that if O'Connor were not a bishop this case would never have come to court. It is not a case of paedophilia, there is no gay angle, it shows no sign of being a systematic abuse process. In its way it could be construed as a kind of a tragic love story. Looking for ecstasy in the wrong way in the wrong place at the right time. As one priest said to me, in what sounded to be a paraphrase of a line from *The Maltese Falcon,* 'We all have something to hide'; and he wasn't only talking about priests.

One of the reasons why Catholics are defending O'Connor is that it is the moment in the pendulum swing when a reaction has set in against the witchhunting tone of the media revelations during the past decade. People will only swallow so much of this solution before starting to emotionally rebel.

The only fact more obvious today than the vulnerability of the Catholic church on this question is that the media is entirely distant from the justice-seeking crusader force its proponents romantically see of themselves on their better days.

Sociologically, in time, the issue will be accurately depicted as one type of major corporation chipping away at another kind of large corporation, the church, at a moment of decline in terms of its moral identity and self-understanding. There is nothing more infuriating than an honest agent found to have feet of clay. Also, statistically, the media is staffed by disillusioned Catholics waiting their turn to get back at mother.

On some visceral level, O'Connor sensed the sacrificial nature of the bloodletting he underwent. While history and society will have their sacrificial scapegoats, they are generally not that pleased about accepting the privilege, even to the point of refusing to apologize.

But that is all right; in the Joycean image we have been able to claw out their eyes. If O'Connor is continuing to claim it was consensual, he may be mistaken but probably was not, at the original moment, entirely deluded.

Doug Todd hit the right note in terms of the Natives as little guys attempting to make a recovery in the face of what they see as the falling Goliath. There is a quote from one First Nations woman who said—"Somebody told me we couldn't challenge the Catholic Church because they have God on their side ... Now it's our turn..." It doesn't require the proverbial rocket scientist to see the seeds of the cyclic rise of a parallel sort of tragic pride.

THE INEFFABLE EXPERIENCE

None of this, of course, has anything to do with authentic religious experience. The ineffable experience of God—as being what religion and spirituality are about—gets lost to view when secular values dominate the perspective. An authentic religious healing has yet to begin on the grand scale between the First Nations people and the church due to all the revisionist anti-colonialist headlines that grabbed centre stage so lamentably, so tragically.

Contrary to Todd's contention, I would claim that the Catholic Church never for a moment understood its role in terms of running residential schools "whose express purpose was to assimilate Indians to European Christian culture," to quote the writer.

The self-understanding of the missionary church in these parts was to bring the Catholic faith in all its triumphalism and shadow, in all its streams of living water and heroic self-sacrificial grandeur, to a people the church felt deserved to have a share in it.

Certainly the cultural baggage came along with it but to maintain that political assimilation was the church's primary purpose is absurd. The church was also hoping to convert the pioneer culture and the nation-state to other values. All the early bishops on Vancouver Island were strongly counter-cultural that way.[240] Certainly Remi De Roo was.

The Second Vatican Council radically and permanently altered the offending triumphalist self-understanding of the Catholic Church. One of the beneficiaries of this attack on paternalism was the Native church worldwide. One of the big-time losers has been the clergy in that their clear roles, prestige, and sense of identity underwent a massive decline which has yet to be properly addressed by the church despite Pope John Paul II's muscular willfulness.

Hubert O'Connor may have taken some faulty action due in part to the confusion this shift created. Beyond the actual incident of the episode, he is largely a sacrificial figure, a scapegoat for a society that is a long way from developing proper procedures to sort through the various levels of culpability in these cases. Until it does there will be a disproportionate degree of blaming; the victims of which—whether First Nations or clergy—will never be satisfied that full justice has been achieved.

5. THE UNION OF OPPOSITES

The myth of the beautiful dying song of the swan appears frequently in Greek and Latin literature and was believed by Socrates, Plato, Ovid and many others, though Pliny expresses doubt about it.

This myth gave rise to the swan's symbolism as bird of the muses. Socrates said that the swan's dying song was one of joy at the prospect of going to its divinity, whose messenger it was.

This section of an entry from a dictionary of symbols[241] underlines a significance that may lend particular relevance to De Roo's life if you happen to subscribe to a certain symbolic analysis of his life and work.

The ambivalent implication—masculine with feminine—of the swan was also well known to the alchemists, who compared it with 'philosophical mercury', the mystic centre and the union of opposites, an interpretation entirely in accord with its archetypal connotation.

This entry goes on to say that the essential symbols of the mystic journey to the other world are the swan and the harp. This would afford another explanation of the mysterious song of the dying swan:

The swan also has bearing upon the peacock, although the situation is reversed. One well known representation of the peacock's meaning is as a sign of the Second Coming of Christ but also as a symbol of immortality and of the incorruptible soul.

The swan/harp relationship, corresponding to the axis fire/water, denotes melancholy and passion, self-sacrifice and the way of tragic art and martyrdom. Conversely the peacock/lute relationship, linked with air/earth is a presentation of logical thought.

If it was the horse that pulled the Sun-gods chariot by day, it was the swan that hauled his bark over waters by night; an allusion useful to the concept of the night battle.[242]

❧❧❧

Remi De Roo's paradoxical life as a conservative who chose a radical left-wing path and therefore possibly planted the seeds of his own reversal can only be properly understood by an in-depth symbolic analysis.

This is in addition to his unequivocal commitment to the Christian mysteries which are centred on the inescapable death and resurrection cycle.

If you profess belief and attachment to such dimensions of reality, they will doubtless at some point come to claim you. The question becomes how are we to understand them in the concrete experience of our mundane life.

How will 'the world' work out its revenge on the holy, in an attempt to claim its innocence with profane experience.

❧❧❧

Despite De Roo's success as a symbolic figure of change in a huge institution undergoing massive internal transformation to its self-understanding, his life's journey was not simply scripted to allow him to set off quietly into the sunset at the time of his retirement.

Other forces were still actively at work, exacting and extracting a price as the cost for so long defying the traditionalist gods and political fates.

De Roo may have been a successful post-modernist figure but the pain and problems of modernism within 20th Century Roman Catholicism would not be that easy to elude through the mere intellectual and moral transcendence that his program manifested in the eyes of his followers.

In the eyes of his enemies within the church he had not so much transcended the model they professed to believe in but he had transgressed lines of authority that define their spiritual life. Therefore he must be brought to heel, if only as an example to the future.

He was not so much a prophetic figure in their eyes as a perverse one. Larry Henderson's woeful yet gloating backpage editorial in the September 2000 *Challenge Magazine*, the country's most consistently cynical traditionalist organ, expressed a nearly demented and definitely dishonest perspective this way:

"It has to be said. The tragedy of our time has been written by those who did not believe. How terribly sad that the bishop who once believed should be the one who gambled away the life savings of the poor. Yet this story is a very important one to be learned.

"When faith goes, everything goes. A priest may once have been the best and brightest of his kind. He rose like a shooting star. And then he discovered how easy it was to fool the world.

"He backed popular causes. He addressed women's movements that demanded women's ordination. He experimented with liturgy. He promoted infidelity. And finally he took money from a closed convent and used it to invest in Arabian horses.

"And all while he saw himself as conscience of the church, always in advance of his times, proposing deviations in belief which upset his people, advocating social experiments which caused defection among his priests.

"Such is the story of many a stormy petrel, who has caused an enormous loss of confidence in the Church, and thinned the ranks of the faithful."

❧❧❧

Now that his active career was complete, the revisionism must begin, his legacy must be expunged, the orchestrated discrediting would be played out. The ghost of 19th Century modernism—a ghost of a ghost—reaching into the 21st Century.

Henderson, a former television news broadcaster who stayed in those trenches a touch too long, becoming a somewhat celebrated right-wing convert to Catholicism, has a field day with De Roo's post-retirement discrediting headlines with his mix of inaccurate generalizations and misdirected shadow projections.

"So why is it happening? I have seen a great deal of this in my life's work, and I have to say it is due to a character flaw which should have been spotted right from the start: the desire to shine, to be popular, to be famous, to be thought intelligent, in a word to be a "front runner..."

"Everyone wants to put God in His place. And where does it all end? In betting on Arabian horses. Now let me tell you something. The age of the front runner and the personality kid is about over."

❧❧❧

The swan was also dedicated to Apollo as it came from the hyper-boreal regions and as a lover of music it was associated with the Omphalos at Delphi; one legend said the soul of Apollo passed into a swan.

Poets were also likened to swans for their sweet songs. Pindar and Virgil were examples of this, Zeno was called the 'learned swan' and Shakespeare the 'Swan of Avon'.

Chapter Seventeen: Traditionally Touchy Topics: Two

1. TRADITIONALISM VERSUS MODERNISM

"As I remember, James Michael Hill died suddenly in 1962. That kindly man had guided this diocese for sixteen years. Clergy, civil dignitaries and others whose lives he had touched filled the cathedral for his funeral. People gathered outside to pay their respects as the city virtually stood still in respect for this man. Those we call 'street people' lined the sidewalk as the funeral made its way to Ross Bay Cemetery—evidence of who he talked to on his long and solitary evening walks."

Monsignor William Bulloch in his candid memoirs *As I Remember* was in a key position to appreciate the change when Remi De Roo replaced a very different sort of bishop, James Michael Hill. Hill happened to have been a former president of the small Catholic university which I attended in the Maritimes between 1969-72.

In the history of Saint Thomas University in New Brunswick, Father Hill is featured as quite an important figure, a 'hero' in the view of many of the English Catholics of that province. This was certainly the view of the author James Fraser, a friend and classmate of mine who wrote this history book during the period we attended STU.

Bishop Hill (1946-62) was deeply committed to the social teachings of the church. This was due to his experience of the Depression Thirties in the Miramichi region of New Brunswick. The Miramichi is still one of many 'poverty pockets' in the province and certainly was during the time I took community development training as a young graduate of Saint Thomas between 1972-75.

Saint Thomas is a sort of younger cousin of Saint Francis Xavier University in eastern Nova Scotia. There the world-famous Antigonish Movement of the Thirties and Forties was, according to

Gregory Baum, "a unique Catholic social experiment of religious materialism."[243]

The Antigonish Movement benefitted the entire region economically[244] and established a permanent infrastructure and attitude about faith and politics in The Maritimes. The success of the movement proved prophetic and enabled other progressive Catholic initiatives in the health care and educational fields there and elsewhere.[245]

In 1986, after the *Ethical Reflections* furore started to subside, St. F X granted Remi De Roo an honourary doctorate in recognition of his contribution to the socially progressive tradition of the Canadian church.

I happened to serve for four years as a social animator with the Catholic Church in the Diocese of Antigonish just prior to moving to Victoria in 1986 and was very impressed with how closely the Catholic clergy in that region could relate to the broader community and were accepted as leaders of such.

For me it was an easy transition to relocate to the style of De Roo on Vancouver Island after Cape Breton. One of the reasons for this close and continuous integration of the priests with the needs of the wider community in Cape Breton was because more than half the population of the region is Roman Catholic and therefore, in its values, is a social democratic culture like Québec. It is the only English-speaking Catholic diocese in Canada where the majority of the population is Roman Catholic. As a result, unlike Victoria, the Catholic culture is self-confident and not readily psychologically threatened.

Also as a result the overlap between the two communities is natural. Since the Catholic population is of highland Scot extraction, mixed with French Acadians, there was a 'natural' openness to the changes of Vatican II when it occurred. The Scottish clan structure is an organically-occurring type of collegial system where the people (with the clergy and religious) are fiercely loyal to the bishop as their chief, but at the same time they reserve the right to forthrightly challenge this same leader.

Bishop William Power originally of Montréal told me he had a very difficult time adjusting to this reality upon being appointed from the Irish Catholic culture of English Montréal where the priest is regarded as a small god, above such candid confrontation.

By comparison De Roo adapted his Belgian-Francophone sensibility into the middle of an English enclave on Vancouver Island. There the church consists of strong contingents of Irish Catholics and the English Roman Church mixed with a few other minority European ethnics, including Croats, Portuguese and Italians.

It was never exactly a marriage made in heaven. To the Anglo majority De Roo would have been considered 'French'.

Monsignor Bulloch gives his impressions:

"Remi Joseph De Roo was ordained bishop of Victoria in the cathedral at Saint Boniface, Manitoba on December 14, 1962 and took possession of his diocese in St. Andrew's Cathedral a few days later. A new regime and a new era had begun.

"The Second Vatican Council was in full swing. Pope John XXIII had called our new bishop to Rome and named him the Benjamin of all bishops for indeed, he was the youngest ..."

One gains the strong impression from Bulloch's autobiography that as a convert to Catholicism he reserved judgment on bishops as something of a necessary evil, with their arbitrary power over his life.

"I did not look forward to being rector of Saint Andrew's Cathedral. Memories of the time I had spent there when I first came to Victoria were not pleasant and I did not expect that much had altered in the interim. I drove into the Cathedral's dirt parking lot. The bricks of the cathedral were still grimy with age. It was not a scene to inspire enthusiasm.

"Home was a suite on the third floor. It was at the front of the house where you could hear the sound of everything that went on in the street, day and night. One window faced the beauty of the cathedral's back wall.[246]

"Bishop Remi De Roo did not live at the rectory, but was settled in a house on Arbutus Road. But I knew that he would breathe down my neck from time to time. After all he was the bishop... But... usually he allowed me to make my own mistakes... Remi and I reached an agreement early on that he would 'bish' and I would 'rect'."

Part of Remi's 'bishing' involved wide travel especially at that time so he would have been grateful to have someone of Bulloch's open sensibility running things as 'rect'. Bulloch's following assignment was to Ladysmith, a sleepy little town an hour north where the church building had gotten itself burned down, as he might express it.

Bulloch's late 1990s memoir features a writing style that is impressionistic, emotive with a flair for the dramatic characteristics of the personality of the author. It provides a good read and useful record if only because he candidly conveys details of the realities De Roo faced from the nature and history of this curious place.

Victoria in its off-the-beaten-path idiosyncratic character has an odd history of threatened canonical repressions and financial affliction. It also has displayed a distinct theological tendency toward Jansenism. Jansenism can be typified as a burdensome scrupulosity among other even less endearing attributes. Fretting would be a natural proclivity for the Jansenist, always watchful and guarded of making a moral error.

A pre-Vatican II dictionary of moral theology describes the moral doctrine of this condemned heresy as "rather obscure." The entry continues: *"Basically it appears as a rigoristic doctrine. One of its dogma consists in diminishing human liberty and debasing nature in order to extol the efficacy of grace. As a whole it is based on the concept of God as a severe and exacting Lord."*[247]

The Jansenist is not quite sure that even God is what he or she is cracked up to be in the benefice department. Hedging his theological bets is one habit. When a priest exhibits the habits of Jansenism, the tragedy of the mental state approaches the gruesome, as Bulloch describes.

Bulloch's paragraphs about one of his pastoral predecessors reveals a candour that is usefully placed: "Father Carl Albury served several years at Ladysmith. Early in his tenure he started a building fund, recognizing that the time would come when the old church would have to be replaced. Now the time had come and he told me: 'I couldn't wish for a better person to spend the $90,000.' Coming from Carl Albury that was the compliment of compliments.

"The successor to Carl Albury was Father Barrett, the epitome of an autocrat. His orders were to be obeyed without question. If they were not obeyed he would place a black cassock on the figure of St. Joseph to show that the Holy Family disapproved.

"When Vatican Council II reformed the liturgy he locked the church, called in carpenters to rip out the sanctuary, placed a small altar in the centre near the people, and announced: "This is how the Church expects us to say Mass in the future." The congregation was horrified and he lasted only six months after that.

"Father Barrett was a true Jansenist, as illustrated by the following incident. A young boy in the parish had bled to death after he fell on his knife point while cleaning a catch of fish. I met Father Barrett in Nanaimo and told him the story because he knew the family.

"He was horrified and asked, "Did you hear his confession? Was he alive?" When I said, "No," his comment was, "Then he must have died in mortal sin." I went ice cold, astounded at such an approach to moral theology. But I said nothing."

❧❧❧

Victoria was far from immune to the difficulties wrought by Jansenism. One of the removed bishops, Bertrand Orth (1900-08) was done so on this basis—accusations of Jansenism. Orth was the bishop who built and paid for the cathedral rectory, or 'The Bishop's Palace' as it was called. While a strong administrator, his moral theology led to serious problems.[248]

If some dioceses like Antigonish seemed predisposed to accept the changes of Vatican II,[249] Victoria was not like this. When Bishop De Roo arrived with the changes required by the reforms of the Second Vatican Council, the problem at the cathedral focused symbolically on the removal of the high altar. He put Bulloch in charge and the high altar became a permanent and central symbol of the tacit resistance in the diocese at that time to the reforms of Vatican II.[250]

The adoption of the vernacular to replace Latin as the language of the official liturgy and the turning around of the altar to face the people were the most visible signs of the shift. The old high altars were elaborate structures that in many cases were permanently fixed to the back wall of the sanctuary of the church. The practical necessity of their removal and the resistance this met became a totemic issue of inner defiance for those who could not accept change to tradition.

Queen of Peace Parish, where my mother grew up in Victoria West, for example, never did remove its high altar. When the traditionalist faction re-initiated Latin Masses in the 1980s, Queen of Peace became their sanctuary for suitable liturgy.

To this day the removal and the manner in which the cathedral altar was handled is a live criticism of De Roo's administrative style. Long a sensitive subject with the traditionalist quarter who turned on De Roo, Bulloch's version, which exonerates De Roo, is as follows:

"Bishop Remi De Roo called me in one day and announced he would be leaving for Rome shortly for the second session of the Vatican Council. He gave me his orders, I groaned mightily. First he wanted the altar removed. Secondly, he wanted the multiplicity of statues (and here I don't blame him) removed from the building and returned to where they should be. Then he instructed me to revamp the sanctuary...

"The bishop was the bishop but little Willie (that's me) was the rector... who knew how much money was available and I wasn't about to borrow any. Therefore with all due respect I changed things a trifle!

"The first order I had received... was to disassemble the main altar and send the pieces to Comox where the monks (who lived in isolation) could build altars for their oratories. I still feel the reverberations of that move. The altar had been built before the opening of the cathedral. There were those who said it had been brought around The Horn, but I found papers, including the signature of the builder, to prove it had originated on the other side of the Johnson Street bridge.

"It was of cedar and had many little niches that held innumerable statues. Of course the statues had to go. I ordered them to be stored, but apparently they went to private individuals—or were sold.

"A statue of Our Lady, the most important one in the church, wound up hanging under the three balls of a pawn shop. I took the full force of the rows over it—even though the responsibility was not mine.

"To protect our congregation during the renovation process, it was necessary for the first time in its history to close the cathedral for a week... The whole place looked like a disaster area when the bishop came home. Fresh from the heady discussions of Vatican II, Remi headed for the church to see what I had wrought. I sneaked off into my own office and sat there waiting. I didn't have to wait long before the telephone rang.

—"Bill, Bishop here. Would you come to my office, please?" Clink. —That sounded a bit chilly, but I wasn't to be fazed. I climbed the stairs to his office and he was sitting there looking unhappy.

—"Bill—"

—"Yes, Bishop."

—"Why didn't you carry out the things I told you to do?"

I looked at him and said, "Remi, if you have that amount of money in your arse pocket—fine, we'll start tomorrow. But I don't have that in our bank account and I'm not about to borrow money without authority."... I think it was then we developed a mutual understanding... we planned carefully and moved slowly... the alterations weren't completed until after I left the cathedral."

De Roo might have been relieved to know that the resistance was financial not theological, a somewhat simpler problem to confront. The theological resisters among the clergy (and there were certainly a number) by and large, were placed in out of the way parishes and not directly disturbed by being forced to conform at any more than their own pace of change—largely backward—allowed. By and large they were senior men of limited ability and vision who arrived at mutually agreed upon pastoral assignments with a committee of their peers.

While this resulted in specific pockets earning the reputation as theological backwaters, there was no coercion. Collegial structures were established, including a priests' senate— one of the earliest in the country[251]—and while the bishop retained a say in placements, much of the spadework was done by the personnel committee in direct consultation with the specific clergy.

While these sorts of developments removed the arbitrary element, they did little to get at the root of the problem where there was the resistant attitude. Some older clerics felt that all this sort of change was at best unnecessary, at worst heretical, and more to do with De Roo himself than Vatican II. It was an attitude which some venerable prelates carried to their retirement stage and beyond.

Michael McNamara, for example, was allowed to carry on for twenty years at Queen of Peace before retiring to his native Ireland. He was possibly the most defiant and obdurate of the resisters.

A more amusing example might be Willard O'Brien, a Maritimer from Prince Edward Island, who directly supervised the actual construction of *Our Lady of the Rosary Parish* at Langford in the early 1950s. Something like twelve churches were named or renamed after the Blessed Virgin Mary in that decade; an indication of the predisposition of the times, following the 'infallible' promulgation of the dogma of the Assumption by Pope Pius XII on November 1, 1950.

O'Brien wrote in *The Torch,* the diocesan newsletter of the day, that the building was put up largely with volunteer labour—as many of them would have been in the Maritimes during the time of his upbringing—and thus the savings were substantial. O'Brien also claimed there was not a day lost to accidents, which the pastor directly attributed to the intervention of the Blessed Virgin Mary herself.

O'Brien's devotion to Mary would have been behind the name change of the parish from Saint Richard's, which admittedly is not a common title for a Catholic parish. It had been named originally for an English benefactor, Sir Richard Scott of Ottawa, which would have jarred Father Willard's Prince Edward Island Irish Catholic sensibility.

While the 1950s saw the naming of every new parish structure in the diocese after Mary, the earlier heritage of non-traditional names, in this case from the 1920s, revealed a colour that was washed away in the Marian conformity of the later era.

Fanatical Mariology is a tested haven for anti-communism within Roman Catholicism and quite a few other odd-ball predispositions. It was a substructure in the religion which could be perilous to ignore. Much of O'Brien's antipathy for De Roo's program was a thinly veiled ideological conflict.[252]

This earlier construction success for Father Willard nearly paled by comparison with his intervention at the nearby Catholic cemetery of Hatley Park. O'Brien was placed in charge of the development of a clergy section. Suitably he delegated the higher ground under a group of elegant evergreens, as the space to be reserved for the burial spot for local bishops.

Unfortunately for his hierarchial designation, there was no bishop who chose to be buried on the westcoast. De Roo's persistent four decades in office would have robbed O'Brien of a number of candidates. As a consequence, in a fittingly fine irony, Father

Willard is now situated in his earthly remains in one of these premium locations. He died unexpectedly on the golf course one Sunday afternoon in the middle 1990s.

At the end of his life he was surrounded by those he considered true loyalists to the faith including the publishers of the dissident traditionalist newspaper, *The Trumpet*.

During O'Brien's last years, he centred his liturgical life at the tiny Saint Thomas chapel at nearby Metchosin, presumably named after an appropriate Roman Catholic saint and not some member of the English ruling class.

2. HERMITS AND OTHER HISTORY

The monks that Monsignor Bulloch mentioned would be receiving the cathedral high altar parts for their Mass-saying purposes in the Comox Valley constitute a significant story in themselves.

In the three hundred years prior to Vatican II the eremitical life in the Western Church had greatly declined. There existed no canonical rights for hermits until the 1983 Code of Canon Law. In the Eastern Orthodox Church, that other great branch of Christianity, the tradition had been maintained. But in the western or Catholic Church it had been eliminated in the reforms following the major adjustment following the Council of Trent (1545-63), the ecumenical council which was called to counter the Protestant Reformation.

The most famous modern monk who had been pressing just prior to Vatican II to have this status reinstated was the author Thomas Merton. Merton, a monk of Gethsemane Monastery in rural Kentucky, became virtually world famous on the basis of his critically-acclaimed autobiography, *The Seven Story Mountain.*

Published in 1948, the book—a sort of modern *Confessions of Saint Augustine*—tells the story of his religious conversion, journey to Catholicism, and eventual life in a Trappist Monastery. The title image is from Dante's image of purgatory where Merton felt he spent a long time prior to entering the church. Thomas Merton eventually wrote fifty books and became the spiritual centre of a popular reform push from the bottom up in the Catholic Church. Much of Vatican II vindicated his ideas, instincts and initiatives.

At the time of his sudden and rather mysterious death while on a trip to Asia in 1968, Merton was considering moving to Vancouver Island to be part of a new hermit community which De Roo had encouraged to set up foundation in his diocese.[253]

A number of monks had left their Trappist and Benedictine monastic communities around the world to converge at the old town of Headquarters on the Tsolum River, near Courtenay, four hours north of Victoria. The movement, fed by the fervour of Vatican II, was under the leadership of Belgian Jacques Winandy who first arrived with one other monk July 16, 1964.

Members of this community included Bernard de Aguiar, a Brazilian who had served with Merton in Kentucky, and Charles Brandt, an American from Missouri, who had been a Trappist at New Melleray, Iowa. They were the most persistent two of an original eight hermits who formed part of a hermit community which "quickly grew to a maximum number of thirteen."[254]

In his 1969 memorandum of history of the founding of the community, Winandy stated: "Besides those mentioned, some twenty candidates presented themselves during a period of five years... without mentioning those who just came 'to see' and the many, more numerous, who wrote for information and were either refused for diverse reasons or who never followed up..."

The ones who did stay included Americans, a Québecer, an Irish from Australia, a native of Martinique and the Brazilian, de Aguiar. In the first five years of their presence on the Island, the twelve thousand dollar property they bought tripled in value and they anticipated establishing a colony of women hermits in the next three to five years.[255] But before this could occur it started to dwindle.

In the early 1960s, Brandt was in correspondence with Thomas Merton who candidly stated his own discontent at Gethsemani. Merton felt that an American corporate model had taken over monasticism there and he wanted to be part of a reform back to basics à la Vatican II:

"It has to be admitted that the monastic life as we have it in the houses of our Order now leaves much to be desired... The consequence is that problems arise... Superiors have tended to regard all such desires with suspicion, on the bases that there have been so many eccentrics and neurotics.

"At the same time even a genuine vocation to a more contemplative life can be made to appear and to act neurotic by a certain type of frustration of his legitimate needs."[256]

The idea of a community of hermits seems somewhat paradoxical but as Merton wrote in the same letter: "The thing we have to remember is that the desire for authentic monastic solitude comes from God and not from man, and that God is working to bring about the realization of conditions in which His will can be fulfilled.

"We all have to co-operate with Him in whatever way we can, and the ways offered may for some reason seem paradoxical. The ability to accept paradoxical and untidy solutions has a great deal to do with the solitary life which is necessarily unpatterned and existential. But if you do come to live as a hermit somewhere, be ready for a grim time and don't expect some of the consolations you are leaving behind."

Merton never did join. He missed a connection with De Roo and Winandy at the Vancouver airport in the fall of 1968 on his last trip. Brandt said Merton was well known for getting flight times confused, so they never did connect.[257] Ironically, given his radical pacifism, Merton only returned from Asia in a coffin in the belly of an American Air force bomber, a paradox itself which fuelled speculation about the cause of his death.[258]

The residual paradoxical tensions Merton alluded to may have resulted in this experiment lasting only a decade in its uniqueness following the Vatican Council. By 2000, only one hermit persists, Charles Brandt, although de Aguiar continued to dwell nearby as a laicized priest. De Aguiar lived a hermetic existence on Hornby Island, as a scholar, artist and pastoral counsellor until nearly the time of his death in November, 1998.[259]

If Merton had decided to join the group, with his dynamic charism, one can only conjecture how something special could have developed from the leadership styles of the avant garde bishop and the world famous writer hermit, perhaps something permanent.

THE CONTEMPLATIVE DIMENSION

It was the work of Bishop De Roo at Vatican II which enabled this worldwide development of western hermit life to begin on Vancouver Island. De Roo made a key intervention in 1965. According to Charles Brandt, it helped re-established the tradition in the Catholic Church after the lengthy hiatus.

In his successful intervention at the Council De Roo stated "the Latin Church is experiencing an ever growing renewal of the life of hermits. It is urgent therefore that the western Church officially recognize the life of hermits as a state of perfection. And Vatican II should make a point of this."

De Roo was quoted saying the hermit fills a prophetic role in the church "reminding us that the building of an earthly city is not the final end of all things. Fleeing the noisy whirlwind of worldly activities, he opens his heart to the Holy Spirit in an atmosphere of calm and interior reflection. Thus he pursues an essential calling of the church, the direct contemplation of God."[260]

'AVANT GARDE'

When De Roo ordained Charles Brandt in November, 1966 the Victoria *Daily Colonist* headline exclaimed: "Hermit-Monks Ordination First in Two Centuries" and called the hermit colony "the only one in North America."

"Bishop De Roo, who has encouraged and supported the unique 20th Century hermitage since its founding in September, 1964, said the ordination would emphasize a facet of religious life neglected by the western church for years and would restore a balance such as is still maintained by eastern and Oriental branches."

"He said Father Brandt and the other solitary hermits of the Hermitage of St. John the Baptist, each of whom lives alone and apart from his fellows on the primitive hermitage acreage... There is little regimentation, for the hermits feel, in the words of Father Winandy that they must guard against the strong tendency of westerners to organize, standardize, centralize and legislate every detail of life."[261]

Thirty-two years later in November of 1998 De Roo accepted the renewal of vows by Charles Brandt at Saint Andrew's Cathedral under a section of the new Code of Canon Law which gives legal status to the hermit state in the Catholic Church. Throughout his career De Roo was consistently seen as counter-cultural, and the contemplative dimension was the root of it. This experiment expressed the ultimate alternative experience of being counter-cultural.

"Before Vatican II there was really no possibility of living the hermit life with the church's blessings," said Brandt who by this time was being celebrated nationally as a 'modern Saint Francis winning awards for environmental care.'[262]

"Asked how he was able to integrate his lifestyle, Brandt said he was inspired by Saint Francis... You just put one foot in front of the other, with no destination in mind."

Vancouver Sun religion writer Douglas Todd goes on to say: "Brandt is a follower and friend of the renowned Catholic monk Thomas Merton, who developed a form of Christian-Buddhist contemplation and encouraged him to become a hermit. Brandt also bases his life's work on Thomas Berry, a noted Catholic eco-theologian."

"With the full support of Vancouver Island bishop Remi De Roo, whom Brandt considers 'avant garde'... It is not an easy thing to do—to discover, as he says in his slow, almost-whispery voice, the deeper inner self—to realize that the human soul and the earth and the Spirit of God are all interconnected, all one.

"Like the monks of the 12th Century, Brandt believes his life of prayer and contemplation is far from irrelevant to the world. 'It's absolutely essential.'"

In his sermon at Charles Brandt's ordination on November 21, 1966 at Courtenay, De Roo gave this summary to the proposition: "The hermetical life is a unique, a select, a relatively rare vocation. Hermits make their lives into an oasis of concentrated prayer and contemplation to fortify the entire Church, the communion of saints. Theirs is a silent witness, a witness of example, of conduct, of action more than of words.

"The witness of those who testify that God alone is the centre of the universe and of all religious aspirations. Hermits remind us, by their lives, of the ultimate meaning of human existence.

"We are not to establish a paradise here below. We are called to a higher destiny in the kingdom of God. This destiny the Hermit proclaims, reminding us by their detachment from all things of the necessary eschatological tension of the Church."[263]

3. 'A CONTEXT OF MUTUALITY'

Charles Brandt only attended specific sessions of the diocesan synod between 1986-91. He was not present at the final ratification round in 1996 although there were a number of proposals to do with the environment confirmed in the final documents.[264] De Roo cited one introduced by Charles Brandt when the bishop described the goal of the synod as "Liberation from Cultural Bondage."[265]

Someone who was present at the final session, although it was her first occasion, was Catholic university chaplain twenty-six year-old Kate Fagan. When De Roo convoked the synod in 1986, Kate Fagan would have been eighteen years of age. By 1996 she had her Masters of Divinity from Notre Dame University in South Bend, Indiana and had just been appointed the third female chaplain in a row delegated by De Roo since 1990 when the sudden death of Father Leo Robert left a vacuum in the position.

In May, 1998 Victoria's *Zoom* magazine, with its subtitle "The People, passions and politics of Victoria," did a cover-story profile of "The Bishop and Ms. Chaplain."

De Roo's first quote about his feminist initiative was: "I can be roundly criticized for doing that but that's beside the point. I have my responsibilities as bishop. One of the biggest questions that the Roman Catholic Church has to face today is the recognition by history and culture of the role of women, not as complementary to men but in a context of mutuality."[266]

The author of the piece typifies the bishop this way: "De Roo is still concerned with political and economic issues... Flawlessly accurate, he quotes 17th Century French philosopher Blaise Pascal to illustrate his beliefs: 'The heart has reasons which reason doesn't understand.' That's one of the big dilemmas today. If we don't bring our heart into unison with our heads, we could very well, in cold reason, destroy ourselves. We have got to come back to a system of compassion and just redistribution as a matter of survival or our democracy's going to collapse. It's a frightening thought."

"One of the weaknesses of Vatican II," he admits, "was that we bishops from all over the world got together and made all these lovely decisions. But then we went home and not so many of us knew how to put that into effect.

"There's a long process of education. We're into that now. It's only been thirty-five years. In terms of the evolution of humanity that's not a long period of time. Some people think it is not enough, some think it's too fast too soon. But its happening. To me, it's an irreversible process."

"Canonically De Roo allowed Fagan to preach, conduct baptisms, weddings and funerals. As a result she gets criticism from both sides: "Naturally I get criticism from those more traditional, who don't want to see things change. Other people who criticize me are of a more liberal bent, who think I am collaborating with the enemy. They see the church as irredeemably sexist and patriarchal and that my playing this sort of role makes it look as if women are more involved and have more influence than they do."

"Both De Roo and Fagan," according to the writer, "are patient, balanced people who bring superb leadership qualities to their job... De Roo recalls his years on the family farm to talk about balance in his own life. His voice catches with emotion and his eyes begin to redden as he describes a memory assisting his father in the breech birth of a calf. I learned an awful lot on the farm just from nature. You learn to wait and let nature have its course."

"I ask them if they can foresee changes in the church forty-five years from now."

"De Roo replies in his customary broad, thoughtful manner: 'Speaking from yesterday's experience, the answer is obvious. It's no. But where are we tomorrow? One of the lessons I've learned is don't try to second guess the future. Things are happening which nobody dreamed would be possible."

"Science has verified that changes occur that appear to be the result of random causes. These gradually build up in tiny parcels of reality and then suddenly, by a kind of osmosis, the change is here. It's a quantum leap. Who knows if there won't be a quantum leap in the church?"

Kate Fagan had this to say about De Roo in the *Island Catholic News* when it published various statements about the bishop at the time of his retirement: "In this historical period of transition within the Church, most bishops seem intent upon choosing a safe path through controversial issues, avoiding any actions that could put them at risk of censure.

"As a result, most Catholics have been disappointed by their bishop's failure to be genuinely responsive to their concerns and pastoral needs. When I tell people about my experience of Bishop Remi De Roo, I am happy to point out a clear exception to this prevailing tendency.

"Bishop Remi's leadership provides many examples of a more courageous leadership. The facet of his vision which has effected me most powerfully is his openness to calling women to lay ministry, and in particular delegating me to provide sacramental ministry traditionally restricted to male priests. His willingness to expand the boundaries in response to pastoral needs in the Diocese of Victoria has had powerful ramifications for my spiritual journey and career as a lay minister."[267]

4. RELIGION AND SOCIETY

A significant intellectual development initiated by the bishop was the establishment in 1991 at the University of Victoria of "The Centre for Studies in Religion and Society." De Roo had an abiding interest in multi-disciplinary studies as a counterforce to the problems created by specialization in science, academia and religion. The centre was a program in this vein. Its first director was a United Church minister who was an expert in Hinduism.

The official opening was September 26, 1993 and the centre claimed to be unique in North America because of its multi-disciplinary nature. Funded from interest drawn on a major endowment by individuals and religious communities including the Anglican, United and Catholic churches, its first director was a scholar who had done research in comparative religion, psychology of religion, environmental ethics and religious pluralism.

All of these fields were constant reading areas for De Roo. In fact the centre is generally admitted to be his brainchild from the initial inception; perhaps dating back to the 1960s when the original concept for an ecumenical college fell through. De Roo has a standing welcome at the centre to initiate new ideas and program ideas. Fundamentally the centre seeks to bridge the gap between academics and the lay public.

Harold Coward, the centre's scholar director, submitted these comments on De Roo at the time of his retirement:

"Remi De Roo keeps up with the latest developments in theology and science better than any member of the clergy I know. In addition, he is very open minded, imaginative and sensitive. As an administrator he is a joy to work with as he can be counted on to find a way to make things happen when the easy legalistic response would result in a blockage. Remi always goes that extra mile."[268]

In retirement De Roo said he hoped to be able to follow his inclination as a scholar; the Catholic church having a long tradition of the man of learning as the natural leader of the community. His luck was to be born into a time that suited his temperament and gifts, allowing his sort of prophetic leadership to have its day. As a result he became a legend in his own time.

Kate Fagan's comment may reinforce the idea that De Roo is a fluke development, that because he is so out of synch with the type of bishop most Catholics assume they will get, he does not belong in the mainstream tradition. As we have seen there is a lengthy precedent even in the Canadian Catholic Church of these sort of prophetic Catholic leaders even—perhaps especially—in western Canada. The abiding question for traditionalists becomes: Is he normative or a peripheral exception? His legendary status as a post-modernist prophetic figure suggests we closely examine this question.

Father Charles Brandt, hermit.

With Muriel Clemenger, left, at the opening of the St. Vincent de Paul Society Ozanam Centre in Victoria. (Jamie Jenkins)

Chapter Eighteen: Smashing The Icon

"And others are those sown among the thorns: these are the ones who hear the word, but the cares of the world, and the desire for other things come in and choke the word, and it yields nothing.

"And these are the ones sown on the good soil: they hear the word and accept it and bear fruit, thirty and sixty and a hundredfold."—Mark 4:19-20.

❧❧❧

Friday, June 2, 2000—*Victoria News* 'Feature' Weekend Edition

Questions raised about politics behind church crisis

De Roo supporters wonder what role politics is playing in crisis rocking Catholic Church

By Mark Browne

Weekend Edition Staff

As retired Roman Catholic Bishop Remi De Roo faces criticism over bad investments he made while bishop of the Vancouver Island Diocese, some local Catholics are convinced that forces within the Catholic church are out to get him.

"There seems to be a concerted effort to discredit him," says Patrick Jamieson, a board member and past editor of the Island Catholic News. *Jamieson is currently writing a biography on De Roo who retired last year after thirty-seven years as bishop for the Vancouver Island Diocese.*

Jamieson is also author of Victoria Demers to De Roo, 150 Years of Catholic History on Vancouver Island.

When news first surfaced that the diocese was $17 million in debt because of unsuccessful investments made by De Roo (involving Arabian horses and a subsequent risky land deal), Jamieson says the way the Roman Catholic Church handled the matter is suspicious.

He says he finds it strange that the National Post *was inquiring if the local diocese was in trouble because of investments made by De Roo a few days before the church made an official statement on the matter earlier this year.*

"The National Post *called and they had wind of it which seemed curious to me because surely they weren't monitoring every Catholic diocese's financial problems," says Jamieson.*

He notes that Conrad Black, the owner of the National Post *who became a Catholic several years ago, and De Roo engaged in very heated debates with each other in 1983 when Canada's bishops addressed the economic and unemployment problems of that period.*

Speaking on behalf of the country's bishops, De Roo expressed views that were very anti-capitalist in nature—something that Jamieson says didn't go off too well with Black.

"It got quite personal," he recalls.

Jamieson says it's important to note that the tides of political conservatism that swept across the Western world in the 1980s posed a threat for the left-leaning social justice policies that De Roo and the Catholic Church in general had endorsed.

As the political power in the Vatican experienced a shift to the right in the 1980s, De Roo became quite unpopular with the right-leaning echelons of the Catholic Church hierarchy who had assumed power, he says.

Jamieson argues that the discrediting of De Roo has its roots in that shift of power within the Catholic Church.

On a local level, Jamieson contends that ill feelings towards De Roo from other priests have a lot to do with a position taken by such priests that wealthy people weren't donating much money to the local diocese because of their opposition to De Roo's left-wing social views.

"There are certain priests here that used to say to me "If we could just get Remi (De Roo) out of the way, the money would start to flow," recalls Jamieson. "So there was this circle in the diocese that was hyper-critical of Remi on precisely those grounds."

But while Jamieson feels that some of the local church hierarchy have been out to discredit De Roo, he stresses he is not convinced that Bishop Raymond Roussin, who took over from De Roo as the Bishop of the Vancouver Island Diocese, is part of that circle. The forces against De Roo have been in play for a long time, notes Jamieson.

However, Jamieson remains critical of how the new administration under Roussin was quick to release information to the media on the diocese's financial crisis and De Roo's involvement. He says the "tradition" would have been for the diocese to initially attempt to resolve the matter "in-house" out of respect for De Roo.

Jamieson says that within a few months of the new administration it had become apparent that the "right wingers" in the diocese had taken control. And that is particularly evident at the meetings the diocese has been holding in an attempt to address the current situation.

"I was kind of shocked and surprised by the level of negativity and antipathy towards Bishop De Roo that comes out at some of those meetings," says Jamieson.

De Roo isn't too popular with the right-wing of the Catholic Church at Saint Boniface in Winnipeg either.

Jamieson notes that when De Roo went there to do some confirmations (a request that the late Archbishop Antoine Hacault made on his death bed) local right-leaning parishioners insisted that it wouldn't be appropriate for De Roo to handle confirmations of children since he was the subject of a canonical inquiry.

As for Re Roo maintaining his silence on the issue, Marnie Butler, editor of Island Catholic News, *says that she has been told by De Roo's lawyer, Chris Consodine, that he will likely come forward and speak up on the matter after the canonical commission releases its findings on July 10.*

Butler suggests that De Roo's reputation is unlikely to be tarnished given that several dioceses across the country are facing financial trouble. Butler says she feels that most people are intelligent enough to see beyond the negative statements being made against De Roo.

Jamieson says he doesn't think that De Roo's reputation will be ruined, while reiterating that there are those among the right wing of the church who simply want the former bishop's name to suffer.

Tom Loring, a longtime social activists in the local Catholic community, says he doesn't feel that De Roo's reputation will be damaged to any serious extent. Most people who find themselves in a position like De Roo is in these days would leave questions to their attorneys, says Loring, who also suspects that there are those in the church that are deliberately trying to discredit the former bishop.

Alan Bailey, a local Catholic and self-admitted big fan of De Roo, says he can only hope that people will forgive De Roo for errors he made in regard to investments made on behalf of the diocese.

While Bailey says it's possible that some right-leaning members of the church are out to discredit De Roo, most Catholics in the community realize that De Roo is human, and like other humans, has made some mistakes.

THE ARABIAN HORSE SAGA

1. FIRST OFF AT THE POST

It was the last Wednesday of February, 2000 I first caught wind of the financial scandal which rocked the Diocese of Victoria during the first year of Bishop Raymond Roussin's episcopacy at Victoria. This next episode, a surprise development, raised many more questions than it answered.

Roussin had been installed gradually as successor to De Roo during the previous twelve months, during 1998. There was a process stretching the solemnization over a six-month period during 1999 as well. De Roo had retired officially on his seventy-fifth birthday, February 24, 1999. The *Island Catholic News* has a series of unpublished photos of the moment De Roo handed the crozier to Roussin. De Roo was in tears, almost as if he could see what was to come.

De Roo was very pleased that "someone as good as" Roussin was selected as his successor. He stated this to me in the cathedral rectory kitchen early in 1997 when I said Roussin's name was being bandied about as a successor. In fact he framed it in negative terms, that we would not be so lucky to get someone as good as Roussin.

Island Catholic News editor Marnie Butler had a strong hunch that Roussin, a member of the Marianist order and the former Bishop of Gravelbourg, Saskatchewan would get the nod. Gravelbourg had been suppressed and attached to Regina due to failing financial support in the traditionally Francophone prairie diocese.

Butler interviewed Roussin early in 1997 at Queenswood Retreat Centre in Victoria for a cover story in ICN. Butler told me at the time she knew he would be the one. She had announced this generally. When she related her intuition, Roussin dismissed the idea, telling her he already had a diocese. She convinced him to sit for a 'cover shot' any way. The diminutive bishop had been on the Island for a Western Bishops' gathering hosted by De Roo in Nanaimo.

At that particular weekend, some of the leaders of the diocesan Catholic Women's League had gotten hold of choir robes resembling red cardinal costumes and served the supper to the bishops dressed as Roman cardinals. According to De Roo, the joke went over well. It is hard to imagine any other western diocese where the bishop would have felt as completely comfortable with this prank and its oblique commentary on the church's official attitude toward women.

❧❧❧

The financial scandal proper was initiated when a special statement was to 'only be read' from the pulpits of all the parishes in the diocese on the first Sunday of March, 2000. It was not to be released in a written form at that time; or earlier. The priests of the diocese had been so instructed at a special meeting earlier in the week.

I was seated at my computer in a studio in Chinatown working on this book when Marnie Butler came to the door. She announced how I could make an easy two hundred dollars for simply tape recording this message from the pulpit for Marina Jiminez of *The National Post*.

Despite the secrecy request—or perhaps because of it—someone had obviously called *The Post* and they wanted to make an offer we could not refuse.

Coincidentally, earlier that day I had been working on the section of the book that deals with the controversy in the late 1980s between Bishop De Roo and Toronto based press baron Conrad Black. Black had taken serious umbrage with De Roo's leadership style on the 'Crisis in the Economy' reflections of 1983.[269] *The National Post* being Black's flagship newspaper, this was an interesting coincidence. As a consequence neither Marnie Butler nor I was disposed to co-operate with the request.

❧❧❧

When Jiminez called the *Island Catholic News*, she said she was sure it was a juicy disclosure, probably sexual in nature but Butler knew it wasn't the case. She had been hearing odd rumours about financial shortfalls at the diocese, something to do with horses but did not think much of it for a variety of reasons. For one thing ICN had never bothered with that side of things in its thirteen-year history.

She also knew that Muriel Clemenger was a horsewoman, and as financial administrator for the diocese she was known to be creative and energetic in her thinking about investments. If Clemenger heard about a good deal in her horse circles, she would try it out. It was in her makeup. If she thought some funds were sitting idle, she could easily move to use them to help the diocese in that manner.

In fact a minor horse cartel was formed among a number of Clemenger's friends and associates, some of whom were close to De Roo, but the bishop himself had nothing directly to do with it.

The comment by Eileen Archer, De Roo's executive assistant for thirty years, bears a certain relevance here: "One characteristic that particularly stands out in my mind is Bishop De Roo's understanding of human nature and his acceptance of people as they are ... He has always trusted people. He assigns a task and expects it will be done. No reminders, no interference. And he encourages people. I for one, have been challenged to do things I didn't know I could."

This quality was precisely why I was happy to try to start an independent Catholic newspaper on Vancouver Island in 1985. I knew that I would never have to be looking over my shoulder, worrying about what the bishop thought. I also knew from our initial conversation on the topic that there would be no money available directly from the diocese; and this suited us both.

More important than money, I knew we would have his trust. De Roo was not a fearful leader at any moment in my experience of him.

2. THE DIFFICULTIES OF THE CASE

Our main contact in the diocesan finance circles was Al Heron, a professional fundraiser hired as a development officer to get donations up in the early 1990s. Heron was very helpful to *Island Catholic News*, coming up with personally creative manners of fundraising for the paper apart from his job at the diocese.

In casual conversation he mentioned he had seen a couple of budget line items that puzzled him, for which he could not get any answers. One of these turned out to be the loss on the Swiftsure Farms investment. Swiftsure was an Arabian horse breeding operation.

Heron's boss Muriel Clemenger was not only appreciated by Remi De Roo for her creative financial work. During Clemenger's last few years at Victoria she was appointed by the Western Catholic Bishops to develop an idea she dreamed up: to form an insurance co-operative to pool their payments. Until then each diocese had made its own insurance arrangement. She reported the savings were substantial.

She and Al Heron managed the co-op after De Roo left office. At that point the new administration brought in its own financial officer, an accountant. Clemenger, who was also aged seventy-five, previously announced she would only be staying until De Roo retired. Al Heron applied for her job but was not granted the courtesy of an interview. It seems there was another plan in the works.

Other regional conferences of Canadian Catholic bishops had more than a passing interest in the insurance pool concept. Clemenger informed me in a conversation during the middle 1990s. The Atlantic Bishops were definitely positive, and even the Ontario bishops were wanting to get involved she said, but the latter group had some technical angles to work out. It was all very bright and positive sounding, especially given what was to follow. It was typical of my experience of her creative inventiveness.

When the investment loss made the headlines, the Western Bishops dropped Clemenger unceremoniously. Shortly after, the Ukrainian Eparch of Winnipeg arrived in Nanaimo to lay off Al Heron. He acted "like a bully," Heron told me in his matter-of-fact collected manner. This was all in spite of the savings Clemenger had creatively instigated. Some definite distancing was going on beyond the simple loss of capital. Heron has since received a financial settlement for 'wrongful dismissal'.

Clemenger and De Roo decided not to contravene the new bishop in public and kept silence on the whole issue despite what was being said and implied about them. Clemenger told me that Roussin and his new administrator asked her at the time of transition not to speak in public in case it contradicted them, and she told me she would honour this agreement which seemed to be logical at the time.

De Roo hired a sharp local lawyer, Chris Considine, to represent him and he did issue a general apology. The public apology meant he would take the fall and not pass any of it on to Clemenger or anyone else at the next level of responsibility.[270] Kim Lunman of the *Globe and Mail* told me in a telephone conversation she did not find any documents in Lacey, Washington, to do with a land investment, that had De Roo's signature on them.

It was the land investment aspect rather than the earlier million dollar loss on the Arabian horse farm that caused the real financial difficulties for the diocese.

The farm loss had taken place in the late 1980s. Investing in the land in the mid-1990s had been part of a recovery scheme that Clemenger devised through the same agent as the original investment, American lawyer Joseph Finley. If there were any other signatures on those documents besides Clemenger, De Roo was protecting these subordinates by his silence and public apology. In effect he accepted final responsibility, by virtue of his office.

❧❧❧

Remi De Roo's character in both senses was the issue at stake here. His was not a nature to give finances, and such, the importance it carried in the secular business world, or the corporate media. In simple terms, he did not really care about money. It was not a pastoral priority in itself.

He also was not going to get into any public dog fights about what had happened, and the details of who had done what to whom. He was not into blaming. I knew this from personal experience. During the six years as editor of the diocesan newspaper, the only editorial suggestion I remember him making was that the paper not cover every "dogfight in the diocese."

As Marnie Butler repeated often enough: "Remi did not care about money for its own sake." This was the reason why she and many other left-leaning converts were drawn to join the Catholic Church during his heyday. He did however tell Butler that he did not feel uncomfortable with financial transactions.

One thing she meant was that while some bishops are noted for their fiscal administrative capabilities, this was obviously not De Roo greatest interest or aptitude; and she admired this about him. To the people around *Island Catholic News*, it seemed like judging the competence of an Old Testament prophet by the tidiness of his cave. It was entirely irrelevant to who De Roo was.

Besides that it seemed awfully coincidental to them that no significant publicly-known problems had arisen until after De Roo left office. In fact the net worth of the diocese had risen astronomically during his four decades.[271] Admittedly this was largely due to the overall development of Vancouver Island, but it seemed he should be given some credit for having the money there to lose in the first place. In addition there was a serious question about under whose watch the real losses had taken place.

3. STOPPING PAYMENTS

Here we are relying on the *Globe and Mail* reporting as contrasted to the local *Times Colonist*. In her June 17, 2000 feature, Kim Lunman points out that the most serious loss was actually due to action taken by the new finance administration team, not by De Roo and Clemenger:

"But the land... never sold and the diocese was faced with $130,000 in monthly mortgage payments. *It stopped paying when Bishop Roussin took over a year later* [italics mine] and the lender, AG Capital Funding Partners of New York, took the church to court in May 1999.

"In March (2000) a judge ordered the land foreclosed and ordered the diocese, Mr. Finley and Corporate Business Park to pay $12-million to AG Capital. The interest alone is now accruing at $7000 per day."[272]

So, according to the *Globe and Mail*, due to a decision taken by the new administration the payments jumped from $130,000 per month to $210,000, escalating the crisis into a catastrophe. In addition, the land was now at risk. In the pages of the *Times Colonist*, which just happened to be owned by Conrad Black at the time, this little distinction was glossed over. The *Times Colonist* was in a feeding frenzy for all the good copy De Roo's purported 'fall from grace' was providing.

In the six month period between February and September 2000 the story made the front page headline of the T-C nineteen times (and the lead page of another section ten times).[273] The tip of the Richter scale may have been reached Saturday, May 27 with: "Ex-bishop gambled assets from convent, De Roo chased losses and had two sets of books, concludes Roman Catholic Church Commission."

Despite the fact that Roussin's last diocese, Gravelbourg, had to be closed and attached to Regina due to financial shortfalls; despite the fact that it was decisions taken subsequent to February 24, 1999 that caused the most serious crisis, De Roo was the only one 'investigated'. In fact he was not investigated at all. He was presumed guilty and it was a blame-affixing exercise that followed.

If there was a moment when De Roo could have started to present his side of the story—an objective moment not driven by media frenzy and pejorative headlines—when he could have been heard in a comprehensive manner, the formal canonical inquiry, requested by Bishop Raymond Roussin and established by the Canadian Conference of Catholic Bishops, would have been it.

After all he had served the CCCB in responsible positions for decades and he had displayed extraordinary gifts of articulation on complex and subtle issues. He would need an occasion like this to explain himself comprehensively, and it seemed simple justice if not courtesy that De Roo would at least be granted the opportunity.

But it was not to be. The changing of the guard was complete.

4. THE COMMISSION OF INQUIRY

The hearings were scheduled on the only days when De Roo had stated earlier he could not be available due to prior commitments elsewhere in North America. The report itself when it did come out reflected only one point of view on the whole matter. It did not indicate that any voices dissenting from the conventional wisdom espoused in the press had been heard at all.[274]

The report could have been written from Ottawa or Toronto, the locations of the principal members of the inquiry group. It entirely reflected the media reports and could have been written from such clippings, saving the price of the plane tickets of these busy and important men.

In interviews prior to the release of the report, Monsignor Peter Schonenbach, General Secretary of the CCCB and a member of the inquiry group, prejudiced and pre-empted his own report with pejorative comment. Canada's top Catholic Church bureaucrat was quoted in the press comparing De Roo's behaviour to that of a gambling addict. Peter Schonenbach was quoted making one-sided statements of fact that he must have known would be interpreted negatively in the un-nuanced reporting of the daily press.[275]

This was a full month before the report was released.[276]

The appropriate way for the CCCB General Secretary to conduct himself on the issue would have been to see that a competent inquiry was appointed, presumably one that had at least one member from western Canada and someone who was knowledgeable about and sensitive to De Roo's pastoral style.

The General Secretary himself should not have served on the board but rather reviewed its findings objectively for the principles of breadth of perspective, balance, objectivity and comprehensiveness. He should not have allowed himself to be interviewed casually on so sensitive a subject, which only served to fuel the speculation that De Roo was being discredited for political reasons.

Schonenbach's actual behaviour was very surprising because the CCCB had distinguished itself with stellar professionalism in its general secretary role, dating back to Rev. Everett MacNeil in the 1960s and 70s and Monsignor (later Archbishop of Winnipeg) James Weisgerber in the 1980s.

5. DIOCESAN FINANCES

In the *Times Colonist* reporting, there was never any indication that a workable payment structure was in place when De Roo left office, one that had been operating well enough. Obviously the loan arrangement was predicated on the premise that the property was valuable enough to cover its cost and would eventually be sold, probably recouping as well the original loss.

The real losses that drove the diocese into desperation mode were due to the subsequent court judgement, but even this was blamed on De Roo. With the *Times Colonist* and *The Post*, from the very start, the wheels had already been put in motion in one definite direction.

As a student of media-church relations, the significant aspect to me was that the *Times Colonist* was privy to information about the diocese that is given to few if any newspapers about the Catholic Church. It had a field day. This attitude toward the windmill-tilting crusader against corporate capitalism by its lapdog press was not something surprising at this point.

Coverage of De Roo in the pages of the *Times Colonist* during the 1980s and 1990s had soured radically compared with the glowing reports of the 1960s and 1970s when 'the boy bishop' could hardly set a foot wrong in the pages of either then-competing papers, the *Victoria Times* and the *Daily Colonist*.

6. ADMINISTRATIVE GENIUS

Victoria was always a pretty small place, and did not require much administrative genius to keep it rolling. De Roo recognized this from his first days when he found the finances run on a rudimentary model, more suitable to an educational institution.[277]

Roussin had come to Victoria from the Saskatchewan Diocese of Gravelbourg, where he had been put in charge in order to close it down. The Franco-Catholic population was no longer sufficient to keep it financially viable so Gravelbourg was suppressed and attached to Regina.

As a result he would be expected to be a touch sensitive about finances, certainly more than De Roo, who after thirty-seven years in charge would be confident of the overall situation.

The most significant aspect of De Roo's financial administrative style was in how he kept certain types—power brokers, high priced lawyers, accountants, financial wizards and money men, et al—from taking over all the key positions in the financial administrative management of the diocese.

He and Clemenger made sure that farmers, ordinary workers and women maintained a balance on such key committees; and, of course, they were not popular in certain quarters for this.[278]

Most other dioceses had capitulated in these areas to 'the experts'. De Roo was always wary of such experts as his battle over the economy with corporate Canada in the early 1980s showed. While this allowed a different model of church to emerge, it also made him a nemesis in those circles; certain 'successful' types who quickly moved in to fill the vacuum.

All these types of people came to make up Roussin's financial-administrative inner circles during this controversy. The shift was functional on two fronts: Control was obtained of the key money matters in the diocese by a select group of experts who never did have that much time for Remi De Roo and his prairie populism priorities; and De Roo was made to wear the blame and thus publicly discredited.

As in the Charbonneau case, De Roo's good nature was used against him. He said he did not want to contradict his successor in public and thereby jeopardize the subsequent bond issue being raised.

Speculation started early that Roussin would not stay in the diocese for many years. Right from the start his health was suffering from the stress of the situation. He also had a serious auto accident that eventful summer of 2000, which added to his nervous stress and physical ailments.

When De Roo had taken over after the death of Bishop James Michael Hill in 1962, the diocese was literally run on a shoestring. It was bankrolled on one annual 'Pentecost' collection. Hill had kept a small college going in rural New Brunswick during The Depression and so knew how to stretch a dollar.

Once De Roo arrived, the financial footing of the diocese was put on a whole other basis and there was nothing of any irregular note for thirty-seven years. On the contrary, he was considered a fiscal conservative, never a lavish spender. Living very simply despite being a 'prince of the church', he was far from being a gambler of any sort.

De Roo's travel money was taken from his fees as a speaker. He took only the same salary as the youngest priest.

Things were not flush but they continually improved over three and half decades. Then a full year after he leaves office, skeletons were supposedly found in the closets by a new administration, one steeped in the practice of forensic accounting.

Not only were these bones discovered but they made a great deal of noise in their rattling. The bad news was released immediately to the regular press. This was the first objective sign that something strange was afoot; apart from the allegations of fiscal irregularities.

7. CHURCH-MEDIA RELATIONS

The Catholic Church is still one of the most secretive organizations in the history of the western world. It does not trust the media. It does not, repeat does not, give away information to the regular media except for a specific purpose. The Catholic press itself is notoriously dull because it is generally the official organ for managing information, which is still a one-way street.

The normal procedure for a crisis of these purported proportions would be to hush it up and protect the former bishop, if only because it reflects badly on the church as a whole. Use of the local Catholic press would be solely to get the story quietly to the effected population—the people in all the parishes and organizations of the diocese which could be relied upon to recoup the loss and keep the affair as quiet as possible.

There would be rumours, of course, but nothing would be confirmed. The loss would be dealt with internally. The Catholic church does not air its dirty laundry in public. A decision to the contrary was taken and there had to be ‘a good reason’ for it.

In other words, the gain had to outweigh the loss of the bad publicity. The greatest gain would be that the shock would result in the loosening of private purse strings. The loss would be the discrediting of a bishop, a retired bishop, but one who in the view of the majority of principal decision makers was easily expendable for any number of reasons.

In the collective view De Roo was a liability that could be cut. In their view he had brought it on himself. He was to blame. That would be affixed indelibly in the public consciousness, the better to open some of those larger and too-long-closed purse strings. In the interviews for this book De Roo himself admitted that certain well-heeled members of his congregation were withholding in reaction to his social stands.

And it worked. Not only did the money pour in but a carte blanche arrangement for any further financial decisions would be granted. Retreat centres could be closed with a minimum of questioning. It was all necessary for the good of the diocese. The fact that Bethlehem Retreat Centre conducted 'progressive' spiritual development courses, now out of favour by Rome, was simply an added bonus.

8. OUT OF THE LOOP

For some reason *Island Catholic News* was entirely kept out of the loop. It was never approached to help with the situation. Further, ICN Editor Marnie Butler asked the diocesan finance people most privy to information to clarify the financial facts "for the record." While they assured complete openness within the Catholic community these "facts" were never forthcoming. Instead the regular media, which in the usual view of the church is seen as unequivocally antagonistic, was fed information and was trusted to fuel and steer the controversy.

In my twenty-five years of experience as a church journalist who was fascinated by this problem of media relations, I have never seen this done before. Normally the Catholic church assiduously avoids even responding to media inquiries on anything so potential damaging as financial irregularities.

At best the media is viewed with suspicion by church personnel because it is seen as unmanageable and asks difficult questions that are based on secular (i.e. non-Christian) values.

Ironically this is one of the areas where De Roo made some positive contribution during his earlier career. As a writer and editor who worked within the Canadian Catholic Church from 1978, this attitude on the part of the church always seemed counterproductive.

De Roo's reputation for exercising a candid style with media interviews was one of the reasons *Island Catholic News* was set up on Vancouver Island. I felt the paper could succeed in Victoria on an autonomous basis, and it had.

As a journalist I knew that De Roo would wait until there was an objective moment, when he could do what he did best, communicate from a position of personal authority. It was only then that he would feel confident in presenting his side of the truth of the situation; of it being actually heard. As the local media hysteria mounted and the blistering pejorative headlines continued unabated, I sensed this moment was slipping away and would never come.

Local antagonism had built up over the years. The very fact he was blamed in public was definitive testimony. Rome and The Vatican were opposed to his style and his program of implementing Vatican II in its intent.

His hope of a balanced objective moment could only come, if it was going to arrive at all, when the Canadian Conference of Catholic Bishops were brought in to do a competent review of the situation.

Nothing would be further from the truth. This report was the hardest blow yet. The top bureaucrat in the Catholic Canadian Church would pre-empt his own report in an entirely prejudicial manner. It was a scandal in its own right but would pass unnoticed in the general mud-slinging frenzy and confusion which kept getting worse and worse for six months and beyond.

9. FACTS OF THE CASE

In the late 1980s a short term loan, lent by the diocese to Swiftsure Farms in Washington, was not repaid. Swiftsure was brokered by a Seattle Lawyer, Joseph Finley and Muriel Clemenger knew him through her horse circles. Clemenger and her brother, a California horseman, both raised Arabians, which are show horses, contrary to the implication of the *National Post* when it broke the story.

The Post reported that the investment was in race horses, and that a later land deal to try to pay off the 1.1 million dollar loss had something to do with a race track. It gave *The Post* its typical spin, that extra salacious twist.

Neither Clemenger nor De Roo ever broke silence to speak on the issue, but Clemenger told me in a telephone briefing that there never was any question of "investing in horses, or buying horses," which at that time in early March, 2000, was the general tenor of the local reporting. I was going to be interviewed on the radio about the financial scandal and wanted to make sure that some of my impressions were accurate, so Muriel Clemenger and I had a conversation.

She said that the arrangement was a short-term loan at a very good fee, "irresistible, in fact." She said the problem was created when the American tax structure around show horses changed at just that time: "You could not believe how fast things changed."

She said that they should have gotten out earlier and maybe only lost half the amount but "Remi felt sorry for the farmer and we stayed in too long. Remi did not want to make things worse for the man."

It was then Muriel Clemenger told me there was never any question of the diocese investing in horses or owning horses: if there was they certainly had their chance when they were owed all that money.

According to Muriel Clemenger it was his compassion that got De Roo in trouble. This was in the late 1980s, and the money used had been from a defunct trust fund set up to look after some elderly nuns who had been left stranded when Mother Cecilia quit the Catholic Church in the 1960s.

Cecilia, an animal protectionist, had a lot of press about her extreme compassion for animals in the local Victoria papers in the 1950s and '60s. Her extremism got her into hot water with the local bishop as well as Rome and she was ordered by Rome in March, 1965 to cease and desist.[279]

De Roo inherited this problem when he took over the diocese and the trust fund was a solution to a difficult situation. Land had been sold that belonged to Mother Cecilia's order and the funds were used to pay pensions for the members of her order.

Perhaps it was a residue of the Protestant Ethic in Muriel Clemenger that did not like to see funds sitting idle; as the few remaining nuns were comfortably supported. Whether it was her Evangelical background that reasserted itself or not, she tried to do something about it. It was these funds that were used for the ill-fated loan. Technically it did not require the usual checks and balances of diocesan funds because it was outside those regular parameters.

This debt was still outstanding in the middle 1990s when the land deal came along as a solution to paying it off. The idea was that the land would eventually sell covering the old debt and making more money to boot. It might have worked out if De Roo was not required to retire at age seventy-five. At that time it still had not paid off.

Al Heron suggested that the monthly payments were of such a size that a larger supporting body may have had to guarantee the loan. It was suggested the Archdiocese of Vancouver guaranteed the loan that required hundred and thirty thousand dollar payments each month.

In the end the Diocese of Victoria was probably large enough to float its own loan and the diocese was able to get a line of credit to make the monthly payments.

This was the arrangement when the new administration in Victoria took over under Raymond Roussin in February 1999. For whatever reasons, the new finance-administration committee were antagonistic to this arrangement and they pulled the plug making the situation that much worse.

On the face of it, there is really not anything very sensational in all this unless you want to dress it up. So why was it all made into a public scandal?

10. THE BETTER REPORTING

The better reporting on the story was done by the *Globe and Mail*. The local daily, the Victoria *Times Colonist*, seemed to get much too close to the story to do an objective job on it.

It was the difference between a story intelligently told with journalistic objectivity; with a beginning, a middle and an end; and some designated purpose to its telling versus one thrown together constantly in a feeding frenzy because the story had proven a juicy one for the local market.

The *Times Colonist* virtually accepted everything the Diocese issued at face value. Their conclusion to the fact that neither Clemenger nor De Roo would give their sides was simply not to provide any counterbalance in their own reporting. It's typical of lazy journalism, encouraged by a publisher's presumed prejudice.

The story hardly got off the front page for months and this seemed to satisfy the *Times Colonist*. In the fifteen years I have been reading it as the local paper of record, The T-C has never distinguished itself with investigative journalism.

De Roo's reputation was dismembered in every day's trouble. I sent three or four lengthy op-ed pieces to challenge the conventional wisdom, but none were published. My letters that were published were short ones on specific points of accuracy. It was all very dismaying. Eventually, after all the damage was done, Don Vipond, a former editorial writer with the T-C, talked them into running an appreciation piece on De Roo, which by its nature did not attempt to address any of the prevailing issues.[280]

Kim Lunman's piece in the *Globe and Mail* had greater balance and integrity.

Her story was datelined Lacey, Washington where the questionable investment property is situated. She told me that while there she found no court records or documents with De Roo's signature on them, perhaps contributing to the sympathy she said she had for him as a figure in the whole debacle.

"The promissory note for the mortgage was signed by the diocese's financial administrator, Muriel Clemenger, who retired at the same time as Bishop De Roo," her piece read.

"Ms Clemenger, a former missionary who now lives in Nanaimo, recently defended the investment to the newspaper *Christianweek*. 'I remain convinced that we'll come out of it all right because it is a good investment,' she said. 'I'm very much at peace and at rest in my own heart.'"[281]

Clemenger said the same thing to me at the time of my earlier telephone briefing: "They say God is in reality, so God is in this somewhere, we'll just wait and see how."

11. WHAT IT'S ALL ABOUT

Such a coincidence that after thirty-seven and half years as bishop, within the twelve months after he left office, so much after all is found to be wrong with De Roo's administrative manner.

Was Rome asleep at the switch for four decades or are we to assume that perhaps, just perhaps, there are some other dynamics at work here? Certainly things lined up well against De Roo.

At the bottom level, locally, nearly forty years of a certain sort of antipathy was finally given its full play. Within the church, there was that block of clergy that chafed under De Roo's leadership style, who badly wanted him gone so that one of their own could have his day.

Add to this traditionalists who resisted Vatican II tooth and nail. In addition, there were recently converted or returned social conservatives who were embarrassed that a left-wing radical was in charge of their church, especially that he received so much adulation and media coverage for views that drove them crazy.

Of course, Rome's disposition was well known. The new top down authoritarianism was in direct opposition to De Roo's advance. Even the normally unflappable De Roo had been expressing concern at just how bad it was getting in Rome, what he had experienced during his ad limina visits.[282] Rome was not a debatable point.

The top level within the church and the local level were all settled in their indigestion. The local situation had shifted further that way with him out of office. But the big surprise was in the middle where he could have expected to be cut a bit of slack.

If there was going to be a neutral forum where he could have his say, it should have been provided by a balanced intervention from the Canadian Conference of Catholic Bishops where De Roo had made such a critical contribution over many decades.

I knew from the start that De Roo would not respond to the media frenzy, that he would not allow the media to set the agenda where he was expected to speak about his side of the affair.

Catholic bishops are a small and exclusive club. They are in the habit of controlling the venue where they have their say. When the Canadian Bishops Conference agreed to do a canonical inquiry, this could be the opportunity when he felt that a neutral opening was available.

But he would never be granted this moment. The report and the reporting process and the inquiry itself was not conceived in those terms. He was too powerful a speaker to be allowed to have his complete say. After all that was what had made him so unpopular with the other side in the first place. He could marshall facts and ideas and insight of analysis in so masterful a manner it made his enemies see red; and his disciples gasp with inspiration.

This was precisely his area of leadership within the church and within Canadian society.

To be able to move such an institution as the Catholic Church in the way he had demonstrably done for fifty years, this required a special set of skills—political skills that got things changed and also made fiercely irate enemies.

❧❧❧

The Editor
Globe and Mail
June 30, 2000

I appreciated Kim Lunman's piece on the Diocese of Victoria's financial woes (G&M 17-6, p. A11). She did a good job of tracking the financial line of the story. Of course there are those who feel that this is really a political story—church politics.

It's interesting, in this vein, that she was only able to find tenuous direct connections between Remi De Roo, Victoria's bishop from 1962 to 1999, with the line of the story. She acknowledges that the earlier financial strategy was entirely the creation of Muriel Clemenger, the former administrator; and it was her job to do such creating.

De Roo had the reputation for 'not caring about money' and for delegating in a manner that included a lot of trust and little if any second guessing. It is interesting as well that the verdict is still out as to whether the property in question will sell; recovering the entire 'loss' as Muriel Clemenger was still convinced it would even after the original story broke in late February. Clemenger and I had a candid conversation about the topic then when I needed to be briefed prior to a radio interview on this issue.

The fact the story was broken by the National Post *bears some close scrutiny. Their reporter called the* Island Catholic News *with what was supposed to be an irresistible offer of two hundred dollars to tape the message that was only to be read from the pulpit the following Sunday. It is amazingly diligent of* The Post *to be closely monitoring the financial troubles of every Catholic Diocese in the country—some seventy in all. As the one who was supposed to be doing the taping, the request made the hairs stand up on the back on my neck in a sudden alertness that something funny was afoot.*

I well knew that the owner of The Post *(and a few dozen other newspapers, including the local Victoria* Times Colonist *at the time), one Conrad Black, was reported in your pages ferociously attacking De Roo in the 1980s over his role in the Canadian Bishops' critique of the crisis in the Canadian economy. It got all rather heavy and personal.*

The Post *angle about race horses became the hallmark headline of the story despite the fact Arabians are show horses. The gambling edge had to get in there. Muriel Clemenger stated to me there never was any question of buying or investing directly in horses. She said it was a "simple bridge financing arrangement with a healthy fee" that went afoul leading to the losses and then to the recovery strategy of flipping the property at Lacey, Washington, which Kim Lunman tracked. Clemenger told me that it was De Roo's compassion for the horse farmer at Swiftsure Farms that would not let her pull the plug earlier.*

Back home here on Vancouver Island, the new diocesan administration was very quick to publicly affix blame to the previous administration and yet I see that Ms Lunman correctly indicated that it was the decisions taken by the new group that resulted in the escalation of the financial problems, caused by the foreclosure and the court ordered jacked-up interest rates. The new administration refused to continue payments thus resulting in the crisis becoming a catastrophe which was all blamed on De Roo despite his being out of office when these subsequent decisions were taken.

Clemenger obviously had a workable payment strategy in place with the Lacey property but it was promptly abandoned, exacerbating the difficulties. Clemenger was requested by the new administration not to speak in public, a promise she keeps to this day.

Even the way the information was released was very curious at best. The clergy were forbidden from distributing the statement, which was only to be read from the pulpit. This reverting to ancient secrecy methodology caused the maximum media curiosity; and subsequent furore, anger and confusion among the general Catholic population.

On the other hand, it worked and Bishop De Roo in the collective view was entitled to wear all the blame. The new financial administrator, by the way, was hired out of the circles in the diocese that had always been hypercritical of De Roo's administrative style. Clemenger was not popular among the traditionalist clergy, either because she was a woman or as a scapegoat for their feelings about the boss; feelings which could not be directly expressed.

Meanwhile back in Rome, as Garry Wills argues in his new book, "Papal Sin" (reviewed by Michael Valpy in your same edition) very little will be tolerated in the way of church reform or progressive theology. Unfortunately De Roo made the mistake in February '99 of announcing such would form a distinct part of his retirement program. Shortly after that he was silenced for the first time in his career when scheduled to speak in Atlanta at a married Catholic clergy conference. Then as now he has suffered in complete silence, knowing this is hardly the time for speaking out, or his program, yet knowing as well how things can shift in the Catholic Church.

Less than twenty years ago he peaked a twenty year run of social and theologically progressive leadership with the 'Reflections on the Crisis in the Canadian Economy' on New Year's Day, 1983. This event made him a household name—fifteen minutes of fame that was extended for fifteen years.

Rome's disposition and the changing of the guard in Victoria are no big surprise nor was the retrograde reaction of Conrad Black who became a Catholic through the back door about the same time De Roo was championing the rights of the unemployed in the early 1980s. De Roo would not be the individual running the church of his choice.

According to Ron Graham's 1990 book "God's Dominion," Black was welcomed into the church by Cardinal Emmett Carter of Toronto without the privilege of the usual one-to-two year discernment process the Catholic Church requires of its entrants. Perhaps Black's theological acumen was the basis for the exemption, with his strong suit the church's social teachings.

The surprise area of attack was the Canadian Bishops Conference which was called in by the new Victoria Bishop, Raymond Roussin, to do a formal canonical inquiry. While their report has yet to be released, its chairperson Rev. Peter Schonenbach, General Secretary of the CCCB, was headlined in the Times Colonist *comparing De Roo's situation to that of a gambling addict. The general secretary thus pre-empted his own report in a prejudicial manner; hardly professional behaviour from the Canadian Catholic Church's top bureaucrat.*

Roussin, by the way, seems a complete innocent in these political matters, as evidenced by the breakdown of his health under the pressure of the financial quandary and the discrediting that De Roo, his friend and colleague, has suffered.

Coming out of Vatican II, the Canadian Conference of Catholic Bishops could be said to have lead the universal church in its celebration and manifestation of collegiality, a central principle emerging out of Vatican II. An apt example was the infamous birth control controversy in 1968. At the time De Roo led the conference in its all but dissenting pastoral application of the papal encyclical 'Humanae Vitae.'

The general Catholic outcry against the teaching by Pope Paul VI created a crisis of confidence in the church's central teaching authority from which the Catholic church is still reeling. Collegiality was the coming of age of global Catholicism, where the local national church would decide how best to apply the papal teachings; but it has all but been abandoned.

In the 1990s Cardinal Ratzinger of the Curia has made it expressly clear that under the present papal regime the national colleges of bishops have no canonical status or authority. So it is not surprising to see the CCCB fold entirely under Roman pressure, although it must be sorely disappointing for De Roo who was a leading figure in the development of the collegial principle both at the Council (1962-65) and in Canada after as a Council Father.

Remi De Roo, a national icon, has suffered from an orchestrated effort to discredit his legacy, to distract him from adding to it. With his linguistic capacity and actual theological acumen, he was once among the very few Canadian Bishops with legitimate papabilia potential. That was all cancelled from 1968 when he crossed the American kingmaker Cardinal Francis MacIntyre of Los Angeles and had his advancement card indelibly soiled in Rome.

It must be very painful for him to be protested against in Saint Boniface, Manitoba recently when parents complained about having children confirmed by a bishop under threat of canonical censure. De Roo, a priest of that diocese, was anointed for succession at Saint Boniface by Archbishop Baudoux, his mentor, but it was never to be, due to the above difficulties. The mitre was passed to his classmate and cousin by marriage Archbishop Antoine Hacault who died of cancer in April and asked De Roo from his deathbed to make his confirmation rounds.

My own intuition about the financial dimension of this story is that there will be, lo and behold, a deus ex machina manifestation and the financial situation of the diocese will be fully restored by the selling of that much-cursed and joked about property. But the permanent impact will be the discrediting of the reputation of Remi De Roo, the actual purpose of the entire saga.

Not for the first time have such cruel, clever politics been so manipulated in the Canadian Catholic Church (or the Diocese of Victoria). Remember Archbishop Joseph Charbonneau, the social justice advocate of Montréal. He 'retired' for ten years to Victoria prior to his death in 1959, and he too refused to speak out about his shafting because he did not want to add to 'the scandal about the church'. I am afraid the scandal of the church is all too apparent to those who have the eyes to see and the ears to hear.

Patrick Jamieson
Victoria, BC
[unpublished]

Annual footwashing ceremony at Easter Vigil liturgy at St. Andrew's Cathedral. (ICN)

PREFACE

AFTER ALL IS SAID

De Roo's very Christianity and prophetic spirituality meant that he could not be entirely surprised at, or by, the crucifixion when it came.

The problem of Remi De Roo is the problem of a post-modernist figure in a barely post-medieval institution and one that is doing its best to head back that way. The tension is inexorable, yet delicious in its drama. His eventual crucifixion by the very institution that created him was all but inevitable.

People forget that Pope John XXIII spent forty years in the wilderness with virtually no assurance he would ever be listened to prior to becoming the surprise choice as pope. The Holy Spirit of truth and justice works even in the Catholic church but not by eliminating the sharp left-right politics.

PART FOUR: REMI DE ROO AND THE POST-MODERNIST CRISIS

The Battling Bishop
By Judy Steed in the Globe and Mail
Saturday May 3, 1986

One of Canada's most outspoken radicals is an unpretentious man in a gray suit and clerical collar... whose passions have carried his influence far beyond his own parish.

The Bishop of Victoria, a driving force behind the controversial 1983 Ethical Reflections... has experienced, in his words, "plenty of hassles" in the past few decades.

The greatest uproar was reserved for the Ethical Reflections condemnation of a North American capitalist system run for the benefit of an elite minority... Bishop De Roo has extended his views in a new book, Cries of Victims, Voice of God*....*

Bishop De Roo does not fit the stereotype of a man of the cloth. In March, on the stage of Massey Hall, he stole the spotlight from Erika Ritter, Pierre Berton and Bob White with a passionate attack on free trade. Last month he was the keynote speaker at the Canadian Union of Postal Workers annual convention where he criticized the freemarket economy.

And within the past six months he has addressed the National Farmers Union in Edmonton, The B.C. Federation of Labour, The Confederation of Canadian Unions and The Canadian Union of Public Employees.

At 62, Bishop De Roo makes a noticeable effort to speak in a contemporary voice, which bears no trace of elitism. He deflects veneration with a casual smile.

"The fundamental insight is that answers will not come from gurus," he says. "Successful people are comfortable with the status quo. The true experts are the ones suffering from our economic structures."

Nevertheless, he is regarded as something of a guru by most people who know him...

Certainly the bishop's view is far from conventional, though he claims it's very much in the Biblical tradition....

"Of course we Canadians are part of what oppresses them. If you are not part of the solution, you're part of the problem." To his critics he is part of the problem... Toronto's Cardinal Emmett Carter does not share his views.

He was initially angered by the Ethical Reflections, and subsequently objected to another of Bishop De Roo's plans—to give women greater responsibility in the Roman Catholic Church.... An advocate of liberation theology, he believes he is being true to the revolutionary teachings of Jesus. "Christians," he says, "are obliged to transform their world."

His words are strong—and effective. "He has expanded my vision and made me ask myself hard questions," says Sister Christine Gaudet, executive director of St. Michael's Hospital in Toronto. For twelve years, Sister Christine administered a hospital in Bishop De Roo's Victoria parish and observed in action "the prophetic stances he takes... He makes you ask: What will this do to people, to workers."

It is no wonder he has been called into boardrooms by angry executives who feel personally offended by his criticism of their corporate activities.

Bishop De Roo responds with some acerbity: "These men trot out their titles and credentials, they see themselves as model Christians, yet they have not made a distinction between the ethics of their company policies and their own lives." The unexamined life, he suggests, can produce collaboration with oppression.

In Cries of Victims, *Bishop De Roo observes, that "in Western society, the dominant culture tends to view life through the eyes of the influential and wealthy who have the power of defining reality... but the basic purpose of sound economics is to serve human needs, not to exploit people for maximum corporate profit....*

"We have made technology and capital our moral and social goals, when they should be means or instruments. They have become ends in themselves, self-serving and independent...If western culture and Canadian society are to be humane and humanizing, then we must dethrone our economic idols."

He deflects the name calling (that critics always receive) by insisting on the "Christian's right to criticize any system—capitalist or communist—and to search for new alternatives." It is the mission of the church, he argues, to assist in this search. "The church must be countercultural."

....He went to Rome in 1950 where his eyes were opened to global issues. "Rome is like the public square of the world." In 1952, back in Manitoba, he began to work with Catholic youth action groups and came under the influence of Canon Cardijn, the father of Catholic Action and founder of the Young Christian Workers movement, which were to have considerable influence in Québec during The Quiet Revolution....

Bishop De Roo is sometimes accused of being opposed to modern times, but he insists he is no machine bashing luddite. "We're not against technology. It's the use... The Bishops are not against trade, markets and legitimate profit. A dynamic economy is essential for a culture to flourish. But the balance has swung too far in favour of the rich and the powerful," he believes....

Chapter Nineteen: The Prairie Populist Sensibility

1. SOME FUNERALS

I happened to attend a funeral during the later period of the composition of this book; a funeral which was held in the next village in Manitoba to where Remi De Roo grew up.

It was all a coincidence. A friend of my family died after retiring to this Manitoba village and I was available to represent them at the funeral. When I looked up on a map, just where it was I had to be for the funeral, it turned out to be the village next to Swan Lake. It's one of those funny accidents that come along to help you write a book; where the universe seems to arrange itself to facilitate the process.

I mentioned this funeral to the bishop at another funeral, that of Bernard de Aguiar at Bethlehem Retreat Centre in Nanaimo, just a few days after returning from Manitoba. De Aguiar, a native of Brazil, was a former Trappist monk who served as a secretarial assistant to the monk and writer Thomas Merton. This was at Gethsemane Monastery in Kentucky prior to making his way to Vancouver Island in the mid-1960s to be part of the historic hermit community which De Roo helped instigate.

By this time I had come to know the bishop quite well over a period of twelve years, operating a monthly independent Catholic newspaper in his diocese and writing a popular-level history of the Catholic Church on Vancouver Island during that period. We were on very friendly if still somewhat formal terms. From earlier experience I had learned this is often the best way with such men in official Catholic leadership positions.

Many—if not most—in the diocese called him 'Remi' but I —without fail—always addressed him as 'Bishop'. Most of our conversations were on the basis of formal exchange of information —on a need to know basis. We were definitely not on terms of intimate personal sharing. Neither of us were very good at small talk; and that was just fine with me.

When I mentioned that I had attended this other funeral in Dunrea, his eyes visibly lightened and he came forth with more of a flow of natural memories to me than I had ever experienced from him. His talk was of his Swan Lake years and Saint Boniface Archdiocese experience.

This episode told me quite a bit about how he too could open up when circumstances allowed but I also knew that there was really no way to arrange such 'circumstances'.

It was an interesting moment because his coadjutor replacement had been named, and he had said he was well pleased with the choice and the process. He told me on an earlier occasion that he did not expect to have such a good choice provided by Rome.

Overall he seemed very relaxed. He was at an event which represented a symbolic closure to his years as an active bishop, his formal episcopacy. It was the death of a hermit who had come to be part of an exciting development in the earliest years of his episcopacy. The re-introduction of the hermit life to the western church was a Vatican II accomplishment, and De Roo had been a principal vehicle.

It drew him to the attention of the world famous Thomas Merton who was said to be considering relocating to Vancouver Island to be part of this unique experiment in hermit life when he was killed on an Asian journey in late 1968.[283]

It had been a proud and historic accomplishment to help re-establish such a hermit community in the western church—the first time in three hundred years.

Charles Brandt, who was ordained for the community by De Roo in 1965, says that the bishop and Jacques Winanady, the head of the Island hermit community, went to meet Merton at the Vancouver airport for the purpose of discussing the idea. Unfortunately Merton had given them the wrong flight details and they never did connect. He died in Bangkok before returning to North America.[284]

2. THE VILLAGE OF SWAN LAKE

Swan Lake, Manitoba is in the southwest corner of the province. It is only about 50 km north of the North Dakota/United States border. Brandon would be the closest centre of any size.

Boissevan is nearby, more south and west toward the Saskatchewan boundary. Somerset and Bruxelles are the names of the nearest villages. They are about the same size as Swan Lake and also populated by De Roos and De Papes, the region where they have made their mark.

In Swan Lake itself, the Catholic church building is difficult to miss. Once past the grain elevator with its elevated printing: "Swan Lake," the church is the most prominent structure.

The village is on a rail line, not directly situated on Highway 23 which passes a kilometre or so to the south. There is a hospital/health centre near the church, one of a number in the general region.

I attended the funeral of my friend at nearby Dunrea, a smaller centre, also just off Highway 23 but to the west. Dunrea is perhaps half an hour away by car. De Roo told me he had a Grade School classmate from Dunrea, so it is all of a region.

The geography around Swan Lake is slightly rolling hills. The town is well kept, neat and orderly, betraying its Belgian roots. The church has large outdoor statuary of Saint Joseph, The Blessed Virgin Mary and the Sacred Heart of Jesus, in the yard facing the street; all major devotions of the past century in Canadian Catholicism.

This would be the church and rectory where Monsignor Deiderich, Remi's beloved and influential pastor—and the person outside the family most responsible for nurturing his priestly vocation—lived and served for many years, all the years of Remi's growing up. This was the man who provided his original model of priesthood.

Outside the little town, less than a mile northward is the village cemetery: Protestant English to the left, Catholic Belgian and French names to the right, driving away from the village.

As you turn to travel the hundred yards or so into the Catholic section, a row of trees and a line of grave markers set the boundary of the cemetery proper. Entering, you go first left and then to the right searching for the familiar names, De Pape and De Roo. There are plenty of them.

Off in the far left hand corner is a statue of an angel guarding the graves of the occupants. It is a real stone angel unlike the one at not-so-distant Neepawa, celebrated by Margaret Laurence's well-known novel of that name. Her angel turns out to be in actuality the figure of a woman; an angel only of her imagination.

But here at Swan Lake, Catholic orthodoxy prevails and it is the traditional image of an angel. From my perspective at the gravestones, behind the angel is the infinite-seeming, endless expanse of the prairie. The angel statue represents the last line of shelter and demarcation against infinity at that point.

IMMUTABLE FORMATION

Bishop De Roo's parents and grandparents share grave markers as couples, signifying the permanent stability of their marriage relationships; the bedrock of the clan structure and of his own immutable formation.

While his grandparents De Roo died only three years apart, his parents' deaths were separated by nearly forty years. His mother's marker would have waited those decades for his father's name.

Having studied the lives of these two sets of progenitor, it seemed a profound if very cold experience—due to a dropping October temperature—to set their gravemarkers in the lens of my camera that Saturday afternoon. Then we hurried on to attend the funeral.

3. DUNREA

The funeral in Dunrea itself was held at St. Felix's, the French Catholic parish church of the village. That liturgy told me something of the Catholic faith of the people of that locality.

My friend who died had been a successful hotelier, rising to the top of his profession; working for a national hotel chain although his career peak was managing the Winnipeg Convention Centre in the 1980s.

For reasons that mystified most of his friends and business associates, for the last five years of his life, Ray settled down in this rural Manitoba village as owner of the hamlet's hotel. When he came to Dunrea his health was apparently not threatened.

The inn was a tiny one actually, with just five rooms used only during hunting season. With one of his sons he operated the bar and restaurant, endearing himself quickly with the local people; insinuating himself successfully into the local community scene in a way only a kindly and extroverted over-achiever could in that context.

The turnout at the funeral was testament to this, as were the words of the priest.

The pastor turned out to be an East Indian, sort of a reverse missioner, with a text-book theology from which he expressed his homely homily. He stated unequivocally that my friend had been spiritually prepared to die at the end. He was peaceful and resolved, his earthly affairs were in order.

His one dependent son, who suffered from a permanent handicap, was taken care of as best as could be arranged on this mortal coil. His personal affairs resolved as fully as possible, he had experienced the good death, in the tradition of 'a fully Christian death': surrounded by friends and family, major issues resolved, in little direct pain, fully conscious of what he was undergoing and reconciled to his departure with the last rites of the church.[285]

I had discovered only while travelling to attend his funeral that he had decided to become a Catholic through the instrumental influence of my family of origin some twenty years previously.

Through a combination of conscious and unconscious reasons Ray had chosen to live out his last years in a part of the province with historic Catholic roots and resources.

The reception in his hotel afterwards, with its plates of homemade sandwiches and small cakes, had a heartwarming working-class ambience about it. The locals and the strangers gingerly mixing, feeling out who each other were.

Ray had been attracted, in the end, to a foundation tradition that framed life, death, birth and infinity; and it was in the same region and Catholic framework of ritual and sensibility that personally formed the first fourteen years of Remi De Roo; who in terms of permanent moral sensibility never left it.

4. SAINT BONIFACE

From there his flight to Saint Boniface for seminary training was along a direct and obvious avenue. Historic Saint Boniface where the original cathedral structure is surrounded by the French graveyard and resting place of Louis Riel, an earlier variety of mystic prairie rebel.

The original cathedral building burned to the ground in 1968, leaving only a symbolic shell and courtyard about the modern, smaller and more practical worship centre that rose out of the ashes. Rather than slavishly duplicate what had gone before, typically Saint Boniface erected a fresh structure, more in tune with the tenor of the times following Vatican II.

This is a diocese which dates back to 1822 as a mission. The historic figures of Provencher, Taché, Grandin dominate the popular imagination; all bishops in the 19th Century, men who served long and difficult terms, some before Canadian confederation. They all have major arterial roadways named after them in the French-speaking suburbs of Greater Winnipeg.

In the 20th Century one local archbishop, Belliveau, served for forty years between 1915 and 1955, dying at Saint Boniface Hospital. His death contains an object lesson and featured Remi De Roo in a more than incidental role.

For seventeen years the young De Roo served as a seminarian and priest under Archbishop Belliveau who suffered a stroke in his later years. The stroke limited his capacity so he was assisted by an auxiliary bishop, Maurice Baudoux, Remi De Roo's mentor.

The day that Archbishop Belliveau died Father De Roo happened to be in his own office in the chancery at six o'clock in the morning when a knock came to the door.

De Roo was in the habit of staying over in his office if he worked late and there were likely to be any early morning school enquiries. This particular morning Father De Roo thought he heard something out of the ordinary and wondered to himself if it was "the old man."

At six a knock came at his door and upon opening it was the archbishop fully dressed asking to be taken to the hospital. Two hours later 'the old man' was dead.

❧❧❧

De Roo told me this story in his expansive mood after the de Aguiar funeral in Nanaimo. He also told me that day he felt he knew the exact moment his upward mobility was sealed. He related both episodes in the same disinterested matter of fact manner. He also smiled as he told me 'that he had not told me this story'.

Belliveau's successor, Archbishop Baudoux, served until 1974 at which point Bishop De Roo had been in Victoria for nearly twelve years, a suitable apprenticeship period if he was going to be further elevated to his home diocese. Instead his cousin by marriage, Antoine Hacault, a classmate and colleague at the Second Vatican Council, was appointed.

There has always been a great deal of speculation on the informal level about why someone of his obvious ability was consistently passed over for promotion when he regularly demonstrated a leadership capacity rare within the Canadian church.[286]

5. SOUTH OF THE BORDER

The answer, it has been strongly hinted, lies south of the border in Los Angeles. The American writer John Gregory Dunne has done an indepth portrait in the *New York Review of Books* of the late Cardinal James Francis McIntyre of Los Angeles. McIntyre was as much a stout opponent of the reforms of Vatican II as De Roo was their defender.

According to Dunne, McIntyre was appointed at the insistence of Cardinal Spellman of New York in his ambition to outflank a number of liberal bishops in the American midwest.

Spellman apparently wanted a flanking west coast ally against what he called the midwest axis in his internal church wars. A close associate of Pope Pius XII, Spellman had more than a little influence on Vatican appointments. By having his ultraconservative chancellor MacIntyre appointed he worked his strategy effectively.

McIntyre was seventy-seven years old when the Second Vatican Council was held in 1962 and he lived until 1970 making life entirely miserable for progressive forces in his archdiocese in the interim.

The most publicized case perhaps, if only because McIntyre was seen to have lost it, was with the Immaculate Heart Sisters, a large and important religious order in Los Angeles, who refused to be bowed and left the diocese in all but total numbers—a remnant stayed as loyalists.

Bishop De Roo had publicly welcomed a number of these religious—known colloquially as The Hollywood Sisters—to work in his diocese at the time of the public controversy. As such he publicly contradicted McIntyre's directives. Informed sources strongly suggest that his copy book in Rome was permanently soiled against him from this time, in 1968. At the time he probably thought little of it.

Douglas Roche, the founding editor of the *Western Catholic Reporter*, based in Edmonton, wrote a story April 4, 1968, headlined: "De Roo Upholds Sisters' Right to Experiment."

It reads: "Bishop Remi De Roo of Victoria has publicly protested against a ruling by the Vatican Congregation of Religious which would severely restrict the Immaculate Hearts Sisters program for renewal.

"Bishop De Roo, who has thirteen IHM Sisters in three convents in his diocese, says he will allow them to continue their experimentation "Unless I get a ruling from the Holy Father personally."

"He said the attitude shown by Ildebrando Cardinal Antoniutti, prefect of the Congregation, could have disastrous consequences" for sisters everywhere.

"The IHM controversy, which has now reached major proportions in the Church in the U.S., began when James Cardinal McIntyre of Los Angeles opposed a temporary experiment in renewal under which the Immaculate Heart Sisters permitted members to wear secular clothing, keep their own hours and find ways of serving Church and society other than by teaching in parochial schools.

"The IHM Sisters said their experiments were a response to the decrees of Vatican II and also to a directive by Pope Paul mandating self-renewal by religious communities. Cardinal McIntyre said they were being disobedient to him in carrying out the reform without his direction, adding they would no longer be "approved nuns" and could not teach in their thirty-five Los Angeles schools next year."

"The cardinal asked the Congregation of religious for a ruling. A letter from sixty-nine-year-old Cardinal Antoniutti sided with Cardinal McIntyre and against the nuns:

- The Sisters "have to adopt a uniform habit" because "the habit pertains to the nature and characteristics of any institute for which it has been approved."
- Every community should meet daily "for some religious exercise in common."
- The sisters should stick to education because that is what they were founded to do.
- They are required to work in "collaboration with the local Ordinary."

"The IHMs appealed the decision to Pope Paul and so far 3,000 nuns of other orders and many groups of clergy and laity throughout the United States have signed petitions in support of the IHM desire to continue experimentation.

"Bishop De Roo, who gave the IHM sisters in his diocese permission to experiment in their apostolate more than a year ago, noted that he was not consulted by the Congregation of Religious —even though one of the Congregation's four points specifies that the IHM Sisters must work in collaboration with the local bishop.

"As far as he is concerned, the IHM Sisters are working in full collaboration with him and will continue to do so..."

6. SAINT BONIFACE REVISITED

The oversight in 1974 and again in the late 1980s when Winnipeg archdiocese was given to another westcoast bishop would be no accidents according to this hypothesis. If it bothered him no one seemed to notice or publicly remark about it.

Bishop De Roo insists that Antoine Hacault is not his cousin except by marriage but is a very close friend. He reserves the category of cousin to immediate blood relatives. Archbishop Hacault himself however had no problem using the broader sense of the term.

In fact he took an unmistakable touch of pride in the connection, of the sort that comes when a figure through accomplishments and reputation starts to approach the status of legend in their own lifetime.[287]

De Roo was with his 'cousin' in April, 2000 when he died of cancer at Saint Boniface hospital. He agreed to take over his confirmation rounds for him and this resulted in a public controversy reported in the pages of Winnipeg newspapers.

The infamous post-retirement tempestuous financial saga was in full form just then and some ultra-traditionalist critics decided to go public with their reservations about his standing in the church. This was due to the formal canonical investigation that was underway at the time.

It was a very ugly and sad commentary at that stage of things. *The Winnipeg Sun* ran full page stories on pages 5 and 4 of its May 26 and 27 editions respectively, headlined: "Uncomfortable pews, Parishioners protest controversial bishop" and "'Mountain out of a molehill, Church official defends BC Bishop."

Police Reporter Greg Di Cresce's lead paragraph of May 26 read: "Members of the Roman Catholic Diocese of Saint Boniface are calling the decision to have controversial Bishop Remi De Roo confirm young parishioners into the faith a travesty."

Two traditionalist parents felt that financial irregularities and investigation by a canon law inquiry were grounds for not allowing De Roo to do pastoral work he had promised Antoine Hacault on his deathbed.

Even traditionalist theology would not support such an action. These people would well know that the Church has long taught that the 'moral' condition of the performing clergy does not effect the efficacy of the sacrament.

The May 27 article quoted Monsignor Peter Schoenenbach's infamous likening of De Roo to that of a gambling addict. As explained in an earlier chapter, by his odd twist, Schoenenbach, the general secretary of the Canadian Conference of Catholic Bishops who headed up the canonical inquiry, prejudiced the findings by pre-empting his own findings with pejorative ad hoc commentary in the media.

William Kokesch, communications head for the CCCB, qualified his views of the issue this way, quoted in the same *Sun* piece:

"It's a shame an issue that involved material rather than pastoral issues is troubling the end of De Roo's career. And it's sad to think it could colour all the top notch pastoral work he has done."

A few days later on June 4, Father Ray Beaudry, a Winnipeg priest, weighed in with a letter critical of the "two self-righteous women Christine Joyal and Brenda Coppell" saying they seemed to be "unaware De Roo ... was an intelligent, dedicated and generous servant of Christ and his people as an advocate for Canada's disenfranchised, unemployed and politically powerless and the Third World poor and oppressed."

"He has graciously agreed to remain among us despite being pilloried. And we are glad he is here."

Challenge magazine editor Larry Henderson went one step better than Christine Joyal and Brenda Coppell in his September, 2000 'Afterword' column accusing De Roo of apostasy.

"When faith goes, everything goes. A priest may have once been the best and the brightest of his kind... He promoted infidelity and finally took money from a closed convent and used it to invest in Arabian horses... The tragedy of our time has been written by those who did not believe."

Henderson does not quite make it clear what it is De Roo or this unnamed bishop does not believe in but that might suit his abstract purposes better. A slightly demented rant using a convenient straw man for the traditionalist comfort of condemning the world once again; and its latest caught-out disciple, a bishop who robs convents to bet on the horses.

The number of factual inaccuracies approximates the charity of tone of the piece. Henderson's anachronistic attitude might seem almost laughable if it weren't for the sort of mischief it tractably inspired in its readers as demonstrated by the pages of *The Sun*.

Winnipeg has been home to *Challenge* magazine since its inception, where it has made a permanent vocation of being a thorn in the side of anyone who differs with its anti-modernist 'theology.'

7. A POST-MODERN FIGURE

THE NEW AUDIENCE

Larry Henderson's pique is transparently with Remi De Roo's status as a famous figure.

In the 1980s and early '90s there arose a sort of celebratory writing about Bishop De Roo which rivalled that of the 1960s and early '70s with one important difference. He was becoming the hero of the unchurched. The earlier reporting and articles were written largely for the church press but at this later stage it was within the left-wing of the secular media.

These articles were in response to his more developed positions in the social affairs arena, which corresponded to that wider community's precepts of proper action for social justice by a church figure.

The articles were written, by and large, from a humanist perspective. These were spiritually sensitive writers who were transparently seeking meaning in their own lives, and world. These searchers recognized in Remi De Roo a sign, a living symbol who spoke to their personal aspirations for integration.

George Mortimore's May 1990 feature in *Canadian Forum* had the focus of "the social vision of Canada's compassionate bishop" and was representative of the genre. Here was a sort of writing revelling in the fact that on the horizon of Canada's increasingly secular landscape was a religious figure with an inclusive vision, articulated in a convincing enough style for ordinary people to understand.

Mortimore utilizes an image when describing De Roo's living quarters where there is an apartment within the larger apartment, the inner quarters where the bishop has his private rooms. In this apartment within the apartment aspect of the story the writer intimates his own personal fascination for the symbolism of the subject.

❧❧❧

"The small brass door-knocker is engraved: "Remi De Roo: Welcome in the name of Christ."

"Martha Wytinck, the bishop's first cousin and housekeeper, is at the door, which opens off the balcony at the top floor of the diocesan pastoral centre... She shows a visitor into a spacious apartment that commands a view of a small body of water called Swan Lake... Mrs. Wytinck remembers her cousin Remi as a small pre-schooler, sprawled on the farmhouse floor with magazines. "He was always reading...

"No religious pictures are in sight, although Mrs. Wytinck says there is a Ukrainian cross in the bishop's own quarters, which are an apartment within an apartment."

"Does he ever watch television? Only at meal times. That is the only time he has to spare.

"Here are three huge scrapbooks, big enough to hold entire newspaper pages. Does Bishop Remi ever look at his clippings?

—No I've never seen him look at them. He's too busy."

❧❧❧

"Swan Lake was a good training ground for leadership and the furtherance of social justice: strenuous labour and the hardship of prairie farming in Depressions years with five sisters and two brothers. He saw his father's survival strategies: playing a leading part in organizing the Manitoba Wheat pool... The family's devout faith. The parish priest recommended a career in the church for the youth whose intellectual brilliance showed through the rural shyness...

"In the scrapbook, the media labels record his changing public image from 'Boy Bishop' to 'Shirtsleeve bishop' to 'Battling Bishop'... The newspaper stories show him delegating wide powers to a senate of priests and a council of lay people, reaching out to Protestant churches and citizens groups in attacking community problems...

"There is his parallel secular job as first chairperson of the BC Human Rights Commission from 1974-77... and the presidency of the Western Conference of Catholic Bishops..."

❧❧❧

"Longtime associate Pearl Gervais recalls seeing him at a Christmas time family gathering learning backgammon from an eight-year-old boy. Another informant noted how at a L'Arche community home for the mentally handicapped, he was observed listening for a long time to one of the residents giving him policy advice."

"Muriel Clemenger, his assistant for finances: 'He's a very comfortable person to work with. He listens. I don't take things to him unless I want that attention, so we both save time and psychic energy. Remi is a person who knows what he is about. It's very clear to him what he is about and he sticks to that, conscientiously and prayerfully. That gives him a deep sense of confidence.'"

❧❧❧

For Mortimore, De Roo is a Christian leader worthy of respect by members of a generation that combine a grudging regard for the ideals of Christianity with an equally healthy skepticism about the relevance of ancient institutions. Mortimore describes a post-modern figure who is able to pungently address the issues and questions of the day, of these times.

A social anthropologist, Mortimore has his own professional integrity and critical political perspective to keep in balance with his burgeoning admiration for De Roo. He traces carefully the evolution of De Roo's experience that lead up to his strong stand of the Ethical Reflections of 1983.

"During the public debate that followed the bishops' assertions, Remi De Roo became an internationally known figure ... pleading his case for an economy founded on humane and moral principles. He lobbied for the ideas in the report.

"Some called him 'the conscience of Canada.' The story reached a turning point when the Social Affairs Commission on May 1, 1985 urged trade unions to take up the cause of women's workers and part-time workers who lacked job security. The report criticized Eaton's for months of stonewalling a group of women workers in their drive for a union contract.

"The frankness of the attack on Eaton's may have alarmed some of the more cautious bishops..."

❧❧❧

"But in practical terms," the interviewer asks, "isn't the deficit an important issue?"

The bishop has been looking downward and to one side in a meditative self-effacing way. Now he switches to high beam and fixes the interviewer with a steady gaze out of the tops of his eyes

"What's 'practical'? he asks. "In other words, 'practical' is what suits the politicians?"

One word has pushed him into an attack mode—a departure from his usual brisk, efficient tolerance. The interviewer, reproaching himself, knows he has fumbled this one.

"What's good for the well-being of the majority of Canadians, what's good for the future of the country, that's what we should define 'practical'... The big issue is redistribution of wealth. Free trade is a global plan to let the multinationals have free rein..."

He interclasps his fingers and fidgets briefly with his wide gold episcopal ring.

"I hope you will ask me something other than economics," he says. "I'm not an economist. I'm a pastor."

"Should churchmen really mind their own religious business and stay out of worldly affairs?"

"That's an obsolete model of Christianity, to cut the human being into slices, one of which would be the spiritual and the other temporal or economic or whatever. A human being is of one piece. Every dimension, including the spiritual, is part of the human being and part of our system."

❧❧❧

What is most interesting about these articles is how, as the writer gets closer to his subject, the nascent hope and innocent expectations are rewarded in their view. To them De Roo does not disappoint on closer inspection.

Diana Hartog, for example, in her local *Monday Magazine* feature four years earlier in 1986, brings to bear certain personal operational circumspection in her perspective in the piece. Hers is an article which reveals directly this effect De Roo can have on the investigator. She does a lengthy introduction and postscript which frame the more objectively written study.

Hartog says in the introduction: "As were many others, I was baptized in the Roman Catholic Church. But whether as a girl of thirteen I took confirmation, I'm not sure: I can only remember the flowing white vision of a dress I might wear, the bouquet of narcissus I might hold."

"For by then I believe my mother had ventured from her family's Catholicism to sample, in swift succession, theosophy, yoga, vegetarianism and Christian Science; a quest that would end in the 1980s with her settled in a reclining chair in front of the TV evangelists, her head resting on the heavy bosom of the political far right.

"But what if? What if she had stuck with the Catholic Church? She might right now be sending funds through the church to South America to assist the oppressed; she might be down in El Salvador on the side of the liberationists."

❧❧❧

Both of these articles, and many others that appeared, are remarkably alike in the heart of the content that make up the factual story. Both are obviously very interested in knowing more about the life of this man, but beyond the facts which read like a set-piece which the bishop has obviously gotten into the habit of reciting when asked.

They are looking to what makes him tick, how he got that way, how deep is his conviction that has caught their interest? What is it all rooted in from his personal experience and his religious creed? Is it for real? Their parenthetic styles are their differences.

Their summaries of his life catch all the highlights we have already noted with little direct personal punctuation on the writer's part. The story each of them tells is not that much slighter than the in-depth interviews Grant Maxwell conducted for this book nearly ten years later; and he did not get much further in penetrating Bishop De Roo's set interpretation, or better, public hermeneutic on his own identity.

Remi De Roo represented a fascinating still point to all these writers but his real depths, psychological depths will not be penetrated by direct questioning. I learned this by a combination of studying Grant Maxwell's six interviews which consistently seemed to leave the real questions begging. But Grant Maxwell is an accomplished journalist, so I came to recognize that he was being subtly, probably unconsciously, blocked by the bishop's extremely intelligent way of steering interviewers.

He simply lets you in as far as he wishes in these formally controlled situations of direct questions and answers. It is a chess match where the superior trained intellect automatically wins.

It is guided by a recognizable Catholic sensibility, one part open honesty, two parts avoidance and unconscious denial of avenues that have never directly seemed useful for a man of action, a scholarly leader; for him to spend time self-studying for the sake of public disclosure.

WHOSE LIFE IS A UNIT

In her 1986 piece for *Monday*, Diana Hartog frames it with the lengthy personal introduction and postscript, so there is a story within a story. For our purposes the frame contains the more interesting revelation.

The central content is approximately the same set piece of impenetrable facts but in the Hartog framework, De Roo's personae is presented as a living legend. He is regarded as accommodating an original integrity that has an unsettling effect on the writer. This is a common thread in the sort of celebratory writing he attracted after 1983. The last section of her introduction reads:

"A month had passed since that Easter Saturday. For weeks I walked around my notes, head turned the other way: procrastination. Or fear. And yet it seemed that everywhere I turned— radio, magazines, TV—the subject came up: the debate between religion and science, articles on dissenting priests on a phone-in show about whether the church should become more involved with politics.

"What had this man—this bishop with his calm serious mien—stirred in me that I wished to avoid?

"From the strength of his convictions, he could afford to speak in moderated tones. He is well informed—exceptionally so —on national and international events... And yet he is only a man.

"And probably a great one at that—in his dedication, in the energy he brings to the Herculean labour of swinging the weight and wealth and profound influence of the Catholic Church to the side of those people being 'spit out' by the market economy... that is why for weeks I warily circled my notes; when you meet a person whose life is a unit, an integrated whole, the experience can be unnerving, for it throws into question your own life."

The writer, a modern woman, a creature of contemporary critical consciousness is paying precise attention to what he says; how and why he says it, and where his ideas come from.

For De Roo dialogue is the only path of truth for the modern critical consciousness to follow; it is the only way into modern prophetic Catholicism for thinking people. He does not attempt to morally browbeat the listener into intellectual subjugation like Pope John Paul II. It is a suitably subtle process of actual engagement. It is through this dialogue that he inadvertently reveals the depth that has had her walking around in circles of avoidance:

"A marvellous thing occurred near the end of the interview. The subject of Jesus came up. Naturally enough. And as he spoke, De Roo's pace quickened, his face grew animated. Here we had the quick of what he was about. We've all known people who grow excited about abstract subjects—politics, economics, religion.

"But all in the abstract: they come alive, their voices grow louder, they make pronouncements, they chase their own tails. And all this time the bishop has been talking in concise, calm tones of general concerns, of the society as a macrocosm.

"Yet when he speaks of Jesus, his expression grows almost eager; he leans ever so slightly forward in his chair:

"Economically, Jesus was always poor; politically he never sought or achieved any power; he was betrayed by his own friends and destroyed by the powers around him. So from a human point of view, his life looked like a disaster.

"He did not succeed in what he set out to do. But it is in the very acceptance of death, out of love, that he proved that love is stronger... Of course we have difficulty grappling with this, because we don't want to believe that life ends in death. We want to be successful."

❧❧❧

The modern seeking consciousness has encountered the graced moment of ancient paradox; an anecdote which illustrates De Roo's integral giftedness. It is a charism that can be spellbinding for a liberal-realist sensibility which emerged out of the crucible experience of the Sixties and Seventies prior to the re-assertion of conformism, and the nativity of neo-conservativism in the Eighties.

But an opportunity was lost in the decade following this 1986 article. The bishop's model of being church, of being Christian, is not the predominant one being put forward by Rome. Dialogue with freethinking seekers was being replaced by assurances for neo-conservatives and reactionaries.

It was tragic in its implications, given the promise of Vatican II. From the late 1980s until the time of his retirement the thrust he developed was blunted by this far from inadvertent shift of emphasis.

❧❧❧

George (Jim) Mortimore writes: "De Roo turned out to be right about the spirit of Vatican II, and the changes in the church; he may also be right about the necessary and impending changes in the world... Perhaps none of this will happen in Canada.

"Perhaps we will be—as Remi De Roo has often warned us we are in danger of becoming—a population divided between a few tycoons and their middle-class attendants, and a body of techno-peasants in a polluted and soil-eroded land.... If new social forms are just a mirage, why did the conservatives spend so much energy denouncing them?

"Could it be that over Remi De Roo's shoulder they saw a vision of 900 million Catholics and several billion others awakening from a submissive sleep and rising up to take control of their economy? Might De Roo and allies be viewed as the first mammals among the dinosaurs."

8. THE RIGHT TO CRITICIZE

To the chagrin of Larry Henderson and other ultra-traditionalist sensibilities, in the seven-year period between January 1983 and 1990, Remi Joseph De Roo dominated the social imagination of the regular media of Canada as no other Canadian church figure had since perhaps the ill-fated Joseph Charbonneau.

Typical of the intense coverage was an in-depth feature and cover story in *Canadian Dimension* of May 1983, a national left-wing monthly out of Winnipeg. The story titled "The Bishops Speak" was a follow-up to a special edition in January 1979 entitled "The Left Hand of God," where the traditionally Marxist magazine was trying to come to terms with the phenomenon of Liberation Theology and the rise of the Christian left in Canada.

Another notable national story was the already cited feature by Judy Steed in the *Globe and Mail* of May 3, 1986, in addition to *The Canadian Forum* profile.

The Canadian Forum was then edited by Duncan Cameron who co-authored a book of analysis with Gregory Baum on the Church's relevant social teachings from the early Eighties period, including the pope's 1981 encyclical and the Canadian Bishop's "Ethical Reflections on the Crisis of the Economy."

The significance of these pieces is in how they represent a presumed fascination by the general population with the figure of the bishop and what he stood for; about the role and possibilities within religious leadership through the developments of the previous decade.

The writers of these pieces could presume the selling point to their editors of a mass appeal and interest. On the other hand when I tried to interest Robert Fulford at *Saturday Night* magazine in the same period, I was not successful. Fulford wrote a note in reply to say he could not understand the public fascination with the man. The main stream had started to turn away by 1986.

The ongoing appeal was to the smaller press when the daily media had turned off after a three year glut of coverage following the blockbuster statement of January 1, 1983. Only the alternative press was interested in what was behind the phenomenon.

The corporate-owned media was taken initially with the surprise of the attack from such an unexpected quarter, then the blistering quality and the thorough preparedness of the analysis; and the subsequent endurance of the depths of the exchange.

There was full and exhaustive coverage for thirty months, to the point where the bishop was a continuous part of the social landscape and an enduring symbol of resistance to the general capitulation to capitalism of the period.

To attack such a sacred cow so convincingly meant that the bishop and the social affairs commission and the staff were ultimately to be treated as pariahs by the establishment and its agents within the church including bishops of another political persuasion.

In the words of one otherwise sympathetic Québec bishop, Bernard Hubert, Bishop De Roo was sounding too much like the NDP, the Canadian social democratic party of the left. This was inevitable given Gregory Baum's explanatory insight on the CBC Radio that the Canadian Church had adapted a Liberation theological model because when the injustice is institutionalised the church must stand on the left.

But the damage had been done to the myth that the church was there to legitimate the given system and from the mid-1980s the bishop was the scourge of the corporate owned media by and large. As a consequence he became the darling of the alternative media in Canada which included some of the better Catholic newspapers and much of the socially concerned media generally.

Judy Steed's *Globe and Mail* feature from May of 1986 caught the central dynamics at play during the hottest period of the Ethical Reflections debate. Her opening paragraphs set the tone of the permanent image of the man, resulting from the media skirmish over a period of three years.

"One of Canada's most outspoken radicals is an unpretentious man in a gray suit and clerical collar who speaks—in the order in which he learned them—Flemish, English, French, Latin, Italian, Spanish and Portuguese. A Manitoba farm boy of Flemish descent, the second of eight children of a conservative father who helped create Manitoba Pool Elevators, Bishop Remi De Roo is a man whose passions have carried his influence far beyond his own parish."

Steed continues: "Observation of reality: that is Bishop De Roo's starting point... Responsibility for the whole family life is what economics and business should be about... We have made technology and capital our moral and social goals when they should be means or instruments... Our model for society is technical rationality... People are seen as objects to be manipulated for the maximization of profit and power...

"He deflects the name calling of critics by insisting "'Christians have the right to criticize any system—capitalist or communist—and to search for alternatives.' It is the mission of the church, he argues, to assist in this search. The church, he says, must be countercultural."

❧❧❧

There is the story within the story with many of these features or as George Mortimore described the bishop's living quarters, an apartment within an apartment in the appropriate *leitmotif* of a labyrinth representing the bishop's life and mind.

In the case of Mortimore, and *Monday Magazine* writer Diana Hartog, their interview with the bishop was also a self-conscious encounter with a hidden part of themselves, an aspect they had left somewhat dormant. The opportunity to write about this subject presented them with a moment for self-reflection.

In Hartog's case she was returning in her focus to some significant stage she had left behind; for Mortimore he wished for a closer encounter with a vital and authentic humanist advocate of admired values. As they each came face to face with their subject they had a rendezvous which can only be fully explained in the analogous terms of religious experience.

This became the fascination of Remi De Roo for many in a generation with socially progressive sensibilities who had all but written off the church as at best a neutral force in the struggle.

In the same issue of *Canadian Forum* there appeared an analysis of post modernism by Gregory Baum. No other figure in the post Vatican II Canadian church more closely resembled De Roo's sensibility and intellectual zest than Gregory Baum, whom Swiss theologian Hans Kung called among the greatest figures in North American Catholicism.

De Roo's critics within the church would often frame their objections in terms of the threat they felt his 'modernism' presented to traditionalist faith. Opponents of the Council reforms targeted his diocese in this same way. Included is the notorious Anne Roche-Muggeridge, a self-described "counter-revolutionary" and opponent of the reforms of Vatican II since its inception. She addressed a conference on the Catholic Counter-revolution in Victoria on May 2, 1987.

Roche-Muggeridge, the daughter-in-law of Malcolm Muggeridge and author of a number of books vituperative toward the Second Vatican Council, said she laid all the blame on the "manipulative, dissenting theologians, the so-called periti" of the Council, who led the bishops astray.

Doubtless she had in mind one such periti, or theological expert, Gregory Baum, known as Canada's leading Catholic theologian and like De Roo, a radical thinker and seminal influence on the Second Vatican Council.

Baum, the author of dozens of influential books, and De Roo conducted continuous dialogue from that time on; ranging through ecumenism and liberation theology to the questions of women's ordination and the Catholic contribution to Canadian socialism.

9. FRIEND AND INFLUENCE

Without argument, the two outstanding post-modernist figures in the Canadian Catholic Church after Vatican II were Gregory Baum and Remi De Roo.

Their careers and personal intellectual development after the experiences at Vatican II kept pace for four decades. De Roo has been highly influenced by the work of Dr. Baum and he, in turn, owes much to the bishop, who widely put into practice the insight of the thinker Baum.

Baum's best work is launched from his experience of the new practices within the church. He does the in-depth research which leads to new insight. Then De Roo picks up on these and puts them into action within the Canadian Church. It's the dialectical process par excellence.

Equally brilliant communicators, their common work stimulated the other along parallel paths. They are the same age and share an entirely liberal-realist sensibility about how the gospel works best on modern consciousness. There is a brightness to this that may be a uniquely Canadian contribution in its style of open creativity.

As early as June, 1965, Michael Jacot wrote a major feature on Gregory Baum in *Sign Magazine*, a major American Catholic magazine. Its principal theme was that Baum strongly promoted 'concrete theology' which "must re-establish contact with the world as it really is—and not as some people think it ought to be."

Especially during that period, 'concrete theology' flew in the face of conventional Catholic practice. Catholicism was rife with romantic idealism about how people 'ought to be'.

Baum is quoted as saying: "Christians—and especially priests—cannot find a way to God today by escaping from society. A priest must use spiritually the ordinary experiences of every day—he must listen to God speaking to him through the community in which he lives."

In Jacot's introduction to the article he wrote of how he happened to bump into Baum in England and found him exactly as

Baum describes a priest should be. This concrete theology, with no abstract distance or apparent contradiction between the words and the actions, is a hallmark of Remi De Roo's episcopacy.

Both men lived out concrete programs, following the direction it lead, in the bishop's case, into social critique at a national and international level. This is what made them so threatening. Theirs was not a theoretical theology that might appeal to a limited number of adherents and therefore have little concrete effect.

In Baum's case, with his unique intellectual gifts, it led him to write and study and publish books on Ecumenism, Church reform, Jewish relations, Catholics and Canadian Socialism, Catholic Social teaching, Religion and Sociology, all the emerging crucial areas in the Christian church as they came along after Vatican II.

No single theologian in Canada has been more strategically well placed in this way, and no bishop-thinker has been more strategically well placed in terms of implementation than De Roo.

They emerged from such different root situations, mixing in the heady atmosphere of the actual sessions at Vatican II in Rome and in the ecumenical movement of Canada in the late 1960s. Baum went to the Council, interestingly enough, as Archbishop Philip Pocock's personal theologian but he also had a chair there as a periti, an official expert theologian. His path to that situation was not a conventional one.

Jacot cites the quote from Hans Kung who said he considered "that Gregory Baum is one of the great men in the North American Church."

In his article titled "Man for Our Times," Jacot explains that Baum was born a Berlin Jew, reared a nominal Protestant and converted to Catholicism while attending a Baptist university, McMaster in Hamilton, where he studied mathematics, read Karl Barth, Carl Jung, Sigmund Freud and Saint Augustine.

His father had been a mechanical engineer and died when Gregory was young, about the same age as Remi was when his mother died, the early teens. Baum told Jacot his first exposure to Christianity was through the reproduction of religious paintings which hung in his entirely secular home in Berlin. With his mother and sister he fled to England in 1939 but was shipped to Canada and spent the first years of the war in an internment camp.

The camp also happened to be populated by diverse prominent German professors who were interned with him. The experience proved pivotal in his formation at a time when "I was very unsure of myself. In fact I didn't think of myself as being anything—I just appeared to exist like a splodge of matter." Through the experience he became rigorously prepared for university.

In the same period he learned through the Red Cross of the death of his mother as a result of privations suffered when hiding out from the Nazis. He later dedicated his second book, *The Jews and the Gospel*, to her memory. He got to McMaster through Mrs. Emma, a well known Canadian United Church worker who sponsored him in 1942 when he was released from camp to specifically go to the school in Hamilton.

He graduated and went to Ohio to teach. This enabled him to obtain his MA in mathematics. While there he was attracted to Catholicism, converted and entered a religious order, the Augustinians. The Catholic church became his family, replacing his dead mother and father.

"I think I became a Christian because my life and background was destroyed. I came from a liberal-bourgeois family. Life had been founded on a beautiful and highly individualistic understanding of society. But there had been a complete breakdown in this society. People I admired now had nothing to say. I realised this was not the real life.

"The meaning of Jesus—the redemptive power that really transforms us—attracted me. I wanted to be transformed. I regarded Christianity as a redemptive doctrine—grace would come, and we would be changed. God would lead us."

Gregory Baum, a man committed to the transformative power of the gospel, had the same 'full participant' attitude toward the Second Vatican Council because he had the privilege to attend.

Jacot writes: "He began to work harder than he had ever done before. He went to Rome eleven times in three years and spent months preparing documents for the Council. Although the documents put before the Council bear no signatures, theologians are able to pick out many of Baum's ideas in those he worked on. This is particularly evident on the document on the Jews."

Bishop De Roo as an often intervening voting member, and Father Baum as expert theologian—the Canadians had their impact.

And after the Council they spread their wings to teach the Council back home. Perhaps no two Canadian council 'fathers' had more wide-ranging influence. In the Toronto and Montréal circuit

"Baum was one of the most sought-after speakers of any denomination."

"I am always deeply embarrassed because I cannot ask the ministers back to our churches," he said at the time. "Prejudice of any sort is something Baum cannot tolerate... it was the basis of his thesis for his doctorate and later became the subject of his first book *That They May be One*, which deals with Catholic prejudice about dissident Christians.

Jacot continues: "His thick book *Progress and Perspectives* deals with ecumenism in a popular way, stressing the need to cut away prejudice within the church.

"Most people when they meet him are captivated. He is an extremely sympathetic and human man, who acknowledges all the faults and idiosyncrasies of today's society... Everyone has a strong opinion about him, but not everyone takes to Baum. One priest once said to me, "All I see outside that man's door is a string of drunks, deadbeats and neurotics."

"Another colleague complained, "Whenever I open the Catholic paper, Baum is saying something. Why doesn't the man shut up occasionally. When I reported this, Baum laughed, 'The man's right.'

"A certain section of Canadian Catholic life has withdrawn from Baum for another reason. Some years ago, a university professor who happened to be a friend of mine, said, 'We should not get too closely connected with Father Baum—he'll end up in trouble for some things he's saying."

These same sorts of quotes (and the 'Catholic' attitudes behind them) were part of the reputation of De Roo in the same interval and in the same way. Their personalities are distinctly different, in itself probably a factor in the strength of adhesion in their friendship.

Both men are survivors of these wars—a gift derived from their adaptability and commitment to personal and professional growth. They were both also very useful to the institution by virtue of their gifts. As such they were able to straddle the two worlds—the church as the 'People of God' and the church as institution.

"One of the most fortunate happenings in Baum's career," wrote Jacot in 1965, "was been his assignment in the Toronto Archdiocese. Many bishops in North America might have failed to understand his new approaches, but Archbishop Philip Pocock, himself a theologian of liberal repute... has been a sympathetic supporter of Baum... he is able to work unhampered.

"Many people have classified Baum as an out and out radical. He is not... 'we must never discard or break down without being sure we are getting something better,' he says

"Baum says he is concerned with theology in concrete terms, not in abstraction. 'Theology should not talk of things as they should be or as they might be, but as they are.'

Baum and the bishop share a fundamental approach. Ideas in the service of action, and action in the direction of needed change. Concrete theology.

❧❧❧

The birth control controversy of 1968 once again had its beginning in 1965.

"Baum's stand on birth control: He writes a chapter in the book *Contraception and Holiness*, edited by a Jesuit archbishop, is rooted in concrete theology," writes Jacot. The question of birth control, is not he says, really part of the gospel.

"'The church's teaching on social and moral life has not the same unchanging quality as its teaching on the Gospel. Moral theology grows and develops according to man's place in history. Therefore I would say that it is time to re-examine thoroughly the positive role of sexuality in married life. If we do, I'm sure that the present ideas on birth control will change.'"

CONCRETE POST-MODERNISTS

In his essay on postmodernism in the same May 1990 number of *Canadian Forum*, Gregory Baum critiques postmodernist theory which he says "stands or falls with their specific interpretations of contemporary capitalism as a subjectless, self-transcending, cybernetic, economic mega-machine. In my opinion, this interpretation is not convincing."

"There are qualitative differences between the free-enterprise capitalism of the United States, the social democratic capitalism of the European Economic Community, the government-sponsored capitalism of Japan and the dependent capitalism of Third World countries.... the analysis does not take into account the irrationalities of contemporary capitalism, including the damage to the environment and the exhaustion of natural resources...

"There is another definition of the post-modern condition for which I have much sympathy... they argue that people have lost confidence in government, business, political parties, labour unions, universities and other major institutions, all of which are run by technocrats.

"Important for these thinkers is what happens in the community and at the base. These people organize in social movements—the ecological movement, the women's movement, the peace movement, the movement for alternative economies and so forth. There civil society resists the dominant technocracies. There people distrust purely scientific reason.

"They rely upon wisdom of their own, based on their experience of exclusion and marginalization. They recognize that they must build their lives around human values disregarded by society, such as solidarity, community, conviviality and spirituality.

"The postmodern theologians treasure the ideas of social responsibility, emancipation and participation. They wish to mobilize the population, strengthen the new currents and influence the course of history... The theologians recognize that a capitalist economy oriented toward unlimited growth is headed for social inequality, cultural disintegration, and ecological disaster.

"What they call for are social movements at the base inspired by an alternative vision of society and a new ethos, a new spirituality that generates universal solidarity and reconciles people to the natural world, its powers and its limitations."

Gregory Baum (ICN)

Remi De Roo and Raymond Roussin, February 1999 at the time of official retirement. (Deirdre Kelly)

Monsignor William Bulloch, right, outside St. Andrew's Cathedral. (Jamie Jenkins)

Chapter Twenty: The Mythic-Poetic and The Mystic-Prophetic

1. BEFORE THE FLOOD

PISCES—*The last of the Zodiac, closely bound up with the symbolism of water and the 'dissolution of forms' (which takes place in the Akasha).*

Neptune whipping up the waves with his trident, and calling forth bulls and horses out of them, is a symbolic expression of the resurgence of cosmic energy from the watery deeps of the primordial ocean.

If Capricorn marks the beginning of the process of dissolution, Pisces denotes the final moment which, for this very reason, contains within itself the beginning of the new cycle.

Related to Pisces are the avatar in the form of the fish of Vishnu in India, and the Chaldean myth of Oannes, the man fish.[288]

Fish have been a symbol of Christianity since the first days of persecution in Rome when, according to movie lore, a Christian would make a curved mark on the ground with his staff, which would be knowingly completed by a similarly curved line if his compatriot was a Christian.

I have argued that Remi De Roo not only modelled a new way of being a bishop and a priest (as documented by the public record) but that more significantly for the church, following the paradigm shift of Vatican II—in this way it preceded and anticipated the Millennium—he modeled a new way of being a saint in the form of a much more ancient idea, the original concept, from the earliest days of the church.

The biblical allusions to sainthood are that it is simply the ones who try to follow Christ. Only much later did it become an official category for a specific sort of pious holiness as formally recognized by the institution.

If religion is a dynamic process of spiritual growth for the adherent, not merely a formal rule to follow to assure a static state of 'non-impurity'—is not merely a set of cancelling double negatives—then the idea of sanctity has also evolved during the great leap forward of Vatican II. De Roo became a saint over and against the worst instincts of the institution of the church.

Prior to the Council, Catholicism was said, by its adherents, to be not so much a set of practices and beliefs but 'a way of life'. After Vatican II the predominant model of this transformed way of life was the path of justice and peace which De Roo was seen to champion.

Martyrs fell, Christian counter-culturalism to the given political order became the norm, so much so that various national bishops' conferences worldwide became closely identified with this struggle; so much so that the left-wing of the Catholic Church became targeted by the powers that be.

Ask the Jesuits and Religious in Central America about their murdered members, men and women who died for the gospel; for gospel values that were more important to them than life itself. Values that were seen to be the life of one's life.

❧❧❧

De Roo was not the originator of this new 'way of being', but he was a prominent example of the new model and a public symbolic figure for it. As such his life has been in the public scrutiny and therefore more accessible for evaluation; more than most others, bishops or not.

MODERN SANCTITY

My own sense of the man was that he qualified on most if not every count. He rose early every day to pray. His early morning calls to the east coast were well known with the three and four hour time difference. He also called people in the same time zone. An early morning call from Bishop Remi disturbed the slumber of not a few more worldly compatriots.

He had the balanced and evenhanded manner of someone whose life is entirely given over to religious practice. As one broadcaster said during their interview: he manifested a self-assured serenity. His physical asceticism was transparently obvious. He ate little, read for hours, spent much time in solitude, took long retreats, attended assiduously to his own spiritual growth: with demonstrated results.

More important perhaps, in terms of his own stated standards: he followed his truth wherever it took him. He was true to the tradition beyond question but because he was so knowledgeable he pushed its parameters, contributing to the innovation of tradition.

His reputation for looking out for the other guy and the little guy are part of the public record. Even critical comments have a ring of accidental praise by default: in how they served to confirm his relentless commitment to his program, the program of the whole Church at Vatican II.

His critics gained fervour as the containment period gave them courage, perhaps false courage but a courage he often remarked upon as proving their conviction about what they said; and this he always admired.

De Roo was a humble man, modest in his manner and ready to correct his position if challenged convincingly. He was not really concerned with what people thought of him, yet was also sensitive of feelings as much as he could be, given his psychological type.[289]

He was a paradoxical personality which might be a sign of this new model of sainthood. He certainly said often enough that the saints were simply the people of God, the same term enshrined by Vatican II.

Many rejected this because it was too collective and not romantically exclusive like the old idea of sainthood. And, of course, the fact the new pope made so many new saints on the old model tended to shroud the emerging concept after 1990.

The new model was felt by many to put too much personal responsibility on them to live up to its standards. The old model usually started with the concession that these saints were above the rest of us mere mortals; which conveniently let ordinary Catholics off the hook. De Roo did not let people off the hook. He challenged everyone to be the most they could be, given their limits and qualities.

2. MODERN DAY PROPHET

Whether he was a saint or not—old model or new—will not soon be settled, maybe it doesn't even matter. Perhaps the shift of Vatican II is all about putting the emphasis on something altogether different than achieving sainthood, of 'saving one's soul' in the old individualistic sense.

What is certain is that he was a modern day prophet, and it is very interesting to study his birth sign in terms of how he realized the outline given there. Born on February 24, 1924, on the cusp of Pisces and Aquarius, on the cusp of the Age of Aquarius.

"This twelfth house of the Zodiac, when transposed by analogy to the existential and psychic planes, denotes defeat and failure, exile and seclusion, and also mysticism and the denial of self and its passions.

"The dual aspect of this symbol is well expressed by the zodiacal sign itself, composing of two fishes arranged parallel to one another but facing in different directions: the left hand fish indicates the direction of involution or the beginning of a new cycle in the world of manifestation, while the fish that faces the right points to the direction of evolution—the way out of the cycle." [290]

It is not difficult to imagine how this applies to De Roo's life. The early years and family formation are the involution period, up to Vatican II. The irony of the attacks by so-called traditionalists on De Roo is that he has been there in spades. He is like a Zen monk in the fullness of his formation in the complete traditional pattern of Roman Catholicism.

We are not speaking here of someone half formed, or who has not been completely through every stage of what the traditionalists call for. He has been there and sees more. He accepted it entirely but evolved past it, just as the entire church did at Vatican II.

The evolutionary aspect meant that he had a key and critical role for the whole church, worldwide. One sign of his sainthood is that he accepted the role even when crucifixion was readily apparent. His is the sacrificial element of Christianity as well, death and then resurrection in its own good time.

In a talk he gave to Corpus in 1995, an informal question-and-answer sort of dialogue, he said that the church was in for a very long Good Friday in terms of the conventional categories of measuring its success. This would be a purifying experience that it would survive and thrive through but it would be painful for the institution and not short in duration.

That particular talk in itself is quite illuminating. It took place in Victoria when the Canadian association of married Catholic priests gathered for their annual conference. De Roo agreed to meet with them informally and have some frank and candid discussion. Most of this chapter will comprise excerpts from that talk.

That 'talk' provides a clear sense of his take on the central issues and questions of the day for the institutional church in its ongoing 'crisis'. It took place just before the closing five years of his episcopacy when for various and necessary reasons he began to wind down his overall program.

His comments are like a synthesis of the two opposing camps in the church; the old ***thesis*** attacked by the new ***anti-thesis*** of Corpus, with his third thesis, or (hegelian) ***synthesis*** coming out of it.

❧❧❧

De Roo was born on the cusp of Aquarius, which is the eleventh sign of the Zodiac. Its allegorical representation, to continue to cite J.E. Cirlot, is:

"A figure of a man ***pouring water*** *from an amphora. This version merely affects the numerical symbolism, it affords clearer proof of the dual force of the symbol in its active and passive aspect* ***(evolution and involution)****, a duality which is of the essence in the important symbol of the Gemini.*

All eastern and western tradition relate this archetype to ***the symbolic Flood*** *which stands not only for* ***the end of a formal universe*** *but also for* ***the completion of any cycle by the destruction of power which held its components together.*** *When the power ceases to function, the components return to the Akasha—the universal solvent—which is symbolized by Pisces.*

In these two signs of the Zodiac, then, the cosmic praylaya, or Brahma's Night, runs its course. Its function, according to Hindhu tradition, is ***to reabsorb into oneness all those elements***

which originally seceded from it to lead separate individualistic existence. *Thus each seed carries the seed of a new beginning.*

The Egyptians identified Aquarius with their god Hapi, the personification of the Nile, ***whose floods were the source of the agricultural, economic and spiritual life.*** *Consequently, Aquarius symbolizes the dissolution and decomposition of the forms existing with any process, cycle or period; the loosening of bonds;* ***the imminence of liberation or through the destruction of the world of phenomena (institutions).****"*

❧❧❧

De Roo's three central vocational realms, the spiritual, the agricultural and the economic are identified here. The farm boy bishop who takes the spiritual path into the economic realm publicly. What is stated here is not any over-reaching claim about messianic qualities—but rather an indication of the instrumental role accepted by the bishop in pointing to the future.

In his last decade in Victoria a constant theme in his public statements within the institution and within the broader community was that we should be seeking at any cost "The Truth."

As shall be evident from his Corpus talk, since what he was talking about was the dissolution of the institution of the church as we know it, he could expect to be attacked and to pay a high cost, but this was the truth as he saw it.

De Roo always distinguished between the 'Realm of God' and the Christian Church as institution. The role of the church was to bring about the former but not exclusively. Outside the institutional church he had encountered many who were as dedicated to the values of the Realm of God and all these were his allies as well as many within the church per se.

❧❧❧

My own theory about the social effect of a particular decade in the 20th Century is that it lapses over into the next one for a few years. For instance, the social impact of the 1950s penetrated into the 1960s until the middle of the later decade. Similarly, the full impact of the 60s was not fully realized until 1975 or so.

It makes sense that social trends do not happen all at once but take time to unpack and be transformed into the next social period.

In this estimation Vatican II which ended in 1965 brought to a finish the agenda of the 1950s. The decade we call the 1960s (including Vatican II) was not brought to its first phase of fulfilment until 1975. Likewise the election of John Paul II in 1978 only came into full consciousness around 1985. Certainly historic facts can be construed to verify this pattern.

Historic facts in Remi De Roo's life can be marshalled to corroborate this thesis. The social justice thrust of the Canadian Bishops in the 1970s came to a head with the mid-eighties public discussion and furore over 'Ethical Reflections.' In this vein, the impact of the 1980s under Pope John Paul II should be looked at from the perspective of the middle 1990s.

In June of 1995 Bishop De Roo held this two-hour question and answer session at the national conference for Corpus Canada, the Catholic married priests organization which happened to be held in Victoria that year. Corpus also intimately involved the wives of the married Catholic priests. Corpus constitutionally includes the wives of the laicized clergy as equal members. It serves as a new model of basic Christian community which De Roo sees as emerging out of the ashes of the old institution.

Five years further on, after his mandatory retirement De Roo was 'silenced' by Rome for the first time in his career. It was on the occasion of being asked to address an international assembly of married priests, the same group but publicly in Atlanta, Georgia.

His 1995 commentary in response to questions from Corpus members is particularly revealing in terms of the silencing that was to follow; which in turn anticipated the major discrediting of the year 2000.

The significance of Corpus lies in the fact that Catholic priests are priests forever but they can have their sacerdotal privileges suspended by Rome. They are still ordained but cannot function as such within the institution because they have to be incardinated in a specific diocese and permission from the local bishop can be withheld and always is if Rome has laicized them. John Paul II ceased the more liberal practice of laicisations allowed by of his predecessors, particularly Paul VI.

FIRST BISHOP

These comments, which are extensive in length to do them justice, will be used to finish this final section on the confrontation of Bishop De Roo's prophetic Catholicism and post-modernity with the Roman Catholic Church of the last two decades of the 20th Century.

They provide a sharp revelation of the style of the man; how he "makes every effort to speak in a contemporary manner, with no trace of elitism," to use Judy Steed's phrase. The 'concreteness' of his theology is apparent from his first word: thus a realist, not into 'Catholic denial' in any sense of the term. It is this very farm-boy realism that got him into hot water with Rome, who did not want to hear much of what he took for granted, saw as obvious.

De Roo was introduced by Island members of Corpus, which has a large chapter on the garden isle. The introducer made a special point to say that De Roo was the first bishop to publicly welcome them to his diocese and to agree to spend time with them in serious dialogue about the issues of the church today.

De Roo's introductory comments were that he did not wish to impose himself on their agenda because he knew how busy they were, and he calls his time with them an opportunity to have a "chit chat."

3. THE LEAST I COULD DO

"The least I could do was to come and say hello. You have been serving the church and dialogue is extremely important particularly in our contemporary context.

"I know I don't have to remind you all of the articles and books and studies that are coming out about how our cherished institutions are crumbling all around us whether we like it or not. Leave it to the historians two hundred years from now to tell us what is happening except that we already have enough information and knowledge and understanding of the dynamics of civilization and the dynamics of institutions to realize the worst is yet to come.

"It's not going to get better right away, it's going to get worse. There are so many signs indicating that some of the major institutions not only in civil society—one thinks of giants like the

United States—but right in the church, people are tightening their positions.

"What makes this thing very very much like past history, on the eve of the collapse of institutions, at the very moment when they are beginning to crumble, you see them bent on reaffirming their power and bringing everything under control and frustrating themselves that somehow they can weather the storm."

SIGNS OF MAJOR COLLAPSE

"Yet I think it is a mistake. I don't think we are going to weather this storm and come out unscathed in the sense of preserving our major institutions as they were in the past. There are too many signs of major collapse. As far as I am concerned— this is my personal opinion—but I think we are into a really heavy session of Good Friday and Easter is a long way around the corner."

At this point he was asked a question about what sort of approach to take to ministry in this period. This person said she was speaking out of a diocesan context where everything he was saying was being denied, where dialogue is forbidden between groups like theirs and others in the church.

"In a generic way, without referring to any specific diocese, without making any judgements about any particular diocese, I think the problem is much wider than any individual diocese. I think it is a global problem. Although it is particularly acute in the whole western world, particularly in what is called the First World. I think there have been cultural explanations which others have dealt with more efficiently and more eloquently than I ever could.

"Let me go back to some recent studies that are pretty well recognized, that carry authority, such as Reginald Bibby's studies. I don't know if you have read his most recent work titled *There Has Got To Be More.* It's worth picking up. In many ways it pretty well sums up what he has been doing.

"The critical thing is that there is a chart on page 16 or 17. You can go to it right away. In a sense the story of the book is right there on one page. It shows that our perspective completely has to change."

RURAL EXAMPLE

"When I was a farm boy in a rural area of Manitoba where the majority were Catholics—not everyone, there were a number of non-Catholics, mostly in the village. We had a few neighbours.

"I remember in those days when one of my cousins, a Catholic, began to go dating with a Protestant girl, it sent shivers through the whole community. That's in my life time. That's not that long ago.

"In those days when we were gathering after Sunday Mass, when we sort of stood around for a while before we took off for home, we were very conscious of anyone in the community who wasn't there.

"And on the way home, even as a little boy I remember hearing my parents discuss about why so-and-so was not at Mass. That was the mood. Not that we judged but everyone was very conscious. Normally you went to Mass. We'd say, well, you know maybe there has been an accident. The horse fell and broke a leg, or the cow fell in the well.

"Something like that. You assumed that there was a pretty serious reason why that person wasn't there because it was taken for granted that everybody just went to Mass. And that began to slip gradually.

"Now Bibby tells us that the vast majority of people who still identify as members of their respective churches—what we once would have called 'good Catholics'—the majority of those are no longer in church on any regular basis.

"So the mentality that I had as a boy, of considering someone who didn't go to church as unusual, is now the other way around. In a sense now it is the minority who are the exception, who are in church instead of being outside the church. And I am not talking about people who don't have any particular religion. I am talking about those identified by Bibby, as considering themselves as good Christians of whatever denomination."

"In other words, still requiring ministry and they do show up for 'rites of passage', as some have called them. That's looking even within our own territory, our own bounds. The majority of those who need ministering to are no longer in church. Now if that doesn't raise a problem pastorally, what does?

"So from that point of view alone, even within our boundaries, we really have to re-examine the whole nature of ministry and that is leaving aside the command of Christ to go preach the gospel, to evangelize all nations."

THE YOUNG

"Also the young people have been telling us for years and indicating with their feet how they feel about church. Several times I have been in front of an audience where these issues came up and inevitably I can get the audience to say a word.

"All I have to do is describe a little bit the experience of people of being in church and ask them to describe it and I know what the audience is going to say immediately—'boring.' I've done it so many times, it's there. That's the feeling. Liturgy for the majority of people, 'boy, it's boring.'

"That doesn't mean there are not good liturgists and that there are not exciting experiences of liturgy. I have had lots of them. It's just that there's a perception in the majority of people's minds, that has become almost taken for granted that our worship is boring.

"Okay, that's enough to communicate our concern for the dimensions of the problem. What is our response to that? Well, I don't think it's simply to shore up the institution and nail tight the loose planks, and put shingles on the roof and that kind of stuff. I'm talking as a farmer, obviously, as a farmer's son."

NEW MODEL OUT OF QUÉBEC

"It's a whole new world out there. It's not all doom and gloom. To me the most exciting things that are happening are happening in the province of Québec. I don't know if any of you have read the studies by the Québec bishops. If you have not then by all means get a copy. There is an excellent English translation of the major study in the province of Québec.

"And there have been two or three recent declarations by various groups working with the Québec bishops. They have put on paper the new model of church and it's exciting. Very exciting.

"They recognize the fact that things are on a downhill slide and they are not going to turn around. Bibby, as you know, is very, very clear how over the last thirty years or so it is on a straight line down. And depending on where you live in the country, you start with what used to be 80-70-60 percent of the majority not practicing, on a slide down—and it's for every church. United Church and Anglican are not doing any better.

"So from the sociologist point of view, the evidence is there. It's not going to turn around in the present time. So it's going to get worse in terms of numerical presence. But also in terms of perception.

"It's understandable. In a world of mass media it is pretty hard to compete in terms of attracting people. Now if you are not going to bring them back by faith, then if you are just competing at the level of popularity, we don't stand a chance against the media.

"So the only area to look, for me, is the re-building of faith, the re-evangelizing particularly. That obviously cannot be done in large congregations. It's not enough to preach sermons from the pulpit. They can be the most glorious sermons and they are not going to bring about a massive turn-about for the faith. We are already preaching to the converted."

"So my perception is that the future lies in rebuilding the church. And I say that in the broadest and most optimistic sense, not a judgmental way because there are already good things in the church.

"I don't think the whole thing needs to be redone. We don't need to reinvent the gospel. We do need to rebuild the faith and to me the only answer to that is the basic communities of whatever form. Everybody has their pet formula for them. There are many different ways to go about them."

4. IT'S A DIFFERENT PERCEPTION

"For instance, it is very pertinent because I left behind me at the office [to come here] Father Jim Sheppard."
[At this point in the discussion there was an interruption because a spider was seen to have landed on De Roo's shoulders but he said it was all right because on Vancouver Island you have to get used to spiders and that practically speaking all spiders on the island were friendly.]

❧❧❧

"Father Sheppard saw me this morning, talking about his future. He is a Jesuit with Latin American experience who came back to Canada and wants to spend the rest of his second career—another one of these Jesuits into his second career—if you will, building up basic communities.

"He's been at it now for more than a year and he has over thirty basic communities on the Island. And they are not the only ones as he himself has recognized. I would guess, as a modest guess, there are at least fifty basic communities on this island associated with the Catholic church and I don't know how many there are of other denominations."

"So there is already quite an extensive development going on right here. To me that's where the future lies. However, the interesting thing—I was discussing this with him—is that many of these basic communities, the majority of whom are Catholic, those are the ones we know—there are many ecumenical ones also, I respect them all and am not judging.

"The point is that among the basic communities that are specifically Catholic, he tells me, that quite a number do not see themselves as related to their parish. That's interesting. That does not mean they do not go to Mass. The vast majority will be in church on Sunday. But they don't see what they are doing as, in a sense, related to, or pertinent to the parish or in many cases even supported by the parish.

"In fact this is going to be my next challenge to the clergy, in the next little while, whether or not they are willing to recognize that this new reality and not pretend they have already got it. A lot of clergy will say: 'Oh yeah we have got basic communities in the parish.'

"It's a different perception and it's a well known fact that basic communities launched by the priests or by sisters generally have a low survival rate. It's fascinating.

"But the most effective basic communities are the ones that emerge from the laity, not under clerical guidance. I am not condemning. I am simply describing what is already apparently statistically proven.

"So that's an interesting feature. Many of these people, who are the most promising people for the future, don't see themselves specifically relating to the parish as they know it. The parish in the eyes of most Catholics is 'the institution'.

"I've heard more than one priest say it's not Catholic if it's not parish. I know a lot of Catholics who will not recognize as Catholic that which is not under parish control. And an occasional bishop who will not recognize as Catholic that which the bishop does not control [*laughter from audience*].

"I've heard that said also.

"I could name one bishop, who is now in heaven, who said it in my presence [*comment 'and he got into heaven!' laughter*].

"It just shows the gracious mercy of the Lord. And also the fact that Jesus was never a parishioner [*laughter*]."

5. JESUS THE NON-PARISHIONER

"Jesus never was a parishioner. Let's not forget it. Never participated in a parish of any kind. In fact, biblical scholars are more and more recognizing that Jesus didn't ever attend what we would call a church. Not in the sense in which we understand church.

"His vision right up to until the Cross was of the renewal of Israel. If you go to the scene in Jerusalem where the Lord wept because Jerusalem would not accept his faith or its mission, which was that the twelve tribes would become the universal religion growing out of the fulfilment of the Judaic heritage.

"That's very clear now that we are more willing to listen carefully to our Jewish brothers and sisters and recognize how much of our Catholic religion is really interlocked and only understandable in the context of the Jewish faith.

"I have the happy privilege of being very good friends with the local Jewish Rabbi and his wife Sue. There is a dialogue going on; on the Island between Jewish and Catholic women so I am kept up to date about that.

"I have had the opportunity to take part in the Shabot (Jewish liturgy) in the synagogue and I was amazed. As I listened to their chanting to all the verses, I was back in seminary. It was the same tonality and the same mood as when we were chanting psalms in seminary in the 1940s."

"All the familiar verses back again. It's fascinating. We have got to recognize more and more that we don't fully understand our own mission if we don't recognize where we came from. Anyway that's another point. I don't want to talk about that right here."

PROPHETIC COMMUNITIES

"In that context I think the most important ministry is to rebuild or to help to develop the basic communities. That's a ministry that comes out of adult faith development and the formation of small communities is the answer.

"Now those communities don't exist in a vacuum. They have to be linked in some specific struggle in the context of the old prophetic tradition in the cause of justice and truth and so forth. So for me the promising dimension is those small faith communities that are struggling with specific issues.

"To rediscover once again the presence of God in that prophetic tradition of the Old Testament which Jesus brought to its fulfilment in those specific struggles for justice.

"So it's not just a question of having people in the parishes praying, much as we need them. That individualistic kind of piety which marks so many of our parishes—that to me is not the future. Much as I admire the people who go to church and pray. That's not where the future is.

"It's in the struggle, because with Christianity becoming a minority, increasingly so in the world, how is the gospel going to be preached to a world which is increasingly conscious of the injustice of society if you don't have people involved in justice and its pertinent dimensions such as peace or whatever."

"All the spheres of life are the critical areas where the gospel needs to be preached or else more and more the leadership that determines the future whether economic or political, cultural, official—is going to drift farther and farther from any kind of gospel values or gospel principles. It's already bad enough. Look at politics, look at economics. Where are the gospel values?"

6. BEYOND THE BIBBY COMPLEX

"Let's shift gears and get out of the Bibby complex. I'll tell you what I mean by that. With all due respect to Bibby—I know him personally and have great admiration for his work—but we must not identify the totality of the issue simply with the sociologists concern for numbers.

"Sure Bibby can tell us the numbers are dropping. I agree we have to take that into account but also recognize that if we stay only there with Bibby, we are still the prisoners of our framework that considers the value of our religion in terms of the numbers of practicing people. We have to get out of that syndrome and that is going to be the most important aspect—to get out of the syndrome of Christendom.

"That European concept that somehow religion was meant to be the most numerous, then the Catholic Church would be the most powerful. We dreamt of the day when the majority of humankind would join the Catholic Church and all that. Well, that's the concept of Christendom. You will not find that in the bible. And you will not find that in the prophetic experience of the early Church.

"That came with Constantine and it is partly responsible for the tremendous physical, material and economic wealth of the institution with which the church had girded herself. And which now are crumbling."

"And here is where I give clear credit to the Québec Bishops. They have seen this. The Québec bishops are not trying to keep their churches open. They are not talking about re-opening churches. They are letting things go. They are rebuilding a new church and it's coming from the grassroots."

FALSE HOPE

"It's hard for us to get out of that old concept. Hard for me as a bishop administrator. I have always seen the church in terms of statistics—how many weddings, baptism, funerals... That's how we have understood how the diocese is growing. I saw how here on the Island our little 10 percent minority started to climb and we are up around 18-19 percent in British Columbia.

"I have no recent statistics but whatever it is. At the same time I am very very conscious that we don't need very many new churches and our congregations are basically no larger than they were when we were ten percent. Also, when I walk into our congregations, particularly at confirmation time I see a whole new phenomenon.

"I assumed that Victoria would become somewhat more pluralistic, like the big cities such as Vancouver, which is already completely changed that way; but on the Island that would be limited to Victoria.

"So I went to Nanaimo, the second largest parish to do a Confirmation service and the priest, a Jesuit, told me: 'Well, we usually call the children forward at a certain point.' So I said OK you tell them when and as he called forth the little children and there was rustling sound as all these little bodies came forward, gleefully, happily and I stared at the group in amazement.

"I started looking in vain for the blond hair. They weren't there, practically speaking. The only blond children I could recognize were the children of a few people I knew personally. All the others were brown and black haired."

"Suddenly it hit me—wow, this is the Pacific coast if you will, it may not be the same in Ontario but certainly is the case here. The nature of the church is changing tremendously. They are here from all over Latin America, Africa, Asia, Filipinos, Vietnamese... The whole colour of the church, and right now the most dynamic Catholic groups are these groups.

"Filipinos, for example, are the most dynamic groups we have got—singing and dancing at events. It's lovely and I am very happy with it but I say to myself: 'Just a minute. This is going to last the space of one generation. And boom, it's going to go down.'

"Because these people have no roots and all these little children of colour with their bright eyes, they are going to become the media generation and I'll bet you that within fifteen years they are gone.

"So let's not build on this. A lot of priests are taking pride in the fact that the churches are full now with Filipinos, Vietnamese. It's going to be a one generation wonder, I think, and they'll be gone.

"So we are back to the Québec question. I don't think we will ever recoup the numbers. I accept the point that even the basic communities need the Eucharist and that is a major problem.

"History devolves. If you look at what has happened in the last twenty-five years. I'm not going to predict what is going to happen but something is going to change. It's becoming more and more clear that we can't stay the way we are.

"But outside the numbers game, accepting the fact that the numbers are going to drop regardless, where is the future coming from? It's going to come from that prophetic tradition. It's going to be the little remnants that is going to rebuild the church. Not the hope for full congregations. That's my main point."

[Intervention and personal question from the group—How does a person like Bishop De Roo survive in the church today? Given the reactionary forces unleashed at present, the cases like Archbishop Raymond Hunthausen, the social action battle, etc?]

7. THE UNCOMFORTABLE LIFE

"Good question. Simple personal answer. I don't speak for anyone else. I am comfortable in my own skin. There is a beautiful French expression to that effect that does not translate well into English. I don't feel persecuted. I am fully aware that I have been doing and said things that not all bishops would agree with.

"I say to the credit of the Canadian bishops as a whole, irrespective of what individual bishops may have said or done or feel. The Canadian bishops as a body have never tried in any way to silence me or bring pressure on me.

"In fact, I said to the credit of several of our leaders, I have had some of, let's say, the powerful men of the Canadian hierarchy say to me, practically, I don't necessarily agree with what you are doing. I personally myself wouldn't feel called to say or do it, but I want you to know you have my support. And I can document that.

"We've had some difficult situations where leaders of the Canadian Church have rallied to my support so I am not coming across with any martyr complex or anything of the sort. It's not comfortable but then who says that life was going to be comfortable.

"I have only one life to live and there are certain things I have learned as a kid on the farm. It's amazing when I look back what one learns as a kid on the farm. Some of the basic laws of life are about suffering and death and the nature of reality.

"When you have been through that farm experience there are certain things you just know; that certain things just are the way they are."

[Intervention from a woman who equated the farm-child perspective of wholeness with that which can be presented by women members of the church, and how that can get lost on the hierarchy]

"I am glad you raised that because you have given me the perfect entrée [*laughter*] for my next point. My next observation to you as Corpus is to get in touch with your feminine values. Get out of your masculine power trip and your identification with ideas coming from and ruled by the head.

"Go to your hearts and bodies. Establish a balanced spirituality and do what your hearts and bodies tell you to do. And don't get lost in the intellectual battles. If there has been anything that I find may have gone against Corpus, having glanced at some of your past publications—not all of them—is that you have placed too much emphasis on fighting battles of the mind.

"The arguments that persuade nobody and only alienate by dividing. That's the weakness of the mind that the more intellectual we get, the more we divide; and then the more we set ourselves up for polarization and argument, right and wrong, and alienation.

"It's all part of the Enlightenment heritage which gave us the beautiful things we call science today and I am not against the Enlightenment but we are beginning to recognize the legacy of the Enlightenment is collapsing around us. We have to rediscover our hearts and our spirits and that's where the feminine values comes in."

A FEMINIST

"I mean this seriously. I have publicly identified myself as a feminist knowing full well the hornets nest that would open [*laughter*]. Because I am completely personally convinced that if I don't get in touch with my feminine values, I'm not a complete human being and I am going to be in these rational boxes which most of our society including the Catholic Church got itself into."

"We are only beginning to see the price the Catholic church is paying for having sidelined the feminine dimension. It's so obvious today it's painful. But it's not going to be settled by reason and that's why we are getting from the Vatican right now, a further avalanche of intellectual material; trying to close every loophole and tighten everything down and make a perfectly clean package.

"And that has its merits in terms of we have to have clear doctrine and all that, including the universal catechism and encyclicals. There is beautiful stuff in that. I am not knocking it.

"It's another sign to me of that male dominated attempt to justify oneself and shore up the institution. But that's not where its going. We have got to get in touch with the heart side. People today are responding less and less to rational arguments. They are responding more and more to caring, compassion and concern and team work which is where the body comes in.

"There is very little now that we can do in isolation. I have the privilege of being associated with a new development at the University of Victoria which is a centre for dialogue between science and religion and that naturally is interfaith. We are discovering there the richness of the diversity of traditions. How we need to regain all that richness.

"When you go back to the Bible, you don't find much rational argument. You do find a lot of heart and the body. So I am appealing for a more balanced approach. So I would say listen to the feminine insights which the women can bring. I don't mean by that just listen to the women and don't listen to the men. That's not what I am saying.

"Listen to those other dimensions. This may be more important for the men to listen to our hearts and bodies because we have by nature been conditioned to think that we are the rational ones. And we limited our rationality to everything above our chins."

"Whatever was associated with the heart and bodies; the soul and spirit enfleshed in the body and acting. We kind of discarded that—a terrible word that we chose—as 'effeminate'. It shows how bad things had gotten in the church.

"I suggest that if you really want to reach people, make sure you develop the feminine characteristics. Here again the word 'characteristics' is a loaded word. I'm not sure we can say one type is masculine and one is feminine. It's a matter of balance."

8. THE PROPHETIC POPE

"One last comment. We are beginning to see how prophetic Pope John XXIII was when his encyclical *Pacem in Terris* in 1963 put the finger on one of the great movements of the future. The emerging role of women. Before most of the feminist scholars wrote their books, John XXIII was already recognizing it."

[in answer to a comment]

"Yesterday I read one of the most disappointing books I have read in all my life. It had been advertised as the ultimate thing to read about American Catholicism, called *Catholics in the Public Square*. Twelve articles by 'outstanding American Catholics in every possible field', including Michael Novack.

"Supposed to be the talks given at a huge rally of Catholics, who proclaim it's time to stop acting like persecuted people and reactionary, instead to affirm ourselves though our great nation and so forth. Beautiful sounding words.

"But as I paged through the book—I read the whole thing in an hour because the further I went the sicker I got—I said to myself: 'This is terrible.' If this is what the leading Catholics in the United States are proposing as the message that the Catholic Church has to give to the United States, we are in deep trouble."

"For instance their total idea of the church was, the personal characteristic of the good Catholic of tomorrow, is fidelity to the pope. The whole church is centred on the pope. There was nothing whatever about the college of bishops, collegiality or the communion of bishops. Bishops were mentioned in passing.

"Next was the struggle [exclusively against] abortion. Right down the line. There it was in the book that was supposed to be the best. Only one article broke the silence and talked about the fundamental insight of Vatican II, about the transformation of society.

"In your Corpus statement, ministry and service is for the church. I know you mean well but if you think carefully what Vatican II says, it reminds us very clearly that our baptismal vocation is primarily oriented to society not to the church."

ONLY AN INSTRUMENT

"The church is only an instrument, not an end in itself. The church is really an instrument for the promotion of the reign of God. I would like you to think seriously about your theological vision. There is a danger that people who read this will remain trapped in that image that Catholics are here primarily to minister in the church.

"That's not what the church is here for. As we see the churches we have known and loved, institutionally crumbling more and more around us, we are going to have to re-awaken to the fundamental mission of Jesus which was not to build a church.

"The mission of Jesus was to proclaim the reign of God and the primary mission of the baptized is not ministry in the church; it's to proclaim the reign of God throughout the whole continent, in whatever sphere they happened to be, whether its astronomy, literature, politics, music, dancing... you name it."

"We're here to proclaim the Good News of the compassionate presence of God in the midst of sin and death and torment. In the collapse of society around us somehow God is still with us on the way to reign.

"That's where the fundamental faith has to be. It's broader than the church. I'm not denigrating the church or I wouldn't be a bishop dedicating my life through the church.

"But to see the church as one means, pre-eminent if you will, but not the only means to promote the reign of God. For all the while the church itself is suffering and the institution is crumbling, there are many other things happening where the reign of God is being promoted.

"In the other world religions, in the sciences—read some of the most advanced scientists today—these physicists are starting to sound like Saint John of the Cross. The key word today is spirituality.

"I read a book the other day of an avant garde think-tank, business people, heavy into economics—heavy into corporations. All presidents and vice presidents of very successful corporations. That book makes it very clear that the think-tank of American business people have focused very very clearly that the future of success in the business world is in the spirituality of their employees.

"They are beginning to boast of it. Any number of articles I have read recently by successful business people where they tell what is the secret of their success. It's not that they know how to make big bucks but that they had a deep spirituality. I knew who I was, as a result I could resist pressure and disappointment and all that."

"It's prayer and meditation and reflective practices. One business person who has the biggest pizza company in the United States. He's a Catholic who sells 54 percent of all the pizzas. One of his secrets is twenty minutes of silent prayer morning and night. That's his fix. Starts his day with twenty minutes of silence before God. This would never have been said fifty years ago.

"Awaken to that. Ask yourself deep down what is fundamentally our baptismal call in the reign of God. Not whether some of us go into the ordained ministry. That is necessary for the well-being of having the Eucharist, but that's not where it starts. That's not the fundamental drive and that's not where you are going to really rally those basic communities in terms of calling them into the ministry of the church."

TOMORROW'S EXPERIENCE

"In response to that I say focus on your audience. Who are you speaking to? If you are just talking to other middle-aged people, in a sense you are talking to yesterday's religious experience.

"You are not talking to the religious experience of today and tomorrow. Now if your focus is to reach somewhat younger people then you gotta remember your language doesn't correspond to their reality.

"Let's not forget that language is born out of experience. Language evolves with experience. That's why you can't have a dead language. History moves, experiences change.

"So language has to evolve whether we like it or not. We have no choice. How are you going to bring in a new language. It's not by redefining the old language. It's by giving people new experiences."

"Out of the new experience they will define the new language. So to me that is the way to get back to the basic communities. It's going to be out of the lived experience of the compassionate kind of relationship, and the all-embracing wholistic experience that only basic communities can provide.

"Out of that will arise the new language that will bring the new experience. And yes, you have to undergo the fact that for a while it will not be understood, but don't talk to yesterdays' generation. It's gone.

"That will be my last comment. It's four o'clock. I have to dash. Who was it that said that beautiful little thing—you've probably said it: 'Yesterday is History, Tomorrow is Mystery, Today is a Gift, that's why we call it Present.'"

SELECTED BIBLIOGRAPHY

[Criteria for inclusion in this bibliography has to do with direct relevance to the subject; mention in the text or footnotes; or authorship by principals]

Abbott, Walter M. SJ, editor, *The Documents of Vatican II*, America Press, 1968.

Arendt, Hannah, *Men in Dark Times*, Harcourt Brace, New York, 1968.

Atlantic Episcopal Assembly, *To Establish a Kingdom of Justice*, self-published, 1978.

Baum Gregory, *Catholic Quest for Christian Unity*, Paulist Press, 1962; *Catholics and Canadian Socialism, Political Thought in the Thirties and Forties*, Lorimer, 1980; *Ethics and Economics, Canada's Catholic Bishops on the Economic Crisis*, with Duncan Cameron, Lorimer & Co., 1984; *Faith and Doctrine, a contemporary view*, Paulist, 1969; *New Horizon, Theological Essays*, Paulist, 1972; *The Constitution on The Church of Vatican II*, commentary by Gregory Baum, Foreword by Abbot Basil C. Butler, OSB, Deus Books, 1964; *The Priority of Labour, A commentary on Laborems Exercens, Encyclical Letter of Pope John Paul II*, Paulist, 1982.

Bernstein, Carl and Politi, Marco, *His Holiness, John Paul II and The History of Our Time*, Penguin Books, 1996.

Bibby, Reginald W., *Fragmented Gods: The Poverty and Potential of Religion in Canada*, Stoddart, 1987.

Bishops of The Netherlands, A New Catechism, Catholic Faith for Adults, Seabury Press, 1973.

Black, Conrad, *Duplessis*, McClelland and Stewart, 1977; *A Life in Progress*, Key Porter Books, 1993.

Boff, Leonardo, *Church: Charism & Power—Liberation Theology and the Institutional Church*, Crossroad, 1985.

Brady, Patricia C., *Has Anything Really Changed? A Study: The Diocese of Victoria since Vatican II*, Woodlake Books, 1986.

Brym, Robert J. and Sacouman, R. James, editors, *Underdevelopment and Social Movements in Atlantic Canada*, New Hogtown Press, 1979.

Bugnini, Annibale, *The Reform of the Liturgy, 1948-1975*, Liturgical Press, Collegeville, 1990.

Bulloch, William Hodsdon, *As I Remember*, self-published, 1999.

Cameron, J.M., *The Night Battle, Essays*, Burns and Oates, 1962; *Nuclear Catholics & Other Essays*, William B. Erdmans Publishing, 1989.

Canadian Conference of Catholic Bishops, *The Code of Canon Law*, Collins & CCCB, 1983; *Ethical Choices & Political Challenges, Ethical Reflections on the Future of Canada's Socio-Economic Order*, December, 1983; *Report of Commission of Canonical Inquiry to Most Reverend Raymond Roussin, SM, Bishop of Victoria, BC,* June 26, 2000; *Training and Role of Christian Social Leaders, Proceedings and Addresses, Sixth Annual Catholic Social Life Conference, November 16-18, 1958, Winnipeg*; *Catechism of the Catholic Church*, Image Book, 1994; *Witness to Justice, A Society to be Transformed, Working Instruments,* May, 1979.

Catholic Theological Society of America, *Human Sexuality, New Directions in American Catholic Thought*, A Study, Kosnik, Cunningham, Carroll, Modras & Schulte, Paulist, 1977.

Cirlot, J.E., *A Dictionary of Symbols*, Routledge & Kegan Paul, 1962.

Clarke, Tony, *Behind The Mitre, The Moral Leadership Crisis in The Canadian Catholic Church,* Harper, 1995; *Silent Coup-Confronting the Big Business Takeover of Canada*, Lorimer, 1999.

Coady, M.M. Rev., *Masters of Their Own Destiny, The Story of the Antigonish Movement of Adult Education through Economic Cooperation*, Formac, Harper and Row, 1967.

Concilium—Theology in the Age of Renewal, Liberation and Faith special issue, June, 1974, Volume 6, Number 10.

Cooper, J.C., *Dictionary of Symbolic & Mythological Animals*, Harper Collins, 1992.

Craig, Mary, *Man from a Far Country, A Portrait of Pope John Paul II, foreword by Cardinal Hume*, Hodder and Stoughton, London, 1970.

Crosby, Michael H., *Celibacy, Means of Control or Mandate from the Heart*, Ave Maria Press, 1996.

Cuneo, Michael W., *Catholics Against The Church, Anti-Abortion Protest in Toronto, 1969-1985*, University of Toronto, 1989.

Curran, Charles E., *Christian Morality Today, the renewal of Moral Theology*, Fides, 1966.

Diocese of Victoria, *Diocesan Report*, November 2001, 16 pages; *Synod—A Core report*, 1991.

Daly, Bernard M., *Remembering for Tomorrow, A History of the Canadian Conference of Catholic Bishops, 1943-1993*, CCCB, 1994.

De Pape, Mary & Thomson, Marguerite, *Belgian Canadian Builders*, self-published 1993.

De Roo, Remi Joseph, *Cries of Victims, Voice of God*, Forward by Hon. Thomas R. Berger, edited by Bede Hubbard, Novalis, 1986; *Even Greater Things, Hope and Challenge after Vatican II*, with Bernard and Mae Daly, Novalis, Ottawa, 1999; *Forward In The Spirit, Challenge of The People's Synod,* Preface by Remi J. De Roo, edited by Grant Maxwell & Pearl Gervais, Diocese of Victoria, 1991; *In the Eye of the Catholic Storm, The Church Since Vatican II*, with Mary Jo Leddy and Douglas Roche, edited with an introduction by Michael Creal, Harper, 1992; *Man to Man, A frank talk between layman and bishop*, with Douglas Roche, edited with an introduction by Gary MacEoin, Bruce Publishing, Milwaukee, 1969; *Of Justice, Revolutions, and Human Rights ... Notes on a trip to Central America*, Diocese of Victoria, April 1980; *The Diocesan Synod as a Means to Develop Doctrine*, ICN Publishing, 2000.

De La Bedoyere, Michael, editor *Objections to Roman Catholicism*, Pelican, 1964.

Dictionary of Moral Theology, Newman Press, 1962.

Dion, Andre, *Tapestry, A Priest's Journey*, self-published, 1994.

Dolan, John P., *Catholicism, a Historical Survey*, Barron's, 1968.

Du Plessix Gray, Francine, *Divine Disobedience, Profiles in Catholic Radicalism*, Vintage Books, 1971.

Duquin, Lorene Hanley, *They Called Her The Baroness, the Life of Catherine de Hueck Doherty*, Alba House, 1995.

Dulles, Avery, *Models of The Church, a Critical Assessment of the Church in all its aspects*, Doubleday, 1974; *The Survival of Dogma, Faith, Authority and Dogma in a Changing World*, Image Books, 1973; *Vatican II and The Extraordinary Synod*, Liturgical Press, 1986.

Egner, G., *Contraception vs. Tradition, A Catholic Critique*, Herder and Herder, 1966.

Flannery, Austin, OP, General Editor, *Vatican Council II, The Conciliar and Post-Conciliar Documents*, Liturgical Press, Collegeville, 1979.

Fremantle, Anne editor, *The Papal Encyclicals in the Historical Context*, Mentor-Omega, 1956.

Gannon, Robert I., SJ, *The Cardinal Spellman Story*, Doubleday, New York, 1962.

Gannon, Thomas M, editor, *World Catholicism in Transition*, MacMillan, 1988.

Gerzon, Mark, *The Whole World is Watching, A Young Man's Look at Youth's Dissent*, Paperback Library, 1970.

Graham, Ron, *God's Dominion, A Sceptic's Quest*, McClelland & Stewart, 1990.

Granfield, Patrick, *The Limits of the Papacy, Authority and Autonomy in The Church*, Crossroad, 1987.

Gremillion, Joseph, *The Gospel of Peace and Justice, Catholic Social Teaching since Pope John*, Orbis Books, 1976.

Gutierrez, Gustavo, *A Theology of Liberation*, Orbis, 1973.

Hanley, Boniface, OFM, *Ten Christians (Cardinal Joseph Cardijn)*, Ave Maria Press, 1979.

Haughey, John C. editor, *The Faith That Does Justice*, Woodstock Studies, Paulist, 1977.

Hebblethwaite, Peter, *Introducing John Paul II*, Collins, 1982; *Paul VI, The First Modern Pope*, Paulist Press, 1993; *The New Inquisition? Schillebeeckx and Kung*, Fount Original, 1980; *Synod Extraordinary, the inside story of the Rome Synod, November/December 1985*, Doubleday, 1986; *The Runaway Church*, Collins, 1975; *The Year of Three Pope*, Collins, 1979.

Hellman, John, *Emmanuel Mounier and The New Catholic Left 1930-1950*, University of Toronto, 1981.

Higgins, M.W. and Letson, D.R., *Portraits of Canadian Catholicism*, Griffin House, 1986.

Howe, Irving, *Literary Modernism*, Fawcett Premier Book, 1967.

Island Catholic News, complete editions 1987 - 2001.

James, William, *The Varieties of Religious Experience,* Collins Fountain Books, 1977.

Jamieson, Patrick, *Victoria: Demers to De Roo, 150 Years of Catholic History on Vancouver Island*, Ekstasis Editions, 1997.

John XXIII, Pope, *Journal of a Soul*, trans. Dorothy White, Signet Books, 1964.

Jung, Carl Gustav, *The Symbolic Life*, Vol. 18, Collected Works, Bollingen.

Kelly, J.N.D., *The Oxford Dictionary of Popes*, Oxford University Press, 1986.

Kostelanetz, Richard, ed. *Beyond Left and Right, Radical Thought for our Time*, William Morrow, New York, 1968.

Kung, Hans, *Does God Exist?*, Doubleday; *Eternal Life? Life after Death as a medical, philosophical, and theological problem*, Doubleday, 1984; *Infallible? An Enquiry*, Collins Paperback, 1971; *On Being a Christian*, Doubleday; *Theology for The Third Millennium*, Doubleday, 1988.

Lapointe, Renaude, *L'historie bouleversante de Mgr. Charbonneau*, Les Editions du Jour, 1962.

Lee, Bernard J., *The Future Church of 140 B.C.E., a Hidden Revolution*, Crossroads, 1995.

Lernoux, Penny, *People of God, The Struggle for World Catholicism*, Viking, 1989.

Lonergan, Bernard, SJ, *Method in Theology*, Herder and Herder, 1972.

Loussier, Jean & Langley Sommer, Robin, editor, *Lost Europe-Images of a Vanished World*, Saraband, 1997.

MacEoin, Gary, *Latin America, The Eleventh Hour*, P.J. Kenedy & Sons, 1962; *No Peaceful Way, The Chilean Struggle for Dignity*, Sheed and Ward, 1974; *What Happened at Rome?, The Council and Its Implications for the Modern World*, introduction by John Cogley, Echo Book, 1966.

Maxwell, Grant, *At Your Service, Stories of Canadians in Mission*, CCCB, 1989; *China, Assignment in Chekiang*, foreword by John Fraser, SFM 1982; *Healing Journeys, the Ka Ka Wis Experience, 1974-94*, Ka Ka Wis 1994; *Like a Chinook, The Calgary Interfaith Story*, Inter-Church Consultants, 1974; *Project Feedback—Signs and Portents in the Seventies, Attitudes at the Canadian Grassroots*, unpublished, Canadian Catholic Conference, November, 1975; Six Interviews with Remi J. De Roo, transcribed, unpublished, 1997.

McBrien, Richard P, *Catholicism*, Winston Press, 1980; and *Encyclopedia of Catholicism*, Harper Collins, 1995.

McDonough, John Thomas, *Charbonneau & Le Chef*, McLelland and Stewart, 1968.

McLuhan, Marshall, *The Gutenberg Galaxy, The Making of Typographic Man*, Signet, 1972; *Understanding Media, The Extensions of Man*, Signet, 1964.

McNally, Vincent, *The Lord's Distant Vineyard, History of the Oblates and the Catholic Community in British Columbia*, Western Canadian Publishers, 2000.

Milhaven, John Giles, *Toward a New Catholic Morality*, Image Doubleday, 1970.

Moroney, E. Catherine, *The Chief Who Danced*, Blue Nun Press, 1994.

Morton, W.L., *Manitoba, A History*, University of Toronto, 1967.

Newman, Cardinal John Henry, *Apologia Pro Vita Sua*, Collins Fontana, 1972; *An Essay on the Development of Doctrine*, Christian Classics, 1968; also Image, 1956 introduced by Philip Hughes; *The Essential Newman, Central Writings*, edited by Vincent Blehl, Mentor Omega, 1963.

Nichols, Peter, *The Pope's Divisions*, Penguin Books, 1981.

Ogle, Rev. Bob, *A Man of Letters*, Broadcasting for International Understanding, 1990; *North/South Calling, an autobiography*, Fifth House, Novalis, 1987.

Pius XII, Pope, *The Pope Speaks, Teachings of the Pope*, Pantheon, 1957.

Rahner, Karl, editor, *Sacramentum Mundi, The Concise Encyclopedia of Theology*, 1975.

Roche, Anne, *The Gates of Hell, The Struggle for The Catholic Church*, McClelland & Stewart, 1975.

Roche Muggeridge, Anne, *The Desolate City, The Catholic Church in Ruins*, McLelland & Stewart, 1986.

Roszak, Theodore, *The Making of A Counter-Culture, Reflections on the Technocratic Society and Its Youthful Opposition*, Anchor Books, 1969.

Rynne, Xavier, *Vatican Council II*, Farrar, Straus and Giroux, 1964.

Schillebeeckx, Edward, OP, *Ministry, Leadership in the Community of Jesus Christ*, Crossroads, 1985; *Vatican II, The Real Achievement*, Sheed and Ward, 1967.

Smillie, Benjamin G., editor, *Political Theology in the Canadian Context*, Wilfrid Laurie University Press, 1982.

Smith, Michelle and Pazder, Lawrence, MD, *Michelle Remembers*, Congdon & Lattes, New York, 1980.

Sullivan, Bede, OSB, *Movies: Universal Language—Film Study in High School*, Fides Publishers, 1967; *Twenty Years After Vatican II*, Diocese of Victoria, 1982.

Szulc, Tad, *Pope John Paul II, The Biography*, Scribner, 1995.

Teilhard de Chardin, Pierre, SJ, *The Divine Milieu*, Harper and Row, 1960; *The Future of Man*, Fontana Paperbacks, 1964; *The Phenomenon of Man*, Fontana, 1959.

Thomas, Gordon & Morgan-Witts, Max, *Pontiff*, Panther, 1983.

Urqhuart, Gordon, *The Pope's Armada, Study of the new ultra-traditionalist movements within the Catholic Church under John Paul II*, Corgi Books, 1995.

Ward-Harris, E.D., *A Nun Goes to the Dogs, A biography of Mother Cecilia Mary, OSB*, Sono Nis, 1977.

Warner, Marina, *Alone of All Her Sex, The Myth and Cult of the Virgin Mary*, Picador, 1976.

Whitcomb, Ed, *A Short History of Manitoba*, Canada's Wings, 1982.

Wills, Garry, *Bare Ruined Choirs: Doubt, Prophecy, and Radical Religion*, Doubleday, 1972; *Papal Sin, Structures of Deceit*, Doubleday, 2000.

Yallop, David A., *In God's Name, an investigation into the murder of Pope John Paul I*, Corgi Books, 1984.

Articles and Talks

Allen, John L. Jr., *Vatican nixes bishop's talk at married priests's conference, National Catholic Reporter*, May 21, 1999, p. 8.

Babych, Art, *Catholic Book Causes Storm*, *Prairie Messenger*, February 24, 1992, p. 3; *De Roo apologizes to native leader*, *Prairie Messenger*, December 18, 1995, Vol. 73, No. 22, p. 1; *Victoria bishop plans for 'next career', The B.C. Catholic, Western Catholic Reporter*, July 5 & 13, 1998; *Vatican bans De Roo's U.S. talk, Prairie Messenger*, May 19, 1999, p. 3.

Baum, Gregory, *A Letter from the Pope*, *Canadian Forum*, December, 1993, pp. 21-23; *Competing Rights: Ethical Reflections on the Quebec language debate, Catholic New Times*, March 5, 1989, pp. 9-11; *The Labor Pope in Canada, The Ecumenist*, January-February, 1985, Vol. 23, no. 2, pp. 17-23.

Bill, Desmond, *Senate of Priests Share Bishop's Rule, Victoria Daily Times,* November 22, 1966.

Breig, James, *Gregory and John picked as History's top Popes, Scholars asked to pick Peter's best successor, Catholic News Service, Western Catholic Reporter*, March 29, 1999.

Brown, Joan, *Diocese Makes Hermit History Again*, *Island Catholic News*, February 1998, Vol. 12, No. 1, pp. 1, 6.

Browne, Mark, *Questions Raised about politics behind church crisis, Victoria News*, June 2, 2000; *Retirement Won't Stop De Roo from Speaking Out*, *Victoria News*, February 5, 1999.

Burnham, Rebecca, *Exiting from the left, a controversial diocese director is dismissed; British Columbia Report*, September 9, 1991, p. 32.

Butler, Marnie, *Bishop Raymond Roussin's first year as Bishop of Victoria*, *Island Catholic News*, April, 2000, Vol. 14, No. 3, p. 1.

Canadian Broadcasting Corporation, *Catholics*, transcript, Spring 1984, Four part series on *Ideas* radio program, repeated Winter 1985; *Pope John Paul II, Papal Tour Canada 1984*, six audio tapes of speeches and radio coverage.

Canadian Catholic Review, Special Edition, *The Papal Visit*, October 1984, Vol. 2, No. 9; Special Edition, *Catherine de Hueck Doherty*, September 1987, Vol. 5, No. 8.

Canadian Dimension, *The Bishops Speak*, May, 1983, Vol. 17, No. 2, *Ethical Reflections on the economic crisis*, pp. 2, 5-9; *Canadian Dimension*, a Special Edition, *The Left hand of God—Who Does Christianity Serve?,* articles by Gregory Baum, Ben Smillie, Bonnie Greene et al, January-February 1979, Vol. 13, No. 5, pp. 28-52.

Catholic Insight, *Humanae Vitae's High Noon, Special report*, July/August, 1998, Vol. VI, No. 6.

Catholics of Vision Canada, *Message to Canadian Catholic Bishops*, *Island Catholic News*, February 1997, Vol. 11, No. 1, pp. 7-10.

Concilium, An International Review of Theology, *Special Edition on dogma*, Vol. 1, No. 5, January 1969, Burns & Oates.

Cottrell, Michael, *John Joseph Leddy and the Battle for the Soul of the Catholic Church in the West, Historical Studies, Canadian Catholic Historical Association,* No. 61, 1995, pp. 41-51.

Crane, David, *Canada's unemployment immoral, bishops charge-Bishops hit problem of our economy right on the head, Toronto Star*, Saturday, January 1, 1983, pp. 1,16A.

Cribbens, Norman, *Roman Catholic Gift 'Handsome Gesture', Victoria Times*, December 22, 1962.

Crowe, Frederick E. SJ, *The Conscience of the theologian with reference to the Encyclical*, *Theology Today*, Summer 1969, pp. 312-332.

Davis, Charles, *The End of Religion, Compass*, March, 1988, pp. 6-9.

De Lavis, Robin, *Historic Island Hermit Monk Mourned at Bethlehem*, *Island Catholic News*, December 1998.

De Roo, Remi, *Agri-culture, Agri-business or Agri-power? A look to the future presentation at the National Farmers Union Convention*, December 2, 1985, Edmonton; *Bishop De Roo Explains Last 35 Years of Change, Council Father Unpacks Meaning of Vatican II, Island Catholic News*, Vol. 11, No. 10, November 1997; *Celebrating the gifts of native church*, *Mission Canada* magazine, Fall 1995. pp. 6-10, special edition on Vancouver Island Native missions; *Will the real Mary please identify herself? (While devotion to Mary is central to Catholic faith, the real Mary is difficult to identify), Island Catholic News*, May & June 1994; *Alternative Foreign Policy in Canada, Forum 2000, New Democratic Party of Canada*, Ottawa, November 1986; *Encyclical has exciting vision of work (four part series), Prairie Messenger,* November 1,8,15,22, 1981; *Faith Does Justice—Proposals for a Justice Spirituality,* Address at Seattle University, July 9-11, 1982; *Letters to Premier Glen Clark,* 1) regarding Bill 31, The Family Relations Amendment Act, 1997, June 20; 2) regarding consulting with spiritual leaders, July 9, 1997; *On the resignation of Bishop O'Connor*, Diocese of Victoria press release, July 8, 1991; *Our God is the God of Life*, Pastoral Statement, Easter, 1985; *Review of Silent Coup, Confronting the Big Business takeover of Canada*, by Tony Clarke, *Island Catholic News*, January 1998, special supplement, page 3; *Statement in Support of Aboriginal Peoples of Canada* (with other B.C. church leaders), October 9, 1985;

Submission to Royal B.C. Commission on Health Services, 1990; *Sermon for Ordination*, June 28, 1992, Saint Andrew's Cathedral, Victoria; *Social Gospel Perspectives on a High-tech Market Economy*, Annual Convention B.C. Federation of Labour, Vancouver, November 26, 1985; *Spirituality: An Ongoing Quest, to Wellbeing*, Vancouver Island, January 21, 1998; *The Christ of Justice*, Talk at Hales Corner, Wisconsin, August 1, 1996; *The Salvation of Rural Life Lies in a Prophetic Church, Compass*, review of *Land and Community* by Alex Sim, July 1989, pp. 41-43; *Towards A People's Agenda, Canadian Labour Congress National Conference,* Ottawa, December 1-3, 1991; *Women in the Church Summation, Conference on Women in the Church, Washington D.C.*, October 12, 1986, published in *Island Catholic News*, under title *Bishop De Roo Identifies Women's Role Challenges*, February, 1987, Vol. 1, No. 1, pp. 6-7.

Diocese of Victoria, *Quinquennial Report for period 1969-73*; *Unto Us a Child is Born, A response to the Provincial Taskforce on Childcare*, March 27, 1991; *Wherever Two or More Women...A Plan for Study, Action, Growth*, Doreen Hunter, ed., 1983.

Dutton, Ian, *Catholics quarrel over doctrine, Faction promotes liberalization of rules through petition, Times Colonist*, March 11, 1997, p. A5; *Reflections of A Bishop—The recently retired Remi De Roo looks back on his half century in the priesthood and the revolutionary shift in the Catholic Church*, Friday, March 5, 1999, *Times Colonist* (reprinted in April 1999 *Island Catholic News*, titled *Reflections of a Revolutionary*).

Embra, Shirley, *University of Victoria holds official opening of the centre for Studies in Religion and Society, Island Catholic News*, November, 1993.

Evans, Donald, *Gregory Baum's Theology of Liberation*, *Studies in Religion, A Canadian Journal*, Vol. 1, No. 1, 1971, pp. 45-60.

Fiedler, Leslie, *The New Mutants*, *Beyond Left and Right*, editor Richard Kostelantez, 1969.

Goodacre, Bill, *Brian Swimme links social organization with a wider cosmology*, *Island Catholic News*, October 1998, Vol. 12, No. 9.

Grescoe, Paul, *A different kind of bishop, Star Weekly*, March 28, 1970.

Guillermoprieto, Alma, *A Visit To Havana*, *New York Review of Books*, March 26, 1998, pp. 19-24.

Haight, Roger, *The Crisis of Modernism*, *Compass Magazine* March 1990, pp. 20-24.

Harnett, Cindy E., *Catholic Newspaper takes own same-sex stand —Island editor refuses to join Vancouver newspaper's call for crusade against proposed pension-benefit legislation*, *Times Colonist*, Thursday, July 30, 1998, page A4.

Hartog, Diana, *A Pilgrim in the valley—Bishop Remi De Roo: The Man in the Grey-Flannel Suit, Monday Magazine*, June 11-17, 1986, Vol. 12, No. 25, pp. 1, 7-11.

Harvey, Bob, *Vatican told bishop speech could create 'great scandal,' National Post*, May 20, 1999.

Hebblethwaite, Peter, *The Popes and Politics: Shifting Patterns in Catholic Social Doctrine; Religion in America: Spiritual Life in a Secular Age*, Mary Douglas and Stephen M. Tipton, editors, Beacon Press, Boston, 1982, pp. 85-99.

Helm, Denise, *Catholic newspapers snub De Roo book, Times-Colonist*, February 4, 1992; *'I'm a feminist', De Roo tells students, Times Colonist*, August 28, 1993.

Henry, Tom, *Catholic Church Drops One, Moves to the Right, Monday Magazine*, August 15-21, 1991.

Hill, Roland, *'I am the Tradition', How The Pope Became Infallible, Times Literary Supplement*, April 2, 1999. p. 9.

Hogan, Brian F. CSB, *The Institute of Social Action and Social Catholicism in Canada in the 1950s, Historical Studies, Canadian Catholic History Association*, No. 54, 1987, pp. 125-144.

Hume, Stephen, *Myth-mashing friar packs punches and cathedral seats, Times-Colonist*, Sunday, March 29, 1987; *Newspaper breaking Catholic law by challenging authority of bishop, Times-Colonist*, Tuesday, April 5, 1988.

Jacot, Michael, *Gregory Baum: Man for Our Times*, *The Sign*, June, 1965, pp. 12-15.

Jager, Manfred, *Word came and you could have knocked him over with a feather, Youngest Shepherd faces Drastic Changes, Winnipeg Tribune*, November 2, 1962.

Jamieson, Eugene, *Faith and Politics, Church and Justice, El Salvador and Nicaragua* (an interview with Bishop Remi De Roo), pp. 8-9, *Prairie Messenger*, September 20, 1981.

Jamieson, Patrick, *Antigonish—The Two-sided Legacy, Toward a New Maritimes*, (reprinted from May, 1985, *New Maritimes)* edited by Ian McKay and Scott Milsom, Ragweed Publishers, 1992, pp. 60-66; *The Bishops Revisited, New Maritimes*, review of *On Economics and The Canadian Bishops* by Walter Block, and *Ethics and Economics: Canada's Catholic Bishops on the Economic Crisis* by Gregory Baum and Duncan Cameron, October, 1985, pp. 14-15; *Who's Minding The Justice Store?*, *Catholic New Times*, April 1993; *'Building Up in Love'—Remi De Roo's 25th anniversary as a bishop*, *Island Catholic News*, special edition, December, 1987; *Cowichan Abel Joe's Creative Spiritual Authority*, *Island Catholic News*, May 1989, p. 8; *Reasoned debate on Abortion law urged*, *Island Catholic News*, March, 1988, Vol. 2, No. 2, page one.

Jedynak, Esther, editor, Synod Coverage, *Island Catholic News*, 1986-91, complete coverage, scrapbooks.

John XXIII, Pope, *Mater et Magistra, Christianity and Social Progress*; *Pacem in Terram.*

John Paul II, Pope, *Christ's Faithful People (Christifideles Laici), Vocation of the Lay Faithful in the church and the world*, CCCB, 1988; *Letter to Women*, supplement to *Island Catholic News*, August, 1995; *The Gospel of Life (Evangelium Vitae) Encyclical Letter on Abortion, Euthanasia and the Death Penalty in Today's World.*

John Paul II, *Faith and Reason*, *B.C. Catholic*, special section, October 26, 1998.

Judt, Tony, *Holy Warrior*, review of *His Holiness: John Paul II and the History of Our Times* by Carl Bernstein and Marco Politi, *New York Review of Books*, October 31, 1996, pp 8-14.

Kelly, Deirdre, *'Creative Solidarity' inspires protest against School of the Americas, Island Catholic News*, May, 1998; *Offerings of the Martyrs: Then and Now, Island Catholic News*, p. 1, March 2000.

Kort, Suzanne, *Bishop emeritus embraces Jewish roots, Island Catholic News*, August 1999, Vol. 13, No. 7, p. 8.

Lascelles, Thomas A., OMI, *Indian Residential Schools—The Historical Perspective*, *Mission* magazine, Vol. II, no. 2, 1995, pp. 181-192 (originally published *The Canadian Catholic Review*, May, 1992).

Lash, Nicholas, *Has pope contravened Church's definitive teaching?*, *Prairie Messenger*, September 16, 1998, p. 19.

Marchand, Gregory, *The Bishop and Ms. Chaplain, The life and career of Bishop Remi De Roo and his controversial appointment of Kate Fagan as UVic chaplain, Victoria Zoom*, May 1998, No. 6, pp. 4-5,11.

Maxwell, Grant ed., *He Asked Their Opinion*, *Long Island Catholic*, Thursday, September 28, 1967; *Behind the Mitre tells one side of Catholic dispute, Prairie Messenger*, April 17, 1995, p.2; *He Was Only Talking The Gospel Truth*, special section of commentary, *Island Catholic News*, Vol. 13, No. 1, February, 1999, pp 5-12; *Life and death on the farm*, *Newest Review*, October/November 1996, Volume 22, No. 1, pp. 34-35; *The life-giving witness of Jim and Marg (Beaubien)*, *Our Family* magazine, December, 1996, Vol. 47, No. 11, pp. 23-29.

McClory, Robert, *At 50, time to take stock of the Christian Family Movement* a review of *Disturbing The Peace—a history of the Christian Family Movement, 1949-74*, *National Catholic Reporter*, June 4, 1999, p. 17.

McKinley, Barney, *The Hermits of Vancouver Island*, *Catholic Digest*, May, 1967, pp. 88ff.

McNally, Reverend Vincent, *Victoria: An American Diocese in Canada*, *Historical Studies* (57), 1990 *Journal of the Canadian Catholic Historical Association*; *Surviving in Lotus land: A History of the Diocese of Victoria 1846-1923* (unpublished), Diocese of Victoria Archives; *Fighting City Hall: The Church Tax Exemption Battle between The City and the Roman Catholic Diocese of Victoria*, *Historical Studies* (74) 1992, *Journal of the Canadian Catholic Historical Association.*

Murphy, Maureen T., *Don't cooperate with Catholic lobby group, Archbishop urges, B.C. Catholic,* January 28, 1997, pp. 1, 3.

O'Brien, Willard J., *Our Lady of the Rosary Parish, 25th Anniversary*, self-published pamphlet, June 20, 1976.

Oosterom, Nelle, *Human rights rest on basis of spirit, De Roo tells rally, Prairie Messenger*, April 26, 1981.

Paul VI, *Humanae Vitae, On Human Life*, 1968; *Populorum Progressio*, 1967.

Ratzinger, Cardinal Joseph, prefect Congregation for the Doctrine of Faith, *Instruction on Christian Freedom and Liberation*, Supplement *B.C. Catholic*, April 27, 1986.

Richards, Ann, *Diocese Furthest Out*, review of *Victoria Demers to De Roo, 150 Years of Catholic History on Vancouver Island*, by Patrick Jamieson, *The Trumpet*, December 1997.

Roche, Douglas, *De Roo upholds Sisters' Right to Experiment, Western Catholic Reporter*, April 4, 1968; *Five Year Report for Pope Published by Bishop De Roo, Western Catholic Reporter*, November 1968; *Laity have a stake in papal elections, review of "The Papacy and the people of God," by Gary MacEoin, Western Catholic Reporter*, June 8, 1998, p. 14.

Ryan, William F. SJ, *Has Catholic Social teaching Had Significant Influence?, Eglise et Theologie*, No. 23, 1992, pp. 13-30.

Sacouman, James, *Underdevelopment and The Structural Origins of The Antigonish Movement in Eastern Nova Scotia*, p. 107 in *Underdevelopment and Social Movements in Atlantic Canada*, New Hogtown Press, 1979.

Scott, Peter, *'Perfect' Catholic Bishop human rights battler, The Victorian*, Wednesday, September 29, 1976.

Somfai, Bela, SJ, *Humanae Vitae, Unhealed Wounds, Two Decades After, Compass*, July 1989, Vol. 7, No. 3, pp. 15-18; *Humanae Vitae, Unhealed Wound-II, Compass*, September 1989, Vol. 7, No. 4, pp. 22-24.

Somerville, Janet, *The People of God on Vancouver Island reconstituting a church, Catholic New Times*, August 1991, p. 5.

Speise, E.A., introduction to *Genesis, Anchor Bible, The Documentary Sources of Genesis*, pp xxii-xxxvii, Doubleday, 1964.

Sproule, Jack, *Rev. Remi De Roo and The Challenge, Catholic New Times*, June 17, 2001, page 3.

Steed, Judy, *The Battling Bishop, The Globe and Mail*, Saturday, May 3, 1986, p. A10.

Steinfels, Peter, *Catholic Group Urges Sweeping Change in Church, New York Times,* February 28, 1990, p. A12, 14.

Tennant, F.R., *The Sources of the Doctrines of the falls and Original Sin*, Chapter one, *The Fall Story and its Exegesis*, Schocken Books, New York, 1968.

Theological Studies, March, 1974, Vol. 35, No. 1, *Special issue on Population 1974.*

Time Magazine, *Pope John Paul II-Man of the Year, 1994, Empire of the Spirit*, December 26, 1994-January 2, 1995, pp. 1, 4, 22-41.

Times Colonist, *Mother Cecilia loses $1.5 million lawsuit*, January 24, 1975, page 15; *Death of Mother Cecilia—Nun's lifelong defiance of authority eventually led to break with Vatican,* March 1989.

Todd, Douglas, *Book ad rejection highlights rift among Catholics, The Vancouver Sun*, Friday, February 7, 1992, p. B2; *Island bishop plays down storm over book, ad ban fans Catholic controversy*, *Vancouver Sun*, Monday, February 24, 1992; *Two Bishops, One Church, A Tale of Two Dioceses*, Section E, *Vancouver Sun*, Saturday review Section, August 2, 1997.

Valpy, Michael, *Thorn in Their Side, Formidable intellectual and practising Catholic, Garry Wills thinks the modern papacy has led his church astray*, *Globe and Mail*, D6, Saturday, June 17, 2000.

Van Zanten, Anke, *Belgium*, in *Lost Europe-Images of a Vanished World*, pp. 76-83, Saraband, 1997.

Vipond, Don, *Great Deeds of A Good Man are forgotten, The Crucifixion of Remi De Roo*, *Times Colonist*, August 20, 2000, p. A7.

Wallace, D. Gail, *Social Justice and the Catholic School Teachers' Association: A Historical perspective of the CSTA in British Columbia, Historical Studies in Education: Teachers and Unions*, Spring 1993, Vol. 5, No. 1, pp. 55-65.

Wills, Garry, *A Tale of Two Cardinals (Bernadin and Ratzinger), New York Review of Books*, April 26, 2001, pp. 24-27; *Fatima: 'The Third Secret,'* New York Review of Books, August 10, 2000, p. 51; *The Vatican Monarchy, New York Review of Books*, February 19, 1998, pp. 20-25.

Woodward, Kenneth L., *Life, Death and the Pope, Newsweek*, April 10, 1995, pp. 56-66.

Young, Gerard, *Deficit beats out inflation as myth, De Roo suggests, Times Colonist*, Sunday, May 23, 1993.

Selected Reporting On Post-Retirement Year 2000 Financial Saga

Browne, Mark, *Victoria News Weekend Edition, Crisis rocks the church,* Friday, March 3, 2000, page 2; *The keeper of the faith,* September 7, 2001, pp. 1, 5.

Dickson, Louise, *Times Colonist, Loan plea upsets churchgoers,* Monday, May 15, 2000, pp. A1-2; *Former bishop silent on debt, Borrow to cover interest and expenses, Roman Catholic Church properties listed*, Tuesday, May 16, 2000, pp. A1, 4; *De Roo offers three-sentence letter of apology*, Sunday, May 28, 2000, pp. A1-2.

Di Cresce, Greg, *Winnipeg Sun Police Reporter, Uncomfortable pews, Parishioners protest controversial bishop*, Friday, May 26, 2000, p. 5; *Mountain out of a molehill, Church official defends B.C. Bishop,* Saturday, May 27, 2000, p. 4.

Ian Dutton, *Times Colonist, Catholics raise cash to ease debt, Campaign nets almost $13 million to undo burden left by Bishop Remi De Roo*, Friday, August 4, 2000, p. B1.

Foot, Richard, *National Post, Bishop retired as an 'unremitting reformer,'* Tuesday, February 29, 2000, page A5.

Harnett, Cindy E., *Times Colonist, De Roo's apology not enough for Roussin, Successor says he's acting fast to improve church accountability*, Sunday, May 21, 2000, pp. A1-2.

Henderson, Larry, *Challenge Magazine, An Afterword*, column, September, 2000, p. 28.

Jiminez, Marina, *National Post, Victoria diocese bought 64 hectares to develop racetrack, $3.5M spent in legal fees and mortgage payments*, Tuesday, February 29, 2000, page A5; *Victoria bishop lost gamble on Arabian mares*, Wednesday, March 1, 2000, pp. A1-2; *Bishop's high risk deal not on the books: Successor, National Post*, Friday, March 3, 2000, pp. A1, 12.

Lunman, Kim, *The Globe and Mail, A blessed pitchman hits up the flock, Victoria parishes hear plea to bail out diocese, The Globe and Mail*, Saturday, May 27, 2000; *Trust Fund for nuns wiped out in Victoria, Pension money used to buy race horses, The Globe and Mail*, Monday, May 29, 2000, p. A3; *The lawyer, the bishop and the money pit, The Globe and Mail*, Saturday, June 17, 2000, p. A11; *Bishop's secret deals 'beyond belief,' probe finds, church report blasts Victoria's Remi De Roo, The Globe and Mail,* Friday, June 30, 2000, pp. 1.

Matas, Robert, *The Globe and Mail, Real-estate deal gone bad divides church supporters, Social activist Bishop De Roo criticized for poor financial management of diocese, The Globe and Mail*, Thursday, March 2, 2000, p. A5.

Paterson, Jody, *Times Colonist, Church land deal raises issue of ethics,* Wednesday, March 1, 2000, p. A3.

Roussin, Raymond, *Island Catholic News, Bishop announces Diocesan Financial Concerns, The full text of the statement read at Sunday masses, February 27th in The Victoria Diocese,* March, 2000, p. 5.

Times Colonist, *Catholic diocese rocked by debt, Investment losses force sale of assets on Island, court action considered*, February 28, 2000, pp. A1-2; *Financial crisis worries Catholics*, Tuesday, February 29, 2000, page C1.

Todd, Douglas, *Vancouver Sun, Successor named for Catholic leader,* February 24, 1999; *Island Catholic church sells land to pay millions in debts,* Monday, February 28, 2000, pp. A1-2; *Ex-bishop admits role in money woes, Remi De Roo has acknowledged a 'major problem' occurred during his Island tenure,* Tuesday, February 29, 2000, page A3; *Fast horses, big deal linked to island Catholic money woes,* Wednesday, March 1, 2000, pp. A1-2; *Probe not personal, Catholic bishop says,* Friday, March 3, 2000, page A3.

Vallis, Mary, *The Province, Church cash woes unfold,* Thursday, March 2, 2000, p. A12; *Bishop probes mystery loans,* Friday, March 3, 2000, p. A16.

Westad, Kim, *Times Colonist, Church took risk on U.S. land, bad investments leave Island diocese in debt*, Wednesday, March 1, 2000, page A1-3; *Church official says bishop approved loan,* Thursday, March 2, 2000, page one; *Secret deals astonished new bishop,* Friday, March 3, 2000, pp. A1-2; *Church debt opens old wounds, financial woes revive touchy political divide*, Sunday, March 5, 2000, pp. A1,6, 7; *Court slaps foreclosure order on church-owned land,* Saturday, March 18, 2000, pp. A1-2; *Commission probes diocese's finances,* Wednesday, March 22, 2000, p. C3; *Church report rips into De Roo, Commission says if former bishop had not retired already, he would have faced papal action for damages that will last generations*, Friday, June 30, 2000, pp A1-3.

Wilson, Carla, *Times Colonist, De Roo admits blame on debt, Former Victoria bishop says sorry, 'acted in good faith'*, Saturday, May 20, 2000, pp. A1-2; *Debt Crisis—Catholics dig deep for ailing diocese,* Tuesday, June 27, 2000, p. C1.

Young, Gerard, *Times Colonist, Diocese asks parishioners for millions,* May 14, 2000, page one; *Bishop pledges closer scrutiny of church funds*, Wednesday, May 24, 2000. pp. A1-2; *Roman Catholics demand answers, the word forgive is far from parishioners' lips*, Thursday, May 25, 2000, pp. A1; *Catholic Diocese in crisis—Landowner in no hurry to help church sell up*, Friday, May 26, 2000, page C1; *Ex-bishop gambled assets from convent, De Roo chased losses and had two sets of books, concludes Roman Catholic Church commission*, Saturday, May 27, 2000, pp. A1,4; *Catholics in Crisis—Mystery Man*, pp. A1-2; *The Promised Land*, C4; *Key Players*, C5; *Money For Horses*, C5, Sunday, June 4, 2000; *Church offered deal to ease debt*, Monday, June 12, 2000, pp. A1-2; *Catholics ease burden of mortgage*, Tuesday, September 19, 2000, pp. A1-2; *Offer to purchase land eases church debt woes*, Tuesday, July 24, 2001, pp. A1-2; *Church deal falls through, Seattle company backs out of deal that would have rid Victoria's Roman Catholic diocese of land in*

Victoria's Roman Catholic diocese of land in Washington, Tuesday, August 28, 2001, pp. B1-2.

Totals: Times Colonist front page—19 times between March 1 & September 1, 2000; other section lead page ten times; number of different reporters—eight.

Remi De Roo introduces Marnie Butler, editor of the *Island Catholic News* to Jean Vanier, 1996. In the background is Lock Mawhinney, founder of Comox Valley L'Arche. (ICN)

INDEX

CHAPTER NOTES

Chapter One: Five (or Six) Facts

[1]*Offerings of the Martyrs: Then and Now* by Deirdre Kelly, p. 1, March 2000, *Island Catholic News*, Volume 14, No. 2. "After Oscar Romero was martyred, Peace Accords were signed and UN Truth Commission Reports were released in 1993. An unsettling number of graduates of the US Army School of the Americas (SOA), the Spanish language training school for Latin American soldiers and officers, had gone on to be implicated in the torture, executions, disappearances and murders that were terrorizing the populations."

[2] *William Power, Bishop Emeritus of Antigonish, as quoted in Victoria Demers to De Roo, p. 305-6.*

[3]*Victoria News* feature by Mark Browne titled "Retirement won't Stop De Roo from Speaking Out," February 5, 1999. Browne also scripted a piece on June 2, 2000 during the discrediting campaign titled "Questions raised about politics behind church crisis." For complete text, see chapter 18.

[4]Monsignor Peter Schonenbach, General Secretary of the Canadian Conference of Catholic Bishops, was quoted as approximating De Roo's condition to that of a gambling addict. This statement unfortunately pre-empted and prejudiced the CCCB canonical inquiry report and was very surprising given the historical precedence of such top bureaucrats for painstaking professional objectivity. It also cut off De Roo's only avenue for formal and objective defence of his involvement or lack of such. Due to this complete surrounding in his situation by those antagonistic to his position or involvement, supporters were quoted as saying "there seems to be a concerted effort to discredit him" [see Mark Browne in June 2, 2000 edition of *Victoria News*] and De Roo decided to keep complete silence as though recognizing the present futility of actually being heard.

[5]Saturday May 20, 2000 *Times Colonist* story titled "De Roo admits blame for debt."

[6]*The Victorian*, Wednesday, September 29, 1976 "'Perfect' Catholic Bishop human rights battler" by Peter Scott.

[7]See *People of God* by Penny Lernoux, subtitled *The Struggle for World Catholicism*, Viking, 1989.

[8]Penny Lernoux, *People of God, The Struggle for World Catholicism*, Chapter One, 'The Way of the Cross,' pp. 5-6.

[9]*Catholic New Times* series on the closing of social justice offices in Spring of 1993 by Patrick Jamieson.

[10]An excellent source on this 'development' is "Absolute Truth," a BBC/Vision co-production television series on Roman Catholicism, 1998 shown on Canadian television through Vision Television.

[11]The post-retirement discrediting campaign may have been that rare exception.

[12]See example of Ria Tritt's letter in Victoria *Times Colonist*, August 23, 2000 in response to feature article by Quaker Don Vipond's praising De Roo's overall contribution after the massive discrediting campaign of the earlier part of the year.

[13]Dutton, Ian, Victoria *Times Colonist*, Friday March 5, 1999 p. B3 "Reflections of a Bishop," 'The Recently retired Remi De Roo looks back on his half century in the priesthood and the revolutionary shift in the Catholic Church.'

[14]*Catholic New Times*, February 14, 1999 p. 3. An introduction to a section of his last book reads: "He is the last Canadian office holder to have been at Vatican II. Indeed, as the *National Catholic Reporter* pointed out recently, he and Pope John Paul II are the last in the world, still in office, to have been at all four sessions."

[15]See "The Diocesan Synod as a means of developing Doctrine," a talk given by De Roo to the North American Catholic Theological Society in 1999 and published as a booklet in 2000 by ICN Publishing.

[16]See pp. 28-29 of Lernoux, Penny, *People of God, The Struggle for World Catholicism*.

[17]McBrien, Richard P., *Encyclopedia of Catholicism*, page 1033.

[18]Bernstein, Carl and Politi, Marco, *His Holiness, John Paul II and the History of Our Time*.

Chapter Two: 1968—The Watershed Year

[19]Daly Bernard, *Remembering for Tomorrow, a History of the Canadian Conference of Catholic Bishops 1943-1993*, page 126.

[20]See Anne Roche's two books *The Gates of Hell, the Struggle for the Catholic Church* and *The Desolate City, the Catholic Church in Ruins* especially the latter which happens to have an index, pp. 97 and 112. As one might guess from the progress implied in the titles, things after Vatican II went from bad to worse for this noted antediluvian thinker,

at least until 1986, the date of *The Desolate City* and coincidently the precise year when John Paul II's containment program fully kicked in. She later added Muggeridge to her last name after her famous father-in-law's (Malcolm Muggeridge) celebrated conversion to Catholicism, possibly under her tutelage.

[21]Chapter Six, *Even Greater Things*, with Mae and Bernard Daly, 1998. This book provides an extensive overview of De Roo's later views and some detail on how he arrived at them, and his own growth path. For example see p. 99 for his candid acknowledgement in the area of his growth in human intimacy.

[22]p. 56, *What Happened at Rome, The Council and its Implications for the Modern World*, by Gary MacEoin, Echo Books, Doubleday, 1967.

[23]De Roo claims that Cardinals Leger and Svenens were more influential.

[24]Vatican Council II, *The Conciliar and post-conciliar documents*, general editor Austin Flannery, OP, p. 952 ff.

[25]On pp. 106-109 of *Even Greater Things*, De Roo explains about this decisive intervention. He acknowledges "we achieved a certain breakthrough in church teaching about marriage at the council" but that he was overly optimistic about the maturity of many couples "who turned toward the hedonistic culture around them with no sense that the church can teach or help them."

[26]Jamieson, Patrick, "Building up in Love," Remi De Roo's 25th anniversary celebration as a bishop, *Island Catholic News*, special section, December, 1987.

[27]See Marina Warner, *Alone of All Her Sex—The Myth and Cult of the Virgin Mary*, Picador, 1976.

[28]Maxwell, Grant interviews from December 1997.

[29]Jung, Carl G., *The Symbolic Life,* Vol. 18, *Collected Works,* Bollingen also *Psychology and Western Religion.* In this latter text Jung's appreciative yet critical essays on the symbolic system of Roman Catholicism reveal his overall positive attitude.

[30]Maxwell, Grant, as quoted in *Victoria Demers to De Roo, 150 Years of Catholic History on Vancouver Island*, p. 332.

[31]"Absolute Truth," four part BBC/Vision Television co-production television series on the Catholic Church since Vatican II, Vision Television, October 1998.

[32]Wills, Garry, *Bare Ruined Choirs*, Chapters 8 and 9, "Paul In Chains," and "Prisoners of Sex," Doubleday, 1971.

[33]Wills, Garry, *Bare Ruined Choirs*, p. 95 *Papal Sin, Structures of Deceit* (footnote p. 103).

[34]*Even Greater Things*, pp. 122-23.

[35]*Our Sunday Visitor*, October 4, 1964; *Western Catholic Reporter*, August 25, 1966; *National Catholic Reporter*, August 31, 1966.

[36]McBrien, Richard, *Encyclopedia of Catholicism*, Harper Collins 1995, p. 1033 "Although committed to the Second Vatican Council, much of his pontificate... has been dedicated to the containment of progressive ideas and practices following from that council. For that reason it has been called a restorationist papacy. Others see him as the first post-modern pontiff."

[37]Gordon Urquhart, *The Pope's Armada – a study of the new ultra-traditionalist movements within the Catholic Church under John Paul II*, Corgi, 1995.

[38]Wills, Garry, *The Vatican Monarchy*, New York Review of Books, February 19, 1998, p. 20ff also *Holy Warrior* by Tony Judt, review of *His Holiness: John Paul II and The Hidden History of Our Time* by Carl Bernstein and Marco Politi, New York Review of Books, October 31, 1996.

[39]Lee, Bernard E., *A Hidden Revolution—The Future Church of 140 BCE*, also *World Catholicism in Transition*, editor Thomas M. Gannon, SJ, MacMillan 1988.

[40]Dutton, Ian, "Reflections of a bishop—The recently retired Remi De Roo looks back on his half century in the priesthood and the revolutionary shift in the Catholic Church," Victoria *Times Colonist*, Friday, March 5, 1999 reprinted in *Island Catholic News* under the headline "Reflections of a Revolutionary," April, 1999.

Chapter Three: Politics and the Church

[41]I attended a small liberal arts Catholic university in The Maritimes during the late Sixties and early Seventies where I became involved with community organizing and social activism on the basis of Catholic Social Teaching. During the Seventies I was trained and employed as a community development worker in rural New Brunswick, did a Masters of Divinity program at theology school out of personal interest and became employed as a writer and editor with a specialty in social

affairs for Catholic publications in Ottawa and Saskatchewan between 1978-82.

[42]*Catholics and Canadian Socialism, Political Thought in the Thirties and Forties*, see Chapter Two, "Papal Teaching on Socialism" by Gregory Baum, Lorimer, 1981.

[43]See essays by J.M. Cameron in *The Night Battle* particularly "Catholicism and Political Mythology;" also in *Catholics and Canadian Socialism* by Gregory Baum.

[44]See *Mater et Magistra*, social encyclical of Pope John XXIII from May 15, 1961 titled Christianity and Social Progress.

[45]See *Justice in the World* by the Synod of Bishops, Second General Assembly (November 30, 1971) p. 513 *The Gospel of Peace and Justice, Catholic Social Teaching Since Pope John*, Orbis, 1975.

[46]pp. 61-64 of Tony Clarke's *Behind The Mitre*, titled "Cat Among The Pigeons."

[47]Ron Graham, *God's Dominion, a Sceptics Quest*, p. 134. Graham is a little shocked at how Black was initiated into the Catholic Church in Cardinal Carter's den amidst champagne celebration.

[48]See p. 63 ff of *Behind The Mitre*, "The Moral leadership Crisis in the Canadian Catholic Church" by Tony Clarke for details on Cardinal Carter's complaints to the CCCB executive about *Ethical Reflections*. Carter was replaced by Aloysius Ambrozic as archbishop of Toronto, who proved even more antagonistic, see p. 23.

[49]Graham, p. 238.

[50]p. 51, *Portraits of Canadian Catholicism*, M.W. Higgins and D.R. Letson, Chapter Two.

[51]Conversation with Eileen Archer, a family friend who served 30 years as De Roo's executive assistant from the time of his arrival.

[52]The 1979 six point pastoral action for social justice plan included the following overall strategy: a) Rediscovering Catholic prophetic faith, b) Participating in People's Struggles, c) Developing a Social Analysis, d) Making Moral Judgements, e) Proposing Alternative Directions, e) Taking Political Action. Tony Clarke writes: "For me, what was particularly exciting about formulating these guidelines was the fact that we had finally developed a practical approach to liberation theology and acting in terms of a prophetic spirituality here in Canada. We also realized that for Catholics to follow these guidelines required conversion to a new religious experience.... While only a minority of Catholics chose to follow this path in the seventies, they

formed part of a new religious movement that began challenging the whole church to revitalize its prophetic faith tradition." p. 18, *Behind the Mitre*.

[53]Carter and De Roo were the only members of the hierarchy included with Mary Jo Leddy, editor Larry Henderson, Morley Callaghan, Marc Lalonde, Richard Cashin and Emmett Hall.

[54]Tony Clarke, *Behind The Mitre*, "The Moral Leadership Crisis in the Canadian Catholic Church," p. 82 ff, Harper Collins, 1995.

[55]See Chapter 3 *Ethical Challenge*, pp. 53-77.

[56]Bede Sullivan, OSB *Twenty Years After Vatican II*, 1982, Diocese of Victoria.

[57]"Ex-bishop gambled assets from convent" read the *Times Colonist* headline of Saturday May 27, 2000, the sub head reads: "De Roo chased losses and had two sets of books concludes Roman Catholic Church Commission." This headline peaked the bad publicity and pejorative reporting on the story. This is the story where Monsignor Peter Schonenbach, General Secretary of the CCCB, is quoted comparing De Roo's condition to that of a gambling addict, thus effectively pre-empting and prejudicing his own official report.

[58]See Chapter 11 of *Victoria Demers to De Roo*, p. 297 titled "Remi De Roo and the Coming of the Synodal Church," also *Forward in the Spirit, Challenge of the People's Synod*, edited by Grant Maxwell and Pearl Gervais, 1991.

[59]For details see Carl Bernstein and Carlo Politi, *His Holiness*, see *Shaking The Empire*, pp. 237-389.

[60]*Prairie Messenger*, September 20, 1981, pp. 8-9.

Chapter Four: The Radical About-Face

[61]McBrien, Richard P. *Catholicism* pp. 657-86; as well as his *Encyclopedia of Catholicism*.

[62]Leonard Cohen, Royal Theatre, Victoria, June 1994.

[63]An excellent depiction of this struggle was done by the BBC in part one of its 1997 series "Absolute Truth," shown in Canada in conjunction with Vision Television.

[64]Xavier Rynne, *Vatican Council II*, Farrar, Straus and Giroux, 1968.

[65]Richard P. McBrien says this of John XXIII in his book *Catholicism*: "It is difficult to exaggerate the role played by Pope John XXIII

in the total event known as The Second Vatican Council, even though he was to die between the first and second sessions (1963)."

[66]*Western Catholic Reporter*, March 29, 1999, by James Breig, Catholic News Service.

[67]Kelly, J.N.D. *The Oxford Dictionary of Popes*, 1986.

[68]*Victoria Times*, October 31 and December 20, 1962.

[69]*Victoria News*, February 5, 1999. Ironically in view of the silencing that would soon follow, the headline read: "Retirement won't stop De Roo from Speaking out."

[70]Maxwell, Grant, *Island Catholic News* December, 1987.

Chapter Five: The Paradox at Victoria

[71]"Word came, and you could have knocked him over with a feather, Youngest Shepherd Faces Drastic Changes" by Manfred Jager, *Winnipeg Tribune*, November 2, 1962.

[72]Rev. Ken Bernard, telephone interview, August 1997.

[73]*Even Greater Things*, p. 13.

[74]See pp. 257-259 of *Victoria Demers to De Roo* (Chapter Nine, "Cody and the Modern Era") for details on this tension in the diocese during the Second World War years.

[75]Victoria had five different bishops during fourteen years between 1923 and 1937, four of whom were quickly elevated to larger centres. For details see chapters 7-9 *Victoria Demers to De Roo*.

[76]Xavier Rynne, *Vatican Council II*, p. 9.

[77]Lajoie, Sigismund, OFM, p. 24, *Island Catholic News*, December, 1987.

[78]Essay in *Beyond Left and Right*, edited by Richard Kostelanetz.

[79]James Sacouman, "Underdevelopment and the Structural Origins of Antigonish Movement in Eastern Nova Scotia," p. 107 in *Underdevelopment and Social Movements in Atlantic Canada*, New Hogtown Press, 1979.

[80]Rev. Richard Renshaw in conversation. Renshaw is a Canadian Holy Cross Father who serves as a general assistant for the Canadian Religious Conference in Ottawa and has been a ethics professor and a missioner to Peru.

[81]The Archdiocese of Vancouver was notorious in its backsliding on the program of the council. It was jokingly referred to as still in The High Middle Ages and as a result, since the containment, has been seen as a model of a sort. The obvious contrast with Victoria has drawn

comparison such as Douglas Todd's *Vancouver Sun* feature from August 2, 1997, E1,4.

[82]The two immediately preceding bishops at Victoria, John Christopher Cody and James Michael Hill (1937-62) had been strong in the area of lay participation if under a more limited model of involvement. See Chapters 9 and 10 of the diocesan history, *Victoria Demers to De Roo.*

[83]"The Diocese of Victoria from 1962 through 1982" by Bede Sullivan, OSB, booklet published by the Diocese of Victoria.

[84]Poor Clares: On A Journey of Biblical Faith, *Island Catholic News*, pp. 8-9, November, 1987.

[85]Six-page *Catholic Digest* article, May, 1967 p. 88ff by Barney McKinley titled "The Hermits of Vancouver Island."

[86]See *Victoria Demers to De Roo, 150 Years of Catholic History on Vancouver Island*, especially the first fifty years when the church's presence was nearly entirely centred on the Native population.

[87]See Bede Sullivan booklet, "The Diocese of Victoria from 1962 through 1982."

[88]p. 6, February, 1999, *Island Catholic News.*

Chapter Six: Advent

[89]Unless otherwise indicated all direct De Roo quotes in this section (Chapters 6-10) are from the Grant Maxwell interviews done in 1997 as research for a book he and I were to write together.

[90]Details on the Belgium roots are from the De Roo-De Pape family history, *Belgian Canadian Builders.*

[91]*Lost Europe—Images of a Vanished World.*

[92]See the *Belgian Canadian Builders.*

Chapter Seven: Nativity

[93]February 14, 1999 *Catholic New Times*, p. 3: "Remi De Roo prepares to retire with bright hope for the continuing legacy of Vatican II."

[94]Conversation with *Island Catholic News*, editor Marnie Butler.

[95] *Dictionary of Symbols* by J.E. Cirlot, 1985, p. 102.

[96]See for example E.A. Speise's introduction to *Genesis of The Anchor Bible, The Documentary Sources of Genesis*, pp. XXII to

XXXVII, also F.R.Tennant, *The Sources of the Doctrines of the fall and Original Sin*, Chapter One "The Fall Story and its Exegesis."

[97]See *The Harper Collins Encyclopedia of Catholicism*, p. 687 ff, 1995 edition or *The Encyclopedia of Theology, The Concise Sacramentum Mundi*, edited by Karl Rahner, SJ pp. 727-730, 1975 edition.

[98]An excellent analysis of this phenomenon within the Canadian context is found in Gregory Baum's *Catholics and Canadian Socialism.*

[99]Compare this with the entirely otherwordly view of the recently beatified Pius IX (1846-78) or his predeccessor Gregory XVI (1831-46), who J.N.D. Kelly called a "good hearted monk with little comprehension of the contemporary world."

[100]Interview with Grant Maxwell.

[101]*Agri-culture, Agri-business or Agri-power? A look to the future presentation of National Farmers Union Convention*, Edmonton, December 2, 1985.

Chapter Eight: Grace Upon Grace

[102]De Roo wrote in an e-mail to Marnie Butler at *Island Catholic News* about this paper which was more radical than anything he might have said to the married clergy: "It is now, as it were, 'on the record academically'. I feel I have achieved a significant step forward in helping to restore the most ancient tradition whereby doctrine emerged from the experience of the believing community, not just 'handed down from above' as some people think."

[103]*Victoria Demers to De Roo, 150 Years of Catholic History on Vancouver Island* p. 146.

[104]May, 1994 *Island Catholic News* pp. 1, 8-9 & June pp. 8-9 (two parts).

[105]*The Symbolic Life*, Bollingen Series, see also volume on the Western Religious Tradition.

Chapter Nine: Ordinary Time

[106]All direct quotes in this section continue to be from the Grant Maxwell interviews unless otherwise indicated.

[107]Jeffrey M. Burns, *Disturbing the Peace—A history of the Christian Family Movement, 1949-74* reviewed in June 4, 1999 *National Catholic Reporter*, page 17 by Robert McClory.

[108]Among De Roo's close acquaintances, these included Romeo Maione, Grant and Vivian Maxwell, Bernard and Mae Daly, Mario and Estelle Carota, Jim and Marg Beaubien among many others.

[109]pp. 20-24 *Compass* March 1990. *Compass,* which was an effort to produce popular level intellectual understanding of the church and theology, prepared a ten month series on the ten decades of the 20th Century at the start of its last decade.

[110]For example in a talk he gave to the Corpus Canada annual convention held in Victoria in 1995 he cited the Québec model since Vatican II as the way of the future for the institutional church.

[111]p. 14, *The Training and Role of Christian Social Leaders by Catholic Social Life Conference*, CCCB, Ottawa.

[112]*Mater et Magistra, and Pacem in Terram* in particular which were addressed to all people of good will, a precedent setting gesture.

[113]The liturgical movement arose after the Second World War and was the key to most of the reform that followed. See *The Reform of the Liturgy 1948-1975* by Annibale Bugnini. The liturgical reform movement of the fifties was actually, perhaps not surprisingly, the central spearhead of what was to come.

[114]Listed by Richard P. McBrien on p. 647 of *Catholicism.*

[115]*Catholic New Times*, February 14, 1999, p. 3.

[116]*A Dictionary of Symbols* by J. E. Cirlot.

[117]"*Of Justice, Revolutions and Human Rights ... notes on a trip to Central America*," April 1980, self-published booklet. He called it his favourite book, although obviously less well known due to its limited production and specific subject matter.

[118]"Angelo Giuseppe Roncalli: A Christian on St. Peter's Chair from 1958 to 1963" in *Men in Dark Times* by Hannah Arendt.

[119]*Winnipeg Tribune* feature by Manfred Jager, November 2, 1962.

[120]p. 273, J.E. Cirlot, *A Dictionary of Symbols*, Routledge and Kegan Paul, 1985 paperback edition.

[121]This is notwithstanding recent Vatican statements by Cardinal Joseph Ratzinger which seems to revert to the old superiority complex.

Chapter Ten: Eastertide

[122]Letters to Grant Maxwell from various Canadians on how they would introduce Remi De Roo, published in *Island Catholic News* as a special section on the occasion of De Roo's retirement, February, 1999, pp. 5-12.

[123]These quotations are all from the Grant Maxwell interviews.

[124]Bulloch's 1997 memoirs, *As I Remember*, are candid in these matters.

[125]Foreward to *As I Remember*.

[126]See Patricia Brady, *Has Anything Really Changed? Doctoral Study of the Diocese of Victoria Since Vatican II*, Woodlake Books, 1986.

[127]See "Victoria: An American Diocese in Canada," by Rev. Vincent McNally, PhD in *Historical Studies* (57) 1990 Journal of Canadian Catholic Historical Association, also his unpublished history of the diocese *Surviving in Lotus Land: A History of the Diocese of Victoria 1846-1923*.

[128]Vincent McNally, *The Lord's Distant Vineyard, History of the Oblate and the Catholic Community in British Columbia,* 2000 and *Surviving in Lotus Land, a History of the Diocese of Victoria 1846-1923* unpublished history of the Diocese of Victoria and also "Victoria: An American Diocese in Canada," *Historical Studies* (57) Journal of the Canadian Catholic Historical Association.

[129]See "Fighting City Hall: The Church Tax Exemption Battle between The City and The Roman Catholic Diocese of Victoria," by Vincent McNally in *Historical Studies* (74) 1992 Journal of the Canadian Catholic Historical Association and "Bishop Sandy's Battles," by Patrick Jamieson, Chapter Six of *Victoria Demers to De Roo, 150 Years of Catholic History on Vancouver Island.*

[130]See pp. 134 & 241 of Ron Graham's *God's Dominion*, McClelland and Stewart, 1990.

[131]ibid.

[132]*Island Catholic News*, December, 1987, p. 8.

[133]In his own way O'Connell conducted himself like an older bishop figure throughout De Roo's 37 year term. He never abandoned his old fashioned manner of the Hollywood pastor, a la Bing Crosby in the films *Going My Way* or *The Bells of Saint Mary's.* Employing the light touch with the drop of humour, and always the moralistic conclusion, O'Connell never seemed to clue to the pastoral approach that emerged out of Vatican II. With his pre-Vatican II textbook theology he was even able to have himself installed as rector at Saint Andrew's Cathedral in his last active years. While there he waged a somewhat successful campaign to conduct the place as he must have imagined it should have been done all along, all in a pastoral bearing that dated from an earlier now outdated era. It was a masterful form of paternalism that at

once ignored most of the progressive developments in theology during the previous fifty years and yet controlled in a behind-the-scenes manner the direction and priorities of the historic parish without wishing to appear directly to do so. Psychologically it was somewhat fascinating as the technique manifested most of the contemporary difficulties of the Catholic Church of the period without ever having to acknowledge them as problems.

[134]"Fighting City Hall," by Rev. Vincent McNally, *Journal of Canadian Church Historical Society* 74, 1992, also in *Surviving in Lotus Land.*

[135]See chapter six, *Victoria Demers to De Roo, 150 years of Catholic History on Vancouver Island* for details, especially claims by Rev. John Barry, chancellor of the Diocese of Antigonish and a distant relative of Bishop MacDonald's.

[136]An interesting example of overlap between the three eras was Monsignor O'Connell who had been Hill's protege and took on the responsibilities of rector of the cathedral parish at the onset of Roussin's arrival in the diocese. O'Connell, whose only brother Martin had been a Federal Liberal cabinet minister in the Trudeau era, ran the parish on the strict basis of deficit reduction. His style was to accept responsibility for dubious debts, ones which had nothing to do with the parish itself but were the result of its heritage nature and the diocesan function of the building. As a result of this directed zeal in his final stage as an active administrator, the parish was reduced to a shell of its former dynamism. Under previous recent rectors there had been a plethora of diverse ministries with appropriate staff. Through unremitting sacrifice of programs and staff budget on the altar of deficit reduction, the parish was eventually reduced to a solitary pastor, the domestic prelate himself. The devolution might be likened to the federal government itself during the same era. O'Connell also championed the cause of fundraising during the campaign to eliminate the debt attributed to De Roo's era, shortly after he left office. The challenge seemed to temporarily strengthen the aging prelate in this direction which would have reminded him of the pre-Vatican and pre-De Roo challenges of the church to survive in 'lotus land'. Unfortunately, he did suffer a stroke in 2001 at age seventy-seven, as rector.

[137]Interview by author with Al Heron, Development Officer, Diocese of Victoria, 1993-99.

[138]There were some notable exceptions, such as Our Lady of The Rosary Parish in Langford. Its parish history, an essay ghostwritten in 1976 by "the one and only pastor of 25 years J. Willard O'Brien" exemplifies the semi-autonomous little empires parishes became under the situation of the earlier times, earlier episcopal styles, fiscal contingencies and the personalities of the pastors. One of its opening paragraphs reads: "This territory only two decades ago was considered the sticks, or back yard of Victoria. Today we take second place to no one spiritually or temporally." Reference to Vatican II reforms reads: "Innovations in the liturgy following Vatican II were weighed carefully and adopted with moderation by a very capable, sage and prudent council. The altar was eventually turned and altar rail removed, but suggestions to remove the large crucifix over the altar and eliminate the statues were met with steadfast opposition." No mention of Bishop De Roo is to be found in the text, with a solitary photo of his face perhaps pointedly placed above Cardinal John Henry Newman's poem, *Lead Kindly Light*.

[139]Ann Richards makes this assertion in her review of the 1997 diocesan history, *Victoria Demers to De Roo* published in the pages of the ultra-traditionalist anti-De Roo newspaper *The Trumpet*. The article, titled "Diocese Farthest Out," appeared in the December, 1997 edition.

[140]*Island Catholic News* December, 1987 p. 15, commemorative edition to mark De Roo's twenty-five years as bishop of Victoria.

[141]ibid.

[142]Paul Blancard, a priest ordained for Vancouver, who later moved to Victoria, was convicted and served time in prison. Subsequently he took treatment, left the priesthood and married, moving away to Ontario.

[143]Probably the most intransigent difficulty De Roo experienced in this area was from locally ordained clergy for whom Bishop Hill and the earlier style were normative. As a result they constantly undermined his more progressive steps by fully exercising their own collegial authority to directly block the implementation in their parishes by foot dragging or to simply stall and not co-operate, sending a mixed signal to their parishioners which encouraged the more obdurate variety of traditionalist.

[144]See *Surviving in Lotus Land*, unpublished history of the diocese of Victoria by Rev. Vincent McNally, in Diocesan Archives.

[145]Garry Wills' June 2000 book *Papal Sin, Structures of Deceit* claims this sort of intellectual dishonesty is the current characteristic papal sin, as compared to the avarice and political power seeking of earlier eras.

[146]*Encyclopedia of Catholicism*, Rev. Richard P. McBrien, Harper Collins, 1995, p. 1033: "Although committed to the Second Vatican Council, much of his pontificate has been dedicated to the containment of progressive ideas and practices following that council. For that reason it has been called a restorationist papacy. Others see him as the first post-modern pope."

[147]pp. 29, 34, *People of God, The Struggle for World Catholicism,* by Penny Lernoux. "As noted by the French theologian Marie-Dominique Chenu, one of the theological stars of Vatican II, the record of the proceedings in the council committee responsible for the key document, Dogmatic Constitution on The Church, showed that Archbishop Wojtyla had opposed a definition of the church as the "people of God." Wojtyla envisioned not a church of the people but a "perfect society" in which laity worked under the direction of priests and bishops to achieve "the truth" of a life lived in faith."

[148]For complete text see *Island Catholic News*, pp. 8-11, February, 1997.

[149]For example, the normally progressive *Catholic New Times* and *Prairie Messenger* reported on the event reluctantly if at all. Official diocesan organs such as *The (Toronto) Catholic Register* and the Vancouver *BC Catholic* condemned the statement outright, virtually sight unseen. Journalistic balance and objectivity took a back seat, in this instance, to protecting the institution from internal criticism. Internal dissent was no longer even news.

[150]See Peter Hebblethwaite's *Synod Extraordinary—the inside story of the Rome Synod*, November/December 1985.

[151]Note dated July 23, 1997 from Remi De Roo to the author regarding twenty minute taped interview by Terry Spence on CFAX Radio in Victoria. Note reads: "Thank you for your courtesy in letting me listen to the tape. I thought you were quite persuasive and handled yourself well. All the Best! Fraternally Remi."

[152]"Bishop De Roo Explains last thirty-five years of change—Council Father unpacks Meaning of Vatican II," *Island Catholic News*, November, 1997; pp. 1, 7-12.

[153]Personal experience of the author. When De Roo reviewed the sections on himself of an earlier book about the diocese of Victoria, *Victoria Demers to De Roo*, he questioned the accuracy of this commonplace statement about Paul VI and his image as a Hamlet figure. The source in this case was the *Oxford Dictionary of Popes* by J.N.D. Kelly.

[154]pp. 95-96 of Chapter Six, "The Tragedy of Pope Paul VI" in *Papal Sin* by Garry Wills for statistics on resistance to *Humanae Vitae*; in addition 87 Catholic theologians signed a statement July 30, 1968 to express their qualms of conscience over *Humanae Vitae* as a teaching document of the church, prior to the September statement of the Canadian Bishops. See "The conscience of the Theologian with reference to the Encyclical" by Frederick E.Crowe, SJ in *Theology Today* Summer, 1969.

[155]Grant Maxwell interviews.

[156]Todd, Douglas, "Two Bishops, One Church," *Vancouver Sun*, August 2, 1997, Section E, Saturday Review Section.

[157]Grant Maxwell letters.

Chapter Eleven: Night Battles

[158]Peter Hebblethwaite *Synod Extraordinary, the Inside Story of the Rome Synod, November-December 1985*, Doubleday, 1986. This write-up on Ogle first appeared as an obituary notice in *Island Catholic News* at the time of his death.

[159]See *The Varieties of Religious Experience* by William James, classic treatment from 1901-02 on the psychology of religion.

[160]Gregory Baum dedicated his 1980 study of *Catholics and Canadian Socialism, Political Thought in the Thirties and Forties* to Eugene Cullinane. Half the pages of Chapter Five "Catholic Support for the CCF in Saskatchewan," consist of details of the Basilian priest's story.

[161]"Retirement won't stop De Roo from speaking out, After more than 30 years as Roman Catholic Bishop of Greater Victoria, Remi De Roo is ready to take his social activism on the road," by Mark Browne, *Victoria News*, Friday, February 5, 1999.

[162]Mark Browne wrote a follow-up piece Friday June 2, 2000 in *The Victoria News* titled: "Questions raised about politics behind church crisis, De Roo supporters wonder what role politics is playing in crisis rocking Catholic Church." See chapter 18 for text of the article.

[163]Details on papal biographies from *Oxford Dictionary of the Popes* by J.N.D. Kelly.

[164]For two other decidedly different considered views of his death see *Pontiff* by Gordon Thomas and Max Morgan-Witts and *In God's Name* by David A. Yallop. Carl Bernstein and Marco Politi's speculations in *His Holiness, John Paul II and the History of Our Time* are also interesting.

[165]*Oxford Dictionary of Popes* by J.N.D. Kelly p. 326.

Chapter Twelve: A World of Paradox

[166]*The Night Battle*, essays by J.M. Cameron, Burns and Oates, 1962. Sermon titled "Faith and Reason, contrasted as Habits of Mind in John Henry Newman, Sermons, chiefly on the Theory of religious Belief, preached before the University of Oxford" (1843). This section was originally written for *Compass* magazine in 1993. The Jesuit magazine commissioned the piece but decided not to print it, paying a submission fee of $500. It was eventually run in the January 1994 edition of *Island Catholic News*, precipitating the strongest profusion of letters in response in the history of that often controversial independent Catholic monthly. The stream of responses to the feature had to be cut off because of space restrictions after three months and several full pages of letters to the editor, both pro and con to its content.

[167]Patrick Jamieson, three part series, Spring of 1993, *Catholic New Times*, edited by Janet Somerville.

[168]Rev. Everett MacNeil, then president of the Catholic Health Association of Canada and a former General Secretary of the Canadian Council of Catholic Bishops was my boss for three years (1978-81) at the CHAC. He was responding at a lunch break to my puzzled pondering about the seeming contradictions of the new pope.

[169]I spent parts of 1993 and 1994 in Romania where the Catholic Church is primarily a Hungarian Ethnic minority amidst a sea of ninety-three percent Eastern Orthodox. The atmosphere is pre-Vatican II with a severely defensive posture in a penitential, moralistic, xenophobic milieu of traditionalist Catholicism. Eastern European Catholicism is completely out of step with the westernized liberal mindset that ensued after The Council.

[170]Theologian Hans Kung called Ratzinger, (a formerly progressive theologian with Kung in the early days of *Concilium*, a progressive

theological journal from the 1960s) "power mad." See *People of God* by Penny Lernoux.

[171]1987 CBC Lectures by Gregory Baum on liberation theology; see also *Catholics and Canadian Socialism* (1980).

[172]See *The Priority of Labour, A Commentary of Laborems Exercens, Encyclical Letter of Pope John Paul II*, by Gregory Baum, 1982.

[173]Michael Valpy, religion reporter, *Globe and Mail*, page D6, Saturday June 17, 2000. In a review of *Papal Sin*, he describes Wills as "omnipresent man of American letters...a talented historian, an investigative journalist, a political commentator and a literary critic... an ex-Jesuit seminarian, a lifelong Catholic layman and a close student of the church and some of its giants: Augustine, Newman, Chesterton."

[174]p. 157, *Catholics Against the Church* by Michael W. Cuneo, in chapter 6, "Revivalist Catholics, Social Justice Catholics, and the Politics of Ecumenism," 1989.

[175]p. 104, *North/South Calling*.

[176]pp. 104-5, *North/South Calling*.

[177]p 151, *Catholics Against the Church*.

[178]pp. 5-10, "Catholics and Political Mythology" in *Night Battle*, essays by J.M. Cameron.

[179]ibid p. 9.

[180]*On Pilgrimage* by Dorothy Day.

Chapter Thirteen: Gathered to the Centre

[181]Reports to Rome for the years 1968 and 1973 stated: for 1968, assets of $848,807 including $390,248 in property and $386,435 in investments of which $341,160 is held in trust. With liabilities such as mortgages payable the net worth of the diocese is $483,193. For 1973, on December 31, assets including both property and investments totalled $1,027,420.70 including liabilities of $228,270.57. With capital gain the net worth is stated as $1,027,420.70.

[182]One of the sad ironies of Vatican II's implementation as an event enhancing the role of the laity is that in many diocese this meant control by right wing business men, lawyers, accountants and monied elite. De Roo kept these people from ruling while he was in power, but the make-up of the 'committee' that 'advised' his successor during the so-called financial crisis and revelations following De Roo's departure was of this type.

The 'crisis' of course served their purposes of gaining control. It was suggested to be more than a coincidence that for nearly forty years the financial management was smooth running but the moment he steps out of office all sorts of crippling problems were said to surface, accepted without question by much of the mainstream media, and put forward by people who had been hyper-critical of De Roo's style, goals and politics all during his regime.

[183]See chapters 6 and 7 of *Victoria Demers to De Roo, 150 Years of Catholic History on Vancouver Island*, for details especially pp. 209-211 & 213-216.

[184]p. 12, February 1999, *Island Catholic News.*

[185]Eight major shifts were listed in the final Synod documents, see *Island Catholic News* of November 1997 for detailed analysis of shifts by De Roo as rooted in Vatican II, pp. 1, 7-12.

[186]My own observations about the significance of the diocesan synod are rooted in my experience of having worked in Catholic Dioceses in Saskatchewan, New Brunswick, Ontario, Manitoba and Nova Scotia and from working with national church organizations as a communications specialist. See *Island Catholic News* March 1990, pp. 7 & 9.

[187]*Has Anything Really Changed? A Study: The Diocese of Victoria since Vatican II*by Patricia Brady, Ph.D, Woodlake Books, 1986.

[188]*Encyclopedia of Catholicism*, pp. 1299-1306, edited by Richard P. McBrien.

[189]*Forward in the Spirit, Challenge of the People's Synod*, 1991 edited by Pearl Gervais and Grant Maxwell.

[190]As editor of the *BC Catholic* Hawkswell refused to advertise De Roo's 1992 book *Eye of the Catholic Storm*, saying it undermined the church, according to Douglas Todd in the *Vancouver Sun* of February 24 of that year.

Chapter Fourteen: Spiritual Predecessors Cullinane and Charbonneau

[191]p. 206.

[192]p. 29 *Political Theology in the Canadian Context.* Ben Smillie writes: "**Agrarian Populism**—The agrarian revolt in the prairies questioned the bondage of a closed future for the farmer trapped by rail monopolies and the consequent high transportation costs. The farmer also faced a federal trade policy which provided protection through

tariffs for farm machinery companies in central Canada but left an unprotected international market for his grains.

"He was also victim of a banking system located in central Canada that loaned money at high interest rates and foreclosed on farmers in lean years. Land policy provided Canadian giants like the Canadian Pacific Railway and the Hudson's Bay Company with tax-free land but left the farmer burdened by debt.

"These grievances were fought by prairie populism, becoming politically visible in The Progressive Party in 1921 and in the anti-party federation idea of the Cooperative Commonwealth Federation (CCF)...The problem with agrarian populism lay in its issue-oriented platform and its abhorrence of political ideology."

[193]The proceedings were published in 1982 as 'Political Theology in the Canadian Context,' edited by Benjamin G. Smillie.

[194]See final chapter of this book titled *Before the Flood* for excerpts from that talk.

[195]The five mainline Canadian Christian Churches formed any number of ongoing and ad hoc joint committees on social justice questions during this period, perhaps the most representative was PLURA, an anagram formed from the first letters of the churches: Presbyterian, Lutheran, United Church, Roman Catholic and Anglican. PLURA funded grassroots social justice projects.

Three representative texts which illustrate this development are *The Gospel of Peace and Justice, Catholic Social Teaching Since Pope John* (1976); *Puebla and Beyond* (1979); *The Faith that Does Justice—Examining the Christian Sources for Social Change* (1977) (see bibliography).

[196]p. 1. *Political Theology*, etc.

[197]p. 3. ibid

[198]p. 3. ibid

[199]For an excellent explanation of this background see chapter two of Gregory Baum's *Catholics and Canadian Socialism*, titled "Papal Teaching on Socialism," pp. 71-96.

[200]Gregory Baum claims this attribute but it was also the deeply held sentiment of my own family of origin who were inspired by Cullinane between 1954 and 1958 while stationed in Whitehorse with the Canadian military. 'Father Gene,' as we called him, served as chaplain to the forces base called Camp Takhini. My youngest brother was named after him as a testament to his spiritual impact on our clan.

[201]p. 160, chapter five "Catholic Support for the CCF in Saskatchewan" in *Catholics and Canadian Socialism, Political Thought in the Thirties and Forties.*

[202]See sixteen page appendix of *North/South Calling*, an autobiography by Fr. Bob Ogle; also remarks by Canadian canon lawyer Frank Morrissey, OMI pp. 34-35 of transcript of Catholics, CBC radio IDEAS program May 6-27, 1984.

[203]p. 248, Lorene Hanley Duquin's *They Called Her The Baroness, The Life of Catherine de Hueck Doherty.* "The following week Catherine received a letter from Father Gene Cullinane, CSB, an economics professor... he told her that something strange had happened to him in Combermere... 'I felt God and experienced God as never before in my life... My eyes were opened and I saw holiness here as I had never seen it anywhere before. A consciousness of the supernatural took hold of me to such an extent that I believed I myself was transformed."

[204]*They Called Her The Baroness, The Life of Catherine de Hueck Doherty* by Lorene Hanley Duquin, see introduction by Rev. John Catoir, p. xvii also Chapter 11, The Dominion of Canada, 1921 p.73.

[205]Catherine Doherty digested the philosophy of Madonna House in what was titled *The Little Mandate* which reads: "Arise — go! Sell all you possess...give it directly, personally to the poor. Take up My cross (their cross) and follow Me—going to the poor—being poor—being one with them—one with Me. Little—be always little... simple—poor—childlike. Preach the Gospel WITH YOUR LIFE—WITHOUT COMPROMISE—Listen to the Spirit—He will lead you. Do little things exceedingly well for love of Me. Love—love— love, never counting the cost. Go into the marketplace and stay with me...pray...fast... pray always... fast. Be hidden—be a light to your neighbour's feet. Go without fear into the depths of men's hearts...I shall be with you. Pray always. I WILL BE YOUR REST.

[206]For a good overview of this see p. 62 ff, *Ethics and Economics* by Gregory Baum.

[207]Peter Hebblethwaite discusses the bankruptcy of the Catholic Social Doctrine discussion in his 1982 article "The Popes and Politics: Shifting patterns in 'Catholic Social Doctrine'" where he says that John Paul II has resurrected CSD for his own ideological purposes after major social Catholic theologians particularly the French Dominican Marie-Dominique Chenu have written it off as too general a vehicle to be effective, favouring instead the approach initiated by John XXIII

who "had a keener sense of history than any other pope of this century." De Roo's contribution was along this line. Liberation theology would be an example of this 'sense of history' approach.

[208]p. 67, *Ethics and Economics*.

[209]See *Catholic New Times* Series "Whose minding the Social Justice Store" by the author and Janet Somerville, April 1993.

[210]Chapter 6 *Revivalist Catholics, Social Justice Catholics, and the Politics of Ecumenism*, p. 148 ff.

[211]p. 178, Cuneo.

[212]In the late 1980s and early 1990s De Roo issued a number of statements around the abortion issue, published in *Island Catholic News*. British Columbia had elected a right-wing populist Catholic premier, William Vander Zalm, who publicized his personal views on abortion, making it an issue in the regular media. This development allowed De Roo to make his own seamless garment policy public. See ICN cover story, March 1988 (Vol. 2 No. 2) or p. 5, June 1989.

[213]A good example near the close of his career was a couple of Alberta academics Patricia Rooke and her husband Rudy Schnell who moved to Victoria and took exception to his record as espoused in the pages of *Island Catholic News* which regularly received their revisionist attacks on De Roo's reputation, record and general value to the Canadian church. Some of their letters were published by ICN, during 2000, others are in my files.

[214]p. 28, Chapter Three, "The Catholic Counterreformation," Penny Lernoux, *People of God, The Struggle for World Catholicism*.

[215]This constant theme that Vatican II had invented nothing new but rather rediscovered practices and insight of the early Christian church was regularly re-emphasized during De Roo's last ten years in office when the attack on the reforms of the council received a new impetus. An example is the May 1994 televised interview on Campbell River community television by broadcaster Joan Brown, another is the February 1999 coverage in *Catholic New Times* of De Roo's retirement plans.

Chapter Fifteen: The Archbishop Charbonneau Saga

[216]Catherine Moroney SSA's version of the Charbonneau saga was published in her own written form in the August 2000 edition of *Island Catholic News* (Vol. 14, No. 7).

[217]My mother Margaret Patricia née Harris was Luca's close intimate since she was a student at Saint Ann's Academy in the late 1930s. Luca stated on videotape at the time of my parent's fiftieth anniversary in 1992 that "The Jamiesons are my second family." Margaret often said to me that Luca had serious reservations about De Roo's administrative style dating from the time of his first arrival.

[218]In the Jamieson family circle she was often saying in her Irish way that she was saving a big kiss for Pope John XXIII when she got to the pearly gates of Heaven, in gratitude for the freedoms he had granted religious women and particularly herself, who was always high spirited.

[219]Author's conversation with Muriel Clemenger in 1993.

[220]For example, Rev. Terrance McNamara, OMI, rector at Saint Andrew's Cathedral between 1986 and 1992, refused to allow *The Trumpet* to be distributed at the cathedral on precisely this basis. Whereas ICN had done two years of groundwork to ascertain acceptance by the parishes, *The Trumpet* presumed it would be granted *ipso facto* the privilege, with a product that was hypercritical of the reforms of Vatican II, diocesan policies and the bishop himself.

[221]"Newspaper breaking Catholic law, defying authority of bishop," feature article by Stephen Hume, staff writer, Tuesday April 5, 1988, Victoria *Times Colonist*.

[222]p. three, *Island Catholic News*, January 1988 (Vol. 1 No. 12).

[223]Monsignor George Martin, a former student of Father Hill and one time President of Saint Thomas University, called him "an eminence, a local hero" in the Miramichi area of New Brunswick. See pp. 270-71, Chapter Ten of *Victoria: Demers to De Roo, 150 Years of Catholic History on Vancouver Island.*

[224]pp. 96-7, Lapointe, *Renaude L'histoire bouleversante de Mgr. Charonneau*, 1962.

[225]A good examination of the shift in the situation of the Catholic Church in Québec is provided in the CBC Radio IDEAS series *Catholics* initially broadcast over four weeks in May, 1984, particularly part three titled "From Prince to Servant."

[226]*Charbonneau & Le Chef* by John Thomas McDonough, 1968; also *l'historie bouleversante de Mgr Charbonneau* by Renaude Lapointe, 1962.

[227]*Catholics and Canadian Socialism*, Chapter Seven, "Catholics in Eastern Nova Scotia," p. 189 ff Baum op cit. On page 202 he says: "The Antigonish Movement was certainly the most original and the most daring response of Canadian Catholics to the social injustices of the Depression. It was based on an alternative vision of society, it was radical and went beyond the church's teaching on several issues, advocated religious materialism and introduced reforms in Canadian society that had explosive implications."

Chapter Sixteen: Traditionally Touchy Topics

[228]June 20, 1997 letter from De Roo to Premier Glen Clark opens: In the spirit of Bill 31, the Family Relations Amendment Act, 1997, and in the spirit of mutual respect, the Catholic community of the Diocese of Victoria asks the homosexual members of our churches and neighbourhoods for their sensitivity and understanding. It is a matter of extreme importance to the men and women engaged in the union of marriage to retain the term spouse which is an historical and traditional description of the sacred commitment to each other through marriage. We believe other terms can be used to describe different forms of commitment between human beings... In the same spirit of respect we ask all heterosexual members of the communities to consider and reach out to their homosexual neighbours...

[229]*A Dictionary of Symbols* by J.E. Cirlot.

[230]See sources used in *Victoria: Demers to De Roo, 150 Years of Catholic History on Vancouver Island,* in particular McNally and Hanley regarding original invitation from Island Natives to pioneer bishops to come to Vancouver Island.

[231]*Island Catholic News*, p. 8, May 1989.

[232]p. 1, August, 1989 *Island Catholic News.*

[233]p. 8 ff. The theme of that issue of *Mission Canada* is "Blending native traditions in faith life—focus on West Coast missions." The De Roo article is titled: "Celebrating the gifts of native church." An article on Saint Ann's is called "Cowichan nations blend native traditions in practice of faith."

[234]*Mission Magazine*, pp 6-10, Volume 14, No. 2, Fall, 1995.

[235]See Vincent McNally's "Fighting for a Foundation: Oblate Beginnings in Far Western Canada 1847-1868," in *Western Oblate Studies 4*, 1995. His history of the Oblates in British Columbia published in 2000 incorporates this material.

[236]CBC Enterprises produced a boxed commemorative series of six tapes of the pope's 1984 Canadian visit.

[237]p. 103, *Has Anything Really Changed* by Patricia C. Brady, PhD.

[238]See *Surviving in Lotus Land—History of the Diocese of Victoria, 1846 - 1923* by Vincent McNally, PhD, available in unpublished form at archives of Diocese of Victoria.

[239]Review Section, *Vancouver Sun*, September 21, 1996.

[240]For detail see my 1997 history of Catholics on Vancouver Island, *Victoria: Demers to De Roo*, particularly the first section on the pioneer bishops of the first fifty years, 1846-1896.

[241]*Dictionary of Symbolic and Mythological Animals*, p. 232 by J.C. Cooper.

[242]See Cirlot's *Dictionary of Symbols*, entries for Peacock and Swan.

Chapter Seventeen: Traditionally Touchy Topics: Two

[243]*Catholics and Canadian Socialism, Political Thought in the Thirties and Forties* by Gregory Baum, Lorimer, 1980 see chapter 7, "Catholics in eastern Nova Scotia."

[244]*Underdevelopment and Social Movements in Atlantic Canada*, 1979, edited by Robert J. Brym and R. James Sacouman, New Hogtown Press, Toronto; see also *New Maritimes* magazine, May, 1985, "Antigonish—The Two Sided Legacy: Catholicism and Socialism" by Patrick Jamieson, pp. 10-12.

[245]The Extension Department of Saint Francis Xavier University at Antigonish, Nova Scotia has a long record of adult education and life long adult learning programs that supported the original Antigonish Movement of the Thirties and Forties up to the present day, including the founding of a Diocesan Health Care Council between 1983-86 which I happened to be instrumental in establishing as its first executive director and organizer.

[246]Bulloch reveals the unaesthetic nature of his earlier unpleasantness at the cathedral was due to false accusations by a fellow priest of paedophiliac tendencies. In reaction Bulloch reveals in *As I Remember* that he had to be restrained from trouncing the man on the spot.

[247]Roberti, 1962.

[248]For detail on Orth saga see pp. 145-154 of *Victoria Demers to De Roo, 150 Years of Catholic History on Vancouver Island.*

[249]A story that is told by Father Stanley 'Stumpy' MacDonald from his experience as pastor at Inverness in Cape Breton concerns Broad Cove, a tiny village which has produced some forty priests for the Diocese of Antigonish including Monsignor Ronald Beaton who served on Vancouver Island between 1915 - 1950.

An eighty year old man when asked if he thought Vatican II had not gone too far with its changes, said just the opposite, that it had not gone far enough. Even in the middle 1980s, after the great defection of the 1970s, Antigonish still had some two hundred and fifty priests (compared to Halifax's forty) including some 35 Father MacDonalds and 25 Father MacNeils', thus explaining the sometimes curious and/or amusing nicknames. [Author's notes from time spent working for Antigonish Diocese between 1983-86.]

[250]When I arrived in 1986 to start the *Island Catholic News*, I had any number of conversations with individuals who felt this was an important 'news story' that I should do something about—how the high altar was disposed of in the middle 1960s.

[251]"Senate of Priests Share Bishop's Rule," November 26, 1966, *Victoria Times*.

[252]p. 293, *Victoria Demers to De Roo*, see also history of Our Lady of the Rosary Parish, Langford by founding pastor Willard O'Brien who carefully explains how "a wise and prudent parish council" under the direction of its guiding pastor very slowly went about the changes required by Vatican II.

[253]See *Asian Journal* of Thomas Merton.

[254]August 24, 1969 "Report on the 'Pia Unio' Hermits of St. John the Baptist, Diocese of Victoria, British Columbia, Canada" by Jacques Winandy.

[255]Winandy memo.

[256]Letter from Merton to Brandt dated September 27, 1964 included in a posthumously published book of letters.

[257]Audio taped recorded interview with Charles Brandt at ICN offices June 1999.

[258]Marnie Butler, editor of the *Island Catholic News* between 1993-2001, who was also a convert to Catholicism, largely drawn by De Roo's prophetic Catholicism and Thomas Merton's writings, said that in her circles at the time of Merton's death, it was assumed he was

assassinated by the American Central Intelligence Agency for his role in the Catholic left's resistance to the Vietnam War. Merton lead an annual retreat at Gethsemani for the leaders of the Catholic left including the Berrigan brothers. His writings revealed a radical pacifism.

Butler was associated with the Centre for the Study of Non-Violence which was founded by folk singer Joan Baez and Ira Sandperl in California. When she announced this during a talk in Vancouver about the life and work of Thomas Merton by Donald Grayston, the general reaction was shock, denial and disbelief from an audience which included Archbishop Adam Exner. Charles Brandt wrote in a letter (September 1, 2001) "The consensus on Merton's death is that it was accidental and not a sinister plot."

[259]See *Island Catholic News* pp. 11-12, December, 1998.

[260]p. 1, February 1998, *Island Catholic News*, "Diocese Makes Hermit History Again, Vatican II Intervention Comes to Fruition" by Joan Brown.

[261]p. 29, *Victoria Daily Colonist*, Wednesday, November 23, 1966.

[262]p. 1, *Vancouver Sun*, by Doug Todd, Thursday, January 30, 1992. Brandt was also interviewed on CBC Radio and television programs featured his message and lifestyle; a lifestyle which combined contemplative prayer, environmental action, social justice advocacy, and teaching Christian meditation as part of his integrative hermitic commitment.

[263]*Victoria Colonist* ibid.

[264]See Final Synod Documents in August, 1991 *Island Catholic News*, pp. 7-13.

[265] *Island Catholic News*, Vol. 5, No. 8.

[266]p. 4, May, 1998 Victoria *Zoom* magazine, Number 6. Cover article titled "The Bishop and Ms. Chaplain, The life and career of Bishop Remi De Roo and his controversial appointment of Kate Fagan as UVic Chaplain."

[267]p. 11, Volume 13, Number 1, February, 1999, *Island Catholic News*.

[268]ibid, p.9.

Chapter Eighteen: Smashing the Icon

[269]See pp. 117-119 of *Behind the Mitre* by Tony Clarke for details.

[270]In a CBC radio interview Chris Considine explained that De Roo's apology meant he accepted ultimate responsibility for the problem but it did not imply he was personally to blame.

[271]De Roo's 'Ad Limina' report to Rome in 1968 was published in the *Western Catholic Reporter*. Financially the diocese was worth $840,000, half of which was in real estate. Five years later the same report had the figure just over a million dollars. At the time of the scandal in 2000 the net worth was over a hundred million dollars. De Roo may have been 'caught out' by this radical escalation of property value during the 1980s.

[272]p. A 11, *Globe and Mail*, Saturday, June 17, 2000 "The lawyer, the bishop and the money pit, It started with a $30,000 investment in horses. The next thing anyone knew, Vancouver Island Catholics were $17-million in the hole" by Kim Lunman in Lacey, Wash.

[273]See bibliography section 'Selected reporting on post-retirement year 2000 financial saga'.

[274]Muriel Clemenger, who spoke before the Commission, stated that she 'was not heard' at the hearing, saying she could have "saved the price of her gas."

[275]Paragraphs from the *Times Colonist* banner headline "Ex-Bishop gambled assets from convent" by Gerard Young read: "The former bishop of Victoria used money from a closed nun's convent to invest in Arabian horses, then later, like a gambler on a bad streak, chased his losses with a risky land deal....As well, the former bishop apparently was operating two sets of books for the diocese, (Monsignor Peter Schonenbach) said.

[276]The date of the "Report of Commission of Canonical Inquiry to Most Reverend Raymond Roussin, SM, Bishop of Victoria, BC" was dated June 26, 2000, Schonenbach was quoted in the *Times Colonist* on page one May 27, 2000.

[277]The overall holdings of the entire diocese in 1968 was less than a million dollars, according to the Ad Limina Report to Rome by Bishop De Roo for the five-year period 1964-1968.

[278]For example, on page 6 of the inaugural edition of the *Diocesan Report* (An Organizational and Financial Report of the Diocese of Victoria, Vancouver Island), of November 2001, not one woman is

named as a member of the seven key finance and administrative committees. Two women are named on the publication committee.

[279]A biography of Mother Cecilia Mary, OSB *A Nun goes to the dogs* by E.D. Ward-Harris was published in 1969.

[280]"The Crucifixion of Bishop De Roo—Great deeds of a good man are forgotten" by Don Vipond, Sunday August 20, 2000, p. A7, *Times Colonist*.

[281]*Globe and Mail*, June 17, 2000. On August 28, 2001 on page B1, the *Times Colonist* carried the headline "Church deal falls through" reporting that an offer of $9.6 million US had not been successful. The approximately $15 million Cdn. was still the estimated market value of the land at this date even after all the confidence-threatening turmoil, validating Clemenger's confidence in the property as a 'good investment'.

[282]After his mid 1990s visit De Roo who met often with small groups and in small group settings where an extraordinary candour was shared about the state of the church, De Roo was saying openly among friends that he felt he had seen the face of evil on his latest trip to The Vatican. He told some confreres that he feared that the next pope would be extremely right wing.

Chapter Nineteen: The Prairie Populist

[283]Taped interview with Father Charles Brandt as well as passing reference in Merton's last book *Asian Journal*.

[284]Taped interview with Charles Brandt, *Island Catholic News* offices, Victoria, September 1999.

[285]See essay "The Good Death" by J.M. Cameron, re-issued in *Catholic Health Association of Canada Review*, fall, 1980, originally published in *The New York Review of Books*, 1976.

[286]For example, a typical comment was made at the time of Raymond Roussin's appointment in 1998 as De Roo's successor at Victoria. Jean-Marc Caron, the French language Radio Canada reporter engaged me in a lengthy conversation on this topic, saying there had to be a story there. He was far from the first individual sympathetic to De Roo's reputation who had the same question, thinking I might have some information and ideas about it.

[287]On October 31, 1997, the 35th anniversary of De Roo's appointment to the hierarchy a testimonial dinner was held in Victoria and Archbishop Hacault attended purchasing a copy of the history of the

Catholics on Vancouver Island. The book had just been published to coincide with the 150th anniversary of the diocese of Victoria which had started out of Red River Colony connections but was actually one year older than Saint Boniface. Bishop Hacault told me how proud he was of his 'cousin' and the historic and personal links with Victoria that evening while I signed his copy.

Chapter Twenty: The Mythic Poetic and the Mystic-Prophetic

[288]J.E. Cirlot, ibid.

[289]*In Even Greater Things* he tells of his discovery that some religious Sisters found him cool, aloof and remote, and how this spurred him on to invest time in personal development workshops, eventually becoming a trainer and teacher in the Enneagram.

[290]J.E. Cirlot, ibid.

Grant Maxwell

Patrick Jamieson was founding editor in 1986 of the *Island Catholic News,* the independent monthly for Vancouver Island. He published a history of Catholics on Vancouver Island, *Victoria: Demers to De Roo* in 1997. The first lay editor of the progressive *Prairie Messenger* in Saskatchewan in 1981, he also served as Director of Communications for the Catholic Health Association of Canada in the late 70s.